Learning
Audio/Video Production

Antonio Manriquez &
Thomas McCluskey

Boston • Columbus • Indianapolis • New York • San Francisco • Amsterdam
Cape Town • Dubai • London • Madrid • Milan • Munich • Paris • Montréal • Toronto
Delhi • Mexico City • São Paulo • Sydney • Hong Kong • Seoul • Singapore • Taipei • Tokyo

Taken from:

Video Production 101 Delivering the Message
Copyright © 2015 by Peachpit Press; Published by Pearson Education

Adobe Premiere Pro CC Classroom in a Book
Copyright © 2014 by Adobe Press; Published by Peachpit, a division of Pearson Education

Adobe Creative Suite 6 Production Premium Classroom in a Book
Copyright © 2013 by Adobe Press; Published by Peachpit, a division of Pearson Education

Adobe Audition CC Classroom in a Book
Copyright © 2013 by Adobe Press; Published by Peachpit, a division of Pearson Education

Adobe Premiere Pro CS4 Classroom in a Book
Copyright © 2009 by Adobe Press; Published by Peachpit, a division of Pearson Education

Guide to Graphic Design
Copyright © 2014; Published by Pearson

Introduction to Computers and Information Technology, 2e
Copyright © 2016; Published by Pearson North America

Exploring Careers for the 21st Century, Second Edition
Copyright © 2015; Published by Pearson Learning Solutions, a division of Pearson Education

Life Skills for the 21st Century, Building a Foundation for Success, Revised First Edition
Copyright © 2015; Published by Pearson Learning Solutions, a division of Pearson Education

Business Communication Essentials, 7th Edition
Copyright © 2016; Published by Pearson

Pearson

330 Hudson Street, New York, NY 10013
Hardcover ISBN 10: 0-13-467974-1
Hardcover ISBN 13: 978-0-13-467974-7

1 17

About the Authors

Antonio Manriquez is the video production teacher for the New Media Academy at the world-famous Hollywood High School in Los Angeles, California. He is an Apple Distinguished Educator, an Apple Certified Trainer, and an Avid Certified Instructor. His education and career in video and cinema production began at the age of 14 when he directed a feature-length film that premiered at the 1997 Sundance Film Festival. He is the founder and executive director of Media Educators of Los Angeles (MediaEducatorsLA.org), a networking organization founded in 2009 and created to educate and empower media arts educators in the greater Los Angeles area. Manriquez also chairs the CUE (CUE.org) Video in the Classroom Learning Network.

Tom McCluskey is a screenwriter, filmmaker, and teacher originally from Astoria, Queens, New York. He is a graduate of Regis High School, Fordham University, and the University of Southern California's School of Cinematic Arts, and he is currently completing his master of arts degree in educational administration at California State University—Northridge. With 15 years of experience teaching filmmaking, he is currently building a video production program at Helen Bernstein High School in Hollywood. He has won numerous awards for his films and screenplays including two CINE Golden Eagle Awards. He is on the board of directors of Media Educators of Los Angeles (MELA). He and his wife, Lauren, have one daughter, Lia Patricia. They live in Tarzana, California.

Table of Contents

Introduction

Filmmaking, media creation, or whatever you want to call it has been with us for more than 100 years. However, it's been only in the past 10 years or so that people gained access to high-quality, inexpensive equipment. Now, almost everyone can create and distribute their own work without the need for expensive rentals or the approval of some executive body, whether that be a production company, a movie studio, or a film-school faculty.

Like never before, the power is in the hands of the masses to create audiovisual pieces that say what they want to say in the way they want to say it.

The main idea of this book is to take the sum of information producers need to make introductory projects and arrange it into ten project-based units, layering in just as much new information as the student needs to complete the next, more complex level of project. It integrates theory with technical information in order to provide you with the most essential knowledge and skills.

If you go through this book in order, you will develop the skills to create 10 different, distinct, and authentic video projects. You will also have learned the media creation process.

How the Book Is Organized

Learning Audio/Video Production consists of ten chapters. Chapters 1 through 6 focus on building the knowledge you need to become a media content creator. Chapters 7 and 8 provide hands-on experience working with Adobe Premiere Pro, a video editing system, and Adobe Audition, an audio editing system. Chapters 9 and 10 cover the skills you need for career success.

CHAPTER 1 provides basic information equipment and storytelling, then progresses into more detail about the types of professionals who work in the industry. It also covers the production workflow, and how to set up and use the most common camera shots for maximum effect.

CHAPTER 2 delves into the history of audio and video production. It expands on storytelling with detailed information on how to prepare a script, and it introduces audio. It also explains copyright protections and how to ethically use someone else's work in your projects.

In CHAPTER 3, you learn how to prepare the many documents required for developing and managing a media project, such as shot lists, scene breakdowns, and budget. You explore the importance of the storyboard, cover the fundamentals of camerawork, and find out how to record a voiceover.

CHAPTER 4 provides an overview of casting and the audition process. It spends more time on audio, including differentiating between the types of equipment, and introduces lighting techniques.

CHAPTER 5 discusses professionalism, and how to prepare for an audio/video production career. It also covers interviewing techniques, for when you are behind the camera as the interviewer and on camera as the interviewee. It also introduces titles.

CHAPTER 6 is all about nonfiction, including documentaries and news. You learn about the role of the documentarian, and the challenges and rewards of developing nonfiction media content.

In CHAPTERS 7 and 8 you have the opportunity to work with Adobe Premiere Pro and Adobe Audition. Premiere Pro is a full-featured nonlinear video editing system you will use to edit and enhance your audio and video clips. Audition is a full-features audio editing system you will use for editing digital sound files.

CHAPTER 9 covers fundamental skills you need for profession success, including decision making, problem solving, and critical thinking. You learn how to use effective communication tools, such as active listening, and how to employ technology to improve your productivity. Other topics include teamwork, leadership, and conflict management.

Finally, CHAPTER 10 provides practical information on finding and keeping a career in audio/video production. It reinforces the importance of academic planning, and reviews the documents you will need for a career search and how to create them. The chapter discusses resources to use in a career search, and how to prepare for a job interview. Finally, it covers skills to use on the job to ensure career success, such as ethics, and professional communications strategies.

Chapters are structured to make the learning process simple and enjoyable. Each chapter begins with a listing of the topics that will be covered followed by an overview of why those topics are important.

Chapter 10 Overview

- Exploring Careers in Audio/Video Technology
- Academic Planning
- Developing Employability Skills
- Creating Career Search Documents
- Analyzing Job Search Resources
- Ethics at Work
- Developing New Skills
- Applying Professional Communications Strategies
- End-of-Chapter Review and Activities

The field of audio and video technology is filled with exciting and interesting careers. In this chapter you will explore the trends, job outlooks, and educational requirements for these jobs. You will also learn about how to use academic planning to prepare for your career and how to develop employability skills.

Next, you will review how to prepare career search documents, including resumes, cover letters, and thank-you notes, and you will be introduced to the process of applying for a job, including how to find job opportunities, how to fill out an application, and how to prepare for a job interview.

Finally, you explore how to be ethical at work, develop new skills, and apply professional communications strategies on the job.

Each chapter concludes with review questions designed to remind you of the most important skills and features you have learned and to test your knowledge of the chapter's key points.

End-of-Chapter Activities

REVIEW QUESTIONS

1. List at least three audio/video technology industry associations that offer work-related certifications.
2. Define employability.
3. List and define at least four career search documents
4. How can you prepare for a job interview?
5. What are six questions you should ask when evaluating and comparing job opportunities?
6. How can you behave ethically at work?
7. What are three ways an employer might provide an opportunity for you to develop new skills?
8. What is an audience-centered approach to communication?
9. What is market research and how can you use it to successfully promote a product?
10. What are four ways you can use business applications to interpret and communicate data, observations, and information?

Review Projects provide an informal way to practice the practical skills covered in the chapter, individually, with a partner, or in small teams.

Review Project 1

Review rules your school district may have for technology use as part of its acceptable use policy. Categorize policies based on appropriate use, vandalism or destruction, and consequences of violations. As a class, debate the benefits and draw-backs of items in the policy, such as censorship and filtering.

Review Project 2

In small groups write a script for a skit that demonstrates ethical conduct related to interacting with others at work, such as client confidentiality, privacy of sensitive content, use of network resources, and providing proper credit for ideas. Perform your skit for the class.

Review Project 3

As a class, discuss personal security guidelines and safety rules and regulations. Plan and practice a safety drill to demonstrate the rules, following all emergency procedures, as needed.

The Portfolio Builder project at the end of each chapter challenges you to complete a themed media content project using the skills from the current chapter as well as skills from the previous chapters.

CHAPTER 10 – PORTFOLIO BUILDER

CREATING A SHOWREEL

Recall that a showreel is a compilation of your best audio and video clips that you make available to prospective clients and employers. In this project, you will create a showreel.

DIRECTIONS

Throughout this book you have been creating audio and video projects. Now, use the skills you have learned working with Premiere Pro, and the knowledge you have acquired about developing quality products, to compile clips from your projects into a showreel that highlights your accomplishments. Use music and titles, obtaining permission as necessary. As you work, ask your classmates and teachers to review the project and offer advice on how to improve it. When you are satisfied with the end result, output it in a format suitable for posting online.

Chapters 7 and 8 include hands-on step-by-step Try It! exercises that allow you to practice what you learn about each feature. Each exercise is introduced so you know what you are going to accomplish in the following steps. Numbered steps make it easy for you to complete each part of the project. Frequent illustrations show you how to select settings, as well as show you results you can use to check your progress.

Exercises include helpful notes and tips that provide information such as alternate methods of performing tasks. Feature boxes include more in-depth information on related topics, tools, shortcuts, and professional methodology.

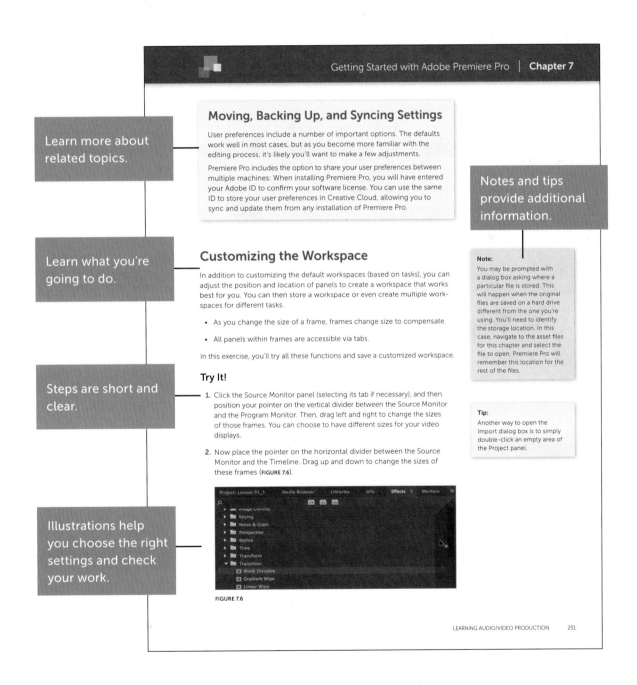

Learn more about related topics.

Learn what you're going to do.

Steps are short and clear.

Illustrations help you choose the right settings and check your work.

Notes and tips provide additional information.

Getting Started with Adobe Premiere Pro | **Chapter 7**

Moving, Backing Up, and Syncing Settings

User preferences include a number of important options. The defaults work well in most cases, but as you become more familiar with the editing process, it's likely you'll want to make a few adjustments.

Premiere Pro includes the option to share your user preferences between multiple machines: When installing Premiere Pro, you will have entered your Adobe ID to confirm your software license. You can use the same ID to store your user preferences in Creative Cloud, allowing you to sync and update them from any installation of Premiere Pro.

Customizing the Workspace

In addition to customizing the default workspaces (based on tasks), you can adjust the position and location of panels to create a workspace that works best for you. You can then store a workspace or even create multiple workspaces for different tasks.

- As you change the size of a frame, frames change size to compensate.
- All panels within frames are accessible via tabs.

In this exercise, you'll try all these functions and save a customized workspace.

Try It!

1. Click the Source Monitor panel (selecting its tab if necessary), and then position your pointer on the vertical divider between the Source Monitor and the Program Monitor. Then, drag left and right to change the sizes of those frames. You can choose to have different sizes for your video displays.

2. Now place the pointer on the horizontal divider between the Source Monitor and the Timeline. Drag up and down to change the sizes of these frames (FIGURE 7.6).

FIGURE 7.6

Note:
You may be prompted with a dialog box asking where a particular file is stored. This will happen when the original files are saved on a hard drive different from the one you're using. You'll need to identify the storage location. In this case, navigate to the asset files for this chapter and select the file to open. Premiere Pro will remember this location for the rest of the files.

Tip:
Another way to open the Import dialog box is to simply double-click an empty area of the Project panel.

LEARNING AUDIO/VIDEO PRODUCTION   251

Working with Data and Solution Files

As you work through the Try It! exercises, you will be creating, opening, and saving files. Keep the following instructions in mind.

- Most projects will require you to open a data file to begin the project. The data files can be accessed from the Navigate IT Web site (www.pearsonhighered.com/navigateit). Select "Student" and browse for "Learning Audio/VideoProduction."

- The data files are named with the chapter number and a file number; i.e., **Ch08_1.prproj**. Data files for the end-of-chapter projects have the initials PB (for Portfolio Builder) followed by the chapter number; i.e., **PB08.prproj**.

- You will be instructed to save the data files with a new name. Saving the file with a new name preserves the original file in case you want to go back and start over or repeat steps as a review.

- You will be directed to include the initials of your first and last name so you can easily locate your files if you have to share a computer. Solution file names will appear in the text with two xx's to stand for your initials; i.e., **Ch08_1_xx.prproj**.

- Follow your teacher's directions for where to access and save the files on a network, local computer hard drive, or portable storage device such as a USB drive.

- Many of the media assets (audio, video, and images) used in the Try It! exercises are provided in ZIP files. To use them, download the ZIP files according to your teacher's instructions and extract the files into a folder. When you open a data file, the Link Media dialog box will display. Select any asset in the Missing Media list, click the Locate button to open the Media Browser, navigate to the folder where you extracted the assets, and click Search. After selecting the matching asset file, click OK. Remaining files for that project should relink automatically.

Chapter 1

Message and Medium

Chapter 1 Overview

- What is Video Production?
- Equipment and Gear Basics
- Telling a Story
- Tools of the Content Creator: Symbols, Clues, and Twists
- Careers in A/V Production

- Production Workflow
- The Shot: Composing for Meaning
- Shooting to Edit
- Postproduction: Putting it All Together
- End-of-Chapter Review and Activities

Message and Medium. These two concepts are the essence of the audio/video production process. The **message** is the story you want to tell. The **medium** is the format you use to tell that story.

This chapter focuses on the basic information you'll need to get started on your first video production. You will learn about equipment and gear, the components of storytelling, and the people who work together to create all kinds of visual content, including movies, television shows, training videos, and animations. You will be introduced to the production workflow and all the different shots you can use to capture the video you need to tell your story.

What Is Video Production?

Throughout this book, phrases such as *filmmaking*, *media creation*, and *video production* are used interchangeably. That's because the information can be applied to the production of a visual poem, fictional film, animation, montage, documentary, training video, commercial, public service announcement (PSA), or anything else that uses moving pictures to convey a subject or an idea. At their root, despite wide variations in style, content, length, audience, and goals, all of these forms are just different types of *content creation*, which means they all have as much in common as divides them, especially when it comes to their creation.

When you make a media piece—any media piece—you are choosing an image or series of images and accompanying sounds to show something to an audience, whether that audience is your best friend or the entire world. When your audience watches your piece, they will immediately begin to try to *decode* your *meaning*. You may not think you are "telling a story" or anything so grandiose if you are simply filming your friend's skateboard trick.

But you are.

Even in the 20-second video of a skateboard trick, there's a progression; something is attempted, and success or failure may result. Your audience wants to find out if the skateboard trick works or not.

Equipment and Gear Basics

Before jumping into an adventure filled with gadgets, gear, and gizmos, consider this fundamental truth about telling a story through the medium of video: it's not about the gear you use; it's about how you use it to tell your story effectively and convincingly.

You could have the latest, most expensive pro camera on the market, but if you don't have a good story to tell and don't know how to use the camera, your project will be no better than average. Mobile devices have brought high-quality video tools into a lot of people's pockets. A high-quality camera alone does not make you a professional videographer.

Here is a general list of the intangible requirements to create successful, professional video:

- An understanding and working knowledge of the controls of your equipment

- A well-organized plan of attack

- An ability to problem-solve calmly under pressure

- An eagerness and curiosity about how things work

- A devotion to detail

- An understanding of the value of safety

- A commitment to reliability and dependability

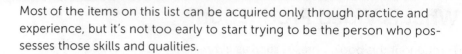

Most of the items on this list can be acquired only through practice and experience, but it's not too early to start trying to be the person who possesses those skills and qualities.

Tools of the Trade: From Mobile Devices to Pro Gear

There are several tiers of equipment available based on price, quality, and feature set. The top tier is **professional-level equipment** (see FIGURE 1.1), tools exclusively used for large-budget feature and television work, the type of gear you'd never hear of anyone buying because it's so expensive that renting is a more practical way to get access to the equipment. In a professional kit, cameras in particular have fewer automatic functions but more physical access to controls through buttons, dials, and switches.

FIGURE 1.1 Hands-on with the RED ONE digital cinema camera.

The lowest tier is **consumer-level equipment** (see FIGURE 1.2) designed for a mass market with a cheaper price tag. Consumer equipment has most of its controls *under the hood*, through automatic functions that allow the user to plug and play easily without a steep learning curve.

Consumer equipment tends to produce a lower-quality product but has the advantage of more resources for support through online tutorial videos created by other users and more responses in support forums.

In between, there is **prosumer-level equipment** (see FIGURE 1.3), hybrids of professional and consumer-level equipment. Prosumer gear hits that sweet spot of high-end features and quality with moderate prices. Equipment in this category definitely holds back on some controls that professional work demands, but what this gear lacks in controls can usually be handled by a workaround. Prosumer equipment has allowed enthusiasts and educational programs to create professional-level work without paying a hefty price or sacrificing control.

FIGURE 1.2 An iPhone mounted on a Zacuto Zgrip running FiLMiC Pro app

FIGURE 1.3 A Sony NXCAM camcorder

It Fits in Your Pocket!

Through advances in mobile technology, smartphones now make capturing video something everyone can do. Smartphone video applications have not only transformed how video is created and distributed but also generated an upsurge in the number of people who have access to the tools to do so.

When video was introduced as a capability of mobile phones, the quality and format was below standard definition (SD) because of the limitations of storage space and the ability of the device. Currently, the resolutions of video captured with mobile devices match the high-definition (HD) standard of television and keep increasing. With professional digital video and cinema quality increasing to ultrahigh definition (Ultra HD) resolutions ranging from 4K to 8K, consumer demand has shot through the roof.

Choosing a Camera to Fit Your Budget and Needs

In professional applications, the purpose of a project helps determine the type of camera that is used for a production. Choosing from the variety of camera types available at affordable prices with their assortment of features, requires an understanding of the capabilities and limitations of each type of camera.

STUDIO CAMERAS

Within television production, large **studio** or **broadcast cameras** (see **FIGURE 1.4**) are used because of the requirements of that type of production. These cameras allow a single-cable connection to a live switcher that includes communication with the operator and a video signal of the program choices of the director to be monitored.

FIGURE 1.4   A studio camera with a teleprompter.

Each camera has a **tally light** that indicates which camera angle the program is switched to so that the operator and the talent are informed. A large **viewfinder** display allows the operator better to detect the focus of their shot and increases mobility.

The camera supports used for studio cameras include large tripods to hold their weight and **pedestals** that use air or hydraulic pressure to allow the camera to move up and down easily.

ENG

Outside of the studio, **electronic news gathering (ENG) cameras** (see **FIGURE 1.5**) are used for news and many other forms of video production. ENG cameras have a shape designed for comfortable placement on an operator's shoulder for handheld use.

FIGURE 1.5   A JVC electronic news gathering camera.

Unlike studio cameras, ENG cameras have a built-in recording mechanism. Before it was possible to use memory cards to record video, these cameras recorded video to cassette tapes, which made the size and power requirements of the camera much larger than other consumer cameras made then or now.

Even as video formats transitioned from analog to digital, ENG cameras still required tape to record the picture and sound until tapeless acquisition became practical and affordable.

To complete the all-in-one design, ENG cameras use professional-grade microphone inputs to record audio, a function that is neither necessary nor available for studio cameras or film cameras.

CINEMA

Film cameras (see **FIGURE 1.6**) require the operator to see the shot through an **optical reflex viewfinder** that forces them to keep their face in direct contact with the device to prevent light leaking in and exposing the film negative.

PHOTO BY YURIY PONOMAREV. SHUTTERSTOCK

FIGURE 1.6 A 35mm film camera

Historically, their disadvantage was only one person could monitor what the camera was capturing. The invention of the **video assist**, or **video tap**, a small video camera built into the camera to *tap* into the view of the lens, allowed directors also to monitor what the camera operator was seeing.

Digital cinema cameras (see **FIGURE 1.7**) don't require a video tap since they are basically a type of video camera. The use of digital cameras in cinema production started with models that looked and functioned like ENG and broadcast cameras. Early use of digital cameras in feature-film production came along with the increase in quality of smaller digital tape formats and the ability to record higher-definition images in the standard frame rate for cinema production.

Cinema cameras have begun to move away from the systems and formats of broadcast video and use new acquisition formats that take advantage of the workflow of feature film production (see **FIGURE 1.8**) and emphasize the need for higher-resolution images that capture a larger spectrum of light and color.

> **Note:**
>
> In the United States, the system for standard definition video is called NTSC, which runs at a frame rate of 29.97 frames per second (fps). Feature motion pictures run at a frame rate of 24 fps. See Chapter 3 for more information on frame rates.

PHOTO BY MARIO CASTRO

FIGURE 1.7 ARRI Alexa cinema camera

FIGURE 1.8 Blackmagic Design Pocket Cinema Camera

Images acquired in raw image formats and new digital cinema color spaces necessitate color correction before being delivered to a viewing audience. This extra step in the workflow makes for higher-quality images than footage shot directly in standard video formats.

A feature that distinguishes film and cinema cameras from most other types of cameras is the ability to switch out wide and telephoto lenses easily (see **FIGURE 1.9**). ENG and studio cameras have a single lens, usually a zoom lens, to use for every shooting circumstance. In recent years, manufacturers have begun to add the ability to switch lenses to some prosumer and consumer cameras.

PHOTO BY BEBOY, SHUTTERSTOCK

FIGURE 1.9 Lenses for cinema and DSLR cameras

CAMCORDERS

Camcorders (see FIGURE 1.10) are like ENG cameras, but for the prosumer and consumer markets. Prosumer camcorders (often called **professional camcorders)** record audio using professional audio inputs and have many manual and custom controls on the body of the camera.

FIGURE 1.10 A Sony HDV Camcorder

Unlike ENG cameras, camcorders are too small to rest on the operator's shoulder and include many more automatic functions to make operation easier for novice users. A feature that originated in camcorders and has made its way to ENG cameras is the swing-out **LCD viewfinder** screen. Touchscreen controls on LCD viewfinders have migrated from the consumer camcorder to professional digital cinema cameras.

As with digital cinema cameras, a certain class of camcorders has come to market that allows the switching of lenses. In video production, familiarity with various types of lens mounts and features was not required knowledge before the introduction of video-capable DSLR cameras.

DSLR

Digital single-lens reflex (DSLR) cameras (see FIGURE 1.11) are the digital version of single-lens reflex cameras used for still photos on film. With increasing resolution (expressed as **megapixels**) and processing capability, digital still camera manufacturers experimented with adding video capture as a feature. This function allowed the user to use interchangeable photo lenses to capture video, much like cinema cameras do.

A major advantage of using a DSLR to capture video is the price of the camera. With prices comparable to—and often lower than—the price of camcorders, these cameras can reproduce professional-quality cinematic images far beyond what most camcorders can deliver. (When pricing a DSLR, keep in mind that the accumulated cost of lenses can drive up the price far beyond the "body-only" price of the camera.)

The DSLR's ability to record audio does not match that of camcorders or ENG cameras, so the use of **dual-system sound**, as in cinema production, is required for professional-quality audio. Recording audio on a separate recorder in a dual-system sound setup requires considerations for synchronizing the audio with the picture in the editing process.

FIGURE 1.11 A Canon DSLR camera

Unlike other video cameras, DSLRs lack the ability to control the zoom lens with a motorized switch, and many have limited or no automatic focus control. For the price, the quality, and their capabilities, DSLR cameras make for great training cameras. Using a DSLR demands that the user have an understanding and active involvement in manipulating its controls to capture professional images.

MOBILE CAMERAS

Even smaller than consumer camcorders and DSLR cameras are pocket camcorders that record video and sound in a device that can easily hide in the palm of your hand. Pocket camcorders are one type of camera that can be placed in the mobile camera category.

Sports and action cameras are by-products of the scale of pocket cameras and are used for capturing virtually any kind of sporting activity. They're also used in professional cinema and television production for stunts and tricky angles. Sports and action cameras specialize in capturing in high frame rates that make movement look clearer and sharper and, when played at slower frame rates, help demonstrate aspects of the physical world that real-time video does not.

Consumer mobile devices, such as smartphones and tablets (see **FIGURE 1.12**), have cameras that take wonderful snapshots and impressive video images. Apps dedicated to adding complete manual and custom control to mobile cameras are making it possible to consider using mobile cameras exclusively for many types of video productions. Accessory manufacturers are creating cases and mounts that convert mobile devices into cameras capable of producing sophisticated projects.

Smartphones and tablets that run apps can edit and upload video to online video-hosting services. With a single device you can write, shoot, edit, deliver, and present a video production without introducing a single other piece of equipment into the process. The ease and low cost of doing so makes it possible for anyone with such a device to use video to deliver their message to the world.

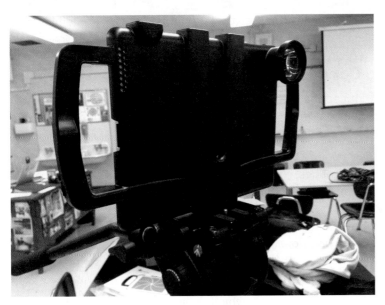

FIGURE 1.12 An iPad in the iOgrapher Mobile Media Case

SOUND GEAR

In Chapters 3 and 4 you will learn about the kind of microphones (see **FIGURE 1.13**) you can use for specific types of audio recording. To get a head start on equipping yourself appropriately, identify the microphone inputs and audio recording capabilities of your camera.

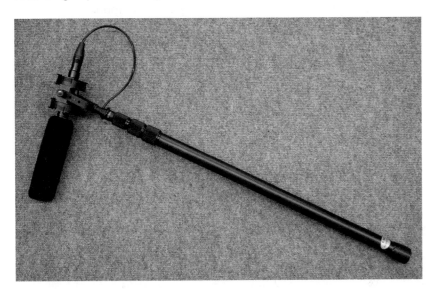

FIGURE 1.13 A shotgun microphone mounted on a boom pole

If your camera does not have enough **audio inputs** or the kind of inputs to fit the microphones you want to use, consider getting a portable digital audio recorder that records audio on memory cards, has professional microphone inputs, or even has a built-in microphone. Some portable audio recorders can be mounted directly on a camera with an output to record reference or backup audio to the camera.

There are even apps that let you use your phone or tablet to record high-quality audio files in the same **uncompressed format** that professionals use.

Cables and Connectors

You may have noticed that a lot of this equipment must be hooked up using cables and connectors. These cables and connectors are used to carry audio and video signals in either analog or digital format.

Analog describes a device that represents changing values as continuously variable physical quantities, such as sound. **Digital** describes a device that processes all information using binary code—1s and 0s. Analog audio is stored electronically as continuous vibrations that are the same as the original sound waves. Analog video is stored as continuous waves of red, green, and blue intensities. It uses varying signal strength to represent brightness. Digital audio consists of sound waves that have been sampled and digitized so they can be used by a computer. Digital video uses 1s and 0s to represent visual images.

There are many different standards, which means there are many different connectors. The differences are usually in the types and numbers of wires, the strength and frequency of the signal, and the physical design of the plugs and sockets.

FIGURE 1.14

FIGURE 1.15

- Bayonet Neill-Concelman (BNC) connectors (see **FIGURE 1.14**) are used for professional video electronics, using serial digital interface (SDI) cable, HD-SDI, or CoaXPress, an asymmetric high-speed serial communication standard over coaxial cable. Coaxial cable (see **FIGURE 1.15**) is commonly used by the cable television industry and for data communications over Ethernet networks.

- Component A/V cable is used to carry analog audio and video signals and is used on HD televisions, DVD players, and Blu-ray players. Basic component cables have 10 connectors. Six are for video and four are for audio.

FIGURE 1.16

- Composite video cable uses a single standard RCA-style jack to pass video signals. It is usually paired with stereo audio jacks. Composite video cables are designed to maximize video signal transfer. They are used with home A/V equipment such as DVD players and televisions.

- Digital Visual Interface (DVI) is used for flat-panel LCD computer displays and digital projectors and is compatible with most computer video cards (see **FIGURE 1.16**). It carries uncompressed digital video in analog, digital, or both.

FIGURE 1.17

- Firewire, also called i.Link or IEEE 1394, is a digital data transfer protocol used on digital camcorders and high-end audio equipment (see **FIGURE 1.17**).

- High Definition Multimedia Interface (HDMI) is a digital connection for transferring uncompressed high definition picture and sound. It is found on home electronics such as televisions and game consoles (see **FIGURE 1.18**).

- Mini HDMI is the same as HDMI but smaller, so it is suitable for digital cameras and camcorders.

FIGURE 1.18

- Mobile High Definition Link (MHL) is used for transferring HD video and audio from portable devices to HD-ready A/V equipment such as a television or A/V receiver.

- Radio Frequency (RF) connectors are used to connect a radio or television receiver to an antenna or to a cable system.

- RCA cables and connectors are used for analog and digital audio or composite video (see **FIGURE 1.19**).

- S-Video is a single jack used for carrying standard definition analog video.

- Universal Serial Bus (USB) is an interface between a computer and a peripheral device such as a digital camcorder, digital camera, microphone, keyboard, or printer (see **FIGURE 1.20**).

- Video Graphics Array (VGA) carries analog video information to flat panel LCD monitors and plasma televisions to display video from a computer (see **FIGURE 1.21**).

- XLR is used in professional audio and video cabling applications.

FIGURE 1.19

FIGURE 1.20

FIGURE 1.21

Accessories and Expendables

Having chosen a camera—often the most difficult choice to make in your gear selection—you still need to add a few essential items to your arsenal. Some of these items could be foregone on informal productions but are never left out of a professional inventory.

Camera stabilization tools such as a **tripod**, **monopod**, a **shoulder mount**, or a **gimbal-based device** (like a Steadicam, Glidecam [see **FIGURE 1.22**], or M VI) can take a novice production from looking like shaky home video to smooth, precise, high-end work.

FIGURE 1.22 A Glidecam X10 bodymounted stabilization system

When choosing a tripod, consider the weight of your camera. A $10,000 150mm tripod designed to hold a pro camera would be overkill if you are mounting a smartphone on it. On the other hand, a $10 photo tripod will definitely not allow you to make smooth movements with a heavier camcorder.

You never know how important batteries for your camera and audio gear are until you forget to bring enough charged ones for your shoot. Never settle for the battery that comes in the box with your camera; always buy more than you think you need, and always keep them charging. Did a battery die on a shoot? Put it on the charger now.

Media such as **memory cards** or **cassette tapes** is like gold. Memory cards of a high class ensure that the camera will be able to write the fast stream of video data being jammed onto it effectively. Tape is cheap; do not reuse tapes unless you like glitches and corruption in your footage.

A **clapboard**, or **slate** (see FIGURE 1.23), is a tool that has two purposes: to label or slate your shot for visual identification during the editing process and to have a matching visual and auditory reference to synchronize picture and sound if they were recorded on separate systems. Slates are usually made of acrylic for use with a dry-erase marker, but there are even apps available that enable you to use your mobile device as a slate.

FIGURE 1.23 A standard slate and "mouse"

Other useful expendables and accessories include the following:

- **Gaffer tape**

- Gloves (slang: *hand shoes*) for protecting your hands from hot lights

- A flashlight

- A multitool

- Pens, pencils, markers

Telling a Story

The journey of a thousand miles begins with a single step. It's not uncommon for those considering a project to wonder what to write about or how to go forward. It can all seem too big, too vague, and too undoable. It's not. You just need to look at your project one scene, one shot, or one piece of dialogue at a time; listen to your instincts; and be honest with yourself about when you are moving in the right direction and when it's time to switch gears.

The great composer Mozart wrote his operas and concertos in ink, supposedly never needing to change a note. Luckily, text-editing programs have an Undo command and a Delete key, and **nonlinear editing (NLE) systems** let you drop in and pull out clips at will.

Don't stress about getting it perfect. Just get it.

Here are a few things to consider as you get started.

In the Beginning

Content creation—whether for a TV series, a feature film, or a documentary—is based on three universal elements.

- The **main character**, also known as the **protagonist** and sometimes the *hero*. For example, the skateboarder is the main character in a skateboarding video.

- The **goal** the main character pursues, such as a great skateboarding trick.

- **Obstacles** to that goal, such as a steep skateboard ramp.

Every video comes down to these three things. There are a lot of other elements, of course, but these three form the skeleton on which everything else builds.

The universal experience of watching media is tracking something that has been established by the content creator to watch. The next time you view anything, see how long it takes for you to understand what you're tracking.

This process works differently, of course, depending on various other factors such as the length of the media. For a television show such as *The Fresh Prince of Bel-Air* (1990–96), the whole series will track something—how street-smart Will Smith handles the changes in his life when he moves from his tough Philadelphia neighborhood to the wealthy neighborhood of Bel-Air.

Every individual episode will track this development in a general way. Additionally, it will track an individual storyline more specifically. The conflict always raises a yes or no question—say, will Will make it onto *The Oprah Winfrey Show*? It gives the audience something specific to root for and against.

PROTAGONIST/MAIN CHARACTER/HERO

Protoganist, main character, and hero are all synonyms (words that mean the same thing) for the main character—the character the story is about.

In *The Matrix* (1999), Neo is the character mostly responsible for making things happen, so he is the main character. Luke Skywalker and Anakin Skywalker in the *Star Wars* film series are other examples of main characters.

Sometimes the protagonist in a media piece is not immediately apparent. At first glance, Frodo Baggins appears to be the main character of the *Lord of the Rings* series of books by J. R. R. Tolkien and films by Peter Jackson, when he has to decide how to dispose of the One Ring, a weapon of great power.

However, over a protracted series of adventures, Frodo's pal and gardener Sam Gamgee really fills out the role of the protagonist better than Frodo. Although Frodo ultimately has to get to Mount Doom to destroy the ring, Sam does pretty much all the heavy lifting to get Frodo there across something like 8,000 pages of books.

One of the most important things to do as a writer/creator is to let the audience know what kind of person the protagonist is. What does she care about? What is she good at? What are her weaknesses? Getting to know the main character is often the first thing that gets an audience interested in a story. You may notice, the next time you watch a show or film, that some aspect of the protagonist's personality is showcased the very first time she appears.

Often, the protagonist in a film or novel has a special skill that will help him or her to achieve the goal. For example, Luke Skywalker in *Star Wars* (1977) is a great pilot, a skill he uses to try to destroy the Death Star.

The hero of the story may be the protagonist, and the protagonist may be a hero, but not always. In *Lord of the Rings*, the most traditionally heroic character is Aragorn, but he is not the protagonist because he is not the most central driver of the mission. Tony Montana in the film *Scarface* (1983) is not heroic, but he is definitely the protagonist of his narrative. Protagonists don't have to be "good guys/girls"; they just have to be relatable and interesting.

GOAL

The goal is the thing that the main character most wants to achieve. This goal can involve beating the villain and/or solving the problem or threat. Goals may change during the story, but usually only if they become deeper, more intense, or richly meaningful to the protagonist.

For instance, Luke Skywalker's initial goal in *Star Wars* is to save Princess Leia. Once the pursuit of that goal concludes, around halfway through the film, the story could be over, except that the quest to rescue her has uncovered a great and immediate threat to freedom throughout the galaxy (a bigger and more intense goal).

Most goals in stories are surprisingly simple, though they don't always start out seeming that way. They're usually things that a large portion of the audience also might want—money and treasure, of course, but also deeper things—love, respect, a purpose in life, freedom.

Goals can generally be broken down into *external* and *internal* goals that can come from the same result. For instance, in the film *Rocky* (1976), Rocky Balboa wants to "go the distance" in his fight against Apollo Creed (external goal) because that will give him back the self-respect he has lost (internal goal).

CONFLICT/OBSTACLES

Conflicts and obstacles are whatever might stop the protagonist from achieving his or her goal. Examples of obstacles include Shrek the ogre's self-esteem in *Shrek* (2001), that Jack and Rose are from different socioenomic backgrounds and also that their ship hits an iceberg in *Titanic* (1997), and that Juliet's family is at war with Romeo's in *Romeo and Juliet*.

Most writer/creators like to have at least a pretty clear picture of who their protagonist is, what their goal is, and what the obstacles might be before they start writing their stories out in detail. Once you have all three of these things, you can begin to generate empathy for your main character. If farmers are in the business of producing crops or dairy products, storytellers are in the business of producing empathy.

Empathy

Empathy is the feeling that makes the audience care about the protagonist. The audience wants that skateboarder to finally nail that trick.

The writer, director, actor, and everyone directly involved with the project make the audience feel that they know the character or even that they are the character. The more the audience identifies with the protagonist, the more involved they are in the story.

Some of the most common ways the writer and director create empathy for the main character include the following:

- Having the main character go after a goal that is *almost* impossible. Examples include Luke Skywalker taking on the Empire, El Mariachi having to fight dozens of hit men in *El Mariachi* (1992), and Rocky wanting to last 12 rounds against the heavyweight champ of the world.

- Having the main character experience a great loss. For example, in *Spider-Man* (2002), Peter Parker's beloved Uncle Ben dies.

- Having the main character experience a great need, such as Rocky's need for self-respect.

- Having the main character exhibit personality traits that people respect, such as bravery, like Luke Skywalker; humor, like Austin Powers in the *Austin Powers* franchise of films; or decency, like attorney Atticus Finch in *To Kill a Mockingbird* (1962).

- Having the main character experience events that happen in real life, such as stepping in a puddle, or missing an important phone call.

Empathy creates engagement and identification between the audience and the protagonist. It binds the audience to the protoganist through the entire story.

The 12 People You Meet in Stories

A good next step when writing your story is to think about the types of characters who will populate your narrative in addition to your protagonist. This section describes some of the most common types of characters in narratives.

ANTAGONISTS AND ANTI-HEROES

The **antagonist** is the character who most gets between the main character and the goal: the mother who doesn't want her daughter to marry below her means in *Titanic*, or the replicant (cyborg) who simply wants to extend his synthetic life in *Blade Runner* (1982). The antagonist is not always a villain, but if the story does feature a villain, the villain is probably the antagonist.

Can the villain be the protagonist? There have certainly been lots of cases where writers and directors switch it up. **Anti-heroes** are villains who inspire audience support despite their illegal or immoral activities, and they include some of the richest characters in media history, including Michael Corleone in *The Godfather* series.

Even the relatively innocent genre of family films has explored the anti-hero in *Despicable Me* (2010) and *Megamind* (2010), where traditionally villainous characters take on the role of the hero, usually attempting some sort of redemption.

THE MENTOR

Sometimes the main character has a **mentor**, an older advisor who gives him some knowledge or training he uses to achieve the goal. Examples of mentors include Morpheus in *The Matrix*, Uncle Ben and Aunt May in *Spider-Man* (2002), Gandalf in *Lord of the Rings* (2001), and Obi-Wan Kenobi in the *Star Wars* movies.

One of the most interesting mentors ever is Hannibal Lector, who some misremember as the antagonist of *The Silence of the Lambs* (1991) because he seemed more villainous than the actual villain (serial killer Buffalo Bill). But Lector actually illuminated the thought processes of the antagonist for the protagonist, FBI agent Clarice Starling. The Lector character proved so popular, in fact, that he graduated to the position of antihero in later films and a television series.

THE ALLY/ALLIES

Sometimes, the hero has an **ally** or second hero who pursues the same goal for a different reason and whose personality, strengths, and weaknesses are different from the main character's. Examples include Quint the shark expert in *Jaws* (1975), who is interested in catching the shark not because he shares the protagonist Sheriff Brody's need to protect his town but because sharks are his obsession. Han Solo in *Star Wars* also wants to rescue Princess Leia like Luke Skywalker does, but for money rather than out of moral obligation.

MIRROR

Mirror characters are similar to the protagonist; they often seem like brothers or sisters. They may be allies or competitors or even obstacles. They exist to illuminate the "dark side" of the protagonist, so the audience can see what the story would be like if the protagonist chose a different path, or to worry about if the story seems heading to an unfavorable conclusion.

Han Solo is a mirror character to Luke Skywalker. Eddie Brock is a mirror character in *Spider-Man 3* (2007). Like Peter Parker, Eddie is a photographer for the *Daily Bugle*; also like Peter, he is transformed into a superbeing, the villainous Venom.

One of the most interesting mirror characters in literature and film comes from *No Country for Old Men* (2007), based on the novel by Cormac McCarthy. The seeming protagonist, Llewelyn Moss, is shown to be the mirror character in one of the most staggering sequences in cinema history, forcing the audience to rethink the entire story.

THE HENCHMAN

The **henchman** is the ally of the antagonist. Oddjob, the well-dressed assassin who slices off enemies' heads with a razor-tipped bowler hat in *Goldfinger* (1964), remains one of the great Bond henchmen. The minions in *Despicable Me* (2010) are popular henchmen that earned their own film.

THE LOVE INTEREST

A **love interest** is a kind of ally who also provides a romantic storyline. Memorable examples include Trinity in *The Matrix*, Lois Lane in *Superman* (1978), and Rhett Butler in *Gone with the Wind* (1939). In some cases, the romantic storyline is the main story; in others, it is supporting. In David Cronenberg's remake of *The Fly* (1986), reporter Veronica Quaife is a love interest, ally, victim, and antagonist to the main character.

THE SIDEKICK

The **sidekick** is a kind of ally who generally provides humor (or brightness contrasted to the protagonist's darkness). C3PO and R2D2 in *Star Wars*, Jimmy Olsen in *Superman*, and Cosmo Kramer from *Seinfeld* (1998) are examples of outstanding sidekicks.

THE TRAITOR

The **traitor** is an ally who turns against the protagonist, usually reversing the likelihood of success. When Cypher in *The Matrix* gives the location of Morpheus' ship to the Agents, things turn grim for Neo and company. Elsa in *Indiana Jones and the Last Crusade* (1989) betrays Indy, making her both a love interest and a traitor.

Traitors can go both ways. Mini-Me starts out as a henchman for Dr. Evil in *Austin Powers: The Spy Who Shagged Me* (1999), but after a squabble, he joins the hero's side as Mini-Austin.

THE BUREAUCRAT

The **bureaucrat** is a character who represents the status quo, the way things are done, and as such is an obstacle for the protagonist, who usually seeks change. Sometimes the bureaucrat can be mistaken for the antagonist, but he is more of a roadblock than a true adversary.

Die Hard (1988) alone has several great bureaucrat characters: Dwayne Robinson, the Deputy Chief of Police; Thornburg, the reporter; and FBI agents Big Johnson and Little Johnson.

THE VICTIM

The **victim** represents the potentially dire outcome of the story if the protagonist does not achieve the goal; for instance, Nemo in *Finding Nemo* might be lost if his father cannot find him. The victim can also be the love interest (Lois Lane in *Superman*), an innocent child (Dana's baby Oscar in *Ghostbusters II* [1989]), or, frequently, the protagonist.

Recall that characters can "change jobs" throughout a story, more than once as the writer/creator sees fit. One of the most interesting examples of this shift occurs in Quentin Tarantino's omnibus masterpiece *Pulp Fiction* (1994), which is made up of several stories involving the same characters. In one storyline, hitman Vincent Vega is the protagonist; in a second, he is the sidekick; in a third, he is a henchman.

Once you have considered the characters you want to populate your story, as well as their goals and obstacles, you will need to organize all the steps of the quest the protagonist will undergo to achieve the objective.

Three-Act Structure

The **three-act structure** is the set of rules for all storytelling, from movie screenplays to television scripts to novels, plays, and short stories. Following these rules allows writers and directors to write scripts and present the information the audience needs in the most intriguing order.

The first rule of the three-act structure is that all stories can be broken down into three separate and distinct parts—previously, you may have referred to them as the Beginning, Middle, and End, but here they shall be known as follows:

- The first act (usually around the first 25 percent of the story)

- The second act (approximately the middle 50 percent)

- The third act (the final 25 percent)

The next three sections define the three acts in a traditional narrative structure.

THE FIRST ACT

The first act identifies the setup: when and where the story takes place, such as Philadelphia in *The Sixth Sense* or the future in *The Matrix*. The first act also introduces the circumstances that pertain to the story, such as the first voyage of the world's largest ship in *Titanic*.

In the first act, the audience meets and learns important facts about the life and personality of the protagonist, especially their strengths and weaknesses. In *Titanic*, Jack is poor but full of life, while Rose appears wealthy but feels dead inside. In *Die Hard*, John McClane is a tough cop who won't give up, but he desperately wants to get back together with his wife and children.

The audience also learns what the goal will be and gets a hint at least of what threat or problem might prevent the protagonist from achieving it, such as a plague, an asteroid, a serial killer, or an iceberg. Also, the villain or antagonist or a bureaucrat is introduced.

You can also think of the threat as the antagonist's goal, which is usually the opposite of the protagonist's goal. For example, in *Speed* (1996), the threat is that a bus will blow up if it goes below 50 miles per hour; therefore, the hero's goal is to make sure that doesn't happen so he can save the passengers.

The moment when the protagonist accepts the challenge of achieving the goal is called the **first act break**. Examples include Luke deciding to leave his planet to try to save Princess Leia in *Star Wars* and Rocky agreeing to fight the heavyweight champion of the world, Apollo Creed.

The first act break is the moment when the main character becomes locked into his or her path and the audience understands what the rest of the movie is about and what the goals and threats are.

THE SECOND ACT

The rhythm picks up and the pace increases in the second act. The main character now tries to achieve her goal but encounters a series of obstacles. Obstacles can include the following:

- *The loss or death of family/mentor/allies*: Dr. Crowe, the child psychologist, grows apart from his wife in *The Sixth Sense*; Luke loses mentor Obi-Wan in *Star Wars*.

- *Personal injury, either physical or mental*: El Mariachi loses his hand; Luke also loses his hand in *The Empire Strikes Back* (1980).

- *The threat turns out to be much worse than originally thought*: The shark in *Jaws* is much bigger than expected; the computers in *The Matrix* seem omnipotent; the Death Star in *Star Wars* is the greatest weapon the universe has ever known.

- *The original method of defeating the villain or threat doesn't work and only makes the threat more serious*: The shark overwhelms Sheriff Brody and his team at first in *Jaws* because the sheriff has underestimated it; first the Air Force and then nuclear weapons fail against the aliens in *Independence Day* (1996).

As you've probably noticed, the two emotions that successful stories elicit in the viewer are *hope* and *fear*. The audience hopes the protagonist will achieve her goal, and fears that she will not.

The second act usually involves a series of ups and downs in which some events bring the protagonist closer to the goal while other events push her further from it.

The ups and downs of the story are most often reflected through a series of twists, reversals, and false hopes. When the U.S. military brings in nuclear weapons in the film *Independence Day*, it gives the audience a false hope that, at least by using such an extreme measure, the aliens can be defeated. In *The Sixth Sense*, when the audience realizes that a major character has been dead all along, this twist changes what everyone has believed so far to be true. When El Mariachi gets knocked out and taken to Moco, his situation is reversed; he goes from being on top of the situation to a captive.

The distinguishing characteristic of the second act is that things get tougher for the main character, whether she is looking for love or trying to save the world. The audience's empathy for the main character grows as the situation gets worse.

The protagonist tries to solve the problem, but the first solutions don't work for whatever reason, and now when things get worse, the audience gets to see what the heroes are really made of.

Eventually, though, the protagonist's strengths, such as perseverance, resourcefulness, smarts, or sheer luck, enable her to defeat the antagonist or resolve the conflict. This moment in the story is called the **second act break**. It usually happens around 75 percent of the way through the story, and it moves the story from the forward momentum of the second act to the even faster momentum of the third act.

The second act break might feature any of the following:

- The main character finally figuring out how to stop the antagonist/threat. For example, Luke and his crew find a weakness in the plans for the Death Star.

- The protagonist figuring out when the threat will strike—for instance, when will the lava hit midtown L.A. in *Volcano* (1997)? This plot device is also called a "ticking clock."

- If the hero's goal intensifies during the second act (*Star Wars*) or changes because of a new understanding of the circumstances (*The Sixth Sense*), the second act break is the moment when the last piece of the puzzle is in place and the protagonist knows what must be done to achieve the goal—for example, help a young boy cope with his abilities in *The Sixth Sense*, or fly onto the Death Star and destroy it in *Star Wars*.

At this point, the audience knows what, when, and usually where and how the big scene/"big showdown" will occur.

The pace picks up as the second act break moves into the third act because this is the first time the protagonist has been sure of what needs to done to finally achieve the goal.

THE THIRD ACT

The third act features the big showdown between the protagonist and antagonist or the big get-together or final goodbye in a love story. The main character must finally go all out with an act of great bravery in a drama or action movie or an act of honesty and compassion in a love story.

Often, the showdown, also called the **climactic scene,** will involve the hero overcoming a weakness that's been discussed since the first act. In *Jaws*, Sheriff Brody, who is afraid of water, gets dumped in the ocean to fight the shark. In *Die Hard*, John McClane must do the only thing he finds impossible: open up to his wife. Superman must overcome kryptonite.

Sometimes, the hero must make a great sacrifice in order to achieve the goal: El Mariachi loses his hand, Jack sacrifices himself to save Rose in *Titanic*, driller Harry Stamper gives his life to save the earth in *Armageddon* (1998).

After the showdown, the hero has won or lost (usually won), and there's been a **resolution** or result, most likely the accomplishment of the goal or perhaps a new understanding or enlightenment. For example, when Luke blows up the Death Star, the resolution is that the Rebels are saved. When Jack sacrifices his life in *Titanic*, the resolution is that Rose is saved and will remember him always. When Austin Powers defeats Dr. Evil, he doesn't get his mojo back, but his story is resolved because he realizes he doesn't need it after all.

Finally, after the showdown, there's usually a shot or scene that lets the audience know things will be okay going forward. For example, Hooper the shark expert and Sheriff Brody paddle back to shore in *Jaws*; the survivors back on Earth mourn Harry Stamper in *Armageddon*.

This final wrap-up after the conflict has been resolved is called the **denouement**.

Tools of the Content Creator: Symbols, Clues, and Twists

The following are a few strategies that content creators ranging from novelists to video producers use to make their stories more interesting.

Symbols are something, usually visible, used to represent something else, usually invisible—for example, a heart for love or a four-leaf clover for luck. The classic film *Sunset Blvd.* (1950) is full of symbols. The title itself could refer to the end of a career or the end of a life. An attacking microphone represents the technology that ended a silent film star's great career.

Irony is a humorous twist in expectations, such as a swimming instructor who drowns. In the film *Citizen Kane* (1941), a woman says to the protagonist, "Well, you know what mothers are like" and he smiles, precisely because he doesn't know that and therein lies the heart of his problem. In **dramatic irony**, the audience knows something the characters don't. In *Kane*, everyone is searching for the identity of "Rosebud," but only the audience is allowed to learn what "Rosebud" really means.

Planting and **payoff**, like foreshadowing in a novel, mean giving the audience a clue as to what will happen later. For example, the compressed air tanks in *Jaws* are introduced as a very dangerous item, which will be meaningful later in the story. In *Citizen Kane*, the first image is a sign in the front of the main character's mansion that says "No Trespassing." When that sign reappears at the end of the film, it is clear to the audience that the filmmakers believe that the truth of a man's life is very difficult to know.

Subtext refers to what is really being said or meant beneath the dialogue. For example, in the film *Annie Hall* (1977), the filmmaker actually writes the subtext onscreen as subtitles as if it is a foreign language.

Repetition and **variation** occur when some element in the story is repeated but varied or seen in a different way to reflect some change in the story. Many elements and themes from the film *The Godfather* return in *The Godfather Part II* (1974), but they have grown darker, reflecting the moral disintegration of the protagonist, Michael Corleone. This repetition is also referred to as a *leitmotif*.

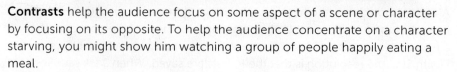

Contrasts help the audience focus on some aspect of a scene or character by focusing on its opposite. To help the audience concentrate on a character starving, you might show him watching a group of people happily eating a meal.

Misdirection is when the writer and director make the audience think something will happen and then insert a twist, as in a murder mystery when the audience thinks that the butler did it because he has a bloody knife, and then he licks it and it turns out to be strawberry jam.

Flashbacks are an example of how to use nonlinear storytelling effectively in filmmaking. Stories by default proceed forward in chronological order. Sometimes the storytellers break the timeline and send the audience back, via a flashback, to see something that happened earlier that is relevant to the current storyline. *Citizen Kane* is told almost entirely through flashbacks from the perspectives of several characters who know a man who recently died.

Careers in A/V Production

Once a writer/director has a story to tell, he needs a crew to help tell it. This section lists some of the most common jobs in media creation. Note that many of these jobs are covered in more detail later in this book.

Executive Producer

The coordinator or overseer of the entire production, the **executive producer** (EP) chooses the project and arranges the financing. He may work for a studio, own the script of underlying property, or in some way be responsible for getting the movie made.

Personality type: Executive producers, like writers, must have or choose a story or big idea that will take over their lives for a substantial amount of time. They should be active readers and viewers and have a sense of the audience or marketplace for whatever project they are choosing to focus on. They must have the business sense to analyze whether the project they have chosen to develop will be competitive in whatever arena it will screen, as well as the drive to put together the best possible team to produce the project.

Producer

The **producer** is a day-to-day boss responsible for making sure everyone else is doing their job. Their responsibilities include the following:

- Assigning responsibilities to individual crew members and checking to make sure they will complete tasks correctly and on time

- Arranging the shooting schedule location by location

- Making sure everything needed to film is ready on schedule

Personality type: Producers need to be extremely organized and able to juggle several issues at once. They must have good planning skills and predict where challenges to their success will come from, solving problems before they erupt.

Writer

The **writer** visualizes the plot and theme; creates the characters, visual descriptions, and dialogue; and communicates with the director and occasionally the actors about specific aspects of the story.

Personality type: The writer needs a good vocabulary and a visual, descriptive imagination.

Director

The "creative boss" of the movie, the **director** does the following:

- Transforms the script into a series of images or shots that can be filmed, and turns thoughts and ideas into pictures and performances. Directors have to hold the whole project in their head to make sure everything that is filmed will work together well.

- Creates or oversees *storyboards* and *shot lists* to let crew members know what the shots are.

- Casts actors who can give the necessary performances.

- Rehearses the actors and crew, giving them constructive feedback

- Oversees the creative process of the film from preproduction through postproduction

Personality type: Directors need to be natural leaders, visually and verbally creative, and focused on getting the job done; they must be supportive of people with whom they work. They deal mostly with the actors, director of photography, camera operator, and producer. All other work on the production is channeled through the director.

Actors/Talent

Actors, also called **talent**, play one or more onscreen roles in a project. An actor is responsible for the following:

- Creating a character including a **backstory**, which is the life that the character lived before the project began. Actors are responsible for developing their role both in the way they look and in the internalized thoughts and emotions they have, reacting spontaneously and believably as the character.

- Practicing and memorizing all dialogue.

- Practicing and memorizing their scenes, including their movements or **blocking**.

Personality type: Actors must be really focused to shut out all the "noise" and stress on a set and just let themselves become the character. They should have good memorization skills and commit themselves, in a mature way, to the things they do. Good actors, like good writers, have active imaginations and love coming up with new things every time they take on a new role. Actors interact mostly with the director and other actors.

Script Supervisor

The **script supervisor** (also known as the **continuity supervisor**) is the offi-cial note-taker on the set and is responsible for making sure that the script is filmed in its entirety, or for noting why anything is changed in the dialogue or the description as filming progresses. The script/continuity supervisor deals mostly with the director, helping to keep the director on task and make sure all of the shots and takes will have good continuity when the editors cut them all together.

Personality type: The script/continuity supervisor must be observant and take good notes.

First Assistant Director

The **first assistant director** or 1st AD runs the set and makes sure everyone is doing their job and staying on schedule. She develops call sheets so that everyone knows where they need to be and when.

Personality type: This crew member must be tough and have good discipline and natural leadership skills and be a good motivator to help eliminate prob-lems that can slow a crew down. The 1st AD deals mostly with the director and the producers.

Cinematographer/Director of Photography

The **director of photography** (DP, or DoP in the United Kingdom), also known at the **cinematographer**, is in charge of the look of the film and the way light and shadow are used to help create the tone or feeling of a movie. He chooses the type of film to create the appropriate look as well as equip-ment to control or shape the light. The DP works mostly with the director and the camera operator.

Personality type: The DP must have good visual imagination and be visually creative and artistic.

Camera Operator

The director designs the shots, but the **camera operator** records the shots; therefore, the camera operator must have especially good communication with the director. The camera operator is in charge of maintaining the com-position or framing, the exposure, and the focus of the shot.

Personality type: The camera operator must be responsible and reliable, steady and focused, and able to learn how to use new equipment and gear when necessary.

Camera Assistants

Camera assistants, or assistant camera (AC), are in charge of the various responsibilities related to the preparedness and use of the camera, including the following:

- Transporting the camera gear (camera, boom pole, microphone, slate, and so on) to the location and back

- Making sure all camera gear including slates, dry erase markers, lens cleaner, and so on is available when needed

- Marking the slate before each new take

- Pulling/changing focus during the take for the camera operator, as needed

- Making sure camera batteries are charged

Personality type: The camera crew must be reliable and responsible and like learning how to use complicated equipment.

Gaffer

The **gaffer** handles the electricity on the set. Professional productions use a lot of electricity for lights and other equipment, so this is an important job where safety is the absolute number-one priority. Student and amateur crews don't always have gaffers but must still be focused on safety whenever dealing with electricity.

Personality type: Gaffers must be technically competent, authoritative, attentive to detail, and well-organized.

Key Grip/Grips

The **key grip** is the boss of the grips. This team builds up or breaks down the lighting rigs used to film scenes based on the DP's wishes, as well as any other gear used by the camera crew, such as the **dolly**. The grip team reports to the key grip and his assistant, the **best boy**.

Personality type: Grips get it done; they set it up, and then they break down the riggings and other lighting gear, which can be hung far above the stage or set. Grips are primarily involved in assuring the safety of everyone on the set. They use effective communication to listen and ask questions. They pay attention to deadlines.

Production Designer/Art Director

The **production designer** collaborates with the director to make sure everything bought or made for the film, such as props and costumes, contributes to the right mood or tone of the film, whether silly or serious. The **art director** works for the production designer and oversees the art department, making sure everything is created to the exact specifications of the design plan.

Personality type: The production designer and art director must have good visual imaginations and be especially demanding before saying that something is right for the film.

Costume Designer/Prop Master

Like the production designer, the **costume designer** and **prop master** collaborate with the director and actors to come up with the right clothing and onscreen objects for the characters to use when filming.

Personality type: These designers must like shopping and have good visual imaginations. They must do their research and be very certain when saying that something is right for the film.

Make-Up Artist/Hair Stylist

Make-up artists and **hair stylists** work with the director and actors to achieve whatever make-up and hair effect is appropriate for the scene, from simple everyday stage make-up to prosthetic effects.

Personality type: Make-up and hair stylists in media are extremely competent and passionate about what they do, yet generally upbeat and pleasant to work with. They are often the ambassadors between the crew and the cast and must keep themselves familiar with trends in make-up and hair but also be knowledgeable about different styles through history and different cultures. They must be ready to style characters from different eras and ages. This is a lucrative discipline, and those interested should consider a program to learn how to develop into a professional.

Production Sound Mixer/Boom Operator

The **production sound mixer** must capture a quality audio recording of the action on the set, typically focusing on the voices of the actors and then the background sound of the location. He must choose the proper microphones and recording devices to get the best, cleanest sound and analyze every location beforehand for potential problems, such as buzzing in the background, street noise, or anything else that might affect recording.

The **boom operator** collaborates with the production sound mixer, wearing headphones so that he can hear the recorded sound and holding the boom pole and microphone over the actors' heads at a downward angle so that their voices are clear and easy to understand.

Personality type: Both of these positions require good hearing; additionally, boom operators should have strong arms as they may have to hold the boom pole over their heads for several hours a day while focusing on the sound quality.

Editor

The **editor** reviews all footage and cuts the movie either on film or using nonlinear editing (NLE) software such as Avid Media Composer, Adobe Premiere Pro, or Final Cut Pro X. The editor functions as the director's second set of eyes, working with the director to create the final finished version of the movie.

When possible, the editor should watch on the set to make sure the director is capturing footage that can be cut together well.

Personality type: Editors must have extremely high and exacting standards and a lot of patience to look through hundreds of takes of shot after shot trying to find "it"—the ideal balance, rhythm, and cut point to perfect the scene. Editing is one of the main jobs that leads to directing.

Assistant Editor

The **assistant editor** (AE) creates the edit log or list of all the available footage, called *dailies*. Assistant editors are in charge of bringing the media into the editing system and organizing it for the editor to find and use it easily. They also may be called on to edit some of the scenes.

Personality type: The assistant editor must have a lot of patience and concentration and be detail-oriented. On a two-hour feature film with a 10:1 shooting ratio (footage shot:length of piece), assistant editors have to log (list) and maintain a mere 20 hours of footage, but assistant editors on reality shows must sort through massive amounts of material, with ratios of 40:1 to 100:1 or more.

Sound Editor

Sound editors cut the music, sound effects, and rerecorded (or "looped") dialogue (ADR) into the film.

Personality type: Sound editors, like video editors, must like working with computer programs. They often have little interaction with the rest of the crew except for the director.

Music Supervisor or Composer

The **music supervisor** helps the director choose prerecorded music that matches the feeling of the scene or comments on it in an appropriate way. Alternately, a **composer** writes and plays music specifically written for the film.

Music is a key component of a successful project, often conveying the emotion that the script or performances sometimes hold back on.

Personality type: The music supervisor or composer must have a sharp ear and a keen sense of how to choose or compose music that captures and amplifies the tone of each scene.

Publicist

The **publicist** determines the best strategy for marketing screenings or exhibitions of the finished work far enough in advance to attract a substantial audience. Depending on the budget of the project, the publicist may create and distribute flyers, posters, or other materials related to the movie or buy ad time on radio and television or ad space in print and on the Web.

Over the last 15 years, social media has become the key to successful promotion of a media piece, with most sizable productions creating a Web site that users can link to through Facebook, Instagram, Twitter, or some other well-trafficked site. The publicist might also organize parties or other social events to promote the project.

Personality type: Publicists should be visually minded and active in social media, and familiar with Adobe Photoshop and other design-oriented software.

Production Assistant

The **production assistant** (PA) is an all-purpose utility player who may be called on to help out with any job that needs doing, from assistant camera to art department to assistant producer. This is the key entry-level job on real Hollywood films and television production companies, both as *office PAs* and *set PAs*.

Personality type: A good production assistant is reliable and always looking for something to do to help the movie.

Entry-Level: Getting a Foot in the Door

Though some preprofessionals eager to begin a career in the entertainment industry disregard production assistant jobs that call for getting coffee and similar menial tasks, these positions are actually an excellent way to learn on the job and watch other people doing their jobs without the whole crew depending on you every second of the day.

Production Workflow: The Three *P*s

In video production, there are three main stages of the process of creating a project: **preproduction**, **production**, and **postproduction**. Don't be fooled by the production-centric titles; each stage is as important as the other. Some jobs on a project are limited to one stage of the production, while the leading positions stay with a project through all three stages.

Preproduction

The preproduction stage begins when a decision is made to create a project and goes through until the start of the production stage. The steps that occur in preproduction include but are not limited to the following:

- Writing the script
- Budgeting the entire production
- Scheduling the shoot
- Fundraising to meet the budget
- Hiring the crew
- Casting the talent
- Scouting locations
- Designing and building sets
- Rehearsing
- Renting equipment

Production

The main phase of the production stage is **principal photography**, when the bulk of the shooting takes place. It is also where the majority of most projects' budgets are spent. The length of the principal photography depends on many factors, such as intended running time of the project, the size of the budget, and the final deadline.

Additional photography, in the form of **reshoots** and **pickups**, is also part of production. Reshoots are done if there is an error or a change to a scene that can't be fixed by any means other than to shoot the scene all over again. **Pickups** are additional shots that are necessary for the scene that were not captured when the scene was originally shot. Reshoots and pickups can occur as part of principal photography or during postproduction.

Postproduction

Postproduction (or post), as the name states, is the stage *after* production, but it doesn't necessarily have to wait until production ends to start. The management and organization of media, the assets and material that make up the images and sound that are put together, frequently occur as the production stage is still happening.

Picture editing is the first phase of post, and in most circumstances (live production excluded) takes a longer time than production. Simple projects that have few to no *visual effects* (*VFX*) have fewer people working than the production stage requires. A project that has visual effect shots, such as background elements over a green screen or animations in the foreground, requires more crew members in post.

Postproduction also includes work on audio, titles and graphics, and color correction.

One More *P*: Protocol

When setting up a shot, there is a standard order or **protocol** that a crew must follow for maximum efficiency. Before any equipment is set up, the director and talent use the stage or location space to block the action. Once the actors are blocked and rehearsed, the camera or cameras are placed for the first shot of the day.

Once the camera is placed, the grip and electric department get to work on lighting the shot. In cases of large or complicated lighting setups and shooting in a studio, the set is prelit for efficiency.

As final tweaks are made to the lighting, the sound crew can position their microphones, making sure they are not seen by the camera and do not cause any shadows in the shot.

A full camera rehearsal takes place for all elements to be blended together before cameras roll. The talent aren't the only ones who have a script with lines to say—the crew does, too! Once everything is working in full rehearsal, the director calls out, "Lock it up."

The 1st AD says, "Quiet on the set, picture up!"

"Picture up" is short for "the picture is up," which means the cameras are about to roll.

At this point, a camera assistant holds the slate or clapboard in the shot with the sticks open, ready to mark.

Once the set is quiet, the 1st AD calls, "Roll" or "Roll sound."

Tip:
The 1st AD might want to ask, "Is anyone not ready?" Asking this is more likely to get a response from someone making a final change that needs just one more minute than asking, "Is everyone ready?"

Note:
When numbering scene numbers on a slate, use uppercase letters to be easily recognized. Also, the letters I and O are skipped to avoid confusion with the numbers 1 and 0.

The sound mixer (or recordist) starts recording and says, "Speed!" That means the audio recording machine has taken up speed. This step is a holdover from the days of analog audio recording when a reel-to-reel recorder took a moment for the motor to get to its proper recording speed.

The camera operator starts recording and also calls, "Speed," "Camera rolling," "Camera rolls," or just "Rolling."

The camera assistant then verbally slates the shot by saying the scene number and take, for example for scene *3B take 2*, the AC would say, "Scene three-baker, take-two."

Before hitting the slate, the AC says, "Marker." If there are separate slates for different cameras, the AC will say, "A-camera mark" or "B-camera mark" before hitting the slate.

The marker is called before hitting the slate, not after, and certainly not during. The purpose of the slate is to synchronize the picture and audio. The sound of the clapboard needs to be clearly heard so the editorial team can match it up to the picture frame where the sticks meet each other.

If there is no audio being recorded, the AC holds his fingers between the sticks to show the editing team that there is no associated audio to search for. Shooting without synchronized audio is called MOS.

If talent or crew are still a little antsy, the director might call for everyone to "settle" before calling, "Action!"

When the take is done, the director calls, "Cut."

To keep things moving, the director immediately states whether to shoot another take or move on to another shot. To shoot another take, the director says, "Back to one," which means back to first position, where everyone was when the shot started. If the take is good and no other take is needed, even for **safety**, the director or 1st AD can call, "Moving on."

Then the cycle continues, until the last shot of the day is complete.

Tip:
If there is a mistake made while hitting the slate, the AC needs to call, "Second sticks," before hitting the slate again.

Note:
An extra take done after an acceptable take is captured is called a *safety take*.

The Shot: Composing for Meaning

The placement of the camera and the type of lens used can be key for telling the story. When motion pictures got into the storytelling business at the start of the 20th century, directors simply placed actors in front of the camera and had them act. The result was a filmed play, and the camera was mostly used as a recording device.

These days, media creators use the camera in countless ways to add energy to a scene or to comment on the action.

A **shot** here is defined as a camera angle—move the camera or change the lens and you're changing the shot—though it can be defined in many different ways, as you will see. Here are some definitions and categorizations.

Shots Defined by Size

Some shots are defined by width, or the lateral range of subjects or action captured in the frame. Each shot plays a role in the sequence of shots that comprise a scene, constitutes a part of the way one or more subjects are framed, or determines where the director wants the audience's attention focused at a given time (see **FIGURE 1.24**).

■ Full Shot	■ Medium Close-up (MCU)
■ 3/4 Shot	■ Close-up (CU)
■ Medium Shot (MED)	■ Extreme Close-up (ECU)

FIGURE 1.24 Basic shot sizes on a human subject

WIDE SHOT (WS)

A **wide shot** is a short-lens shot used to establish space, as in a master shot, or a whole location, as in the opening of a film (see **FIGURE 1.25**). One of the key things video producers want to do, especially in the beginning of their project, is to establish where it is taking place and then again, once the location changes, to reestablish that.

FIGURE 1.25 Wide shot

FIGURE 1.26 Full shot

FULL SHOT

A **full shot** gives a full-body view of the subject (see FIGURE 1.26). The top of the frame is slightly above the subject. The bottom of the frame is just underneath the subject's feet. The shot allows the viewer to see the relationship between the subject and the location of the scene.

FIGURE 1.27 3/4 shot

3/4 SHOT

A **3/4 shot** (pronounced "three-quarter") is slightly closer than a full shot (see FIGURE 1.27). The bottom of the frame cuts off at around the knees. The shot is loose enough to see enough of the subject's full body movement without bringing attention to the placement of the subject in the surrounding space.

FIGURE 1.28 Medium shot

MEDIUM SHOT (MED)

A **medium shot** is a head and upper-body shot, where the bottom of the frame cuts off at around the waist of the subject (see FIGURE 1.28). It may be considered the workhorse of media creation since many directors use it most commonly to handle dialogue-heavy scenes. Medium shots comprise more than 50 percent of most films.

MEDIUM CLOSE-UP (MCU)

A **medium close-up** is like a medium shot, showing the head and the upper body, yet the bottom of the frame cuts off halfway between the waist and the shoulders (see FIGURE 1.29).

FIGURE 1.29 Medium close-up

CLOSE-UP (CU)

In a **close-up**, the face of the character fills the frame, with the bottom of the frame cutting off right below the subject's shoulders (see FIGURE 1.30). This brings the audience very close to the character in a way that can seem uncomfortable or claustrophobic, which is why it is mostly saved for scenes of emotional importance or to convey suspense.

FIGURE 1.30 Close-up

EXTREME CLOSE UP (ECU)

A **macro lens** is used to magnify something in *extreme close-up* (see FIGURE 1.31) and make it fill the screen. An example is an ant on someone's skin or a blade of grass. Showing the audience something closer than they would ever typically see it can have a disquieting effect.

FIGURE 1.31 Extreme close-up

FIGURE 1.32 Long shot

LONG SHOT (LS)

The main action is far away from camera in a **long shot** (see **FIGURE 1.32**). This distancing effect makes the audience look into the shot to figure out what is happening, and it can also be used to contrast a character with their environment.

FIGURE 1.33 Two-shot

TWO-SHOT

The **two-shot** can be an MS, CU, or WS where two characters speak to each other and both of their faces featured in the shot (see **FIGURE 1.33**).

FIGURE 1.34 Over-the-shoulder shot

OVER-THE-SHOULDER (OTS)

This is a type of two-shot used frequently for conversations. **Over-the-shoulder** shots are generally done in pairs, each one focusing on a character on one side of the frame and the listener's shoulder on the other side, as if the camera were sitting on it like a parrot on a pirate (see **FIGURE 1.34**).

Shots Defined by Angle or Lens Height

Besides an **eye-level** shot, in which the lens is at the same height as the subject's eyes, there are terms for shots that look up, down, or in a rotated view at the subject.

HIGH-ANGLE SHOT

The camera is above the subject in a **high-angle shot**, which is frequently used to emphasize the smallness of the character and make it seem as if the world is out to get them (see **FIGURE 1.35**). One example of this would be a frightened little leaguer stuck deep in right field from the point-of-view of a ball coming toward him.

FIGURE 1.35 High-angle shot

LOW-ANGLE SHOT

In a **low-angle shot** (see **FIGURE 1.36**), the camera is below a character, looking up.

FIGURE 1.36 Low-angle shot

OBLIQUE SHOT/DUTCH ANGLE

An **oblique shot**, or Dutch angle, is a shot that is rotated either left or right with a tilted horizon (see **FIGURE 1.37**). Its purpose is to give the audience a sense of disorientation.

FIGURE 1.37 Oblique/Dutch angle shot

Shots Defined by Camera Movement

Camera motion, or the lack of it, are crucial components of visual storytelling and directorial style. One of the key conversations the director has with the camera operator and cinematographer is whether the camera should move during a scene because the position of the crew and the placement of the lights depends on this variable.

HANDHELD CAMERA VS. CAMERA ON STICKS (TRIPOD)

One of the first decisions you make is whether it's best to shoot your scene handheld or to lock the camera down on a *tripod* or three-legged stand. A handheld camera allows you easy, faster movement, though you should make sure the **image stabilizer** on your camera is turned on if you plan to move the camera. Keeping the camera on the tripod (slang: *sticks*) preserves the composition of your shot better.

TRACKING SHOT/DOLLY SHOT/TRUCKING SHOT

A **tracking shot** means the camera stays with the characters, or moves onto or off of them as they move within the scene. A dolly (see **FIGURE 1.38**) is a platform that the camera and tripod stand on to move smoothly, and dolly tracks are what they move along. Some low-budget filmmakers use a wheelchair as a dolly. A more expensive alternative to a dolly and dolly tracks is a gimbal-based stabilizer, such as a Steadicam rig that stabilizes operator movement.

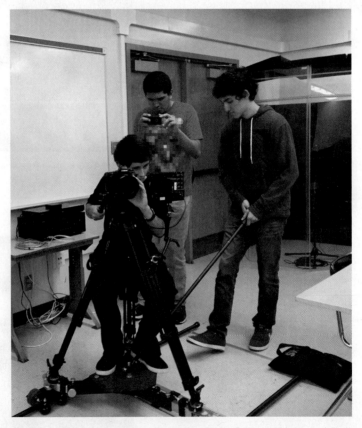

FIGURE 1.38 Students using the Indie-Dolly Systems Universal Dolly

A crane is a device that can raise your camera up over a scene or drop it down. The shot at the end of many films where the hero walks through a devastated Las Vegas cradling the newborn he just saved as the camera lifts up over the scene is a **crane shot**. A slider can be mounted on a tripod or tripod-crane hybrid to move the camera around and up and down as an alternative to using the dolly or going handheld. Drones are increasingly being used to capture shots from above, particularly moving shots.

PAN/TILT

A **pan** (see FIGURE 1.39) is the horizontal (left-right) movement of the camera from a stationary point. A **tilt** (see FIGURE 1.40) is the vertical (up-down) movement of the shot.

> **Tip:**
> Sometimes too much panning and tilting or handheld camerawork can make the audience dizzy or confused!

FIGURE 1.39   A pan-right shot

FIGURE 1.40   A tilt-up shot

Changing Subject Size

Changing the size of the subject of your shot is a great way to make an audience think about what they are going through in that moment. The following are the main options the director and media creator have for changing subject size.

ZOOM IN/ZOOM OUT

There are two simple ways to change the size of the subject in your shot. The first is by **zooming** in or out (see FIGURE 1.41), changing the lens on the camera from a **wide-angle lens** (which shows a lot of the space right in front of the camera) to a **telephoto lens** (which shows space further away from the camera), or vice versa.

FIGURE 1.41   Zooming in or zooming out

The camera might zoom in on a character during a moment of surprise or intense emotion for instance, when he finds out the baby isn't his in a soap opera.

Some directors don't like to use zooms because wide-angle and telephoto lenses photograph space differently, which can throw off an audience. Telephoto lenses flatten space; wide-angles emphasize space.

PUSHING IN AND PULLING OUT

An alternative to zooming is to move the camera toward or away from the subject. This technique is called **pushing in** (toward the subject) or **pulling out** (away from the subject), and it takes a bit more work than zooming in, especially because you have to change focus, or rack focus, when you change the distance between the camera and the subject during the shot, which can be tricky.

DOLLY ZOOM

Occasionally, a media creator will use the difference between a wide-angle and telephoto lens to their advantage, putting the camera on the dolly, pulling it away from the subject, and zooming in on the subject at the same time (or vice versa). This technique leaves the subject the same size but changes the space around them and seems to turn the world around the character "inside out." This is called a **dolly zoom** shot.

Shot Defined by Job

Similar to special teams in football, there are some shots that have a special job in a scene.

INSERT SHOT

An **insert shot** is a close-up of some detail in the scene, such as a watch or something besides the main action that has some relation to the scene. For instance, a shot of 20 cigarette butts on the ground might tell the audience that the character who's smoking has been there a long time.

ESTABLISHING SHOT

An **establishing shot** is an **extreme wide shot** to show the audience where the story is taking place. Usually you will find these at the beginning of a film and then throughout as the location changes.

REACTION SHOT

A **reaction shot** shows a character's reaction to what has just been said. As with over the shoulders or two shots, these can also be described as CUs or MSs.

POINT-OF-VIEW SHOT

In the **point-of-view shot**, the camera shows what a character is seeing of the scene. A point-of-view (POV) shot is actually three shots in sequence:

1. A CU of someone's eyes
2. What they are seeing
3. Their reaction

REVERSE ANGLE

A **reverse angle** matches a previous shot from the opposite angle. Reverse angles are used most commonly during dialogue scenes or interviews that cut back and forth between two reverse angles to maintain the flow of the conversation and allow the editor to control the rhythm of the scene.

Shots Defined by Camera Action

Shots can also be described in media production by what the camera is doing during the shot to accentuate what is happening in the story.

RACK FOCUS SHOT

In a **rack focus** shot (see **FIGURE 1.42**), the focused or clear portion of the image changes during the shot from one part of the frame (for instance, the end of the barrel of a gun) to another part (the eyes of the man about to pull the trigger). Note that in professional productions, an assistant camera operator must change the focus during the shot.

Foreground in focus   Background in focus

FIGURE 1.42   The effect of racking focus

SLOW DISCLOSURE SHOT

A **slow disclosure**, or **slow reveal**, is a tracking shot in which more information comes into view over time. One example is when the camera in a POV shot tracks past drops of blood on a carpet, and after a moment a dead body is revealed.

FAST-MOTION SHOT

Shooting half as many frames or fewer per second (for instance, 12 fps for film, 15 fps for video) and then playing back at normal speed, **fast-motion** shots are generally used to show a process condensed into a smaller amount of time, such as the construction of a building. They are also known for generating humorous effects in early comedies of the "silent era." This is also called **undercranking**.

SLOW-MOTION SHOT

Shooting twice as many frames or more per second (for instance, 48 fps for film, 60 fps for video) and then playing back at normal speed will slow onscreen time, which can convey intensity during key moments such as a car crash. This is also called **overcranking**.

FREEZE FRAME

Like slow motion, **freeze frames** give the audience extra time to think about what's going on and let them know it's important. Sometimes this effect is used during credits to communicate to the audience that these are the significant characters in this story, so pay attention to them.

SUPERIMPOSITION

A **superimposition** (see FIGURE 1.43) is actually two shots laid one on top of the other showing both images at the same time. It connects the two images somehow and asks the viewer to make the connection.

FIGURE 1.43 A superimposition shot

Master and Coverage

The **master shot** is the main shot of the scene, usually the widest and almost always the first one filmed. The master shows all of the main action of a scene. It establishes the space of a scene, including what is onscreen and what is off-screen, and shows where everything is relative to everything else.

Every scene in a project has one master shot and then however many shots of *coverage* of that master as the director feels they need or can afford.

To understand coverage, think of the scene you're shooting as a jigsaw puzzle. As a director, the first thing you plan is the master shot. At least with this shot, you should have a recording of the whole scene.

Then ask yourself, what else do I need to show to get the right effect from this scene? Two over-the-shoulder shots? A reaction shot from the guy down the hall who hears the conversation? An insert shot of the clock?

Every other shot or camera angle besides the master constitutes coverage of the scene. And it's not just the scene that's covered; it's you, as the director or producer, protecting your scene from boring the audience.

Shooting to Edit

Media creators organize shoots around simple logic. When you're in a location, you shoot all the scenes at that location if you can. When you're shooting a scene, make sure you know what that scene is about, such as a character's frustration, and make sure you get the reaction shot that lets the audience make a connection to that character and that feeling.

Continuity

The majority of media projects rely on the illusion of **continuity**. That is, Shot A is followed onscreen by Shot B, and once the editors put the shots together, the audience will believe that B follows directly after A, without any break in time or space, even if the two shots were done three weeks apart, in different states.

This illusion is a continuity of time and space created on film or video as a mirror image of the real three-dimensional world. Editors, who cut the picture together, must look at the storyboards and work with the director to make sure the shots will work together to create this alternate world.

If the shots don't work together and there seems to be a jump forward or backward in time, this discontinuity is referred to as a **jump cut**. Sometimes, in a music video, fight scene, or chase scene, editors use jump cuts on purpose.

The following are some rules for maintaining temporal (time) and spatial (space) continuity.

ONSCREEN AND OFF-SCREEN SPACE

Space in a movie is essentially fake. A movie screen has only two dimensions —height and width—but has to create the illusion of a three-dimensional space within it. This effect is accomplished by showing the audience where things are relative to each other on- and off-screen and then by maintaining a consistency about these relationships. This is called **orientation**.

When the director envisions a scene, he has to be aware of *all* of the space in the scene, including the part in front of the camera and the part that is happening offscreen as well.

In some scenes, such as a party scene, action progresses in various areas of the scene simultaneously and is covered by different shots. The director must rehearse the scene in its entirety, remembering which moments on one side of the room are happening simultaneously with other moments across the room so that the character positions, background action, and overall continuity match from shot to shot. Characters should be able to walk out of one shot into another shot, and this all has to cohere with integrity and continuity.

MATCHING ACTION

Directors might use a dozen or more shots to document a single action, such as Ripley being chased through a spaceship in the film *Alien* (1979). Each of those shots must match the others in terms of the lighting, the speed at which the characters move, the energy of the actors' performances, what the characters are wearing, and so on. The director will occasionally check with the continuity person or the video playback to make sure.

The editor must match the action from shot to shot by finding a **cut point**, which is a frame (still image) in which to cut out of Shot A and another frame to cut into Shot B that will hide the edit and maintain the action with no break in time or ellipsis. The goal of the editor as he reviews the footage is to find a **seamless cut**. Seamless cuts are also referred to as **transparent continuity**, which means that if the editor does his job well, the audience does not even notice the cuts.

STAGELINE/180° RULE

The **stageline** (a.k.a. *the line, the 180°,* or *the* **axis**) (see FIGURE 1.44) is an invisible line through the main axis of the action, for instance, the line from the eyes of one person to the eyes of the person to whom they're speaking. This line of action provides the orientation the audience uses to figure out where things are, left or right, in front or in back of something else.

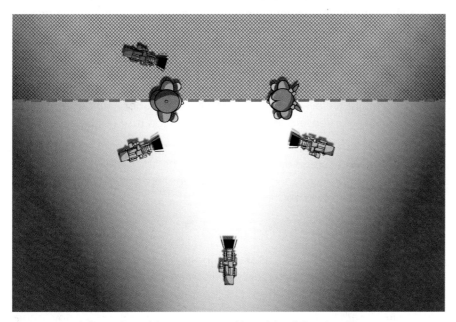

FIGURE 1.44   A floor plan with cameras on either side of the stageline

The rule of the stageline, also known as the **180° rule**, states that once the line is set, all shots—CUs, MSs, WSs, whatever—must be taken from the same side of the line in order to maintain the viewer's orientation of left and right.

Let's say you're shooting a dinner scene. If you want to cover (get coverage of) the scene with two matching over-the-shoulder (OTS) shots, you must make sure to shoot them from the same side of the stageline. You can see in Figure 1.44 how these shots would balance each other.

When cut together, it will appear that the man and the woman are actually talking to each other. Note that he stays on the left and she stays on the right side of the screen even though you have changed the camera angle.

Compare this scene to an example in which the stageline is crossed. Imagine what the scene will look like when these two shots are edited together. The man and the woman are now both on the same side of the screen—they will "pop" on top of each other on every cut!

Once the stageline has been set, it can be changed any of the following ways:

- Moving/dollying the camera across the line during the shot, which will establish a new stageline

- Moving the actors during the shot, which likewise will establish a new stageline

- Cutting to an insert shot (such as a clock) with no left/right orientation, which reboots the orientation in the viewer's mind

SCREEN DIRECTION

Another aspect of space orientation that media creators must be aware of is the rule of **screen direction**, which says that if an object such as a car or a train is moving from left to right, that object will continue to move from left to right in following shots unless it stops and turns around.

To see the object moving from right to left suddenly will upset the audience's orientation. They might think it's a different object headed toward the first object. They might believe time has passed between Shot A and Shot B. They will try to make sense of it, but their explanation may not be accurate.

As you can see from Figure 1.44, if you follow the rule of the stageline, you will maintain correct screen direction. Crossing the stageline will reverse screen direction. Not maintaining correct screen direction is a common problem for new directors.

EYELINE

Eyeline refers to the direction a character looks off-screen, left or right, and will also orient the viewer to the space off-screen and also whether other objects or people are left or right of the onscreen character.

When filming a car chase or conversation around a lunch table, or any scene involving more than two characters, it's not uncommon for directors, camera operators, and script supervisors to discuss eyeline—"What was the eyeline of the last scene, left or right?"—to make sure characters are looking the right way off-screen toward each other.

BLOCKING

Blocking is the movement of actors or the camera during the scene. For instance, an actor may enter a room, stop, find the person he is looking for, cross to a seat next to her, and sit down. The director may tell the camera operator to pan across the room to pick up the actor entering and then pan back with the actor and tilt down as he sits.

The director rehearses the blocking with the actors and camera operator because, even though the actors' movements should look spontaneous, the actors need to "hit their mark" on every take so they'll be in focus. Likewise, the camera operator's moves must be equally rehearsed.

If the actors or cameraman are out of step or miss their mark, either the shot will be out of focus or the composition will be ruined. For instance, a head may appear in front of another head instead of next to it.

Tip:
The camera assistant may put down a piece of tape that the actors can see out of the corner of their eyes.

Postproduction: Putting It All Together

This section provides an overview of the entire post workflow, with enough details about certain steps that you can work through a simple project, such as the example project at the end of this chapter.

A general workflow for postproduction includes the following:

1. Ingesting and organization

2. Assembly (rough cut)

3. Feedback

4. Revision and trimming

5. Final cut

6. Audio sweetening and mixing

7. Titles and graphics

8. Color correction

9. Delivery

Ingesting and Media Organization

Ingesting is the process of bringing any form of media into the editing system, especially when the footage was acquired in a nontape format (see **FIGURE 1.45**). Ingesting footage from tape is called **capturing**.

FIGURE 1.45 SD cards are one of many forms to deliver nontape media

Once ingested, the media is represented in video-editing applications as **clips**. Before any editing is to begin, each clip needs to be identified and labeled to be easily located.

The more footage to be ingested, the more critical the need to label and organize footage. In traditional video-editing applications, clips and other media assets are organized in **bins**. Bins are just like folders or directories in a computer file system and take their name from the physical cloth-lined bins that were used in film editing.

All digital video is encoded with some **compression type**. A compression type or **codec** (short for compressor/decompressor) is chosen based on the purpose of the video.

Mobile devices tend to record video in the same codec that is used to deliver directly to the Web by keeping the file size low. H.264 is one of the most commonly used codecs for web video and acquisition on both mobile devices and DSLR cameras. Compression of this type tends to be heavy and can result in the loss of image quality.

Most editing software can work with footage that was acquired in codecs that have heavier compression. Doing so demands more processing power from the computer. There are other codecs available that are higher quality and less demanding on the processor but that create larger file sizes.

The conversion of media from one codec to another is called **transcoding**. Depending on your choice of editing software and the power of your computer, you can either manually transcode your media, allow the software to automatically transcode in the background, or not transcode at all.

Putting the Pieces Together

Assembly is the process of combining all your best footage in a sequence for a first cut, or rough cut. Assemblies are usually longer than the finished product is intended to be.

Feedback is required, especially when working with a client, to get different critical perspectives on the work. The editor can receive notes from the director, producers, the client, and even executives for changes to the cut.

The project goes through **revision** and **trimming** according to the notes received. With each new cut, another round of feedback occurs until the program is ready to be called a **final cut** and the picture is locked.

A **picture lock** is the point at which picture editing is complete and the project moves onto work that doesn't affect the running time or duration of the project. If changes to the picture that affect running time need to be made after this point, it's possible to make those changes, but doing so can upset the multiple processes occurring simultaneously afterward, particularly in sound/music editing and visual effects.

Audio mixing and sweetening in professional video productions are done by a separate post audio crew once the picture is locked. At this stage, any audio elements not added by the editor, such as sound effects and music, are edited into the project.

Sharing Your Project

How you share or deliver your project to your client or audience depends on how you intend to distribute it. Some video-editing applications have direct upload options to online video-hosting services such as YouTube or Vimeo (see **FIGURE 1.46**).

FIGURE 1.46   The built-in sharing options in Apple Final Cut Pro X

Conversion to a more compressed codec for Internet delivery such as H.264, called **encoding**, is needed to keep file size down for quick transfer. Because of the nature of the encoding process, compressing media into a smaller file size while maintaining an acceptable quality can be time-consuming, especially if you have a long program.

Once compressed, you will have a single file containing all the edited clips, titles, graphics, effects, and audio in one compact stream, ready to be delivered through the Internet, stored on the cloud, or copied onto a flash drive or external hard drive.

Platforms and Options

The tools to edit video have changed considerably since the days of tape-to-tape linear editing. **Linear editing** used at least two videotape recorders to copy each shot from the camera source to the program tape one by one. It required the editor to place each shot in the order in which it was meant to be seen.

If a shot needed to be added to an early part of a program, the rest of the program from that point on needed to be edited again. The editor needed a clear game plan as to how the program and each shot should be laid out. Creating a simple effect such as a dissolve required the second shot to be copied on another video tape to be played back on a third videotape player to be played back simultaneously to perform the effect.

Editing on a computer in a **nonlinear editing (NLE)** system allows the editor to move shots around in any order without losing any previous work.

Working on a NLE must have felt miraculous to those who had previously edited on linear editing systems.

In the 1990s, the film and television industry began to adopt editing on NLEs. The two most popular editing systems at the time were *Avid* and *Lightworks*. Avid Technology, Inc., still holds the title of the standard for professional editing systems in film and TV production.

Lightworks is also still around. It may not be as widely used as Avid Media Composer (see **FIGURE 1.47**), but it is one of the most affordable video software programs available.

PHOTO COURTESY AVID TECHNOLOGY, INC.

FIGURE 1.47 Avid Media Composer

In 1999, Apple, Inc., released Final Cut Pro. Digital video (DV) cameras could be connected to a Mac computer using a FireWire cable to capture picture and sound without any loss of quality.

Final Cut Pro was sold at a fraction of the price of the established competitors, which caused a disruption and a bit of a divide in the industry. Video production companies and documentarians used Final Cut Pro because of its affordability and ease of use, whereas TV and film editors continued to use Avid's editing applications because of their established base, support, and reliability.

The same year that Final Cut Pro was released, Sonic Foundry released Vegas Pro, a Windows-only NLE, which was acquired by Sony in 2003.

The team that originally created Final Cut Pro was hired by Adobe Systems, Inc., to create another entry in the competition, Adobe Premiere (now Adobe Premiere Pro), which was released in 2003.

To add yet another set of options for editing your project, mobile apps for phones and tablets are becoming more powerful and capable of handling high-quality video to create professional-level projects. Apple iMovie for iOS (see **FIGURE 1.48**) becomes more feature-rich with each update. Film editor Dan Lebental, A.C.E. (*Iron Man*, 2008), developed TouchEdit, a video-editing app used on professional productions that fits into established workflows. Adobe also has its own editor for the iOS platform, called Premiere Clip.

PHOTO COURTESY APPLE, INC.

FIGURE 1.48 Apple iMovie

The market for the tools to deliver your message using video is being flooded by new and creatively designed solutions. It can be overwhelming. It is difficult to say which video-editing solution is the right one to use, since factors such as budget and choice of operating system apply differently for each user and each production.

Ultimately, if pursuing a professional career in postproduction, it is a good idea to learn to use as many platforms as you can, because the evolutionary history of postproduction tools proves that nothing settles and unexpected change lurks around every corner.

End-of-Chapter Activities

REVIEW QUESTIONS

1. Explain what is meant by the message and the medium.

2. How have advancements in smartphone technology impacted video production?

3. Explain the difference between professional-level, consumer-level, and prosumer-level devices and give an example of each.

4. List at least five types of video cables and connectors and explain how each is most commonly used.

5. Define the terms analog and digital.

6. What is a protagonist?

7. Explain the purpose of each act in a three-act structured script.

8. What are the three Ps in the A/V production workflow?

9. What is a shot? Explain at least three types of shots.

10. What are the nine steps in a general postproduction workflow?

11. How and when is client feedback incorporated into the workflow?

Review Project 1

Select one of the careers described in this chapter. Conduct research to learn about the selected career, including educational requirements, job outlook, skills, and responsibilities. When your research is complete, use a word-processing program to write an audio script for a commercial about the career. Read your script to a partner or to the class.

Review Project 2

With your teacher's permission, work in pairs to identify and correctly set up video and audio equipment available in your classroom or lab, using the correct cables and connections. Document the steps you use by writing a how-to guide or manual.

Review Project 3

With your teacher's permission, work in teams to set up and record a variety of shots using a camera or camcorder, as described in this chapter. Start with a team meeting and assign different jobs to each team member, such as writer, director, actors, camera operator, etc. You may use video or still photography. Using a word-processing program, write an audio script that describes each shot, and then record it. Show your video to the class. If you use still photography, use the images and the audio to create a presentation and show it to the class.

CHAPTER 1 – PORTFOLIO BUILDER

TEN-SHOT SELF PORTRAIT

A video blog (*vlog*) lets you *share your daily life with others* using images and sound. Most vlogs take the form of a single-shot self-interview. The more proficient ones are more stylized, including music and creatively shot images. The best vlog episodes are the ones that tell a story and come from the heart.

DIRECTIONS

There is no subject you know better than yourself. In ten shots, you will create a one-minute self-portrait video that tells the story of how you identify yourself, what you're interested in, what you're passionate about, and what you want for your future. Show the world who you are.

1. Write a list of the ten things you feel describe you and with which you identify.

2. Reorder the list so that it reads like a countdown to the most important item on the list or the one with which you most closely identify.

3. For each item on the list, describe a shot that you plan on creating to represent each item on the list. Be specific about the shot size and type of angle, such as "A high-angle full shot" or "An eye-level medium close-up."

4. Using any camera you have access to, stage and shoot each image on your list at least three times so that you have some options to choose from when you edit. You can capture the shots in any order that's practical.

5. Using the camera microphone, record a self-interview shot in which you list off the ten items and why you identify with them or how they relate to your self-identity. Be brief; you have only 60 seconds.

6. Using any editing software you have access to (desktop or mobile), assemble your shots together in the order you listed.

7. Add some music to the edit—your own if you're a musician.

8. Export the video from your editing software and share it with the world on the online video-hosting service of your choice.

Chapter 2

Investigation and Exploration

Chapter 2 Overview

- The History and Evolution of Audio and Video Production

- Creative Vision

- Accuracy Counts

- Developing Treatments

- Writing and Formatting a Screenplay or Script

- Know Your Rights: Copyright

- Developing a Soundtrack and Score

- Ethical Use of Someone Else's Work

- Postproduction: Incorporating Audio

- End-of-Chapter Review and Activities

This chapter starts with an exploration of the history of audio and video production. It moves on to the process for investigating and researching a topic to ensure a project has technical, historical, and emotional authenticity.

This chapter also explains how to draft the technical documents that serve as the blueprints for the project, including treatments, scripts, soundtracks, and scores.

Finally, you learn how to make the most of the postproducion process to improve your project.

The History and Evolution of Audio and Video Production

There is no way to cover the entire history of motion pictures and all other forms of media across all platforms and all genres, mentioning every innovation over the past century plus of filmmaking in a single book, let alone in this one chapter.

However, by exploring some of the most important events, breakthroughs, trends, and developments in the audio and video production industries, those studying audio and video production can gain a better understanding of the technology, skill, and creativity that go into the process.

The New ABCs

Media creation is a form of communication based on a language that has been constantly evolving over the last 100 years across every developed nation on the planet. At different times, the most remarkable innovations in method or style have come from the United States, France, Russia, Germany, India, Mexico, China, and many other countries as well.

Filmmaking is both one language and a thousand languages. It is extremely personal, and it is global. The language of visual communication is an ongoing dialogue that re-engages every time someone releases a media project. Every time a new project goes out into the world, it has an effect. Sometimes the effect is a ripple; other times it is a giant wave.

Every audio/video project makes use of the innovations that have come before. Every once in a while, an artist comes up with a new way to communicate something that has never been done before and the result is a change in the entire experience.

One example is the "bullet time" shot in *The Matrix* (1999), which moved 360 degrees around a character during a freeze frame, suggesting the slowing of time except for the camera and one other element in the shot, a bullet.

That shot and the concept behind it were not invented for *The Matrix*, but that film popularized it for a worldwide audience. The filmmakers used something they had seen before in an innovative and visually exciting way, and as a result it was quickly adopted and overused in other projects, turning into a visual cliché in family films and commercials.

The following are just a few of the highlights of the history of media creation over the last 125 years. It is recommended that you seek out and review the specific examples referenced throughout so you can see and hear what the fuss is all about.

First Steps and Early Breakthroughs

As early as 3200 BCE, Sumerians, Egyptians, and Mayans employed a series of visual characters, or **hieroglyphs**, to communicate stories pictographically (see **FIGURE 2.1**). Pictures stood in for letters and told a story.

Photography, which means "writing with light," developed over many years, from the pinhole camera concept invented by Aristotle in the fifth-century BCE to early heliographic engravings, the earliest known photographic process, which began in the 1820s. The invention of the **camera obscura**, a sealed box with a hole in one side to allow light to reflect from outside into a flipped image inside the box, led to the invention of the first camera by Frenchman Joseph Niépce in 1826 (see **FIGURE 2.2**).

FIGURE 2.1 Hieroglyphs on Egyptian stone tomb

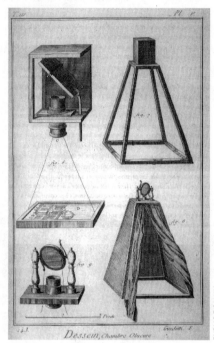

FIGURE 2.2 Camera obscura

Refrigeration, the internal combustion engine, and the personal computer are frequently listed among the greatest inventions of all time, but the camera and, later, the motion-picture camera are perhaps the greatest cultural breakthroughs in history. Before the first cameras came into use, painting, drawing, and sculpture had served as the primary media for representing people, stories, and the world around them for thousands of years. Practically overnight, the process of interpretation changed, and a much more realistic alternative to all of these was available. No longer did people need to paint or draw their surroundings. For the first time, they could create a much more exact reproduction of the images that eyes transmit to the brain.

It's no coincidence that new, less representational styles of painting such as impressionism and expressionism flourished in the wake of the invention of photography. While the camera could now capture and depict reality, these styles allowed artists to represent the world in ways that the camera could not.

Before long, every other art form from the novel to the play needed to retrench or find a new identity in the wake of photography, and its flashy cousin, motion-picture photography.

Action! Advent of the Motion Picture

The development of photography into motion photography came about as a result of a bet. In 1872, California governor Leland Stanford hired photographer Eadweard Muybridge to take a series of photos of a horse running on a racetrack to determine whether the horse ever had all four hoofs off the ground at the same time.

To settle the bet, Muybridge set up a series of cameras along the track and had each attached to a wire that would break and develop an image when the horse raced by. The still photos were viewed in sequence, and the process is considered the primary leap from photography to motion pictures (see **FIGURE 2.3**). (By the way, if you were wondering, galloping horses *do* have all four hooves off the track at the same time.)

The next major innovations in motion pictures came from the great American inventor Thomas Edison and his collaborator W.K.L. Dickson with the Kinetograph camera in 1893, and across the Atlantic in France where the Lumiére brothers developed their own camera, the Cinematograph, in 1895 (see **FIGURE 2.4**).

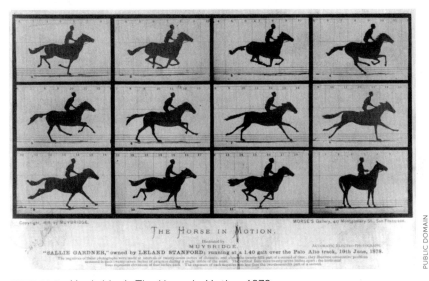
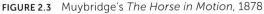

FIGURE 2.3 Muybridge's *The Horse in Motion*, 1878

PUBLIC DOMAIN

FIGURE 2.4 A poster for the Cinematograph

These cameras ran a continuous roll of film into a dark chamber, exposing one frame of film to light and then stopping, advancing the film another frame, and exposing it again so that the series of still images, when played back at the same speed at which they were recorded, would create the illusion of a moving picture.

LIFE IN TWO DIMENSIONS

These pioneering artists are generally credited as the first filmmakers. Their movies lasted from a few seconds to around a minute, and they documented everyday events, such as workers leaving a factory or a round of a boxing match.

They had no synchronized sound of any kind and were typically accompanied in theaters by a live organ. They were more like documentaries than fiction films, and their appeal came from their magical representation of real life as a two-dimensional moving image projected against the screen or wall.

It is in "two dimensions" because the film frame and the screen have real width and height but only the illusion of depth. Of course, this illusion has challenged filmmakers ever since the dawn of filmmaking. Only recently, after more than 100 years, has three-dimensional (3D) filmmaking become a significant aspect of the film-going experience.

Before 3D, filmmakers had to rely on **z-axis movement**, which is when a person or object moves toward or away from the screen, creating the illusion of depth (the x- and y- axes are the length and height of the image).

A funny story about z-axis movement at the dawn of the motion-picture era comes from an urban legend about the first screening of the Lumiére's film *Arrival of a Train at La Ciotat Station* (1896). This film, as advertised, showed a train arriving at a station at a time when audiences were not quite sure what they were seeing (see **FIGURE 2.5**). As the train got closer, the story goes, the audience was not quite sure that they were safe in their seats. They jumped out of their seats so the "train" would not plow into them!

FIGURE 2.5 A frame from *Arrival of a Train at La Ciotat Station* (1896)

A STEP TOWARD THE STAGE

As audiences became familiar with motion pictures and the novelty of merely seeing any moving image wore off, the focus of produced films came from the dominant visual storytelling form of the day, which was theater. The shooting of a play was typically in a static or still wide shot. The actors would walk into frame, deliver their lines, and walk out.

During this time, filmmakers used the camera simply as a recording device, and dialogue was delivered via the use of written **title cards** between the scenes. This allowed audiences across the country to see the finest stage actors of their day, but visually it didn't make use of all the power the camera had and was not at all as interesting as what was to come.

MÉLIÈS THE MAGICIAN

Georges Méliès was arguably the most imaginative and innovative filmmaker during this first decade of film, pioneering many special-effects shots, using the power of film editing to make characters appear and disappear, and using multiple exposures and time-lapse photography, as in his most famous film *A Trip to the Moon* (1902); see **FIGURE 2.6**.

FIGURE 2.6 An iconic frame from *A Trip to the Moon* (1902)

According to legend, Méliès' delight in trick photography began when his camera jammed while a car was passing in front of it and restarted when a hearse was passing, so when he watched it back, it appeared that the car simply became a hearse. This magical transformation was very exciting to Méliès.

A GIANT STEP FORWARD

The next artist to revolutionize the young art form was Edwin S. Porter, whose groundbreaking work *The Great Train Robbery* (1903) had so many new tricks, it must have seemed as if it had traveled back to audiences from the future. Its innovations included the following:

- First film to *pan* (turn) the camera from left to right or right to left

- First film to crosscut between two storylines occurring at the same time

- One of the first attempts to color a film frame-by-frame by hand

One could argue that cutting from scene to scene and expecting the audience to follow the logic of the narrative is the single greatest leap in the history of media production. Porter's film really jump-started the grammar of visual communication that was to take hold and set the stage for what was to come over the next 100 years.

THE CONTROVERSIAL PIONEER

D.W. Griffith was one of the first filmmakers to attempt the production of longer, feature-length films and to embrace the use of the close-up in films. He was the first blockbuster film producer. Though he was the preeminent director of his time, Griffith may be best known for the racism in his magnum opus *The Birth of a Nation* (1915); see **FIGURE 2.7**.

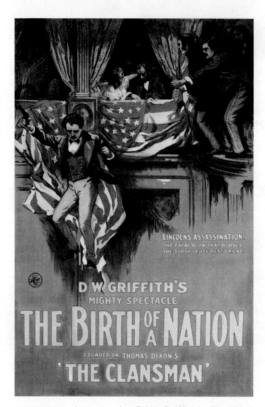

FIGURE 2.7   A poster for D.W. Griffith's *The Birth of a Nation*

This film, based on the novel and play *The Clansman*, depicted the origin of the Ku Klux Klan in a heroic light and sparked massive protests everywhere it was shown. No one disputed Griffith's mastery of cinema, but 100 years later, *The Birth of a Nation* remains one of the most hated films in history.

BIRTH OF THE STUDIOS

For its first 20 years, the motion-picture industry steadily grew up on the East Coast, primarily in New York and New Jersey.

By 1910, the movers and shakers of the American film business left the East Coast for sunny Los Angeles, where they could shoot almost every day, and entrepreneurs from other industries such as Samuel Goldwyn (MGM Studios), William Fox (20th Century Fox), Adolf Zukor (Paramount Pictures), Louis B. Mayer (MGM Studios), Carl Laemmle (Universal Pictures), Harry Cohn (Columbia Pictures), Jack and Harry Warner (Warner Bros.), and Walt Disney (Walt Disney Studios) developed the first movie studios, empires that continue to dominate the industry to this day.

AND WHAT OF EUROPE?

European countries were busy developing their own media cultures and master storytellers, whose styles were sometimes crafted to contrast with the "Hollywood" style.

Chief among these many movements was the expressionism of German cinema, best represented by Fritz Lang in films such as *The Cabinet of Dr. Caligari* (1920), the Soviet montage theory seen in the editing experiments of Lev Kuleshov and Sergei Eisenstein's *Battleship Potemkin* (1925), and the impressionistic French cinema of Jacques Feyder and Able Gance (see **FIGURE 2.8**).

FIGURE 2.8   Poster art for *The Cabinet of Dr. Caligari* (1920)

STUDIOS, SYNC SOUND, AND COLOR

By the end of World War I, Hollywood had become the dominant worldwide force in motion pictures and popular culture. The most significant technological development of this time was the invention of a **synchronized sound system**, which began in 1927 in films such as *The Jazz Singer*.

For the first time, audiences could hear characters speak on film! Performers who had been seen but not heard suddenly had to use their voices. As a result, careers were made and lost solely based on one's quality of voice during this transformative period. It is documented expertly in three great Hollywood classics: *Sunset Boulevard* (1950), *Singin' in the Rain* (1952), and *The Artist* (2011).

The other most significant technical step forward was the development of color film processes, which started with filmmakers hand-painting individual frames of their movies and evolved into the two- and three-strip Technicolor process that eventually provided rich combinations leading to the production of some of the greatest color films ever made, including *The Wizard of Oz* (1939) and *Gone with the Wind* (1939).

RISE OF THE STUDIO SYSTEM

The emergence of the *studio system* refers to the industrialization of the top movie studios during the 1920s.

The major studios, in collusion, exerted maximum control over the production and eventual commercial success of their films by doing the following:

- Building huge soundstages where most filming would take place.

- Developing the *star system*. The studio bosses realized the success of their business depended on the audience identifying with certain performers that they would then look for in movie after movie. They groomed actors, transforming them into stars and signing them to long-term contracts that took away their right to make films for other studios without their bosses' approval.

- Developing the means of distribution and exhibition of their product, creating a vertical monopoly and limiting competition from newcomers. By 1939, there were 15,000 theaters in the United States, all showing the product of a handful of studios.

This arrangement lasted into the 1950s until decisions in a series of court cases (beginning with *United States v. Paramount Pictures*, Inc. in 1948; see **FIGURE 2.9**) required distribution and exhibition companies to be separate entities. During this time, however, several genres or categories of entertainment became the specialty of one studio or another: gangster films at Warner Bros., musicals at MGM, horror and monster movies at Universal, and animated films at Walt Disney Studios.

FIGURE 2.9 The original front gate at Paramount Studios in Hollywood

THE EUROPEANS STRIKE BACK!

As international distribution picked up after World War II, more European films were finding international audiences after screening at festivals such as the Cannes Film Festival in France. Though Hollywood films and American movie culture had dominated world cinema for decades, other countries were gaining increased access to the worldwide audience and forcing Hollywood to take notice.

The most significant of these was the French *nouvelle vague*, or "new wave," in which crews used lighter cameras and gear for quicker production to make more vital, less formal films that challenged sensibilities and were shot like low-budget documentaries.

Filmmakers such as Francois Truffaut and Jean-Luc Godard, who were inspired by Hollywood films, inspired in turn a new generation of American mavericks to explore more sophisticated and complex stories with less simplistic heroes.

THE SCREEN GETS WIDE

Every time the audience started to get bored with the clichés of visual communication, Hollywood came up with some technical improvement to bring them back. When television became popular in the 1950s and brought moving pictures into American households free of charge, Hollywood changed the shape of the screen from squarish (like TV) to the Cinemascope widescreen 2.35:1 aspect ratio and then later introduced the U.S. widescreen cinema-standard 1.85:1 ratio, both of which are still in use to this day (see **FIGURE 2.10**). This wider space emphasized the epic nature of films and gave directors a new space dimension in which to visualize.

1.33:1

1.85:1

2.35:1

FIGURE 2.10   Examples of three standard aspect ratios

CURRENT TRENDS IN THE FILM, AUDIO, AND VIDEO PRODUCTION INDUSTRIES

Technological advancements in gaming, film, and television, and the way people consume audio and video content are currently the major forces driving trends in the audio and video production industries. Technology such as immersion experiences and virtual reality are having a major impact, as audio and video producers must find ways to develop 3D audio and video products for immersive, real-space environments.

Trends in delivery methods, such as a move away from broadcast television to online streaming or mobile device based content, are also affecting audio and video producers. Developing vertical audio and video that can run in multiple environments including television, computer, and mobile device, is increasingly important.

General trends in technology, such as increased processing power and smaller systems also impact the audio and video production industries. As already mentioned, smartphones can be used to capture studio-quality sound and video, and that quality will continue to improve. This drives the need for easy-to-use postproduction software and apps that can also be used on mobile devices to create professional-quality media content.

Creative Vision

You have a reason for everything you do. It reflects some need you have. You eat when you are hungry. You sleep when you are tired. You play when you are bored.

Media creation fulfills a need, too: the need to express yourself, to perform, to be heard, to improve the world, to be part of a larger dialogue.

Do you think that when William Shakespeare wrote *Romeo & Juliet* in 1595 (or thereabouts), he knew that in 2017 ninth-graders in Midland, Texas, would be reading, performing, and analyzing the balcony scene? Probably not.

The point is, you are unlikely to know when you develop an audio/video production if it will catch on, transcend its origins like a Molière play or a *Seinfeld* episode, and stake a claim to relevance far beyond what its creators might have originally imagined.

But that does not mean you should not have a vision. You, as a creator, should be clear at least with yourself about what you want your work to do once it is out in the world. Do you want to share it with only your closest family and friends? Are you hoping it will go viral online? Will you one day be walking the red carpet and accepting a Golden Globe or Academy Award?

One of the most inspirational stories about a writer and his work concerns Sylvester Stallone and the script for *Rocky* (1976). Stallone had kicked around as an actor and was almost 30 years old without anyone giving him the chance to do what he knew in his heart he could achieve on screen.

So, he wrote a script for himself and, against tremendous odds, found a studio that wanted to buy the script and make his film—only not with him in it. Not a rich man at that time, Stallone responded with an act of great character. He demanded that he play the lead role as a condition of selling the script. Eventually, the studio agreed to his terms, and the results validated everything Stallone had ever thought about himself. The film won three Academy Awards, including Best Picture of 1976.

Having creative vision will help you identify and achieve your goals. You may have to wait, or struggle, or sacrifice, but if you can see the light at the end, you will have a path to follow to succeed.

Accuracy Counts

Every project that ever landed successfully has its own process, and the key to its completion and its success is that its creators knew what they needed to know and learned what they needed to learn before they went into production.

You are responsible for the accuracy and validity of your project. You must get the facts right and present them truthfully. That means if you are making a statement in your public service announcement (PSA) that 15,000 dogs are left homeless every year in Los Angeles County, you should thoughtfully consider this problem from several angles and ask the following questions:

- Why does this happen?

- Is there a way to improve the situation?

- What appears to be the best way?

- Where am I getting my facts from?

- Why do I consider this source to be trustworthy?

Down the road, you might have "people" to gather information and check facts for you, but for now you are on your own. You are most likely to use the Internet to research a project. Be aware that not everything posted online is valid and accurate. Learn how to use critical-thinking skills to evaluate information for accuracy and validity. Practice identifying fraudulent Web sites that use **propaganda**, which is information used out of context to try to mislead and influence thinking, or that depend on assumptions to make a point. An **assumption** is something that is accepted as true even if there is no factual proof.

When you evaluate information, look for the author's name and credentials and whether or not he cites his sources. Identify whether the information is objective, which means it is balanced and fair, or if it is designed for a purpose, which means the author is trying to promote a particular viewpoint or to mislead the audience. And, finally, check for spelling and grammatical errors, which might indicate the author is not a professional.

You should also be aware that as a content creator you have the opportunity to spread propaganda of your own. Be mindful of how it might affect the way your project is received, and as a result, how you are received.

Most media creators, when they are starting out, don't have a lot of money or a lot of connections. But they all have one thing that may be worth millions of dollars and peace of mind over the course of a career: their reputation.

How does a writer, producer, or media artist develop a solid reputation? Sometimes it is by being recognized as honest and truthful. Sometimes it's by having a clear vision, or a way of seeing things that opens up other people's eyes. Vision is a key component of all types of leadership, and media creation is a type of leadership.

Key strides against racism were made over the past century by the song "Strange Fruit," written by Abel Meeropol and sung by Billie Holliday; by the career of baseball player Jackie Robinson and the progressive leadership of Dodgers owner Branch Rickey; and, most impactfully, by the life, writing, and leadership of Rev. Dr. Martin Luther King, Jr.

Each of these transformative leaders engaged an audience through the use of media, and each of them changed the world. Their style and their venue may have been different, but they are comparable in the integrity of their vision.

What gives work integrity? Honesty, accuracy, vision, and validity.

Whatever research or investigation you do for your project, you need to consider the source and whether it would stand up to the scrutiny of others. If you are working on a project celebrating the career of Bill Gates, remember that his Wikipedia page once referred to him as the devil and, even worse, gave him a funny mustache. Yes, Wikipedia can be publicly edited, and so it's not to be trusted without supporting evidence.

So, what can you trust? Online look for .edu and .gov domain names. Here are a few specific sources that have passed the test for objectivity:

- NPR
- PBS
- C-SPAN
- BBC
- Reuters
- The New York Times

Developing Treatments

Many writers first develop an outline of their screenplay or script, known as a **treatment**. A treatment consists of a list of scenes and a short summary of what happens in each scene. Once the treatment is complete, authors write each scene in more detail with the visuals and the characters' dialogue included in the final screenplay.

In the Beginning

One key way writing a script is different from other types of writing is that you must organize content into scenes. A **scene** is a unit of action in one location and time—for instance, breakfast at the Aguilar house, a graveyard at midnight where the vampires rise up, or a car chase along the railroad tracks.

Think of a scene as a unit in your story like a quarter is a unit of a dollar. It usually takes about 30 scenes to make up a feature-length screenplay or movie. Remember, every time you go to (or *cut* to) a new place and time in your screenplay, you are actually beginning a new scene.

There are as many ways to begin a story as there are stories to tell. Writers generally have some sense of the protagonist or main character, the goal they are going after, and the obstacles that will get in their way. You may want to introduce the main character in their environment first or introduce the villain doing the very thing that will force the hero to chase him down.

Developing Your Main Character

Remember that character (personality type) determines action. The things that your main character *does* tell the audience what kind of person he *is*. In video, actions really do speak louder than words.

For example, if Luke Skywalker in *Star Wars* had been a better soldier, he would have left on his tracking computer during the climactic scene. Had he left on his tracking computer, he probably would have missed getting his shot at the Death Star. Had he missed his shot, the Rebel Planet would have been destroyed.

The main personality trait of the main character (lazy, brave, generous, selfish) should become clear to viewers quickly in the beginning of the story. The next time you watch a movie, look and see. The writer usually demonstrates it during the first scene the character is in.

Recall that the special kind of *empathy* that exists between the main character and the audience is based on hope for the main character.

The **character arc** is the overall change in the main character from the beginning to the end of the story as a result of the action in the story. This is also called the "hero's journey." Here are a few examples:

- Michael Corleone in *The Godfather* (1972): From Ivy League college boy to mafia don

- El Mariachi in *El Mariachi* (1990): From singer to mercenary

- Neo in *The Matrix* (1999): From geeky hacker to cyber superhero

- Austin Powers in *Austin Powers* (1996): From swinger to husband

What's the Big Idea?

The **theme** is the idea behind the story or lesson of a movie or written work, such as "to thine own self be true" (*Hamlet/Star Wars*) or "slow and steady wins the race" ("The Tortoise and The Hare"). Like your main character and your goal, the theme should be one of the first things you determine for yourself as you start to write your story.

Unlike stories, themes don't need to be original. Any important lesson you want to get across has probably been around since the beginning of storytelling in one form or another. The theme shows what you, the writer, think is important. Is it more important to take care of families or friends, or is a person's main responsibility actually to himself? Is it all right to lie to get out of a tight spot?

Your story will tell the audience your opinions about the world you live in, so make sure it reflects your real feelings.

Often, a physical change (Michael Corleone's broken jaw, El Mariachi's busted hand) reflects the spiritual/emotional change in the main character.

Other times, a physical journey (Austin Powers to Las Vegas, Neo to see the Oracle) will reflect the emotional/spiritual journey of the main character.

Your goal when you sit down to write is to create the most interesting and entertaining story you can. Many scripts, including those written by experienced and talented writers, have the same problems, and these are things you can think about when you write your story.

Troubleshooting

Probably the most common problem in screenplays is the use of clichéd scenes or characters, which seem so familiar and unoriginal that they bore the audience or, worse, take them out of the story and make them think about the writing. The challenge of writing or any art is to be original yet relatable.

Another problem is a story with an unlikable or uninteresting main character. It's not that the main character has to be nice. Tony Montana in *Scarface* (1983), and Michael Corleone in *The Godfather* (1972) are not always nice people. Yet they are interesting not just because of what they do but why they do it.

A common type of "bad" main character is the passive main character, who neither does anything nor seems to care much one way or another about what happens. Ask yourself as a writer, "Why is an audience going to care enough about this character to stay and watch what happens to him?"

Finally, scenes—particularly endings—that seem to come out of nowhere are big problems. Writer/director M. Night Shyamalan had a massive success with *The Sixth Sense* (1999), which relied on a wonderful twist that surprised most viewers but nonetheless made perfect sense within the context of the story. He followed up with a twist-a-thon of films—*Unbreakable* (2000), *Signs* (2002), *The Village* (2004), and *Lady in the Water* (2006)—that, while occasionally scoring box-office success, often left audiences scratching their heads because of the implausibility of their endings.

Remember, as a writer, that you are building a story like an architect and engineers build a house. If you start to build a two-story house and then put a 70-story apartment building on top of it, it'll collapse just like a story will if it isn't built with the right foundation and good, solid, high-quality materials.

Writing and Formatting a Screenplay or Script

A **screenplay** (or teleplay) is a script, or written version of a film, video, audio, animation, or television show, indicating specifically what the audience is seeing (what is onscreen) and hearing (on the audio track). Because of this, a screenplay reads like the combination of a novel and a technical document like the blueprint of a house.

Screenplays will differ from writer to writer depending on their style, what kind of project it is, and how many descriptive words the writer chooses to use. The rule of thumb is to be succinct and to the point in your descriptions so that the reader can breeze through your script in approximately the amount of time it might take them to watch your final project.

The Four Components of a Screenplay

Although screenplays may differ based on the style of the writers, if you look at them as technical documents, they can usually be broken down into four main parts.

- Scene heading, which is also called a slugline

- Scene description

- Transition

- Communication

SLUGLINES

Every scene in a script must start with a **slugline**, which is a capitalized heading that provides three key pieces of information: the setting, which is either interior (INT.) or exterior (EXT.), the location, and the time of day. You skip a line before and after each slugline to designate the start of a new scene.

Sluglines are designed to give important instructions to the key personnel, including the director, producer, cinematographer, production designer, and sound designer. Here's an example:

```
INT. CROWDED SCHOOL HALLWAY - DAY
```

Let's break this part into three parts.

- INT. indicates that the scene occurs inside (INT./interior). EXT. would indicate it is outside (EXT./exterior). The producer adds up the number of pages that take place inside (on stages or locations) and outside (backlots or locations) and budgets for the correct equipment and personnel for each.

- CROWDED SCHOOL HALLWAY: Describes where the scene takes place in a few words. Save any longer visual clues for the scene description.

- DAY or NIGHT: Indicates when the scene takes place. You can also use DAWN, DUSK, or NOON. However, anything more specific (11:38 p.m.) should go in the scene description.

Remember, skip a line before *and* after the slugline so it stands out from the rest of your script.

Some scenes start inside and go outside, or vice versa. In that case, you write INT./EXT. or EXT./INT. to indicate both.

You might want to intercut between two locations in one scene, which you would write in by placing these words along the left margin of your page, skipping a line before and after this description:

```
INTERCUT WITH (PREVIOUS SCENE)
```

SCENE DESCRIPTIONS

Scene descriptions describe the scene exactly the way the camera shows it. They set up what the characters are doing physically, and how they interact with each other and their physical surroundings. Unlike novels, which can take the reader inside the mind of their characters, it's important in scripts to describe the picture on the screen *visually* and avoid phrases like "Luis and Marco have been best friends for years," using instead, for example, "Luis and Marco give each other a secret handshake," which is something you can see or hear on film.

When you write a scene description, use the present tense, and include only the most important details. Be brief and clear, telling the reader just what he needs to know to get across the necessary information in the scene. Insert a blank line between paragraphs and keep paragraphs to no more than six lines. One rule of thumb is to break each paragraph where you want the camera to cut.

Each time a new character is introduced, type the character name in all uppercase letters. You may also capitalize certain words for emphasis, such as sound effects.

Here's an example:

```
"THREE BLACK BUTTONS"

FADE IN:

INT. CORRUGATED METAL SHACK - DAY

SHADOWS. TINY STREAKS of DUSTY LIGHT
PIERCING THROUGH.

SFX: A low and menacing MOAN.

A finger-thin flashlight BEAM illuminates
the far wall.

Hanging on the wall we see C-CLAMPS, a
HACKSAW. A BELT SANDER.

Spattered and dripping BLOOD.
```

You may notice that the scene description doesn't always follow traditional sentence structure and may involve things such as sentence fragments. It comes down to style. Here's a more traditional example:

```
The THIEF climbs into the expensively furnished
living room - full-length mirrors, a terrace with
a view of Central Park. He listens for any SOUND
and, hearing none, puts on NIGHT VISION GOGGLES.
```

Note:
The Courier 12 pt. font is the standard font for typing screen-plays and teleplays.

Also notice that, in this example, certain words are capitalized within the scene description:

- The first time a character is introduced: "The THIEF"

- Sound effects: "A car BACKFIRES"

- An indication of what the camera should do: "We PULL BACK TO REVEAL Sam standing behind a lamppost in an MCU."

- An important prop: "NIGHT VISION GOGGLES"

TRANSITIONS

Transitions, or scene breaks, tell the reader how you want to go from scene to scene. As with sluglines, you skip a line before and after each transition.

Except for FADE IN: at the front of a script, you place transitions flush right along the right margin of the page so they stand out visually, like this:

FADE IN:

CUT TO:

DISSOLVE TO:

FADE TO BLACK.

Here are some descriptions of the major transitions and what they are used for:

- **CUT TO:** means one shot begins exactly where the previous one ends with no overlap of the visuals.

- **FADE IN:** means a fade from a black screen into the first shot of the movie.

- **FADE OUT:** or **FADE TO BLACK:** is usually the last shot of a film, where the image gradually disappears into the blackness. Fade-ins and outs take the audience into the story. Occasionally, a show might fade to black and then leave the screen black for a moment before fading up into the EXT. scene. This (along with other elements) may suggest a passage of time, though it would be up to the writer/director to then clarify how much time has passed.

- **DISSOLVE TO:** is when a shot disappears (fades out) as another shot appears (fades in) and the two shots overlap and occupy the screen together for a moment. This is typically used to connect two images in some way, such as when a singer on the left side of the screen singing a duet dissolves into her partner singing along on the other side of the screen, and the two characters, apart in "space," are united graphically onscreen and seem to be looking at each other.

A dissolve can be used for many purposes. Its main attribute is that it is not a cut; it has a different feeling, particularly based on the length of the dissolve, and may require the audience to wonder why the show is going from shot to shot or scene to scene in a different way.

- **WIPE TO:** is when a line moves across the screen, usually either horizontally, vertically, or diagonally, and it lays one shot down on top of another as it goes. Wipes are rarely used in quality productions.

COMMUNICATION

The three main types of communication in a screenplay are as follows:

- *Dialogue*: One character speaks to another, several characters speak to each other, or a character addresses a group.

- *Narration or voiceover*: Either a character from the piece or the omniscient (all-knowing) narrator who is not part of the story speaks directly to the audience without being seen. This is written as follows: JENNY (VO) or JENNY (OC) or JENNY (NARRATION), where OC means off-camera.

- *Interior monologue*: The characters "speak" to themselves. Usually, the audience hears their thoughts over an image of their face. This is written as follows:

```
                    DAVID
               (thinking)


     Oh God, it's the first day of school!
     What am I doing here? They're all
     gonna laugh at me! Where's my first
     class?
```

When writing communication, you include the speaker's name in all uppercase letters, 3.5" from the left edge of the sheet. Follow it with the vocal direction, or parenthetical descriptions of how they say their dialogue, 3" from the edge. Below the direction you type the actual dialog, indented on the left and right sides. Industry standard is 2.5" from the left and right edges of the sheet. Here is an example:

```
                    JOHNNY
               (bored)


     I'm bored! I'm getting the heck out
     of here! Don't tell me what to do!
     You're not my mom!
```

Note that in this example, there is really no need for the parenthetical, since Johnny is stating that he's bored. Use parentheticals only when the meaning of the dialogue might be unclear.

When you put it all together, it looks something like **FIGURE 2.11**.

```
EXT. EAST SIDE HELIPAD - DAY

Jimmy waits, alone. He takes a vial of pills out of his
pocket, opens it and swallows two, dry.

Gillespie and Morrow appear. The three men cross to where
their prisoner, GRIFFIN, waits for them in the custody of two
Riker's Island guards.

                    GILLESPIE
          Sure we can't stick around a couple
          extra days? We could bring them up
          to date on what we've been doing,
          like cultural ambassadors.

Morrow signs the guards' voucher for their prisoner.

               GUARD ONE
          Thank you, sir.

The guards take off. Gillespie tries to get a rise out of
Griffin, who stares intently at Jimmy.

               GILLESPIE
          Comfortable?

               MORROW
            (re: the pilot)
          He'll shuttle you to JFK. You're
          traveling to China first class.

               GILLESPIE
            (impressed)
          First class...

               MORROW
          Hong Kong PD will meet you at
          Beijing and ferry you to the
          island. Once you drop him off,
          you're done. Good luck. See you in
          a few days.

               JIMMY
            (uncertain)
          Thanks.

                                        CUT TO:
```

© TOM MCCLUSKEY 2014

FIGURE 2.11 A page from the screenplay *Rapid Descent* (2014)

PREPARING AN AUDIO SCRIPT

An audio script is necessary for documenting narration or voice over recording. In a two-column script, video information, such as a description of the shot, goes in the left column and the audio script goes in the right column. Dialogue is typed using standard sentence case and is double-spaced.

Sometimes audio and video are combined in one column, with formatting used to differentiate between the two. Video descriptions are single-spaced and in all caps. The audio portion of the script is standard sentence case and double-spaced.

In both script formats, instructions for the narrator are in all caps, separated by parentheses, and words to emphasize are underlined. For example, if you want the narrator to emphasize the words "really" and "big" and wait a beat between them, you would write: `really (PAUSE) big`.

Know Your Rights: Copyright

You see that little © symbol to the right of the image for Figure 2.11? In reality, it has as much power as the *S* on Superman's chest. **Copyright** is one of the single most important concepts for the novice media creator to grasp. It actually refers to a series of rights that the creator of any piece of media automatically has in regard to that media, including the following:

- The right to produce or reproduce the copyrighted work

- The right to prepare derivative works based upon the work

- The right to distribute copies of the work to the public

- The right to perform a copyrighted work publicly

- The right to display the copyrighted work publicly

This means that if you write, compose, or design something, you are the one who has the right to exploit that work commercially and to make money from its reproduction. Naturally, if someone disputed your copyright claim and it came down to a lawsuit, the hearing board would try to determine which parts of your work are both original and yours.

The U.S. Copyright Act of 1976 (and a few pieces of legislation since) clarifies the protections that are guaranteed to the owner of a copyrighted work. Technically, you own the copyright to anything you create from the moment you write it, as long as you are not infringing the copyright of someone else.

However, to protect your copyright or to simply clarify that you are the one who created your work, it may be worthwhile for you to register your work with the U.S. Copyright Office. You simply send them a copy of your completed work along with their fee, which depends on what type of work it is, and they will protect it. **FIGURE 2.12** shows an example of a copyright form.

It would naturally help, of course, if you were ever to bring a lawsuit for infringement against another party for violating your copyright in your work, to have a copy of your work on file with the U.S. Copyright Office.

Additionally, the Writers' Guild of America (WGA), an organization that protects the rights of writers, will register your script as a sort of protective backup to the copyright office. As a professional writer, when you "go out" with your script (try to sell it), a lot of potential buyers may see it over a short period of time, so you may want it to be as protected as it can be.

Certain types of work like TV shows, films, screenplays, songs, paintings, and computer software are protected by copyright. Certain designs would be considered trademarks rather than original artwork but would then be protected by trademark law. A **trademark** is another type of intellectual property—a symbol, sign, or expression that is associated with a commercial product or a corporate entity and cannot be used by another individual or business.

Certain types of creative work, like names of songs, books, and band names, are not protected by copyright law.

Form VA

Detach and read these instructions before completing this form.
Make sure all applicable spaces have been filled in before you return this form.

BASIC INFORMATION

When to Use This Form: Use Form VA for copyright registration of published or unpublished works of the visual arts. This category consists of "pictorial, graphic, or sculptural works," including two-dimensional and three-dimensional works of fine, graphic, and applied art, photographs, prints and art reproductions, maps, globes, charts, technical drawings, diagrams, and models.

What Does Copyright Protect? Copyright in a work of the visual arts protects those pictorial, graphic, or sculptural elements that, either alone or in combination, represent an "original work of authorship." The statute declares: "In no case does copyright protection for an original work of authorship extend to any idea, procedure, process, system, method of operation, concept, principle, or discovery, regardless of the form in which it is described, explained, illustrated, or embodied in such work."

Works of Artistic Craftsmanship and Designs: You may register "Works of artistic craftsmanship" on Form VA, but the statute makes clear that protection extends to "their form" and not to "their mechanical or utilitarian aspects." The "design of a useful article" is considered copyrightable "only if, and only to the extent that, such design incorporates pictorial, graphic, or sculptural features that can be identified separately from, and are capable of existing independently of, the utilitarian aspects of the article."

Labels and Advertisements: Works prepared for use in connection with the sale or advertisement of goods and services may be registered if they contain "original work of authorship." Use Form VA if the copyrightable material in the work you are registering is mainly pictorial or graphic; use Form TX if it consists mainly of text. **Note:** Words and short phrases such as names, titles, and slogans cannot be protected by copyright, and the same is true of standard symbols, emblems, and other commonly used graphic designs that are in the public domain. When used commercially, material of that sort can sometimes be protected under state laws of unfair competition or under the federal trademark laws. For information about trademark registration, call the U.S. Patent and Trademark Office, at 1-800-786-9199 (toll free) or go to *www.uspto.gov*.

Architectural Works: Copyright protection extends to the design of buildings created for the use of human beings. Architectural works created on or after December 1, 1990, or that on December 1, 1990, were unconstructed and embodied only in unpublished plans or drawings are eligible. Request Circular 41, *Copyright Claims in Architectural Works*, for more information. Architectural works and technical drawings cannot be registered on the same application.

Deposit to Accompany Application: An application for copyright registration must be accompanied by a deposit consisting of copies representing the entire work for which registration is to be made.

Unpublished Work: Deposit one complete copy.

Published Work: Deposit two complete copies of the best edition.

Work First Published Outside the United States: Deposit one complete copy of the first foreign edition.

Contribution to a Collective Work: Deposit one complete copy of the best edition of the collective work.

The Copyright Notice: Before March 1, 1989, the use of copyright notice was mandatory on all published works, and any work first published before that date should have carried a notice. For works first published on and after March 1, 1989, use of the copyright notice is optional. For more information about copyright notice, see Circular 3, *Copyright Notice*.

For Further Information: To speak to a Copyright Office staff member, call (202) 707-3000 or 1-877-476-0778. Recorded information is available 24 hours a day. Order forms and other publications from the address in space 9 or call the Forms and Publications Hotline at (202) 707-9100. Access and download circulars, forms, and other information from the Copyright Office website at *www.copyright.gov*.

FIGURE 2.12 An excerpt from Form VA, application for copyright, from the U.S. Copyright Office

Copyright Vs. Plagiarism

Most students will already be familiar with the concept of plagiarism, which is presenting someone else's work as if it is your own without citing the original source. Copyright infringement is theft, and it might potentially be considered a crime if the work that was infringed upon was deemed by a judge to have real commercial value.

Developing a Soundtrack and Score

A defining aspect of the motion-picture medium is its inclusion of other media, music being one of them. Unfortunately, instruction on the specific methods of writing and recording a piece of music goes beyond the scope of this book.

Rather, this section will focus on the understanding of how a musical **soundtrack** and **score** can be used to enhance and strengthen the delivery of your message. You will learn how to identify the right kind of music for your video and how to communicate and work with musicians to create the score (see **FIGURE 2.13**). You will also learn about the ethical and legal use of music that was not originally created for your video.

FIGURE 2.13   Student recording a piano track for a video score

Using a Score

The terms *soundtrack* and *score* are frequently used interchangeably. Originally, the term *sound track* was used to define the entire completed mix of audio that accompanies the motion picture. As record albums of music used in films began to be sold to the public as a separate product from the film in the early 20th century, the entertainment industry began to use the contraction *soundtrack* to describe the music in a film's sound track. Today, the most common use of the term *soundtrack* refers to songs in a motion picture, as opposed to a musical score.

A *score* is music that is intended to play in the background of a motion picture's sound mix, usually recorded by an orchestra specifically for that film (see **FIGURE 2.14**). Its purpose is to support and enhance the mood, tone, and emotional impact of a scene. A score guides an audience's emotional understanding of what is happening onscreen. The music can set a specific mood, like suspense and anticipation in a horror film, excitement and energy in an action scene, or melancholy in a scene where there is loss or death.

Note:

Albums of music from a motion picture are also called *original soundtrack* (OST).

FIGURE 2.14 A full orchestra at work in a scoring session

Music in motion pictures is not just limited to instrumental compositions; songs also serve an important purpose. For scenes in which there is no dialogue, a song with lyrics that reflect the action or emotion of a particular scene can be effective. Songs bring an element of poetry to the collection of media that is integrated into a motion picture. Filmmakers can use a song in its entirety as the foundation of an entire sequence or montage.

There are some films whose soundtrack is made up entirely of songs or prerecorded music, with little or no original score. The soundtrack for the Mike Nichols film *The Graduate* (1967) is made up entirely of popular songs written and performed by Simon & Garfunkel. Director Martin Scorsese frequently uses this approach to film music, most notably in *Goodfellas* (1990), *Casino* (1995), and *The Wolf of Wall Street* (2013). Even in *Shutter Island* (2010), Scorsese used prerecorded music that sounds like original score, mostly because a large chunk of the music was used in other films.

Directors don't fill their films' soundtracks with songs just because they like them. They often choose songs that locate the story or segments of it at a specific point in time. Two examples of this are *Forrest Gump* (1994) and *Almost Famous* (2000).

On the other side of this spectrum, you can choose to not use any music at all in your video. Master of suspense Sir Alfred Hitchcock was able to prove that a thrilling suspense film could be made with the complete absence of music. He tested this theory most notably in *The Birds* (1963). Instead, composer and longtime collaborator Bernard Herrmann designed the sound of the film using sound effects of birds instead of music only three years after creating one of the most memorable horror movie scores in *Psycho* (1960).

Musical Themes

The most popular film scores contain a memorable musical theme or **leitmotif**. A **musical theme** is a musical phrase that repeats and is usually attached to a character, a place, or a time in a story. What music comes to mind when you read the name Darth Vader? How about when you think about sharks? Or dinosaurs? The composer of the memorable themes used in the *Star Wars*, *Jaws*, and *Jurassic Park* series is John Williams, who is considered the master of the film score theme.

The videos you create, especially if you are creating a series, might have an opening theme and a closing or end credit theme. The number of musical themes you have in your video depends on the structure and themes of your story. You might choose to have a single theme that repeats but varies in style to support the mood of each scene. The Jean-Luc Godard film *Contempt* (1963) uses a single two-and-a-half-minute theme, composed by Georges Delerue, repeated throughout the film.

Spotting Cues

The first step in the process of adding music to your video is spotting the cues. A **cue** is the term used to describe both a piece of musical score and the moment in the video at which that piece of music begins. **Spotting** describes the process of identifying where those cues go, listing how many cues are needed, and writing a description and purpose for each cue. The document created to organize the music in a production is called a **cue sheet** (see FIGURE 2.15).

> **Tip:**
> Remember that there is no rule forcing you to put wall-to-wall music throughout your video. Sometimes just the sound of the environment is enough to create the appropriate mood for the scene. If you want your project to play like a Puccini opera, feel free to "through-compose" your music.

FIGURE 2.15 Blank cue sheet template

A director works with a music editor and composer to create a cue sheet, which is then used by the postproduction team to keep track of the music in a show. The document evolves when multiple sources of music are used and the management of rights and ownership require additional information to be added to the sheet.

Working with a Composer

As a videomaker, you will find yourself collaborating with a variety of people with expertise in different crafts. Some of the folks you will work with are working primarily at a technical level, such as the camera department or lighting technicians.

Others you may work with, like your actors or talent, work mostly on an emotional level. How you communicate with either type of collaborator requires a bit of code-switching. You don't speak to your friends the same way you do to your parents. When you are working with a composer, you have a unique hybrid of both qualities because music can be very technical but is mainly concerned with what Stanley Kubrick called a progression of moods and feelings.

When collaborating with a composer who is providing an original score for your project, remember that even though she might be entering the process late in the production, she is an integral part of your team. When beginning work with the composer, share your passion for the project. Enthusiastically express in detail your intentions in making the video. Discuss the meanings, subtext, symbology, language, rhythms, visual design, challenges, triumphs, what you had for breakfast, and so on.

The more the composer understands what went into the project, what it means, and what it is intended to deliver to an audience, the better equipped she'll be to create music that is, at the least, appropriate. Ideally, she'll create a new element that enhances the story and message beyond what you imagined was possible.

It can also help to share with your composer examples of other sources of music you like, to give her a better sense of what you are hoping to achieve. It's not uncommon for a director and editor to use temporary music they intend on replacing later during the postproduction process. Such guide music is called a **temp track**.

> **Tip:**
> When sharing an export of your project to a composer, make sure to have a timecode (TC) burn-in window for reference. To do this, drop a timecode reader or generator filter or effect on your sequence.

Ethical Use of Someone Else's Work

Must you use original music for your project, or is it OK to drop in a track of a popular song? What about incorporating a Disney animation, or an Andy Warhol graphic design? An understanding and familiarity with copyright law and fair use will help you identify options for the acquisition and use of such content.

Give Credit Where Credit is Due

A common occurrence with student films is the use of popular songs without proper legal permission. Frequently, students will justify the use of these songs by using arguments such as "But I paid for the download, so it's my copy" or "No one's gonna see it; it's just a school project."

The problems with these arguments are as follows: first, if you bought a copy of the song, what you own is just that, a copy. You purchased the right to play the song for personal use. It will cost more for the rights to reproduce the song in your video for public viewing.

You insist that you are an upstanding and ethical student videomaker, but you really, really want to use that popular song in your video. It just won't work without it. So, what do you do? For starters, you must respect that the work of the musical artist, just like the work you are creating, is **intellectual property**. Intellectual properties are creations that were formed through the work of the mind, such as written work, art, music, designs, or inventions. This work is protected by **copyright law**, which grants the creator of the copyrighted work the exclusive right to control how the work is seen, listened to, used, or delivered to the world.

So, you use a copyrighted song in your video. What's the big deal? At best, your video is removed from online video-hosting sites because of its use of copyrighted music. At worst, you can find yourself being named in a copyright infringement lawsuit, which may result in a significant fine. You also risk losing your reputation.

Does this mean you can never use copyrighted music—or graphics and animations? The answer is no. Follow these guidelines to legally and responsibly acquire and use copyrighted material:

1. Find out who owns the work.

2. Receive permission from the content owner in the form of a **licensing agreement**.

3. Pay for the work, if payment is part of the agreement.

4. Credit the creator and owner of the work.

LICENSING AGREEMENTS

There are a few different licensing agreements you can make with the owner or creator of copyrighted work you want to add to your project. You can ask for **master use synchronization rights** (or **sync rights**), **broadcast rights**, or a limited option such as **festival rights**.

Master use or synchronization rights agreements allow you full use of the copyrighted work to be synchronized with your project and part of your soundtrack. The licensing agreement you sign could be for perpetuity (until the end of time and existence) or limited for a specific period of time, as in **FIGURE 2.16**.

Broadcast rights are similar to master use, except they limit the use of the licensed material for broadcast use only. Other options are even more limiting. For instance, if there is a song you want to use but you can't afford the full sync rights, you can arrange an agreement like festival rights, which will allow you to use the music in your project as it goes to festivals or contests. Once your project is purchased for distribution, you must make a new agreement to pay the full amount for master use synchronization rights.

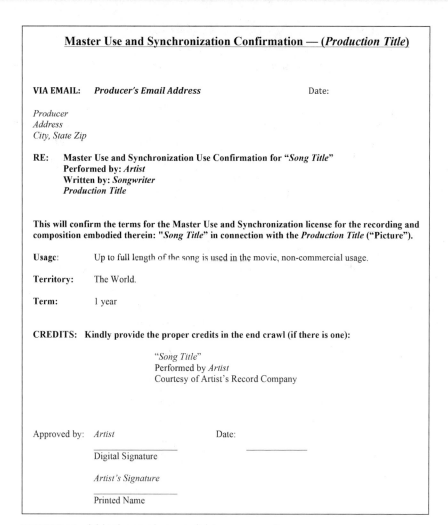

Master Use and Synchronization Confirmation — (*Production Title*)

VIA EMAIL: *Producer's Email Address*   Date:

Producer
Address
City, State Zip

RE: **Master Use and Synchronization Use Confirmation for "*Song Title*"**
Performed by: *Artist*
Written by: *Songwriter*
Production Title

This will confirm the terms for the Master Use and Synchronization license for the recording and composition embodied therein: "*Song Title*" in connection with the *Production Title* ("Picture").

Usage: Up to full length of the song is used in the movie, non-commercial usage.

Territory: The World.

Term: 1 year

CREDITS: **Kindly provide the proper credits in the end crawl (if there is one):**

               "*Song Title*"
               Performed by *Artist*
               Courtesy of Artist's Record Company

Approved by: *Artist*   Date: _____

               _____
               Digital Signature

               Artist's Signature

               _____
               Printed Name

FIGURE 2.16 A blank sample sync rights agreement

FAIR USE

Perhaps you are not able to get in touch with the creator or owner of copyrighted music you want to use, or, worse, you just don't want to ask for permission. There are legal, ethical, and appropriate reasons for the use of copyrighted material in other creations without permission. This is called **fair use** in the United States and **fair dealing** in other countries.

Fair use is not law the way copyright is. It is a doctrine that is part of copyright law that permits the use of previously published materials, provided that a particular set of conditions are met. When you use previously published work in a new creation, it's considered to be a **derivative** of the original. To make sure your use of someone else's intellectual property without permission is defined as fair use, you need to assess four factors in your use of the copyrighted work.

- The purpose of your creation must be for noncommercial use such as educational or school projects, news or journalism, criticism or social commentary, or comedy or parody.

- The work you are copying must be relevant to what you are creating.

- The amount of the copied work should be minimal and not make up a major percentage of the new work.

- What you create must not have a damaging effect on the value of the original work.

It's also important to make sure that what you are using from someone else's creation is changed in some way. It is fair use to incorporate a small part of a copyrighted song in a new song that is remixed and has a different style and form from the original, but it is copyright infringement if you use a large portion of the song and it's not changed in any way.

ROYALTY-FREE AND PUBLIC DOMAIN

No one will argue that creating an original score solely to fit the needs of your video project is ideal. With some projects, especially starting out as a student, you just don't have the time or the budget to commission or compose and then record an original score. That is when you must rely on music, animations, and images that are either **royalty-free** or in the **public domain**.

Royalty-free work is creative work designed to be used freely without concern of paying for licensing fees. Responsible use of royalty-free work requires crediting the creator. There are many royalty-free libraries available online that have affordable, and even free, music, images, and photos for you to use in your video projects.

Intellectual property in the public domain includes works whose copyrights have expired. The amount of time a property right lasts depends on the copyright laws of the country of origin. For example, in the United States, copyrighted works created after January 1, 1978, do not go into the public domain until 70 years after the author's death. If the work was produced for hire or created by a corporation, copyright protection lasts for 95 years after its publication or 120 years from the year of its creation, whichever comes first.

Some artists actively contribute to a growing collection of media under **Creative Commons licenses**. Creative Commons licenses allow artists to set specific guidelines in regard to how their work can be shared, transformed, or redistributed both commercially and noncommercially.

PERSONAL PRIVACY LAWS

One more aspect of content acquisition and use that you must consider when developing your projects is personal privacy. Not everyone wants to be in your video. Not everyone wants to share his image with the world or have his words broadcast over the Internet. The Constitution of the United States guarantees the right to privacy. That means that individuals have the right to determine how their image, words, and other personal information is collected and used. This law also prevents the unauthorized commercial use of an individual's name, likeness, or other recognizable aspect of a person. Commercial use means you are going to make money from the image.

Although capturing a photo, recording, or video of someone in a public place and using it in a project may be allowed, it may not be. Therefore, it is always a good idea to obtain a signed **release**, which is a legal consent form that provides you with authorization to take and use the image.

Don't Go Into Room 237!

An interesting case of fair use comes from the making of the independent documentary **Room 237** (2012), about the theories of hidden meanings in Stanley Kubrick's 1980 horror masterpiece **The Shining** (1980). The film's visuals are almost completely made up of footage from **The Shining**, whose copyright is owned by Warner Bros. Entertainment lawyer Michael C. Donaldson has been quoted in estimating that the use of "a mere 30-second clip from a studio film can cost between $6,000 and $8,000."

Doing the math, that would mean that **Room 237** director Rodney Ascher should have paid Warner Bros. around $1.2 million to $1.6 million in license fees for the use of the footage from **The Shining** had he asked for permission, which he didn't. Rather, he had argued that the use of the footage fell within fair use because the purpose of the documentary was the criticism of the original work; using footage from **The Shining** in a movie about **The Shining** couldn't be more relevant. Although the documentary is created mostly from footage of the original work, no one is going to confuse which film is which. Furthermore, Ascher argued, the creation of **Room 237** could only add to the appeal and value of **The Shining** and get more people to watch it.

Postproduction: Incorporating Audio

Following the basic postproduction workflow allows you to get a simple project based on visuals from footage on a camera to a finished video online. It also lets you make the most of the soundtrack elements in your project by taking the next step in making your project better through the use of audio.

Layering Audio

There was a time when nonlinear editing systems (NLEs) limited the number of layers of audio that an editor could add to a sequence. Today, the limits still exist, but they depend on the power of your hardware rather than the functionality of your NLE. Without any practical limits, there's no reason to not take advantage of being able to add overlapping elements of audio to your project, even when editing on a mobile device.

Organizing the layers of audio is usually done by the following categories:

- Dialogue (or production audio)
- Music
- Sound effects
- Voiceover or narration

In track-based editing software like Avid Media Composer or Adobe Premiere Pro, to add layers of audio, you have to add **audio tracks** before attempting to add audio clips (see FIGURE 2.17). Audio tracks or channels are pathways for audio clips to travel on. Audio clips that are synchronized (or *synced*) with video clips are placed in these audio tracks, separate from video tracks.

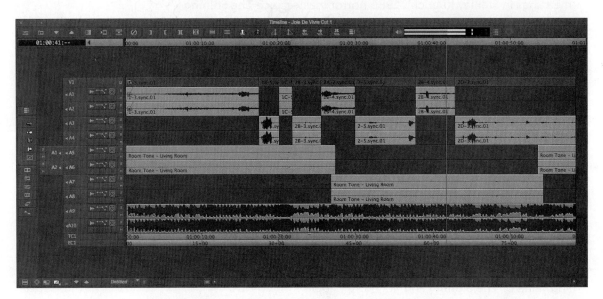

FIGURE 2.17   Timeline of a track-based editing application (Avid Media Composer)

Audio that is recorded with picture simultaneously is called **production sound**. The purpose of this track-based approach is to keep all the elements organized. The organization is useful in that you can toggle elements on and off or so you can deliver your edit to a different audio editing and mixing application that needs to follow the same organization.

In non-track-based editing software, such as Apple Final Cut Pro X, your timeline is a free-floating workspace where audio clips can be layered and connected to any other clip above or below them (see FIGURE 2.18). Production sound is embedded in the video clip segment to avoid potential problems of throwing the audio out of sync with the picture that was recorded at the same time. Audio clips connected or layered in a project can still be organized by labeling which *role* the audio clip serves. The relationship between production sound and the video can be changed so that manipulation of the timing or length of production audio can differ from the synced picture.

The number of tracks assigned for dialogue or production audio depends on how many microphones were simultaneously used to record the audio. It would be safe to dedicate at least four tracks to allow for *checkerboarding* and *room tone*, explained in the "Mixing" section later in this chapter.

Note:

Voiceover recording is covered in the Chapter 3, "Vision and Voice."

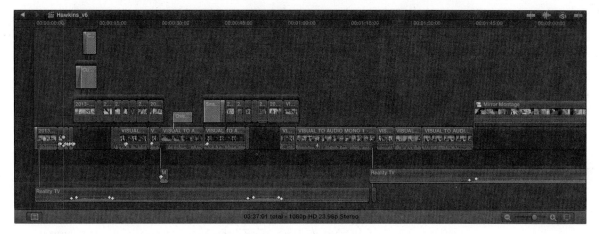

FIGURE 2.18   Timeline of a non-track-based editing application (Apple Final Cut Pro X)

Sound effects and music are usually created in two-track stereo, so the number of tracks will depend on how many layers of each you plan to use, times two.

Voiceover or narration can be included in the dialogue tracks or can have dedicated tracks assigned for it.

Sound Design

The number of tracks you will need for your project is based on how complex your **sound design** will be. Stop and listen to the sounds in the area you are in right at this moment. Try listing everything you hear. Your brain has the capability of focusing on different sounds individually, even if they are around the same volume or coming from the same direction. Here's a list of what you might hear in a classroom of students quietly reading that you can individually pinpoint:

- Fluorescent lights buzzing

- Air-conditioning vents humming

- A classmate coughing

- Pages of a book turning

- Feet shuffling

- Someone sighing heavily

- Another class laughing in the room next door

- Someone else holding back laughter near you

- Paper being crumpled

- Someone whispering

Those are just some of the sounds you might hear in a quiet classroom. Each one of these things could be considered a **sound effect**. Sounds such as the fluorescent lights or air-conditioning vents are called **atmospheric** or

ambient sounds. If that was a scene in a video, those two pieces of audio would take up at least four tracks, two for each stereo clip. The other sounds on the list are specific isolated sounds, also called **hard sound effects**.

Where you place, how you use, and what volume level each sound in your project has is determined by your sound design. If a scene like the one described is focused on one student increasingly unable to focus on her work, you might start the scene with the isolated sound effects playing at a realistic volume level but have the sound repeat.

As each sound on the list is heard, you might increase the level of the effect so it's slightly louder than the sound before it. Each additional sound can progressively increase in volume and in repeating frequency until it becomes an unbearable, *hyper-real* cacophony, letting the audience experience for themselves just why your character is having so much trouble focusing on her classwork.

A scene like the one just described could take about 24 tracks of sound to design for the desired result. Imagine how many tracks an action movie must have, where each character's weapon has two tracks each! In the film *Good Will Hunting* (1997), director Gus Van Sant used 100 tracks of audio for a fight scene on a playground basketball court that lasted less than two minutes.

Finding all the sound effects you need for your project can be time-consuming. Ideally, during production you have a list of the ambient and isolated sound effects you need prepared so that you can record them at the same time and in the same place as you shot the scene. Time and budget don't always allow for such luxury, so recording these sounds later during postproduction is completely acceptable.

When searching for sounds that are difficult to record or when crunched for time, you can use prerecorded sound effects from a sound effects library. Some editing software includes a sound effects library with commonly used sound effects for your convenience.

Mixing and Sweetening

The word **sweetening**, in video production, means to add a small number of sound effects that enhance the project and clean up anything distracting about the sound.

The process of mixing and sweetening can occur as you edit picture and can continue as you add other audio elements. Once all the audio you *think* you will need is edited in, you can officially start the process of mixing and sweetening.

While editing and adding essential audio elements, you might have already taken the time to change the volume levels of clips that conflicted with sounds that need to be heard. Perhaps you've invested time in making sure the levels of your dialogue clips sounded consistent from one clip to the next. This will save you a bunch of time when you start mixing and sweetening.

Note:
Follow the same rules and guidelines for using sound effects recorded by others as you would for music, as mentioned in the "Copyright and Fair Use" section.

Tip:
Don't be overly concerned with the levels on the audio level meter. Your audience will not be watching your project with meters. Trust your ears.

Ideally, with some understanding of the audio level meters and the delivery standards of audio mixes, you won't have to redo much of the work you've already done.

The *audio levels meter* in your editing software has some important numbers to understand. Digital audio level meters top out at 0 decibels (dB). **Decibels** are how audio levels are measured.

Depending on the type of program you are creating, the average level your program should have could be either -20dB (pronounced "minus twenty") for professional television and broadcast or -14dB for web video and other video productions. Audio level meters have green, yellow, and red indicators to highlight the safety of a sound's volume (see **FIGURE 2.19**).

Simply put, if the audio is in red and it's supposed to be a whisper, the level is too *hot*, or loud. That red area should be reserved for the louder sounds in life such as explosions, gunshots, crashes, or your mother telling you to take out the garbage. Dialogue, music, and voiceover should stay in the green, only slightly visiting the yellow zone.

Once you understand the audio level meter, the first official step in the mixing and sweetening process is to start what is usually called a *dialogue edit*. It is best to do this process with headphones.

The first step is to mute all your tracks that don't have dialogue or voiceover in them. If you've organized your tracks or labeled your roles correctly, this should be easy to do. An alternative to muting tracks, especially if there are a lot you have to mute, is to *solo* the tracks you want to monitor.

Once you do that, you can start **checkerboarding** your clips. When two audio clips have a cut and are placed together, sometimes that cut will be audible because the difference between the ambient sound abruptly changes. To fix that, alternate which tracks each clip goes on. This is called *checkerboarding* (see **FIGURE 2.20**).

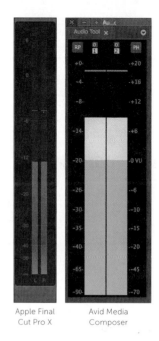

Apple Final
Cut Pro X

Avid Media
Composer

FIGURE 2.19 Audio level meters from two different video-editing applications

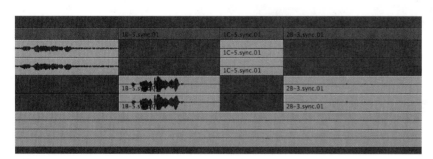

FIGURE 2.20 Checkerboarded audio clips

Then, lengthen the duration of each clip to have them overlap (see **FIGURE 2.21**). Be careful not to lengthen the clip so much that you hear anything unwanted; they should be just long enough to extend the pause in audio.

Using either audio fade transition effects or volume keyframes, fade out the outgoing audio clip and fade in the incoming audio clip (see **FIGURE 2.22**). **Keyframes** are like pushpins on a rubber band. You need to have at least two pushpins to change the line from point A to point B.

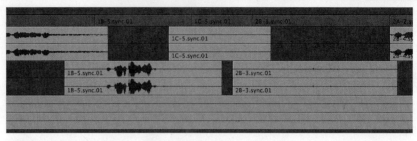

FIGURE 2.21 Audio clips overlapped

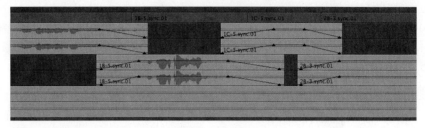

FIGURE 2.22 Audio clips overlapped with fades

Tip:

You will know the importance of room tone only after needing to use it during audio editing and mixing. It will feel like an inconvenience recording room tone, especially when a scene is done shooting and the crew wants to start wrap.

Tip:

If an atmospheric sound effect is not long enough, feel free to duplicate it onto another set of tracks with a fade and overlap to loop the effect. If the effect is too short, the loop might sound unnatural.

When playing back the scene, you should not be able to detect any cuts in audio. If you hear any gaps or voids in audio, edit in some **room tone** with fades overlapping the audio around it. Room tone, also known as *ambiance* or *ambient sound*, is audio of the location the scene takes place in with everyone remaining silent.

During production, be sure to take the time before wrapping to record 30–60 seconds of room tone in case you need to use it in your audio mix.

Using keyframes, you can also bring down the audio level of distracting loud sounds, like certain words spoken too loudly, claps, or prop sounds (see **FIGURE 2.23**).

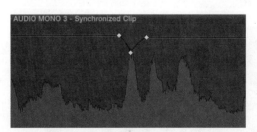

FIGURE 2.23 Keyframes used to reduce the audio level of a peak

Playing back the sequence without sound effects or music, the cuts between audio clips should no longer be detectable. Your work as an audio editor and mixer is like that of a ninja. If someone notices what you've done, you have failed at your job.

Once you are satisfied that your production audio sounds smooth and consistent, unmute the sound effects tracks, take off your headphones, and start listening to your project with audio monitors or speakers. If any sound effect is too loud or makes it difficult to hear important production audio, *do not* raise the volume of the production audio. Rather, lower the volume of the sound effect. Most sound effects need to have their levels lowered to sound natural.

Go through the sequence and lower the levels on all the sound effects so that they provide the desired result for the story and your sound design.

Unmuting the music is the next step. Just like with sound effects, if the music is clashing with other important sounds, lower the music. Novice sound mixers tend to mix the music a little too loudly. This might be because they are so familiar with the story at this point; they aren't listening as carefully as a first-time audience member would. As great as the music is, if it distracts the audience from hearing important information, then it is harming your story rather than enhancing it.

Give the mix a few listens, with the picture and without. Try listening to it on a different set of speakers. Export a copy and play it on a television set. Different listening environments will show different flaws in your mix. Take notes and be an effective ninja sound mixer.

End-of-Chapter Activities

REVIEW QUESTIONS

1. List at least three current practices and future trends affecting the audio and video production industries. Write a paragraph analyzing the practices and trends.

2. What is copyright and how does it affect content you acquire for use in your projects?

3. What is fair use and how does it affect content you acquire for use in your projects?

4. How are trademarks different from copyrights?

5. What is personal privacy? How do laws protect it?

6. What is intellectual property?

7. What are four key elements required in a video script or screenplay?

8. What is the difference between a one-column audio script and a two-column audio script?

9. What is propaganda?

10. What is score?

11. What is production sound?

Review Project 1

With a partner, create a timeline in which you summarize key points in the history and evolution of the audio and video production industry. Share your timeline with the class in an informal presentation.

Review Project 2

Using the information in this chapter and additional information you find online, write a report explaining the beginning and evolution of audio, video, and film. As you conduct research, use critical-thinking to evaluate the information you find for accuracy and validity. Record your sources so you can create accurate citations. Use a word-processing application to create the report. In your writing, use correct grammar, punctuation, and terminology. At the end of the report, create a glossary in which you define the industry terminology that you use and a works cited page or bibliography in which you list your sources.

Review Project 3

Using the information in this chapter and additional information you find online, prepare a formal presentation. Use presentation software to illustrate and describe how changing technology impacts the audio, video, and film industries. As you conduct research, use critical-thinking to evaluate the information you find for accuracy and validity. Record your sources so you can create accurate citations. In your writing, use correct grammar, punctuation, and terminology. At the end of the presentation, include a glossary in which you define the industry terminology that you use and a list of your sources.

CHAPTER 2 – PORTFOLIO BUILDER

PUBLIC SERVICE ANNOUNCEMENT (PSA)

A PSA is a short video, usually 30–60 seconds, that tells a story and delivers a message. At the surface, the least a PSA sets out to do is bring awareness to an issue or inform the audience of a problem. A successful PSA, however, not only brings awareness but effectively makes a *call to action*.

DIRECTIONS

In teams, research a social issue or problem and use that research to develop a story that contains a message and a plan for action.

1. Identify a social issue or problem in your community that needs a change, and have it approved by your teacher.

2. Research the issue. Use the Internet, but also reach out and talk to people who can help provide information. Evaluate the information for accuracy and validity.

3. As a team, write a treatment for a story you can tell visually, without dialogue. Show, don't tell. Most importantly, make sure it is clear what the viewer is being asked to do to solve the problem.

4. As a team, write a 30-60 second script. Remember that a properly formatted script times out to about a minute a page. Your PSA script should be no longer than one page.

5. If you are not creating your own music, find a royalty-free piece that appropriately matches the tone of your story and message. Get the proper permission, if necessary.

6. In your team, assign roles for crew and talent and then shoot your video.

7. Create any title cards or text and record them as part of your video. Creating your own titles with art supplies will add uniqueness to your video. Use one of your title cards to credit the creator of the music you chose to use.

8. Start your editing by laying down the music track. Edit in your shots, keeping in mind that you have chosen a specific running time.

9. Add audio tracks and fill them up with atmospheric sound effects and specific action sounds where necessary.

10. Mix your audio. Make sure any sound effects you've added don't conflict with the music or call attention to themselves, unless that is the intended effect. The same goes with the music. If any sound effects are important to the story and can't be heard, lower the music levels.

11. With your teacher's permission, post the video online and share the link with friends and family.

12. Show the video to organizations related to your PSA topic; they might want to make mention of it on social networks or even embed the video in their Web site.

Chapter 3

Vision and Voice

Chapter 3 Overview

- Developing the Idea
- Stepping Up to the Plate: The Pitch
- Getting it On Paper

- Fundamentals of Cameras and Camerawork
- Recording a Voiceover
- End-of-Chapter Review and Activities

This chapter explores the process of developing longer projects. It also provides in-depth technical information on cameras and lighting to help you refine and improve the quality of your shots and covers the ins and outs of voiceover narration. These topics will help you to control your image and the quality of the narration that accompanies it, leading to work that should reflect a higher level of experience and sophistication and the greater number of options available to you as an audio/visual artist.

Developing the Idea

When you are developing your idea, the two production skills of communication and organization become the keys to your success, so much so that you *cannot* succeed without these skills (see **FIGURE 3.1**). It's worthwhile to take some time to define the actual *goal* of your project because that can determine how much effort, resources, time, heart, and cash you put into it.

FIGURE 3.1   The director and the technical director operate the master control desk.

Why Am I Doing This?

The first question to ask yourself is: Why am I doing this?

To some, this might seem like a theoretical query without much practical application, but really, it will help you define your goals. You also need to ask yourself the following questions:

- Where will it be shown?

- Who will see it?

- What kind of companies or organizations might be interested in buying/optioning/supporting/helping me secure funding?

Young artists just starting out as producers and storytellers can benefit from listing some of the things they want to do with their finished work, such as the following:

- Expressing themselves

- Winning film festivals and contests (see **FIGURE 3.2**)

- Communicating outrage

- Making friends laugh

- Meeting other people who like doing video projects

- Documenting heritage, history, and cultural pride

FIGURE 3.2   Winning an award at a festival

- Completing senior portfolios
- Earning scholarships
- Examining a social problem
- Earning respect
- Gaining confidence
- Obtaining jobs or internships

Media artists find out who they are by figuring out who they care about and what they love. So if you are ever having a hard time getting started on a project, take a minute and ask yourself the following questions:

- What do you love?
- What do you care about?
- What makes you mad?
- What is worth paying tribute to?

Where Do You Begin?

Once you have determined what you are interested in, you must figure out what will make your film interesting to watch and who will do the watching. In other words, you have to think not only about the intention of your project but who will like it and where it will be seen.

A crew recently completed a short video project called *Guilty* about a young man who needs money for college. The only way he thinks he can get it is by stealing iPads and other expensive gadgets.

This project came about because that group was discussing gangster and crime genre movies that they liked, such as *Scarface* (1983) and *Dead Presidents* (1995). Soon they found themselves discussing and watching excerpts from older films such as the original *Scarface* (1932) and *The Public Enemy* (1931), which inspired these artists to transfer their unfinished piece to black and white.

They were all inspired by the material and the project to do their jobs with dedication and the desire to learn and do well. As a result, they completed a work that was exceptionally polished and compelling.

The director won scholarships to college media programs and was accepted into a leading arts program in Hollywood.

However, despite its high quality, the work was not accepted into many festivals because of its 15-minute length. Most festivals are looking to program student works that are 12 minutes and shorter.

The filmmakers discussed a couple of strategies for shortening their piece, but ultimately they decided they weren't interested in making changes because the original film had captured what they wanted. For them, making the film they wanted was more important than getting into a film festival.

With that end result in mind, as you choose and then refine the subject of your project, ask yourself what it is about the topic that is most interesting and original to you. Virtually all projects, from PSAs to shorts to feature-length blockbusters, have something in them that the filmmakers felt was interesting to themselves and to an audience.

Even sequels to big-budget extravaganzas change some elements to keep the movie-going experience fresh for the audience, though these projects have the added challenge of reproducing whatever it was that made the original work so sequel-worthy.

Harper Lee based her Pulitzer Prize–winning novel *To Kill A Mockingbird* (1960) on her life growing up in the South, exploring topics such as rape, racism, the legal system, and mob justice through the eyes of a ten-year-old protagonist. It was not an autobiographical work based on her life but rather her attempt to write what she knew so that her work would have the authenticity and detail of real life.

She expected her book to be rejected or cause a mild scandal, but its steely, accurate depiction of Southern racism broke through and caused a massive sensation. She created one of the great fictional representations of human decency and courage in the character of attorney Atticus Finch.

It is a good idea to develop projects based on your own life and passions because those details are what you know best. Details make stories. That said, if your passion is to write about the life of a World War I flying ace, you should follow your passion and let the details come from the quality of your research.

The writer and director of *8 Mile* (2002) based that film's fictional story on some aspects of the life of Eminem, who starred in the film. Some critics felt that the movie lacked a third act because after the audience sees the main character Jimmy "B-Rabbit" Smith overcome his fears and freestyle brilliantly, they don't then go on to see him become a huge success, selling out stadiums and making a lot of money, as his real-life counterpart did.

This was a creative choice on the part of the producers and director, who didn't want to produce a feature-length hip-hop video, choosing instead to focus on the artist's internal creative and personal struggles.

Stepping Up to the Plate: The Pitch

Generally speaking, when *pitch* is used as a verb (outside of a baseball game), it means to attempt to sell something. When used as a noun in the world of media and entertainment, a **pitch** is a summary of your project that communicates to anyone who hears it the essence of what makes it good... in 25 words or less (see **FIGURE 3.3**).

A pitch is a tool that you keep in your utility belt that will help you to do the following:

- Sell your project to someone or some company looking for that kind of project

- Attract cast and crew members who are talented and looking for quality projects to work on

- Refine or change your idea if you are not getting the kind of response to it you would like

FIGURE 3.3 A writer pitching to a producer

Traditionally a pitch is short and to the point. Ideally, it is a single sentence that captures the essence of the story, such as, "A sheriff who is afraid of water must stop a shark who is killing beachgoers in a Long Island community." Or, "A group of soldiers try to find one missing private who is the last survivor in his large family." Or, "A boy strikes up a friendship with an alien from another planet."

What to Leave In, What to Leave Out

The pitch will typically describe the *main character* of your story, the goal that character is pursuing, and the main *obstacles* that get in the way. The main character, or *protagonist*, is the one the audience relates to throughout the story.

Whether or not you get all the information about your main character into the pitch, it's your job as the writer to know what is most interesting and original about your main character and to weave it into your pitch. You will know how successful your pitch is when it achieves what you wanted it to or when it ultimately fails to do so and you must choose either to refine it further or to abandon it in favor of something else.

Sometimes writers come up with a pitch before they write the script for their project. Occasionally, if the idea of the story itself is interesting enough, writers are even able to sell well-crafted pitches to production companies that may then pay them (or someone else) to write the screenplay.

Selling a project with a single sentence can be the writer's version of winning the lottery. Disney Pictures paid $3.5 million for a pitch called *Lightspeed* before a script was written. Disney management did so because they loved the pitch; had a relationship with the writer, Terry Rossio, who had written the *Pirates of the Carribean* movies for them; and knew that the business potential for this project was extremely high (the *Pirates* movies have made almost $4 billion worldwide). Even though $3.5 million is a lot of money, the choice to pay it for a pitch before the writer sold it to another studio was considered a sound business decision for the company.

However, before anybody sets out to write that one great sentence and retire, note that the great majority of **green-lighted** projects not only sell and are produced based on completed screenplays but that those screenplays have often been rewritten over the course of several drafts.

In fact, most big-budget projects were developed across several different drafts written by different writers, with an organization called the *Writers Guild of America (WGA)* brought in at the end to determine who wrote what and who gets the main credit for the finished script. The WGA is a **labor union** for writers of content for television, movies, news, documentaries, animation, and new media. It includes the WGA, East (for writers living east of the Mississippi) and the WGA, West (for writers living west of the Mississippi). Labor unions are formed to protect the rights and interests of workers. There are many other labor unions representing other categories of audio and video production workers.

Successful Pitching Strategies

The main way writers use their pitches is to communicate the essence or best part of their project and to make sure that any changes they make along the way as they develop it are in keeping with whatever their project is really about.

Some other strategies for successful pitching include the following:

- Starting your pitch with a question related to the main challenge faced by your protagonist. For example, "What if everything you thought you knew about your life turned out to be a lie?" This engages the listener from the beginning.

- Bringing the listener to an interesting or mysterious part of your story and then switching to another portion, creating a cliffhanger in your pitch.

- Speaking openly about what drew you to this story if asked.

- Taking feedback on the project openly, even if the comment does not, at first, seem like a good idea. Feedback from others can help you refine and perfect your pitch, and your story.

Processing Feedback

It's important to listen to and process feedback and criticism you receive to apply an objective point of view to your work. Was something confusing to your audience? Would scenes make more sense if they happened in a different order? The pitch can help you clear things up and determine what you can fix during revisions.

However, think carefully about feedback before embarking on a wholesale rewrite. Feedback can be constructive, or destructive. You want to be true to your story and yourself. Keep in mind that the person giving you feedback has his own interests, opinions, and agendas that don't necessarily reflect your own. Also, sometimes people just feel a need to say something, and their feedback may or may not be useful, or constructive, criticism.

On the other hand, if your pitch keeps getting the same response over and over—for instance, "I'm not buying this, and neither will anybody else"—you may want to consider what specific aspects of your narrative are getting between you and a fantastic finished media project. Writers typically refine pitches over time based on feedback that they receive, just not all at once.

It is a good idea to jot down any ideas you get, sit on them a bit, and then consider whether they will make your story *better* or just different. Anyone can have a good idea, but it is your responsibility as the writer or creator of your project to determine whether the constructive criticism you just heard gets your project where it needs to go.

Pitching from a Template

Finally, the pitch is a tool you use to determine whether anything new you want to introduce—a scene, a character, a motif—fits into your project. If you come up with an awesome new white-haired wizard character named Zandalf but your pitch is "A repressed mom and housewife regains joy in her life when she discovers kickboxing," maybe save Zandalf for the next script.

The following is an example of a template for a pitch. Some who read it may find it cynical to think that all stories can be reduced to one paradigm. However, all projects have to take some aspects of the human experience and funnel them through a particular set of characters, experiences, and subcultures.

As a result, virtually every project from *Titanic* (1997) to *Blue Velvet* (1986) to *Los Olvidados* (1950) to *Finding Nemo* (2003) to *Friday* (1995) can be diagrammed using the following template. Try it yourself with a movie, TV show, book, or play you know well and see!

Sample Pitch

"Hi, my script is about _____, who is a very interesting character because s/he _____. She/he is living an ordinary life doing _____ when something extraordinary happens: _____.

S/he must learn how to _____ or achieve _____, or a disappointing outcome will occur: _____.

The character sets out to _____ but is thwarted when _____ gets in their way, and our hero must come up with a new plan or else _____ will happen as things are quickly getting worse.

After going so far by _____ and sacrificing so much including _____ we wonder if s/he will be able to ultimately overcome their last and greatest challenge, _____ _____, which forces them to go all out and do something they would've previously thought was impossible: _____.

I think the most amazing scene is when the main character _____, and the most moving or thoughtful scene is where _____. These are the scenes that will most thrill the audience and make this a memorable experience for them.

Get It on Paper

Like many important events in life, the making of a video project is attended by lots and lots of paperwork. Artistic paperwork. Business paperwork. Organizational paperwork. Understanding the various types of paper you will be filling out or asking others to fill out is key to successfully developing your media business or career.

In audio and video production projects, forms and paperwork are key to planning and time-management. Time really is money on a shoot, and knowing how to read, create, and fill out forms used in video production will help you be prepared and stay on schedule.

The Project Triangle: Fast, Good, and Cheap

All the documents described help you to have a more organized, clear, articulate production with nothing left to chance. The saying from production—"Fast, good, and cheap...pick any two"—actually comes from the Project Constraint Model (see **FIGURE 3.4**). Here are a few examples of how it plays out in the world of filmmaking:

- **If you want it fast and good, it won't come cheap.** The second and third installments of the *Pirates of the Caribbean* movie series were shot at the same time without a break, which cost a lot of money but allowed the producers to complete both sequels much faster than if the whole cast and crew had gone away and then come back together a year later to start it all up again.

- **If you want it good and cheap, it won't be fast.** Filmmaker Robert Rodriguez jump-started his career by making the feature-length *El Mariachi* (1992) for the jaw-dropping sum of $5,000 by doing virtually every job in the movie he possibly could himself, including the special effects. He later wrote a book about the experience called Rebel Without a Crew, which is a must-read for young filmmakers.

- **If you want it fast and cheap, it won't be good.** There are many, many projects that starred people not known for acting but famous for other reasons—for example, Hulk Hogan and other wrestlers—or that have titles that leave you scratching your head, such as Killer Klowns from Outer Space (1988).

You might watch these titles out of curiosity or for amusement, or even rent them accidentally, but don't be shocked if they aren't very good. Some movies get made because producers have access to professional wrestlers or an excess of clown makeup.

FIGURE 3.4 The project triangle

Shot Lists: The Grocery Lists of Production

At the least, the director should come to the set with a **shot list**, which is a list of camera setups to use to record a scene.

A typical (and simple) shot list might include a wide shot (WS) of the scene that shows the location as well as the actors in the scene; two medium shots (MSs) of the main actors shot from opposite, matching angles; and two close-ups (CUs) of the same action (see **FIGURE 3.5**).

The shot list for a scene might be written up as follows:

Scene 5:

5	Master Shot – School Library
5a	MS – Eric and Andre (OTS – over-the-shoulder Eric)
5b	MS – Eric and Andre (OTS – over-the-shoulder Andre)
5c	CU Eric
5d	CU Andre

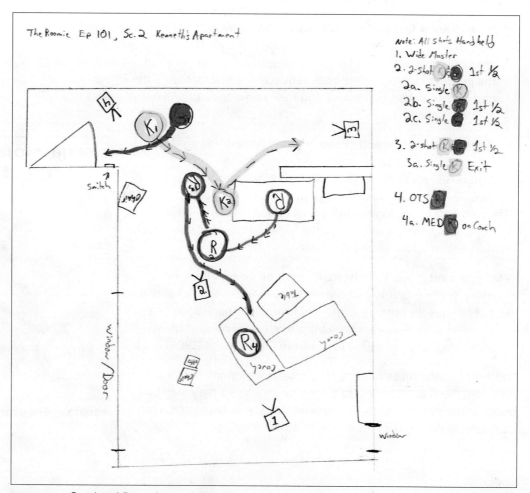

FIGURE 3.5 Overhead floor plan and shot list

The producer and first assistant director have to check this list against their schedule and make sure they have the time to shoot the various setups listed on the shot list. If they don't have the time, they have to prioritize the most important shots and leave the rest for another day.

Many behind-the-scenes featurettes (on DVDs, Blu-ray Discs, YouTube, and so on) include examples of shot lists as well as storyboards that you can review, but they are easy documents to create on your own. When you are the director or producer, it really puts your crew at ease when you can show them you are organized and know (more or less) what and how much you intend to shoot on a particular location for a particular scene.

Script Breakdowns

When a script is in preproduction, the unit production manager or line producer marks up the script using various colored highlighters to determine exactly what is going to be needed to record every scene, and then, as the schedule is determined, when the individual cast, crew, and objects will be required to be on the set to shoot.

As the first assistant director creates a production board and a shooting schedule based on the number of script pages in a particular scene and a certain location, he determines what will be needed and when. The line producer and unit production manager attend to the many technical details necessary to be ready to shoot (see **FIGURE 3.6**).

Charts of all the required elements for a particular shooting day, called a **script breakdown**, detail everything that is necessary and accountable for each day of shooting. This might include the 1966 Mustang convertible used for a getaway, or it could be a photograph sitting on a nightstand that has to be filmed and framed before it can be filmed again during the production of the actual scene.

A crew was shooting a short that all took place in one large executive's office. The entire film consisted of one long scene. It was shot over three weekends, and there was a fish tank in the office that contained a fish that ate other fish, as a visual metaphor for how this main character of the executive "ate" other executives in meetings. The only thing was, it was expensive to rent a fish that ate other fish.

The Problem with Precutting

As a student filmmaker, you should shoot everything you can from a particular angle once you've set up that angle. When you're shooting HD video, setting up cameras and lighting takes much more time than the actual recording of your scene. Consider shooting your whole scene from every angle that you have lit for. Your editors may thank you. It's much, much easier to have something and not need it than it is to need something and not have it (or organize a reshoot).

Color Code	Scene Breakdown Sheet Date: 11/10/98
Day Ext. – Yellow Night Ext. – Green Day Int. – White Night Int. – Blue	Prod. Company: __Cattle Prods.__ Page # _14_ Production Title: _"The Sin Eaters"_ Pg Count _3 1/2_

11	COMMERCIAL ST. / ROUNDUP, MT	EXT./INT.
Scene #	Scene Location	Int. or Ext.
CODY & SETH SHOW UP IN ROUNDUP, MT		Night
Description		Day or Night

CAST Red 1 MARK CODY 2 SETH CODY	STUNTS Orange N/A	EXTRAS/ATMOSPHERE Green TOWNSPEOPLE (25)
	EXTRAS/SILENT BITS Yellow GUN SHOP OWNER ROUNDUP RESIDENTS (12)	
SPECIAL EFFECTS Blue N/A	PROPS Purple PRESCIPTION PILL CONTAINER WALL OF GUNS	VEHICLE/ANIMALS Pink 1962 FORD THUNDERBIRD (WHITE)
WARDROBE Circle 1 JEANS / WESTERN SHIRT 2) WORK PANTS / T-SHIRT STESON HAT	MAKE-UP/HAIR Asterisk	SOUND EFFECTS/MUSIC Brown
SPECIAL EQUIPMENT Box	PRODUCTION NOTES Underline MAGIC HOUR FILMING.	

FIGURE 3.6 Script breakdown

As a result, the crew developed their shooting schedule around the fish. For the first two weekends, they shot the angles around the executive's desk at the other end of the office and didn't shoot any angles that would show the fish tank even in the background. On the last weekend of shooting, they recorded every angle that included the fish.

Often, when it comes to costumes, props, and so forth, line producers will try to get multiples or doubles of whatever they need because things happen, and line producers need to be prepared.

The script breakdown is a complete list of all the categories involved in the production of a particular scene:

- Locations
- Actors
- Background actors (extras)
- Props

- Costumes
- Vehicles
- Stunt performers
- Makeup and hair

In the finished script breakdown, each of these necessary elements has been color-coded and organized by category for each individual scene.

There are software applications such as Movie Magic Scheduling and Jungle Software that will allow you to create script breakdowns fairly easily. Not all crews go to the trouble to create script breakdowns. Most prefer simple lists of cast, crew, props, and so on. But there's no denying that your production, however big or small, will run more smoothly if the producer releases, in advance, a complete list of what is required to shoot and when it is needed.

Shoot Around Your Most Challenging Scenes

The truth of production planning is, you shoot out of sequence in whatever order makes the most sense depending on the availability of your actors, your location, and whatever else you need to make your scenes work.

Yes, but...Is It in the Budget?

The **film budget** for any media project lists how much every element of the production will cost, including the cast, crew, props, costumes, insurance, catering, and everything else.

The costs to produce a project can range from nothing to a few hundred dollars for a video resume to $1,000 for a wedding video and from $5,000 for *El Mariachi* (1992) to $220 million or more for big-budget blockbusters like *The Avengers* (2012). Whatever amount of funding you need to complete your project, a detailed budget is an incredibly useful tool to help you determine where to spend what you've got to get the most bang for your buck (see **FIGURE 3.7**).

Low-budget filmmakers know that sets, props, costumes, locations, and humans may come cheap or free, but the three things that always cost are *food*, *insurance*, and *gear*, including whatever you do to get your cast a version of their work to show. These are the basic costs of doing business.

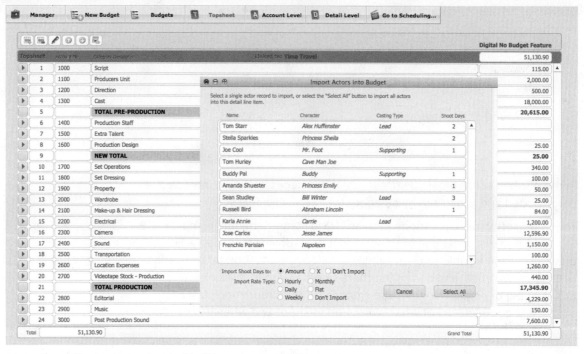

FIGURE 3.7 A film budget created with Chimpanzee production software

Of course, the real trick in effective filmmaking is to get great things shot for free or cheap. All successful indie producers know this. And you might be surprised to learn what you can get for free or cheap once you set your mind to it.

Actor and director John Sayles (*Return of the Secaucus 7*, 1980) and horror auteur Orin Peli (*Paranormal Activity*, 2009) are just two examples of producers who saved a lot by writing a movie they could shoot in their own homes.

Where Are You Supposed to Be? The Master Schedule

The **master schedule** or **shooting schedule** lists each day of production, what scenes are going to be shot, how many pages are planned to be covered on that day, which cast members need to be available, and what the location is, along with other critical information (see **FIGURE 3.8**).

There is no Oscar or Emmy award for the assistant director (who typically serves as schedule-keeper), but the shooting schedule is as important as any other technical document in the making of a project. Many production companies require all producers to have an approved schedule with locked locations before shooting can begin.

Call Me: The Call Sheet

The **call sheet** is a form filled out daily for each day's shooting, which contains all the key information for the cast and crew: where they are shooting, who has to be on set that day, the contact information for all the key personnel, and, most importantly, what their **call time** is—in other words, what time they have to be on set.

SOURCE: JUNGLE SOFTWARE

FIGURE 3.8 A shooting schedule in stripboard form created with Gorilla production software

Call sheets are documents crew members need to prove they worked on particular days, either to confirm their income or to satisfy union requirements (see **FIGURE 3.9**). All levels of crews are well-served in creating call sheets in order to avoid any producer said/production assistant said disagreements. With the call sheet, everyone knows what time they need to be there.

It is a good idea to set a call time an hour before you plan to start shooting, especially if you need to allow time for hair and makeup.

Punctuality

This is a good time to talk about the importance of punctuality. There is nothing more crucial to the morale of a crew or production team than to have everyone on set on time.

Punctuality is the number-one thing that employees in every industry— but particularly in the entertainment industry—can attend to in order to improve their employability and to hold on to jobs. Its importance cannot be overestimated.

If your crew has to sit and wait for one person in order to do their jobs, that person has probably made a roomful of professional enemies.

The entertainment business is a word-of-mouth, reputation-based business. Get an alarm clock and leave for work an hour early the first week. If that gets you to work only 20 minutes early, that means you would've been 40 minutes late if you hadn't allowed that extra hour.

The good news is, in film, television, and other media, if you are punctual, reliable, a good listener, and a capable person, you can eventually find a niche where your skills and your interests come together and start to build a nice career for yourself.

Time Travel

Call Sheet	April 16, 2012	HOSPITAL	Time Travel Films
CREW CALL	Day 1 of 5	Cedar Sinai Hospital 1234 Beverly Glen Beverly Hills, CA 90215	1234 Back in Time Delorean City, CA 90023
7:00 AM	Sunrise: 6:00 AM High: 74° Sunset: 6:30 PM Low: 54°		1st Assistant Director: Nicholas
Breakfast: 6:30 AM	Sunny and Clear	PARKING Parking R Us Park in Lot A only	Producer: Timothy Terraces Director of Photography: Quincy
First Shot: 8:00 AM Camera Wrap: 6:30 PM Crew Wrap: 7:00 PM			

*** No Smoking anywhere on the set ***

Scs.	Set		D/N	Pgs.	Location	
1	INT. HISTORY CLASS		Morning	1 /8	Jefferson High School	
2	EXT. SCHOOL CAFETERIA		Day	2/8	Jefferson High School	
3	INT. ALEX'S ROOM		Afternoon	4/8	Studio 4B	

Role Played	Cast	Makeup	Call Time	Contact	SWF
1. Bill Winter	Sean Studley		7:00 AM		
2. Alex Huffenster	Tom Starr		7:00 AM		
10. Mr. Foot	Joe Cool		7:00 AM		

Crew	Name		Call Time	Contact
PRODUCTION				
1st Assistant Director	Nicholas Nuckles		7:00 AM	
Producer	Timothy Terraces		7:00 AM	
Director	David Dublin		7:00 AM	
CAMERA				
Director of Photography	Quincy Quayle		7:00 AM	(818) 444-1212
ELECTRIC				
Gaffer	Jake Jibby		7:00 AM	
ART				
Art Director	Gina Guru		7:00 AM	(323) 555-1212/gina@gmail.com
MAKEUP/HAIR				
Makeup Supervisor	Karen Knightly		7:00 AM	karen@gmail.com

Shot Information				
First Shot: 8:00 AM	First Meal From: 1:00 PM	First Meal To: 2:00 PM	Aft Shot:	Camera Wrap: 6:30 PM
Last Shot: 6:00 PM		Second Meal To:		Crew Wrap: 7:00 PM

Locations & Address Info	
Jefferson High School	9076 Jefferson Lane
Studio 4B	1090 Cullen Avenue

Atmosphere	Standins
Man on Street - 8:00:00	Scott Woska - 7:30:00
Kid in Park - 9:30:00	Ron Blum - 7:45:00

Advanced Schedule: 4/17/2012		D/N	Pgs.
14	EXT. SOUTH OF FRANCE	Afternoon	/8
21	EXT. ROMAN COURTYARD	Night	/8
22	EXT. CASTLE COURTYARD	Evening	/8
23	EXT. CASTLE COURTYARD	Evening	/8

Notes

Hospital
1234 Beverly Glen, Beverly Hills, CA 90215

RADIO CHANNELS				
1: Nurse/Medic	2: AD's	3: Locations	4: Security	5: Electrical/Grip
6: Grips/Construction	7: Camera	8: Art/Prop	9: SFX	10: Crowd
11: Costumes	12: Transport			

REQUIREMENTS			
ACTION VEHICLES	As per Mick Jones (323) 555-1234		Tom's limo to be set at 8:30 AM
ARMOURER	As per Costumer (310) 555-1212		Suit and Helmet fitting at 10:00 AM
ART DEPT/SET DRESSING	As per PropMaster (818) 555-4545		Ready set at 8:30 AM
CAMERA	As per Claudia Raschke (323) 555-5656		Equipment check at 7:30 AM

TRANSPORT						
DRIVER	PICKUP	PASSENGERS	FROM	TO	FOR	

Page 1   Rev. 1

FIGURE 3.9   A call sheet

Location, Location, Location: Obtaining Location Permits

A **location permit** is a signed document that allows you and your crew to shoot at a particular place at the times and under the conditions that have been agreed to previously by you and the owner or representative of that location (see **FIGURE 3.10**). In professional filmmaking, locations have to be rented for a fee agreed upon between the production company and the owner.

STUDENT VIDEO PRODUCTION LOCATION RELEASE

PROJECT TITLE: _____

PRODUCTION DATE (S): _____

Permission is hereby granted to the producers of _____ to use the property located at the following address:

_____

_____

for the purpose of filming scenes for the project listed above on the above dates only. Permission includes the right to bring equipment and crew members onto the property and to remove them after completion of the work.

The undersigned hereby assigns to _____ its agents, clients, licensees, principals, and representatives the right and permission to copyright, use, exhibit, display, print, reproduce, televise, distribute and broadcast for any lawful purpose, in whole or in part, through any means without limitation, without inspection or further consent or approval by the undersigned of the finished product.

_____ hereby agrees to hold the undersigned harmless of and free from any and all liability and loss which _____ and/or its agents, may suffer for any reason, except that directly caused by the negligent acts or deliberate misconduct of the owner of the premises or its agents.

Agreed By:

_____
Signature of Authorized Property Representative

_____
Project Producer

Date: _____

FIGURE 3.10 A location permit

The location permit spells out the rights you have, such as to shoot in a particular place from a certain time to a certain time. It may also spell out the specific area in which you and your crew may record or not record—for example, in the living room but not the foyer or the bedroom.

In addition to location permits, the crew may want to put up signs around the location indicating exactly what times the location will be used so that people know to be quiet or avoid the area at that time.

Actor Releases

An **actor release** (sometimes known as a talent or model release) is a consent form signed by a performer to allow their image to be used in conjunction with the presentation and promotion of a media project (see **FIGURE 3.11**). The actor is agreeing legally to be recorded and to show up in the movie as the director and producers see fit. This is required by privacy law, as discussed in Chapter 2.

PRODUCTION COMPANY: _____

STUDENT PRODUCTION
ACTOR RELEASE FORM

The undersigned hereby assigns to the above mentioned production company, its successors, assigns and licensees the right to use my image, likeness and voice and name in connection with the production titled:

_____

Also, for the producers to exhibit or exploit the production listed above in any media which currently exists or may exist in the future. I also assign the right to use any images of myself in promotion of the picture.

I agree that I will make myself available to film on the dates agreed upon between myself and the producers.

Additionally I agree that I will make myself available for the rerecording of my voice in conjunction with the production.

I understand that I will not receive any monetary compensation for my participation in this project but will be provided with a finished copy of the project.

Agreed By: _____
Actor Signature

_____
Project Producer

DATE: _____

FIGURE 3.11   An actor release form

There is a tremendous need for contracts such as location permits and actor releases even on student productions where there is no money involved because people sometimes change their minds after you've already filmed them. Without this documentation, a lot of work, time, and money could be wasted, and a cast and crew of many people could be demoralized into not finishing their project.

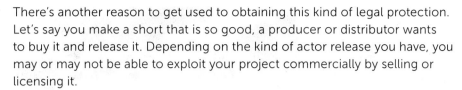

There's another reason to get used to obtaining this kind of legal protection. Let's say you make a short that is so good, a producer or distributor wants to buy it and release it. Depending on the kind of actor release you have, you may or may not be able to exploit your project commercially by selling or licensing it.

Although you need actor releases for professional filmmaking, filming a public figure, such as a senator or a business leader, in a public place, such as a city street, for your documentary, can be done without a release.

Storyboards: Pictures of Your Movie

Storyboards, which depict your audio/visual project in comic book style, are a curious hybrid of technical document and artistic accomplishment.

For Hollywood movies, directors collaborate with storyboard artists to draw out the whole script shot by shot and scene by scene before production begins. The idea is to communicate every possible aspect of each shot—lens length, lighting, time, composition, filtration, and so on.

Creating storyboards helps the director immensely as a visualization exercise. It also lets key cast and crew members see what the project will look like even before they shoot it. Storyboard artists work in a variety of media, including pencil, charcoal, pen and ink, watercolors, and 2D and 3D animation software.

By providing this information to the cast and crew, storyboards allow key creative personnel to minimize the number of items they need to ask the director about.

Virtually every big-budget Hollywood project since the beginning of the Walt Disney Studios in 1923 has used storyboards extensively to streamline its production workflow, save time, and cut costs.

In low-budget projects, directors sometimes choose not to use storyboards and just shoot on the fly. Or they may have an artistic friend draw either storyboards or **overheads**, which are an overhead view of the whole set showing where the camera, actors, and key props need to be placed.

Some projects, such as documentaries, are less suited to storyboards because the shooter is never sure what they are going to record until right before they go out, making such visual pretreatments impractical.

However, other types of projects including commercials, PSAs, and corporate training videos use storyboards increasingly for the same reasons as their bigger-budget cousins: to save money and time.

FIGURES **3.12**, **3.13**, and **3.14** show a few examples of storyboards.

The world we live in is increasingly visually oriented. For this reason, storyboards, photomatics (photographs instead of illustrations), animatics (images roughly sequenced together to suggest the effect of movement), and other types of previsualizations have grown in influence.

There are software programs for storyboarding, and there's also pen and paper.

FIGURE 3.12 A storyboard (left) and the corresponding shot from the film (right) *Double Header*

FIGURE 3.13 Another storyboard from *Double Header* (left), with its corresponding shot (right)

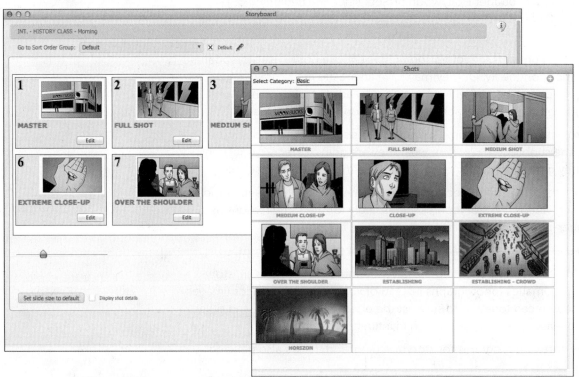

SCREENSHOT: JUNGLE SOFTWARE

FIGURE 3.14 Computer-designed storyboards created with Chimpanzee production software

Fundamentals of Cameras and Camerawork

When you learn how to drive, you need to acclimate yourself to the controls so that you can focus on the road and not get overwhelmed with trying to remember what gear to shift into. Learning to operate a camera is no different—you will never get the shots you want if you wait until the action has begun to learn what all those buttons and dials and rings and settings are for (see **FIGURE 3.15**). Most of the time you are going to use a digital camera and not an analog camera, but it is a good idea to start this section by exploring the difference between the two.

FIGURE 3.15   Students at work on a RED ONE digital cinema camera

Analog vs. Digital

Recall that analog describes a device that represents changing values as continuously variable physical quantities, and that digital describes a device that processes all information using binary code—1s and 0s. For example, a record player reads the bumps and dips in the grooves of the record and translates the information into an audio signal. An audio CD player, however, reads the 1s and 0s stored in files on the CD and translates the information into an audio signal.

Analog camcorders use an electrical signal to record video and audio signals as an analog track on magnetic tape. The video tape formats associated with analog recordings are VHS, VHS-C, 8mm, Hi8, Video8, Betamax, and SVHS.

Digital camcorders record information in binary code on a variety of media types. Until recently, they used tape, DVD, and even hard drives in formats such as MiniDVD, Digital8, MicroMV, and DVCam, but flash memory is quickly becoming the media of choice. Flash memory is small, lightweight, and relatively inexpensive. Common flash memory formats include Secure Digital (SD), Secure Digital High Capacity (SDHC), and SDXC.

One major difference between analog and digital recordings is that when you copy an analog recording, you lose quality, but when you copy a digital recording, you do not lose quality. Also, to work with an analog recording on a computer, you must import it, and convert it to digital format, whereas a computer can read a digital recording as is.

The Lens

The **lens** is the optical component of a camera that allows images you see in front of you in physical space to be delivered to the component that actually captures those images. There are a few controls on the lens that you need to know how to operate, but first you need to know about some of the differences in the more common lenses used in video production.

If you've been using the camera on your mobile device and have had to zoom in, you may have noticed that the quality of the image decreases as you zoom. The image gets blurry and noisy. The reason for that is simple: The zoom function on your camera is digital, not optical. To put it more simply, it's not really zooming in; it's cropping the image or scaling up to show a smaller part of the image more closely. This is not necessarily a bad thing. If you do not want to lose any quality when using cameras with a fixed lens and need to have your subject appear larger on the screen, you just get closer to it.

Professional cinema cameras, DSLRs, and prosumer video camcorders have the ability to switch out lenses to meet the needs of the shot. A lens that has a single angle or perspective is called a **prime lens** (see FIGURE 3.16).

On camcorders, studio video cameras, and electronic news gathering (ENG)–style cameras, there tends to also be just one lens, but it is a **zoom lens**. The zoom lens allows the operator to change **focal length** without switching out the lens (see FIGURE 3.17).

FIGURE 3.16 A 50mm prime lens

FIGURE 3.17 A Canon zoom lens for an ENG-style video camera

FOCAL LENGTH

Whether you are using a zoom lens or a prime lens, your lens will be identified by a handy number that is used to determine how wide or narrow the angle of the lens is. That number is the **focal length**, which is usually expressed in millimeters (mm). The number refers to the length between the **focal plane**, the element of the lens where light comes into focus, and the electronic sensor of the camera, or **image plane**.

There are three types of lenses identified by focal length: the **normal lens**, the **wide lens**, and the **long lens** (see FIGURE 3.18).

- A normal lens has a focal length roughly equal to the diagonal size of the sensor. A normal lens is called that because shots using it appear similar to human sight, or "normal."

- A wide lens (or **wide-angle lens**) has a shorter focal length than a normal lens and a wider angle of view. An extremely wide lens has distortion at the edges of the frame, making what would otherwise be straight look curved. The fisheye lens, used in many a skate video and peephole point-of-view (POV) shots, shows this distortion clearly.

- A long lens (or **telephoto lens**) has a longer focal length than a normal lens and a narrower angle of view. This lens allows the operator to frame the subject tighter or appear closer without having to physically get closer. The long lens also changes the perspective in a way that compresses or shows less of the background.

| Normal | Wide | Long |

FIGURE 3.18 Three lenses of various focal lengths

PRIME LENS

A lens that has a single focal length is a prime lens. Prime lenses, especially normal or wide primes, are smaller and lighter than zoom lenses.

You might ask, "Why would I ever want to use a prime lens over a zoom lens?"

The answer is simple: quality. For a zoom lens to be able to have a range of focal lengths, it requires more optical or glass elements inside of it to work. With more parts come more chances for loss of quality and, most importantly, decreased speed. More speed does not mean it gets the job done faster. Glass that is "faster" (or with a more open **iris** or larger **aperture**) allows a lens to effectively bring in more light to a sensor so that you can shoot in low light for your horror masterpiece or with a higher shutter speed for your action extravaganza.

That being said, high-quality zoom lenses exist; they are just more expensive. Lenses that are considered slower can be quite effective with the right light or by changing the sensitivity of the image sensor.

ZOOM LENS

Having a zoom lens with a good range of focal lengths can be convenient. Switching out lenses takes time that you often don't have in the middle of a shoot. It's also important to keep in mind what a zoom lens was designed to do: change the focal length of a shot as the shot is happening, giving the appearance of getting closer or pulling away without having to physically move the camera (see **FIGURE 3.19**).

You will notice on zoom lenses that are controlled with a **rocker switch** (so named because it rocks back and forth) that there is a *W* and a *T* at either side. The *W* is for wide; the *T* is for telephoto. These lenses have a mechanism called a *servo motor* (or *servo* for short) that allows the operator to control both the direction of the change of focal length and the speed of the movement.

FIGURE 3.19   Rocker switch for servo motor on Canon zoom lens

Novice camera operators, once they've discovered this control, tend to get a bit zoom-happy. The quick use of the zoom lens to move in and out of different shot sizes is appropriate to see in documentary and news footage because those are functional movements of the shot. Quick zooming is also common in music videos and action movies for stylistic reasons. When productions include overuse or unnecessary use of the zoom, it tends to give away to the audience that they are watching the work of a beginner.

The Image Sensor

The part of the camera that takes the light and color delivered by the lens and captures it, converting it to an electronic signal, is called the **image sensor** (see **FIGURE 3.20**). Early video cameras used cathode ray tubes to capture images in an analog format.

PHOTO BY DENIS DRYASHKIN, SHUTTERSTOCK

FIGURE 3.20   CCD image sensor

Later, video cameras began using the **charge-coupled device** (CCD), which allowed for higher-quality image capturing and smaller cameras. Professional video cameras would capture the image using three CCDs, one for each of the three primary colors of the additive color model (red, green, and blue). The combination of the three primary colors can create a representation of other colors.

Most current video and digital cinema cameras use the **complementary metal-oxide semiconductor (CMOS)**, which can capture images with more image detail, more of a range between light and dark, and with more color detail. This range is frequently referred to as **dynamic range**.

Focus

Focus is how you control the clarity of the video you record. When something in your image is *in focus*, it is clear and defined. This is called **sharp**. When something is out of focus, it is fuzzy, and called **soft**.

You may have experimented with some of the settings and controls of your camera and figured out how to turn on the **manual focus** or auto-lock feature. With automatic focus, the camera does its very best to set the focus so the image is as sharp as possible. This is a great feature, if neither the operator nor anything in your image is moving. Consumer and prosumer camcorders handle autofocus fairly well. Cameras in mobile devices tend to distractingly pulse in and out of focus with the movement.

As an operator, you determine what is in focus in your shot based on the distance the subject is from the image plane (where the sensor is). On professional productions, a camera assistant uses a tape measure to determine the distance the desired focal point is from the camera. If that subject or the camera moves closer or farther apart, then it might be desirable to change the focus setting. This is called *pulling focus* (see **FIGURE 3.21**).

FIGURE 3.21 Follow focus knob on a RED ONE digital cinema camera

When shooting an event that you do not have complete control over, you can focus using the method that news shooters and videographers have always used.

1. Zoom in all the way on the subject. If the subject has eyes, go for that. When we have a conversation with someone, we tend to look at their eyes.

2. Use the **focus ring** on the lens to get those eyes as sharp as possible (see **FIGURE 3.22**).

3. Zoom back out and frame your shot.

FIGURE 3.22 Focus ring on a Canon zoom lens

Sensor Size

Once, there were standard film gauges of 35mm and 16mm (see **FIGURE 3.23**) and standard video sensor sizes of 2/3" and 1/2". With those sensor sizes, it was easy to predict what a 50mm prime lens would look like on any camera with those sensor or film sizes. Now with so many different cameras being used for professional video production, there is a little more math to consider.

FIGURE 3.23 35mm and 16mm film strips

You might say, "I'm shooting with a Canon DSLR, so a 50mm lens should look the same as it did with traditional 35mm film cameras."

However, even within one brand or kind of camera, the sensor sizes can be different from model to model. For example, the Canon 5D series has a sensor that has been labeled 35mm full frame, whereas the Canon Rebel series has a sensor labeled APS-C sized, which is a smaller sensor. Any lens with an APS-C sized sensor is 1.6 times cropped compared to the same lens on a camera that is full frame.

A larger sensor size does not always translate to more megapixels or higher quality. New sensor sizes, both larger and smaller, have been introduced at a steady rate. There is a good argument that a sensor that can capture light and color with more dynamic range is better than one that captures at a higher resolution.

Exposure

Exposure can be described as a way to control how bright or dark an image is or control how much light the lens is delivering to the image sensor. Aside from adding or subtracting light, there are three factors involved in controlling the exposure of your image: iris, **shutter speed**, and **ISO** or **gain**.

Exposure is a key setting on a camera that is better left to manual control. By default, most cameras have automatic exposure on. Much like autofocus, auto-exposure can produce the undesirable effect of the image getting lighter and darker depending on what is in front of the camera.

IRIS

The *iris diaphragm* of a camera lens functions the same way the colored part of the human eye does: It regulates the amount of light traveling through the lens. In the center of the iris is an opening called the *aperture* (see **FIGURE 3.24**). The measurement of the size of the opening of the aperture is labeled by *stops*, most commonly **f-stops**, using an **f-number**.

FIGURE 3.24   Lens aperture ring on a Canon zoom lens

Here is where it gets tricky. The larger the f-number, the smaller the aperture is, letting through less light. The smaller the f-number, the more open the iris is, allowing more light in (see **FIGURE 3.25**).

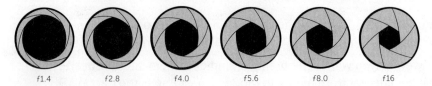

| f1.4 | f2.8 | f4.0 | f5.6 | f8.0 | f16 |

FIGURE 3.25   Aperture sizes with corresponding f-stop numbers

Recall that some lenses can be described as *fast*. Each lens has a range of aperture sizes that determines whether the lens is fast or slow. A lens that is capable of an f-stop of f1.4 or f2.0 can bring in more light than a lens with a range that starts at f4.0 and consequently is considered a fast lens.

So, how do you know what f-stop to set your lens to? That's all going to depend on what you want your image to look like, what is considered good exposure, and how you set the other two factors that determine the exposure of your image.

SHUTTER SPEED

Regardless of how they may appear, the images you have been shooting do not move. Movement in film is all an illusion. Surprise! A motion picture is actually just a series of still images shown in such quick succession that it only appears to move. In fact, traditionally, there have been tiny gaps of darkness in between all those still images that last as long as the image itself.

For example, cinema cameras that shoot at 24 **frames per second (fps)** capture each still image or frame for a duration of 1/48 of a second. The mystery of why the gap of darkness for the other 1/48 of a second in between is answered by understanding the shutter. For half of the time you are sitting in a movie theater, you are sitting in darkness.

The **shutter** is the mechanical device on a camera that allows light to travel from the lens to the image sensor for a specified amount of time. Historically, on cinema cameras that captured images on film or celluloid, the physical strip of film needed a chance to move without light hitting it so that the captured images would not get blurred (see **FIGURE 3.26**).

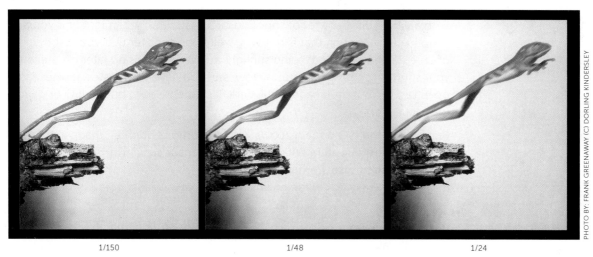

| 1/150 | 1/48 | 1/24 |

PHOTO BY: FRANK GREENAWAY (C) DORLING KINDERSLEY

FIGURE 3.26 Motion blur on a subject in motion at three different shutter speeds

So, for 1/48 of a second, the film stood still and captured the image; then for the next 1/48 of a second, the film would move to place itself for the next frame to capture. This would repeat for the duration of the shot or until the film rolled out. The human brain has to deal with a lot of sensory stimuli that could be very distracting. The reason people see the images and the illusion of movement—instead of those moments of darkness in between frames—is because that's how brains work. The term that folks in this industry have settled on for this phenomenon is *persistence of vision*.

The shutter speed on digital cameras does not necessarily need to be set at half the speed of the frame rate but can be set at the same speed of the frame rate to allow more time for light to hit the image sensor. Doing so gives the footage a different appearance. The longer the shutter is open, the more *motion blur* is visible on the image, especially if the subject or camera is moving quickly. With a faster shutter speed, images appear sharper but require more light to expose well.

ISO/GAIN

> **Tip:**
> Just like with focus and iris, if your camera has an automatic gain control (AGC), you should turn it off.

On digital cameras, the measurement of an image sensor's sensitivity to light is labeled by a system called *ISO* (from the International Organization for Standardization). A baseline ISO on most digital cameras is ISO 100. A doubling of ISO speed (for example, from 100 to 200 or from 400 to 800) is equivalent to one full *f*-stop on a lens.

On video cameras, typically with CCD sensors, the setting is called *gain*. Gain is the electronic amplification of the video signal and is measured in decibels, just like audio. The baseline gain is 0dB. Each +6dB of gain is equal to one *f*-stop.

When shooting with great amounts of light—for instance, outdoors on a sunny day—you might want to set your iris at a high *f*-stop. Your shutter speed might be at twice the speed of your frame rate, maybe higher, especially if you are shooting a sporting event. You might even place a **neutral density (ND)** filter on the lens, which acts like sunglasses for your camera. With these shooting circumstances, there would be no practical reason to have your ISO or gain at a high level.

With a whole different set of shooting circumstances, you might find yourself shooting in a location that is not very well lit or discover that you lost track of time and have started losing sunlight quickly. There is no filter on the lens, your shutter speed is acceptably slow, and you have your fastest prime lens open to *f*1.6, but the image is still dark. It's time to bring up the ISO or gain (see **FIGURE 3.27**).

Bringing up the ISO or gain allows you to capture a brighter image in low light, but there's a catch. With more image sensor sensitivity comes more grain or **image noise**. Perhaps that works for your project stylistically, or maybe it's just not acceptable, which means you are just going to have to add more light.

By bringing up your ISO or gain, you also risk capturing images with less color saturation.

| 0dB gain | 9dB gain | 18dB gain |

FIGURE 3.27 Representation of image noise at three different gain levels

Depth of Field

To begin to understand what filmmakers and photographers mean when they refer to "depth of field," follow these steps:

1. Close one eye.

2. Hold your thumb in front of your face and focus on it.

3. Without moving, try to focus on what's behind your thumb, the background.

4. Now focus back on your thumb.

This is called **rack focus** (see FIGURE 3.28).

FIGURE 3.28   The appearance of a rack focus using a narrow depth of field

A rack focus can be accomplished only if you are working with a narrow *depth of field*. So far you have been controlling what the audience sees by using the size of the shot and framing only what you want to show. This is two-dimensional control. When you want the audience to focus on a specific subject or plane of vision, you must have an understanding of depth of field. The amount of the field of view that is in focus is the depth of field. Another way to define it is the amount of distance in the *z-axis* that has acceptable sharpness. The simplest way to define it is as how much of the shot *isn't* blurry.

There are three main factors that determine the depth of field of your image or how much is in focus: focal length, aperture size, and sensor size.

- Wide lenses, or lenses with a short focal length, tend to have a wider depth of field compared to long lenses that have narrower depth of field.

- An open aperture or a low *f*-stop number can have a narrower depth of field, where a more closed aperture with a higher *f*-stop number has a wider depth of field.

- Larger image sensors, like the full-frame sensor on certain DSLRs or the ever-growing monstrous sensors from camera companies such as RED Digital Cinema, have a narrower depth of field. Smaller sensors that are found in video camcorders make it easier to have a wider depth of field.

White Balance

In the additive color system, adding equal amounts of the three primary colors—red, green, and blue (RGB)—will create white. **White balance** refers to the balance of RGB to represent white.

As with persistence of vision and motion perception, the human brain likes to give the illusion of consistency. Different kinds of light have different colors. If you don't pay too much attention to it, you might not notice. The color of light from indoor practical house lamps is *warmer*, or more orange, than the light from the sun, or *daylight*. Daylight is *colder*, or more blue. Fluorescent light that you will find in most classrooms and offices is somewhere in between (see **FIGURE 3.29**). You can adjust the balance of RGB using the white balance setting so that white objects actually appear white.

6800° K	Shade or Heavily Overcast
6800° K	Overcast Sky
6500° K	Daylight
5500° K	Camera Flash
4000° K	Fluorescent Lamps
3700° K	Clear Sky
3200° K	Tungsten
2000° K	Candlelight

FIGURE 3.29 Kelvin chart: color temperature is measured in degrees Kelvin

There are automatic white balance settings on most cameras, but just as with focus and exposure settings, using these settings puts your image at risk of shifting in an undesirable way. If someone in the shot is wearing a very warm-colored top, the entire image can turn colder, showing color that is inaccurate.

When setting the white balance of your camera, you have three options. For shooting with indoor or *tungsten* light, the preset may have a symbol that looks like a lightbulb, ☀. For outdoor shooting in day, the daylight preset looks like the sun, ☀. For shooting in that in-between color of fluorescent light or just for the assurance of accuracy, use the custom setting, ◣, which sort of looks like a boat or a box that split in two to reveal another box (see **FIGURE 3.30**).

To set the white balance using the custom setting, follow these steps:

1. Zoom in your camera (or fill the image) with a white card or a flat surface that is mostly white. Make sure that the white card is in the same light that your main subject is in or the light that you want the camera to represent as white.

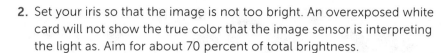

2. Set your iris so that the image is not too bright. An overexposed white card will not show the true color that the image sensor is interpreting the light as. Aim for about 70 percent of total brightness.

3. Press the "set" (or OK or execute) button. Usually something blinks for a brief moment.

4. Reframe your shot, get your exposure back to the appropriate level and ask the camera assistant who is holding the white card to come back behind the camera.

> **Note:**
> Not every camera can have its custom white balance set like this. Check the instruction manual to make sure you are doing it correctly.

FIGURE 3.30 Other icons for different white balance presets on a DSLR camera

Recording a Voiceover

An important element in many video productions is the voice of the narrator. In many projects, there may be no better method of delivering your message and letting your voice be heard than to speak directly to your audience. In the writing stage, you spend a substantial amount of time and care crafting the words that will be heard by your audience and creating the images that accompany them. It is only fair that an equal amount of effort is applied to the recording of the audio.

Mic Check: One Two, One Two

The cost of professional studio microphones used in **voiceover** recording can range from a few hundred dollars up to a few thousand dollars. With this wide range, there are only two considerations that will determine what you should use to record your voiceover: your budget and your ears (see **FIGURE 3.31**).

Over the past few decades, as desktop audio recording has become more popular, affordable microphones that plug directly into computers without additional special interfaces have entered the market. Having to go to a music store or electronics shop is no longer the only way to get recording equipment that can produce professional results (see **FIGURE 3.32**).

Once you have narrowed down the options within your budget, you could compare specifications or read online reviews. Perhaps you find a microphone that has great specs and loads of great reviews, but you should hear it to believe it. Try the gear before you spend your hard-earned cash. Most importantly, though, trust your ears.

PHOTO BY VADIM PO., SHUTTERSTOCK

FIGURE 3.31 Studio microphone with pop filter

PHOTO BY MARSHALL ELECTRONICS

FIGURE 3.32 USB condenser microphone connected to a tablet

Choosing Headphones

A good pair of headphones, or *cans*, is also a crucial piece of equipment to make sure you have when you record. The enormity of options available can be overwhelming. Perhaps you spent a small fortune on a fashionable set of headphones that really enhance the bass of the music you listen to. That does not necessarily mean they will be a good choice for monitoring when you are recording.

Tip:
When purchasing a pair of headphones for recording, ignore what they look like—it only matters what they sound like.

When choosing a pair of headphones, just like when choosing a microphone, first consider your budget. You want a pair that has an almost flat frequency response, meaning one in which there is no discernible enhancement of the high or low frequencies or pitch. Choose over-ear headphones instead of earbuds. Larger audio drivers (the little speakers) will provide more accurate monitoring. Compare different pairs using the same source of audio, like your favorite song, and trust your ears. A good pair of headphones will sound good at low volumes. A *really* good pair of headphones will reveal layers of your favorite song that you didn't know were even there (see **FIGURE 3.33**).

FIGURE 3.33 Student editing with a pair of Sony MDR-V6 studio headphones

Selecting a Location for Recording

Before you record anything, find a location where the answers to the following questions are all "yes."

- Is the location quiet?

- Is it still quiet?

- Will it stay quiet?

Listen carefully for at least 30 seconds. Is there any ticking or buzzing? If so, can the cause of this sound be turned off? Are there any other sources of noise outside of the space you are recording in? Can they be controlled? It's not the end of the world if unwanted sounds occur in between words or during pauses in the recording. They can be edited out.

The irreparable problems are the noises or unwanted sounds that are audible at the same time your voiceover artist is speaking. It's always easier to record another take rather than trying to filter the noise in post.

Tip:

Holding the palm of your hand right in front of your face when you speak can give you an indication of what your voice sounds like when close to a microphone.

When speaking at a normal volume, does the room sound *alive*, like the walls are talking back to you? Do you hear any echoing? This happens when a room has large flat surfaces that bounce the sound around the room (see **FIGURE 3.34**).

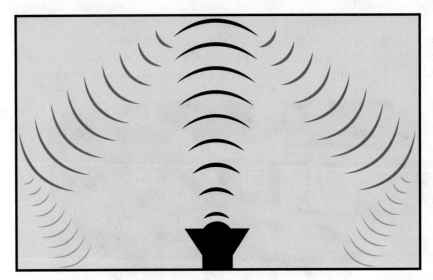

FIGURE 3.34   Alive room: sound bouncing off walls creating an echo

It's best to be in a space that sounds *dead.* That means sounds are absorbed by the objects around the room, keeping echoes from occurring (see **FIGURE 3.35**). If you don't have access to a professional sound booth, you could record in a closet. The smaller the space you're in, the less chance there will be for unwanted noise to creep into your recording.

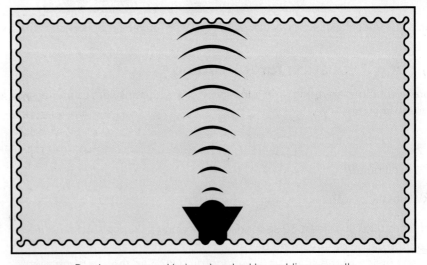

FIGURE 3.35   Dead room: sound being absorbed by padding on walls

Recording Voice

The closer the voiceover artist is to the microphone, the more profound and deep the voice sounds. A naturally deep voice is enhanced by the speaker being about an inch away from the microphone. If that's not the tone you want in your narration, back off the mic a bit.

Even at a safer distance from the microphone, there can be some distracting pops from the speaking of hard letters, like the letter *p*. Those pops are called *plosives* and are caused by air traveling rapidly from the performer's mouth. They can be minimized by using a *pop filter*, also called a *popper-stopper*.

When you are recording a voiceover, have the performer turn away from the mic when taking breaths because they can be distracting to the listener. Breaths can also be edited out in post. Lip-smacking is also much more noticeable when the microphone is close to the performer's mouth.

End-of-Chapter Activities

REVIEW QUESTIONS

1. List at least three forms used for project planning in video production projects.

2. List at least two forms used for time-management in video production projects.

3. List at least five categories of items included in a script breakdown.

4. What is the difference between analog and digital formats?

5. What are two advantages digital camcorders have over analog camcorders?

6. What is a storyboard and how does it contribute to a successful production?

7. What three types of lenses are identified by focal length?

8. What is focus and how is it used?

9. What is exposure and how is it used?

10. What is white balance and how is it used?

Review Project 1

Prepare a pitch for a video project you would like to create. Pair up and deliver your pitch to your partner. Provide constructive criticism to your partner about the pitch. Revise your pitch based on the feedback you received and deliver it again. With your partner, discuss how and why you changed, or didn't change, your pitch based on the feedback.

Review Project 2

Use the Internet or buyer's guide magazines and catalogues, as well as reviews, to research various microphones. Create a table or chart to compare features such as type and pickup patterns, as well as the cables and connectors that each type requires. When your chart is complete, use the information to write a recommendation about which one you would purchase and why. Trade your written copy with a classmate, and proofread it for correct grammar, spelling, punctuation, and terminology. Trade back and edit your document based on your classmate's feedback to correct the grammar, spelling, punctuation, and terminology.

CHAPTER 3 – PORTFOLIO BUILDER

VISUAL POEM

The Visual Poem project is designed to allow you to stretch your imagination and exercise your style and creativity. The concept is simple: Make a video that visualizes the ideas, images, and language of a poem written by a notable poet or author.

DIRECTIONS

Following these steps, use your newly developed skills of production organization and planning, full camera control, and voiceover recording, along with skills you've learned on the previous projects, to make a video that shows you have a firm grip on the language of visual storytelling:

1. Choose a poem from a notable poet or author or write your own. Have it approved by your teacher

2. Analyze the poem. Write a few sentences describing what the poem means to you and what you think the poet intends it to mean.

3. Record a voiceover narration by reading the poem out loud into a microphone. Make sure your narration uses appropriate tone, emphasis, volume, and pacing.

4. Script it out. For each line of the poem, describe what actions and/or images would be ideal to express the ideas, meaning, theme, and subtext beyond what just the words mean. Using the two-column script format would work best.

5. Storyboard it! Using the description for each shot written in your script, draw what those images should actually look like on the screen.

6. Plan your shoot. Create every single document that a professional production would require. That means a schedule, a budget, shot lists, and call sheets.

7. Record your video. Having scheduled enough time, experiment with the controls of the camera. Be curious and try things that you think you might not even use in the finished video. If it doesn't work, don't use it!

8. Start your edit by laying down the voiceover. Edit the appropriate image over each line of the poem. If you have more than one shot per line, try cutting them in. If it works well with the pace and rhythm of the poem and how you performed it, then be happy you shot more than you thought you needed.

9. Add sound effects and music that you created and recorded or are royalty-free.

10. Present your video to the class, or, with your teacher's permission, upload it to a Web site.

Chapter 4

Design and Execution

Chapter 4 Overview

- Casting
- Production Audio
- Production Design and Art Department
- The Look of Film

- Lighting for Narrative
- Postproduction: Creating a Montage
- End-of-Chapter Review and Activities

This chapter covers the importance of several areas where exacting standards and attention to detail are needed to complete a polished, interesting piece of work. Casting your project, designing it, costuming it, and lighting it are all key steps to creating a work worth seeing, thinking about, and talking about. However, no matter what level of lighting gear, props, and actors you have access to, the key determinant to the quality of your finished work is your vision and your perfectionism.

Casting

The director is the creative boss of the film crew, and as such is the crew member most responsible for tying together the work of many other talented professionals to create the best, most unified whole.

The director's three main responsibilities toward the project are as follows:

- To visualize the script, designing the camera shots necessary to tell the story and translate the script into pictures and sounds

- To **cast** the best possible actors to play the various roles in the project

- To direct those actors to give performances that are appropriate and build the project to a proper culmination

Many directors, including Martin Scorsese, agree with the great theater and film director Elia Kazan that *casting*—finding just the right actors to play the roles in a project—is 90 percent of their job (see **FIGURE 4.1**). It has often been said that if a director does that, the rest will work itself out.

FIGURE 4.1 Cat casting for Roger Corman's *Tales of Terror* (1961)

Casting for a media project will be done either by the director or by a **casting director**. The casting director is probably the job known by the fewest people outside of the media industry that carries the most power. They have so much power, in fact, that when playwright David Rabe wrote his landmark play about Hollywood, *Hurlyburly* (1984), the three main characters were all casting agents and casting directors.

You might be asking yourself, if casting is one of the three main responsibilities of the director, where does the casting director fit in? Just as the editor applies a fresh set of eyes to the footage shot by the director and the crew, the casting director is the primary crew member trying to connect the director and producers to the right actors. Interestingly, though the job of director is still dominated by men, casting directors tend to be women.

The casting director schedules and oversees **auditions**, deals with actors' representatives, and creates a **casting breakdown**, which will list all the roles that are being cast, like this:

- **Jenny** (mid-20s): A housewife feeling the pressure of domestic life, itching for a little excitement.

- **Balin** (early 30s): A career con artist for whom no grift is too big or too small. He's beginning to feel his age and wonder whether there's anything for him beyond changing towns and names every few weeks.

- **Fenton** (late 40s): A master manipulator who plays everyone against everyone else and sits back until the dust clears.

Casting can lift a project or sink it. The director needs to determine during the actor's *audition*, or tryout for the role, whether they have the qualities and the abilities to get across whatever the character is feeling, thinking, and doing.

Some actors have a mercurial ability to transform themselves into almost any role. Actress Meryl Streep is the best example of this. She has played a Polish immigrant living in Brooklyn in *Sophie's Choice* (1982), the editrix of a major fashion magazine in *The Devil Wears Prada* (2011), chef Julia Child in *Julie & Julia* (2011), and British Prime Minister Margaret Thatcher in *The Iron Lady* (2013). She has been nominated for an incredible 18 Academy Awards for acting and won three.

Actors may go to great lengths to convince the casting director that they could play a role.

One example of this is Rachel McAdams' audition for the lead role in *The Notebook* (2008). McAdams, at that point, had appeared in supporting roles in a number of films including *Mean Girls* (2006), and since she was trying out for a lead role, she was going to really have to nail it to win the role over more well-known actresses.

The honesty and emotional reality she brought to the audition no doubt impressed the casting director and the director enough to feel confident casting her. Her performance and the worldwide success of that film turned her into a movie star.

Another great casting story involves the film *The Public Enemy* (1931). Originally, director William Wellman (his film *Wings* won the first Academy Award in 1927) cast actor Edward Woods in the lead role of gangster Tom Powers and assigned the role of Powers' sidekick to an unknown actor, James Cagney. However, in rehearsals, the director and producers saw that Cagney had more charisma and seemed more like a forceful and interesting criminal and switched him to the leading role. Cagney became a movie star.

A final casting example that may be more familiar involves the making of the first *Iron Man* (2010). Director Jon Favreau wanted actor Robert Downey Jr. to play the main role, and Downey felt very capable to play it; however, the actor's troubled personal history made the producers reluctant to cast him as a lead in such a big-budget project for which there were high expectations.

An Actor's Life

A major part of an actor's job involves sending out headshots or composite sheets and resumes. The headshots or composite sheets show him playing various representational roles. The resume lists all parts he has previously played and where, where he trained, and any special skills he might have, such as riding horses, whistling, or dancing, that might be useful for certain roles.

Actors send these to agents who might want to represent them (typically for 10 percent of their acting income) who may then send the information to casting directors on behalf of the actors.

The life of an actor before he has a track record of success can be a difficult grind of going from audition to audition and sending out hundreds or even thousands of headshots while trying to land that one role or get that first paying job in the entertainment industry. Depending on the level of production, an actor can invest a whole day or several days on an audition, depending on how many callbacks there are.

Actors also invest a lot of heart and yearning as they wait for their break. It can be emotionally draining for hopeful young actors to hear "no" again and again and then get up, dust themselves off, and jump back into the arena. But any working actor will tell you that that is exactly what you need to do in order to be successful: Keep auditioning, keep training, keep networking, and get yourself out there until someone has the right part and you can show the world what you can do. It's not for the weak of heart.

Downey agreed to screen test for the role (which he ordinarily might not have done due to his stature as an actor), and everyone could tell from his audition that he was the only actor who could embody the complicated identity of Tony Stark/Iron Man. The decision to go forward with Downey may be the most pivotal piece of casting in 30 years because *Iron Man* launched a series of the most successful and profitable films in history, the Marvel Cinematic Universe.

The Audition Process

Auditioning can be nerve-wracking regardless of which side of the table you're sitting on. As a director or casting director, you're desperate to find the performer who can elevate the character as written on the page and bring that character to life on the screen. You may even feel, as some creative types do, that unless you find just the right actor to create that one-of-a-kind role in your project, you can't even move forward with it.

As an actor, you're looking for the chance to use your gifts to create someone and something real, beautiful, and memorable...and maybe get paid... and maybe put something out there impressive enough to get you hired for another role and get even more opportunities.

This is why many actors, when they are just starting out or even after they've been at it a while, are willing to try out for or submit themselves for student films or amateur productions with no pay, where their only compensation is a copy of the finished project that they can showcase on their reel.

In fact, even some well-known actors will participate in a no-budget project if they think the script is really something special, or that the writer, director, or producer is someone worth working with.

To start the audition process, the word has to be put out that there is a project in need of a cast. Most of the time, producers list their breakdowns and project information in periodicals like *The Hollywood Reporter* or *Variety* or on Web sites such as *http://backstage.com* and *http://actorsguide.blogspot.com*.

Once you have actors to consider, there are several popular formats for auditions. Three of the most used include the following:

- Actors read a prepared **monologue** (speech)

- Actors read a **side** (page) from your script

- Actors perform an **improvisation** based on a general understanding of the characters and situations the actors are trying to portray

Improvisation means acting spontaneously in character without a script. It's considered such an important talent for actors, comics, and even writers to have that many acting programs and classes dedicate a considerable amount of time to it.

After auditions, as casting director you may decide to hold a second round of auditions known as **callbacks**, which continue until you have found the best actors to cast in each role. Then, you negotiate contracts.

Production Audio

Recall that *production sound* is audio that you record at the same time you're recording the picture. Any production sound you've included in your projects so far may have been recorded using the *on-camera mic*, which is the microphone built into the camera or one that is mounted on the camera. The sound you record from the on-camera mic can be useful for reference; it may also provide a great source of ambient sound. But when it's important to hear what someone onscreen is saying, the closer the microphone is, the better. Doing so will take a few more tools and a crewmember dedicated to the job (see **FIGURE 4.2**).

Managing the Environment

Take a moment to notice the different sources of sound around you now. Even in a quiet space, people naturally tune out many sounds that a microphone picks up. If you're a crew member in the sound department of a production, it can become a real chore managing the shooting environment to get the best sound possible.

FIGURE 4.2 The boom operator at work on a wide shot

Unlike humans, microphones and audio-recording devices are objective about the sound they hear and pick up. A microphone can't tune out unwanted sounds to focus on what's important. When recording sync sound, you must make sure the only sound that can be picked up by the mic is what is most important onscreen.

Recording what is important does not mean recording every sound that would occur onscreen. For example, if you're shooting a scene where two people are having a conversation in a café or restaurant, realistically there would be environmental sounds including the other patrons' conversations, kitchen activity, servers moving around, music playing, and so on.

To get the best sound for the scene, every sound other than the characters' voices and movement should be silenced. By recording only the voices of your talent, isolated from all other sounds, you will have complete control over the balance of volume levels in your sound design.

Then, you can add the walla track and source music to your edit after the scene is cut together to maintain the illusion that the scene took place in one uninterrupted moment in time. **Walla** is the term used for the atmospheric sound effect of a crowd in a particular place. **Source music** describes music that would authentically be playing where the scene takes place, such as dance music in a club scene.

Keeping your crew and background talent quiet is the easiest part of the job of managing the sound where you shoot. A harder task is making sure all fans and air-conditioning are turned off when the camera is rolling. In a tight space, with a lot of people crammed in and perhaps hot lights working like space heaters, this can contribute to an uncomfortable situation.

Does the air-conditioning really need to be off when you're shooting? Yes, it does. There are other common machines that make a difference in the quality of recorded audio. Computers tend to hum and whir, as do refrigerators.

PEAS, CARROTS, AND RUTABAGA

The walla track was named because a crowd murmuring sounds a bit like "walla-walla-walla-walla." In the United Kingdom, the parallel term is *rhubarb*. This is because *background* actors, or *extras*, are instructed to mimic speaking by mouthing the word "rhubarb" over and over again.

In the United States, the popular phrase to ask extras to mouth is "peas, carrots, and rutabaga," most likely because of the need to suppress obscene or offensive language reaching the audience inadvertently. Even during the silent movie era, actors had to be careful what they said because audience members skilled in lip reading could understand what they were saying.

The more noise you allow onto your production audio recording, the more filtering and loss of quality occurs to the audio in postproduction.

If you're hearing unwanted sounds from a source outside of your direct control, such as a neighbor playing loud music, it's time to meet someone new and make a friend. With your most sincere smile, go to the source of the sound you'd like to have stopped and ask ever so kindly if the source of the sound can be put on hold for the specific amount of time you need it to be off. Explain why it's important to have the area quiet.

Most people will understand. Just make sure to say thank you and to let them know that the quiet is no longer required.

Which Mic When

When recording audio for a video project, there are a few different types of microphones you should be familiar with and know how and when to use them. Microphones are categorized using different criteria such as what use are they designed for, whether they require power, and in what pattern or shape they *pick up* sound.

DYNAMIC MICS

One microphone most people are familiar with is a **handheld microphone** *(or mic)* used in *public address* systems (PA systems) and vocal music per-formances. These microphones are most commonly placed in the **dynamic** category, which means they do not require power to deliver sound to the recording device (see **FIGURE 4.3**).

The reason these microphones don't need power is because they are designed to be positioned very close to the source of the sound. You may see these microphones used in news-style interviews, held by vocalists singing a song, or used by a public speaker talking to a large audience.

Aside from those examples, there aren't too many other instances when it's acceptable to see onscreen talent holding a microphone. Imagine an intimate scene with a couple passing a mic between each other when they need to speak.

PHOTO COURTESY OF MARSHALL ELECTRONICS

FIGURE 4.3
A dynamic handheld vocal microphone

For picking up dialogue while maintaining a high standard of sound quality and keeping the microphone out of the frame, there are some other microphones to consider.

SHOTGUN MICS

A **shotgun mic** is one of the most essential tools of the audio recordist or mixer on a video production. These mics are so named because they have a long, cylindrical shape and are placed on a mount that has a handle similar to that of a firearm. Most often, they are placed on a **boom pole** to get the mic close to the sound source while keeping it out of the camera frame.

Shotgun mics (see **FIGURE 4.4**) are in the **condenser** category. Condenser microphones require power to operate. One example of power used for shotgun mics is **phantom power**, commonly at 48 volts (V), which moves like a ghostly spirit up from the recorder, or receiving end, through the same microphone cable that brings the audio signal back down. These mics are designed to pick up audio from a distance, which is why they are long and require power.

COURTESY SENNHEISER ELECTRONIC CORP.

FIGURE 4.4 The Sennheiser MKH 416 shotgun microphone, the workhorse of the industry

Unfortunately, microphones can't avoid unwanted sounds the way a camera can frame out unwanted objects, although some are built to be more discriminating than others. Shotgun mics are designed to be **unidirectional**, meaning they have a **pickup pattern** (or **polar pattern**) that allows the mic to pick up the sounds from a narrower angle or a single direction. By contrast, **omnidirectional mics**, like most handheld dynamic mics, pick up sound fairly evenly in all directions (see **FIGURE 4.5**).

This is both an asset and a liability. There's great advantage to a mic that muffles down sounds outside of the pickup angle. But it also requires careful and accurate placement of the microphone to ensure a minimally acceptable quality of sound.

BODY MICS

Another microphone that you will find handy is one that can be clipped directly on the talent. It can be placed in a visible location, or it can be hidden. It is the **lavalier** microphone, or **body mic** (see **FIGURE 4.6**).

The lavalier microphone can be hardwired or used as part of a wireless kit that consists of a **transmitter**, which stays with the talent in a pocket or is clipped to a belt or waistband, and a **receiver**, which is connected to the audio recorder or camera.

Note:
The pattern referred to as unidirectional is technically called
hypercardioid, because the
pattern is heart-shaped.

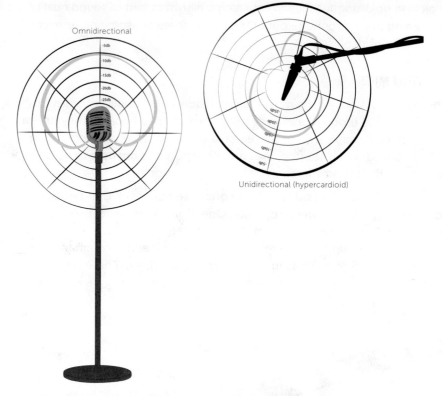

FIGURE 4.5 Pickup patterns of an omnidirectional mic and a unidirectional mic

Tip:
When using a wireless kit for
your audio, ask your crew, the
talent, and anyone else around
to turn off their phones and
mobile devices to avoid inter-
ference coming through the
recorded signal.

FIGURE 4.6 Wireless microphone kit with lavalier mic

A lavalier mic can be either omnidirectional or cardioid. A cardioid lavalier
requires careful placement on the subject. Considerable turns of the head
can have an undesirable on-mic/off-mic effect.

Building Sound Relationships

Sound, particularly background sound, is one of the main areas in which you, like so many before you, will depend on the kindness of strangers. You will need the help of people not directly working on your project, and here are a few tips for getting it:

- Tell people beforehand what you are going to do and how long you need them to be quiet. The same individuals who might feel imposed upon if you presume they will be quiet when you tell them to will generally be supportive if you ask nicely.

- Cheerlead for your project by building interest and support in the community where you shoot. This could end up helping you in countless ways. All producers have to be public relations experts and get folks excited about their project. People are mostly pretty supportive and curious about shooting crews so long as they are not causing excess traffic or behaving in other inconsiderate ways.

- If you say you're going to be done in an hour, be done in an hour. Don't cut corners with the truth to achieve your own production needs. This can be very tough. Producing a large amount of output within a short timeframe is the norm in production, and the pressure can be intense. However, content creation is a relationship business, and the downsides of goal-oriented, short-term deceptions are many. One low-budget crew was allowed to shoot at a restaurant so long as they purchased food there. They didn't buy enough and were not allowed to return to shoot their coverage shots. They had to reshoot the scene from scratch somewhere else.

- Be proactive and clear in your communication. Don't assume that anyone new to your production, especially a bystander, knows anything about what you need or about the way production works. Word of mouth plus the quality of your work is what will lead you to your next gig, and anyone who was serious about a career in media has played the long game by being a straight shooter.

When putting a mic on your subject, don't be shy about asking the person to route the lavalier cable up through their top. It's okay to see the clipped lavalier mic on a subject, but you don't want to see the wire hanging down over the subject's top.

A lavalier microphone has a clip for secure placement on clothing. Setting up which direction the clip opens might depend on whether the subject is male or female. The buttons on men's and women's apparel are different. For men, the buttons are on the right; for women, they are on the left.

Using a Boom

In most shooting circumstances, you will likely ensure the greatest flexibility in microphone placement by using a boom or boom pole. A **boom** is an extension arm to a microphone stand, or a rod alone, to allow a microphone to be moved during the shot.

The **boom operator** is responsible for holding and placing the boom where it is needed without getting it into the frame and without creating any shadows in the shot. The boom consists of several parts: a fishpole, a shock mount, and the microphone itself.

A **fishpole** can have several telescoping sections that allow you to extend the pole to get the microphone into position.

Shock mounts (see FIGURE 4.7) are made in many varieties. Their purpose is to hold the microphone with elastic suspension to keep vibrations on the boom or stand from creating unwanted noise in the signal. Most shock mounts use rubber bands that need to be twisted to hold the microphone firmly in place.

COURTESY OF AUDIO-TECHNICA U.S., INC.

FIGURE 4.7 Shock mount

Follow these guidelines to properly operate the boom (see FIGURE 4.8):

- Place your control hand (right if right-handed, left if left-handed) on the bottom end of the pole.

- Your other arm will be your weight-bearing arm, holding the pole as you would a cue stick.

- Hold your arms in a "U" shape and directly above your head.

- The boom should remain parallel to the ground. If held diagonally, the pole might sneak into the corner of the frame and not be noticed by the camera operator.

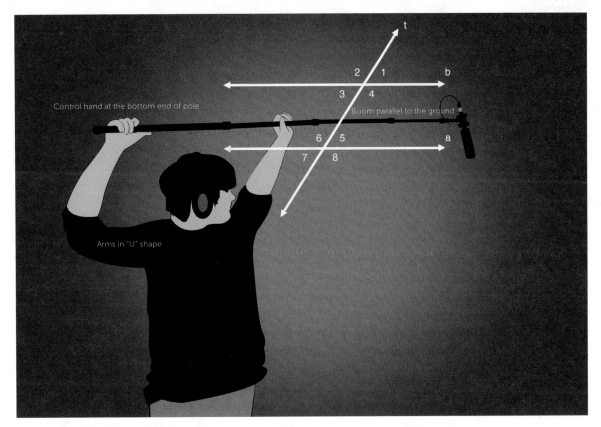

FIGURE 4.8 Ideal form of operating boom

The job of boom operator requires stamina more than strength. Height and a good reach are helpful too. Operating boom also requires you to have dialogue memorized. In a scene with two people speaking, the microphone has to be pointed at the person who has a line *before* they speak. If you wait for someone to start speaking before turning the mic, then you risk the beginning of lines being off-mic.

Here are some more considerations when operating the boom:

- When extending the fishpole, keep each section in equal lengths to balance the strain of the weight equally.

- With twist locks, it's best to start at the lowest section and then work up when extending. Start at the top and work down when shortening.

- If you need to extend the pole to its furthest length, bring in each section about an inch from fully extended to keep the locks from straining.

- When not in operation, collapse the fishpole and place it horizontally on a flat surface. Leaning a fully extended boom on a wall is asking for trouble.

Audio Cables and Connectors

Connecting a microphone to a camera or audio recorder requires use of cables. The most common cable used in professional audio recording is a cable that has **XLR connectors** with three pins at each end. XLR connectors allow for a **balanced audio connection** and therefore longer-distance runs with less noise in the signal. A cable with XLR connectors (see **FIGURE 4.9**) is required for phantom powering a microphone.

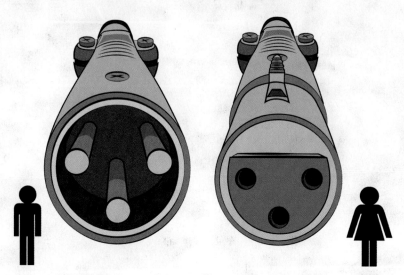

FIGURE 4.9 XLR connectors

A cable is made up of wires. Each wire is made up of thin strands of copper. This design allows for flexibility of the cable, which is why you can loop cables in circles or lay the cable down flat on the ground. The tiny strands in the wires in the cables can break, especially if the cable is wrapped poorly or the cable is bent at sharp angles. The more breakage in the wires, the less quality the signal of audio will transmit. When enough of the strands in a wire break, a complete loss of signal occurs, resulting in a **short**.

To avoid damage to your delicate audio cables, wrap the cables in even and consistent loops, avoiding any figure-eight shapes, knots, or bending. The **over/under cable wrapping method** is ideal.

So, if wire strands make up wires and multiple wires make up cables, what happens when two cables are combined into one? It is called a **duplex cable**. A duplex cable has two connections, which allows a boom operator to have a single, beefier cable running to the recorder.

One connection is for the microphone; the other is for the boom operator's headphones so that they can monitor the audio being recorded. Duplex cables designed for boom have a box with a belt clip (see **FIGURE 4.10**).

When recording audio on a mobile device, a consumer camcorder, or a DSLR camera, you will likely use cables that have *mini connectors*, also called *mini phone connectors*, that have a diameter of 3.5 mm or 1/8". For two-channel stereo connections, the 3.5 mm connector is called a **mini TRS connector**. These are the same connectors used for consumer headphones and earbuds. Another variety of this connector, the kind used for mobile phones that have a built-in microphone, is called a **TRRS connector**.

All of these connections are **unbalanced audio connections** and cannot support phantom powering the microphone. When using these connections, the microphone must be either dynamic or powered by another source, like an AA battery.

FIGURE 4.10 Duplex cable for boom

How to Adapt

Just because you don't have XLR connectors on your recorder doesn't mean you can't use microphones that require an XLR connection. If the microphone has a compartment for a battery, you can treat it like a dynamic microphone and use an adapter.

Search for a mini TRS male-to-XLR female adapter (see **FIGURE 4.11**). They are quite affordable and do the job well. Also on the market are adapter boxes that can mount on a camcorder or DSLR, that have two XLR connections, and that can even phantom power the microphone (see **FIGURE 4.12**). These are much more expensive but can give you the professional connections and controls you need to step up your audio game.

When connecting a professional microphone to a mobile device, adapters for TRRS connections can split the mic input and headphone output so that you can connect your microphone and headphones separately. Some audio manufacturers have designed professional grade shotgun, handheld, and lavalier microphones for connecting to mobile devices and have a built-in headphone jack for audio monitoring (see **FIGURE 4.13**).

FIGURE 4.11
Mini TRS male-to-dual
XLR female audio adapter

FIGURE 4.12
Wooden Camera A-Box mini TRS
male to dual XLR female adapter
box for DSLR camera rigs

FIGURE 4.13
Mini TRRS-to-mini mic jack and
mini headphone monitor jack for
mobile devices

Production Design and Art Department

Do you know the name Cedric Gibbons? He is one of the most successful and award-winning art directors in Hollywood history. He won 11 Academy Awards and garnered 39 nominations. In fact, he designed the Oscar statuette itself. Yet, even though many millions have watched and loved his films, including *The Wizard Of Oz* (1939), *Little Women* (1939), and *Gaslight* (1944), far fewer know his name or many others on the crew beyond the actors and maybe the directors.

The director gets the lion's share of the credit when a project is successful, but in reality, many artists and technicians must coordinate their magnificent work behind the vision of the director.

The **art director** or **production designer** along with the director of photography are the key crew members who determine, along with the director and producers, the particular aesthetic, or look, of the piece: overall dark or light, bright colors or muted, sharp or dream-like, and so on. (see **FIGURE 4.14**).

ILLUSTRATION BY ANDREA DIETRICH

FIGURE 4.14 An art director's rendering of a boutique set

In addition, the production designer must serve the script as the director does, including the following:

- Making sure each prop and **set piece** is appropriate to the time and place of the project. Peter Lamont, production designer for the film *Titanic* (1997), went back to the blueprints of the ship itself to re-create the dining saloon, grand staircase, and other sets as accurately as possible, even contracting with the companies that designed and made the original rugs, furniture, and China plates for the real Titanic. They basically had to re-create the most remarkable ship ever created...again...in order to destroy it for a film.

- Making sure that every item suggests whatever is necessary about the character or the environment in the scene. In the TV show *The Wire* (2000), Jimmy NcNulty is an exceptional Baltimore detective whose personal life is a mess, as reflected by his post-divorce studio apartment dominated by a dirty mattress on the floor.

- Occasionally, the production designer has to create a whole world from the imagination of the filmmaker. Some directors, such as Terry Gilliam (*Brazil*, 1982) and Tim Burton (*Alice In Wonderland*, 2012), envision alternate realities in which everything onscreen is relatable without being familiar. Everything comes from their imagination; everything needs to be designed.

The production designer is responsible for the overall look of the film and coordinates the contributions of key personnel, including the art director, the set decorator, and the costume designer, to make sure that everything is consistent (see **FIGURE 4.15**). The *art director* oversees the art department, which consists of all the people who make everything that needs to be made for the project. For example, the **set decorator** decides what needs to be bought and what needs to be made for the sets.

ILLUSTRATION BY ANDREA DIETRICH

FIGURE 4.15 An art director's rendering of a bedroom set

The **costume designer** must be every bit as particular as the production designer regarding the wardrobe of the actors. The right costuming can communicate as much about a character's personality, status, priorities, cultural background, wealth, and even connection with other characters as the actor's performance.

Like production design, costuming transports the audience visually and texturally into the world and story of the production. Depending on the time period or location of the piece, costume design and creation may involve numerous stages of development, including the following:

- Researching the place or period as needed to assure the accuracy of the costumes

- Drawing a costume plot or a list of all the costumes required for the shoot for every character

- Agreeing on the fabrics and other materials to be used to create the costumes and finalizing the design

- Making all costumes, accessories, and so on, for the production

- Keeping track of them throughout production and keeping them in proper condition for every scene

Each individual project dictates the specific requirements of costume design. For instance, if one scene features a fight between six characters on a dusty road, each character may need to have multiples of their costume at varying stages of dustiness so that different parts of the scene can be refilmed as necessary. For low- to medium-budget productions, costumes may be purchased rather than made, still within the parameters set by the costume designer.

In the history of costume design, there's one artist arguably more dominant than the aforementioned Mr. Gibbons. Designer Edith Head won eight Academy Awards out of thirty-five nominations for films including *All About Eve* (1950), *Sabrina* (1954), and *The Sting* (1973). She didn't design the Oscar, but she did get an Oscar nomination for a film called *The Oscar* (1966). And, she was turned into animated character Edna Mode in *The Incredibles (*2004) (see **FIGURE 4.16**).

PHOTO BY DOUG KLINE/CC 3Y 2.0

FIGURE 4.16 The iconic Ascot dress of Audrey Hepburn in *My Fair Lady* (1964) designed by Edith Head

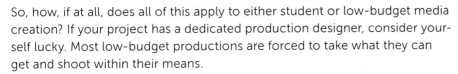

So, how, if at all, does all of this apply to either student or low-budget media creation? If your project has a dedicated production designer, consider yourself lucky. Most low-budget productions are forced to take what they can get and shoot within their means.

But that doesn't mean production design goes out the window. Quite the contrary. Sometimes access to an interesting location or set of props or costumes inspires the production of a media project. The imminent closure of the Thornhill Square Mall in Ontario, Canada, inspired George Romero to use it as the shooting location of *Dawn of the Dead* (1978), the sequel to his wildly successful zombie flick *Night of the Living Dead* (1968).

The Look of Film

Analog videotape was introduced and used professionally from the early 1950s onward in television as a cost-saving alternative to shooting on film. Sadly, the process was still so expensive that early videotape was used over and over again, and many hallmarks from the birth of television were simply erased or taped over.

With the developments made by Sony Corporation in the 1960s, shooting on video became standard for certain types of programming including sports, news, and situation comedies shot on sets.

Video production is an entirely different recording medium than film. Film is a chemical process with an electronic component. Video recording was originally done using analog signals. This process was replaced in the early 1990s by digital recording in which images are captured and stored in a binary format (zeros and ones), typically at a rate of 30 frames per second.

Recall that the film process involves shooting a set number (usually 24) of individual *frames per second* (fps) with a camera and then running them back through a projector at the same rate.

Note:

The 24p frame rate is so popular for those who want to make their video productions look like film that many HD video cameras keep their "cinema filter" (aka 24p button) right next to the power switch for easy access.

Safety First, Safety Last, Safety Always

Even the simple plugging in of a lamp or the holding of a light near an actor's head must be approached with caution. Lights can start fires, or cause burns. There are many risky situations that may arise while using equipment during media creation. Always follow all safety rules and procedures when dealing with the following:

- **Tripods**: Are the legs and the tilt control locked down?
- **Cables**: Are they flat on the ground and taped down so no one can trip over them?
- **Lights**: Are they hot?
- **Electric plugs**: Are they properly plugged in?
- **Stands**: Are they weighted down with a sandbag?

Even with the utmost care, accidents happen. Be familiar with all emergency procedures, and be prepared to follow them should an emergency occur.

Film has a look and a feeling, a grainy texture that video historically has lacked. **Standard-definition video**, with a resolution of 720 x 480 pixels, had a slick, glossy look, but **high-definition (HD) video**, with a resolution of at least 1280 by 720 pixels, is capable of reproducing the textural look of film. This has made HD the standard for broadcast production. HD and standard video formats also differ in the aspect ratio (4 x 3 for standard and 16 x 9 for HD), scanning (interlaced only for standard and interlaced or progressive for HD), and frame rate (29.7 only for standard and variable for HD).

However, nothing stays the same for very long in the world of media creation. Video game producers and visionary film directors James Cameron (*Avatar*) and Peter Jackson (*The Hobbit*) have begun filming in a **high frame rate** (**HFR**) format running at 48 fps, which creates an almost startlingly lifelike image.

You can change several settings on your HD video camera to create a more filmic look, including the following:

- Set your shutter speed at twice the speed of the frame rate: 1/48th of a second (or whatever is closest, 1/50 on most DSLRs)

- Turn off the edge enhancement

- Shoot with a shallow depth of field by choosing a fast lens ($f2.8$ or lower) and adjusting your f-stop appropriately (wide aperture/low number)

- Set your frame rate to traditional film rate of 24fps (a.k.a. 24p, 23.976, or 23.98)

Lighting for Narrative

In the beginning—the beginning of film, anyway—**cinematography**, or the lighting of the set, was done by the director, the creative boss of the project. Over time, this role evolved into a new job, called *cinematographer*.

To this day, the cinematographer, also called the *director of photography* (DP, or DoP in Europe), is the closest partner to the director in terms of creating a look for the film and visualizing the script. The cinematographer is not just the head of the camera department; he also heads up the grip and electric departments. This overall design is supported by thousands of decisions of what to shoot with and how. All these decisions follow from two related questions: Given the goals of this particular project, what should be seen (or not seen), and how should it look—bright or dark, colorful or washed-out, sharp or soft? This is the plan the DP constructs with the director and then executes.

Control the Image

To craft the look of a particular media project, the cinematographer makes a number of choices, including the following:

- Which camera to use, depending on cost, ease of use, durability, image quality, and desired workflow

- What aperture or exposure level, white balance, and shutter speed to set the camera at to record the scene

- What length of lens to use to record the scene and whether to use one fixed focal length (prime) lens or a zoom lens

- What lights to use and where to place them

- What sort of **filters**, **gels**, and **scrims** to place in front of the lights to control the amount of light falling on the scene as well as the color of it

MASTERS OF DARKNESS

The cinematographer is the boss of the camera, grip, and electric departments and needs to be clear about how a shot or a scene should look at a particular moment in the story. If your lighting is supposed to be realistic and natural, then you have to ask yourself, where is the light that is illuminating this scene supposed to be coming from? Is it coming from a lamp or the fluorescent lights on the ceiling or from the sun?

The chief lighting technician (CLT) or head electrician of a production is known as the *gaffer*. The gaffer's responsibilities include the following:

- Implementing the lighting design of the DP and the director (and sometimes contributing to that design)

- Managing and coordinating the lighting crew and gear on set to create whatever lighting effect (lightning, projector flicker, sunset) the DP has called for

- Delegating some of the responsibility for the proper setting up of lights to their assistant, known as the **best boy**, who will then oversee the electricians

While you may not have access to a full range of advanced lighting gear, including light kits, c-stands, flags, and so on, you will still want to control the lighting to whatever degree you can. Controlling lighting helps you create the image you have visualized and match the tone or feeling of the piece.

This can be done in a variety of ways. You might be surprised at the degree to which, with just the lighting options available to you in a typical room, you can create a wide range of lighting conditions that may serve your project well.

Here's an experiment you can do. Sit your subject (actor) at a table. Plug in a desk lamp or other open bulb light source so that you're able to move it around the head of your subject. Light sources, like lamps for home use, are called **practical light sources**, or **practicals** for short.

First, place the light directly in front of the subject so that the subject is lit from the front, and observe the lighting pattern and shadows across the face of your subject. Observe the effect you get from front-lighting your character with single-source lighting (see **FIGURE 4.17**).

Tip:
For safety's sake, do not place the light too close to the subject or you might blind your subject!

Now, place the lamp on the side of your actor and see what that does to the light level on the near and far side of their face and the shadows that this directional light creates (see **FIGURE 4.18**). Notice that any motion of the lamp up or down, rotating around the head of your subject, or moving closer or farther away from their face will change the quality of the light falling on them from hard to soft, as well altering as the shape and contrast of the shadows under their chin, nose, and so on.

FIGURE 4.17 Single-source lighting from the front

FIGURE 4.18 Single-source lighting from the side

Now, lift your light up above the head of your subject so that it shines directly down onto the subject (see **FIGURE 4.19**). See what that does to the brightness levels on the top and bottom of the character's face as well as the contrast levels of the shadows under their eyes, nose, and mouth.

FIGURE 4.19 Single-source lighting from above

Place the light on the other side of your character's face and see what that does to the brightness levels on the left and right sides of your character's face as well as on the shadows.

See whether you can notice any difference when you place the light on one side of the actor's face as opposed to the other side in terms of creating a more suitable look for your project. Look carefully. Most actors, it is said, have a "good side" of their face, which is preferable to film them on.

Tip:

"Look carefully" is good advice for every part of the process in video production.

Finally, try placing the light under the chin of your actor to get that spooky horror movie look (see **FIGURE 4.20**).

FIGURE 4.20 Single-source lighting from underneath

By placing the light closer to your actor, you should achieve a softer quality of light on the subject's face. By placing the light farther away, you should create a harder shadow and a higher contrast or contrast ratio (the ratio between the lightest and darkest portions of their face) across the face of the actor.

Now repeat your experiment if you can with a small work light from a home improvement store and a *China ball* (aka paper lantern) by placing that on top of your light (see **FIGURE 4.21**). This creates a nice, omnidirectional soft light that is pleasing for low-light shooting that will really give your work a professional look (see **FIGURE 4.22**).

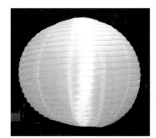

FIGURE 4.21
A China ball
with a light inside

FIGURE 4.22 Low soft light with a China ball

As you can see, when shooting with digital video cameras, there is a lot you can do to control the lighting design of your scene. All you have to do is control the light that you have by positioning the subject relative to the light sources you cannot move. You can also exert greater lighting control on certain types of shots such as close-ups (CUs) and medium close-ups (MCUs) than you can on wide shots (WSs) in this way.

Your **key light** in these situations is the main light on your subject. Any other lights that you use to fill in from another direction are naturally called your **fill lights**.

In the accompanying photos, the actors have been staged and lit as if they are in three different genres or styles of film project: comedy, film noir, and drama. All three shots were staged with available light or one stage light, and transformed by simply changing the position of the actors and turning the available lights on or off.

The styles of lighting have different names. **Studio lighting** has a moderate contrast without domination by dark or light areas of the frame and is used most often in dramas (see **FIGURE 4.23**).

FIGURE 4.23 Studio lighting—bright and shadowy areas

High key lighting, where the overall lighting of a shot is very bright without a lot of contrast, is mainly used for comedies like *Bring It On* (2000) or *Austin Powers* (1997) and most sitcoms (see **FIGURE 4.24**).

FIGURE 4.24 High key lighting for comedy

Low key lighting frequently uses mainly shadow areas and low light to dominate the frame (see FIGURE 4.25).

FIGURE 4.25 Low key lighting for film noir

All of these philosophies of lighting originated with cinema but remain in use because digital cameras have a dynamic range of up to of 16+ f-stops between the brightest and darkest parts of your frame, allowing high-definition video to be lit like film.

This sensitivity to light lets you see more of your frame without having to light everything. If you're using lights, you can light your subject more softly without losing picture detail. Best of all, the viewfinder and external monitor will show you immediately what your shot will look like.

HOW TO MEASURE LIGHT

Lighting professionals on a set will use a variety of **light meters** to measure the amount of light around their subject, including **reflectance meters**, which measure the light coming off the subject, and **incident meters**, which measure the light falling on it (see FIGURE 4.26).

FIGURE 4.26 A digital light meter capable of incident and reflected light metering

Since digital video cameras show you the exact quality of the image that you are going to record on your viewfinder or external monitor, you can rely on what your eyes are showing you as to whether you are recording the quality of light that suits your piece.

If you do find a reason to use a light meter on your media project, once you plug in your ISO and shutter speed, they will show you what aperture to set your lens at by measuring light in **footcandles**. One footcandle is the amount of light that one candle would throw on an object 1 foot away from it. There are apps for your phone or tablet that are useful light meters (see **FIGURE 4.27**).

You may want to meter light using an **18% gray card** to guarantee accurate and consistent exposure from shot to shot.

DOING A LOT WITH A LITTLE

Just as with production design, you have a lot of opportunities to control your lighting, even if you're restricted to using available light. Consider positioning your actor in such a way as to take advantage of the quality and the direction of the light that is available. For instance, the strongest lighting source available to you when shooting outdoors is the sun.

Depending on where your action is staged, your actors might wind up with an exposure problem if the bright light of the sun is behind them. This is called being **backlit**. The contrast of the brightly lit background and your subjects in the shadowy foreground is too high to get a balance of both areas in the shot (see **FIGURE 4.28**). Either you bring the exposure up to expose the foreground correctly, thus making the background **blown out** or overexposed, or you expose for the overall image, leaving your foreground subject in silhouette. If your goal is to show that your character is mysterious and shady, then you're good to go. If that's not your intention, by repositioning your actors at a different angle relative to the position of the sun and adding a simple tool to your arsenal, you can light them more successfully, depending on the feeling and tone of your scene.

FIGURE 4.27 A screenshot from the Pocket Light Meter iOS app

FIGURE 4.28 An underexposed scene outdoors

Additionally, one of the simplest pieces of lighting equipment to acquire is a **bounce board** (see FIGURE 4.29), which is either a white, silver, or gold reflective board you can get in a camera store or a foam board or **foamcore** you can get at an art or office-supply store. You can use it to reflect sunlight in order to add or fill in light to your subject when you're filming outside or to fill in the shadow so as to provide a pleasing contrast of light on your subject (see FIGURE 4.30).

FIGURE 4.29 Using a bounce board

FIGURE 4.30 More light on the subject

A Balance of Light and Dark

The use of light can be a central metaphor for the state of being of your character. Characters in relative darkness and shadow might be seen by the audience as evil or mysterious. Characters standing in bright light may seem more heroic or stalwart. Characters who are standing partially in light and partially in shadow seem to be between two states of being, between good and evil.

In *The Godfather: Part II* (1974), cinematographer Gordon Willis used the lowest lighting imaginable for a scene in which the protagonist, Michael Corleone, considers whether to do something so terrible it will mark him and change him forever.

Willis chose to underexpose the character in the shot, making him dark and difficult to see, reflecting the darkness of the spiritual space the character is in as he considers committing what is for him the ultimate sin. Willis pushed the envelope of what was considered acceptable lighting, and when the film won the Academy Award for Best Picture in 1974, it validated that audiences were ready for more sophisticated visualization.

In a scene from the earlier *The Godfather* (1972), Willis lit the character of the elder Vito Corleone in very low light and primarily from above so that his eyes stayed in deep shadow and it was difficult to see into them, which made him all the more mysterious to another character who comes to him for help.

However, there's no one right way to create a mood, whether it be suspense or joy. In *Rosemary's Baby* (1968), evil acts are committed in brightly lit apartments without having the characters sneak into shadows. Cinematographer Bill Fraker took a different approach than Willis, emphasizing the matter-of-fact, everyday, almost boring nature of evil that the director and the cinematographer wanted to get across.

What Color Is Your Light? Using the Kelvin Scale

Recall that the Kelvin scale is used to set the white balance on a camera. You may remember that the following values correspond to the most common lighting scenarios:

- 1,850° K: Candle light (warmer, redder)

- 3,200° K: Studio lights and flood lights

- 4,000° K: Late-afternoon sunlight

- 5,000° K: Fluorescent light

- 5,600° K: Daylight

- 6,500° K: Overcast daylight or shadow area on sunny day (cooler, bluer)

Professional film crews have various ways of making the colors of light match when shooting with different types of light sources. They may gel the windows to make the light coming in match the color of the practicals in the room. If you have access to gels, you can do this. Alternately, you can make one of the following accommodations:

- Choose to restage your actions in an area lit by only one lighting source

- Use the custom white balance setting and balance on a white card that has a blend of both light sources on it so that neither will appear too far from what the eye would perceive

- Set your white balance for the area where most of your action plays in the shot and then color correct the other portion during editing

If you follow the latter plan or find when watching your footage that the color of the lighting does not match, Apple Final Cut Pro, Adobe Premiere Elements, and Adobe After Effects, among other editing software, have color correction panels that should enable you to match your footage pretty closely.

Postproduction: Creating a Montage

In the medium of motion pictures, the most essential part of the process is editing. Even for home videos, just removing the moments where the camera shakes, the image is out of focus, or nothing important is happening on the screen would improve the viewing experience a lot. Having some music playing underneath would be great, too. Actually, having the whole collection of video cut down into small bits and fit into one song would make for a memorable and fun video. That video could be called a **montage**.

The Strategies of Montage

The term *montage* comes from the French word meaning *assembly*. Montage describes a sequence that uses a collection of short clips to show a passage of time. This allows a storyteller to show a multitude of related events in a shorter period of time, thus compressing time for the viewer.

This compression of time is what makes the medium of the motion picture so powerful and effective as a method of message delivery. Commercials are a great example of how a message is delivered with a story through compressed time, for instance a limit of 30 seconds.

The most famous example of montage can be found in the film *Rocky* (1976), where legendary editor Richard Halsey compresses Rocky's weeks of training into the length of a memorable piece of musical score.

This sequence set the standard for the training montage. Montages are typically named after the type of progression they depict. Another popular montage is the shopping or getting-dressed montage, as seen in *Pretty Woman* (1990). Yet another is the epiphany montage, where a character recalls moments from throughout the film to come to a major realization, as edited masterfully by John Ottman in *The Usual Suspects* (1995). *Clueless* (1995) created a montage that was both a shopping and an epiphany montage.

MAKING FAST WORK

The music video has been credited with the biggest change in proving that a viewing audience can perceive a message through a series of rapidly cut images. MTV (formerly Music Television) premiered in the early 1980s and became at one point the singular platform for the experimentation of a new form of motion picture. Directors who started their careers making music videos and commercials transitioned into feature films and brought their fast-cutting techniques with them.

With directors such as Ridley Scott (*Prometheus*, 2012), Michael Bay (The *Transformers* series), David Fincher (*The Social Network*, 2010), Spike Jonze (*Where the Wild Things Are*, 2009), Michel Gondry (*Be Kind Rewind*, 2008), and Gore Verbinski (*The Pirates of the Caribbean* series) all coming from the fast-paced music video format, it's no wonder that video today is so much faster-paced than the films of 30 years ago.

A 2011 study by researchers at Cornell University on the change in pace in films over the previous 75 years found that the number of shots in motion pictures has tripled and the average length of each shot has decreased by a third.

This increase in the speed of cutting and shortening of shots is obvious in blockbuster action movies, but it has trickled down into an astonishing variety of genres in the world of new media.

MAKING SHORT WORK

The extent to which media makers have demonstrated how compressed time can be, while still telling an effective story, continues to push beyond the limits of what was thought possible. The comedy film series *5 Second Films* took the absurd idea of telling a funny story in five seconds and made a name for themselves doing just that.

Not taking it as a joke, the *Vine* video-sharing service, started in 2013, not only challenged the world to tell stories in six seconds but also popularized a new aspect ratio of 1:1 (a perfect square).

THE KULESHOV EFFECT

Soviet film pioneer Lev Kuleshov developed the theory of editing that is the core foundation of the motion picture, known as the **Kuleshov effect**.

The Kuleshov effect is the phenomenon that two images, having no intentional connection or relation to one another, will create new meaning and interpretation simply by being seen sequentially, or *juxtaposed*. Many filmmakers, including Alfred Hitchcock—who referred to the Kuleshov effect as *pure editing*—believed that the juxtaposition of shots, more than the composition of any individual shot, was the truest magic of cinema.

The most popular example of Kuleshov's demonstration of this theory starts with a close-up shot of a man, an actor who stares off-screen with a blank or ambiguous expression. By cutting this shot together with a shot of a bowl of soup, then back to the man, the effect is the audience perceives that the man is hungry (see **FIGURE 4.31**). The same shot of the man intercut with the shot of a child in a coffin gives the illusion that the man is sad (see **FIGURE 4.32**).

To drive the point home, juxtaposing the same shot of the man with a shot of an attractive woman reclining on a chaise lounge gives the audience the idea that the man is feeling lustful (see **FIGURE 4.33**).

Is the man actually feeling any of the suggested emotions? Does it really matter? What matters is that the audience naturally looks for a connection in the images, which means that you as a storyteller have a powerful tool for bypassing your audience's rationality and reaching them via their subconscious mind. Just remember to use it responsibly.

FIGURE 4.31
The Kuleshov effect: hunger

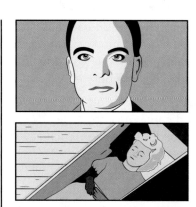

FIGURE 4.32
The Kuleshov effect: sadness

FIGURE 4.33
The Kuleshov effect: lust

The Tough Love of Trimming

In the same way it is said that writing is rewriting, editing is reediting. The workflows for projects in the previous chapters gave no suggestion to do any **trimming**, or creating new cuts or drafts of your work.

As you were editing those projects, you may have noticed errors which you then went on to correct. Some common errors include jump cuts, flash frames, and repeated action or dialogue when cutting from one shot to another.

The primary reason a project needs trimming is to control its pace or timing. At a basic level, cutting for a specific program time motivates a cut after the assembly stage. A commercial might need to be exactly 30 seconds. A program that has to fit into a half-hour TV slot needs to have a **total running time** (TRT) of 22 minutes to allow time for commercials. Student film festivals and video contests commonly have running time limits for submissions.

One of the many great things about new media video platforms is that there are virtually no standards for how long a video should be. The problem is that, according to numerous studies, the human attention span is shrinking.

With the popularity of the Skip Ad button and Vine videos, knowing how to trim a project is more important than ever.

Before moving forward and sharing some trimming methods, consider a broader definition of the term *trimming*. The popular definition of the verb *trimming* is the clipping or removal of small bits to shorten the project. An alternative definition as a noun is decoration or garnish. Trimming a sequence most certainly will include the shortening of segments in your edit, but will also include the addition or substitution of footage, such as when adding decoration or garnish.

One more important consideration is to **version** your sequence or edit. Versioning is the duplication of your edit to keep a backup reference of your edit at a specific point in the workflow. This insures you always have a copy of the version that came before.

If your rough cut or assembly is called *ProjectName_v1*, duplicate the sequence and name the copy *ProjectName_v2*. You can also add a brief description to the version, such as *ProjectName_v1_assembly* or *ProjectName_v2_directors-cut*.

Am. Hist. X.

An interesting case of trimming gone to an extreme comes from the making of the film **American History X** (1998). The film was the feature debut of director Tony Kaye, who had previously built his career directing commercials and music videos, having earned six Grammy nominations. Taking the role of cinematographer as well as director, Kaye shot nearly 200 hours of footage for the feature.

The rough-cut assembly had been positively received by the studio New Line Cinema, with only a few notes for revisions. Perhaps because of his sensibilities as a short-form director, Kaye had taken the rough cut and cut it down to a fast-paced 87 minutes. The studio and the film's star, Edward Norton, who felt this director's cut played like an "after-school special," took control of the film and ultimately released the film at a 119-minute run time.

Kaye was so unhappy with the cut of the film that was ultimately released that he filed a lawsuit against the studio and petitioned to have his name removed from the film, suggesting he be credited with the standard replacement pseudonym of Alan Smithee or the less standard Humpty Dumpty.

TRIMMING

To understand the various ways to trim your footage, you must become familiar with some terms first.

Because of the variety of methods and technology in picture editing evolving over time, there are numerous ways to describe simple editing concepts. For instance, the juncture between two clips or where a cut occurs is called an **edit point**. Each side of that juncture can also be called an edit point.

Actually, there are many other terms for that single-frame location. The **out-point**, **end**, **tail**, or last frame of an outgoing clip can be called the **A-side** of a cut. The **in-point**, **start**, **head**, or first frame of an incoming clip can be called the **B-side** of a cut (see FIGURE 4.34).

> **Note:**
> Reordering or swapping clips can also be considered trimming.

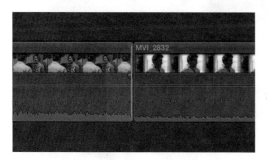

FIGURE 4.34 The two sides of an edit point

Once you get comfortable with the different terms describing an edit point and begin to use them consistently, you can move on to understanding the ways to change those edit points. There are four basic trims that can be made to a single clip (see FIGURES 4.35-4.38).

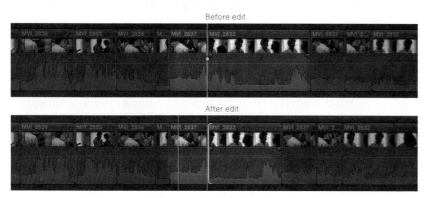

FIGURE 4.35 Shortened at the head

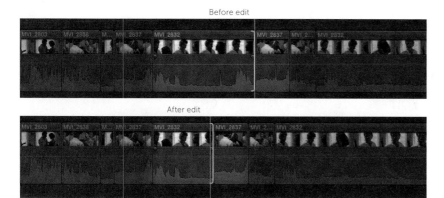

FIGURE 4.36 Shortened at the tail

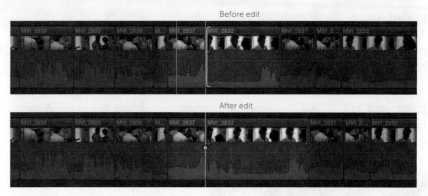

FIGURE 4.37 Lengthened at the head

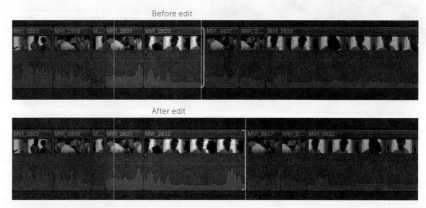

FIGURE 4.38 Lengthened at the tail

At times there will be material in the middle of a clip that you want to remove. In film editing, this was called a **lift**. In nonlinear editing, a lift, which is performed with the Delete or Backspace key, will leave a gap in your edit. If you're cutting with a system like Final Cut Pro X that has a *magnetic timeline*, then deleting a selection or entire clip will not leave a gap. To avoid leaving a gap, you can choose an **extract** or **ripple delete**.

Here are two methods to remove, lift, extract, or delete footage from the middle of a clip.

- Select a range, either with a range selection tool or with the I and O keys, and then perform a lift, extract, or deletion.

- If you like a more tangible approach that feels like you're actually doing something physical, use a **blade tool** to cut the clip segment into pieces. You can then select pieces to delete, move, or reorder.

RADIO EDIT

When cutting a dialogue scene, an effective approach to managing its pacing is a technique called a **radio edit**. To create a radio edit, play back the assembly version of the scene, but turn off the video track first (see **FIGURE 4.39**). Can't turn off the video track in your editing software? Try closing your eyes instead. By focusing only on the audio of the scene, you can more easily notice unnecessary pauses and redundancies in the content of the scene.

FIGURE 4.39 The Video Track Monitor button in the timeline in Avid Media Composer

You might trim it tighter for a fast-moving scene, or you might find that the pace doesn't let the audience breathe. Perhaps a line of dialogue doesn't quite make sense where it was originally intended. Moving some of the lines around in a different order might help you find a different meaning to the scene or just make it weird and incomprehensible. After experimenting, turning the video back on will reveal some issues with the cut, such as continuity errors or jump cuts.

Tip:
To turn off the video in a track-based NLE, locate the track-enable button in a patch panel or the video track monitor button in the timeline.

SPLIT EDITS

Once you've completed your radio edit, a trimming technique that will take your edit to professional-polish level is the **split edit**, also called **L-cuts** or **J-cuts**, named because of the shape the clips resemble after the trim is made.

A split edit is made when you need to leave the audio edit in place but transition the video sooner or later than the audio. This is incredibly useful to see reaction shots that could inform the audience of a character's thoughts.

In a J-cut, the audio transition occurs before the video transition (see **FIGURE 4.40**). This is a good way to start hearing an off-screen character while holding the picture on the character who has just finished speaking. J-cuts are commonly used to show a character's reaction to being interrupted before cutting to the person who has taken over speaking.

In an L-cut, the video transition occurs before the audio transition (see **FIGURE 4.41**). Doing this lets you show a character reacting to another character as they finish speaking. L-cuts are commonly used to see a character at the moment they process what another character is saying, while waiting their turn to speak.

Not every edit point requires a split edit, but it's good to experiment so that you don't leave your sequence going back and forth predictably like a tennis match.

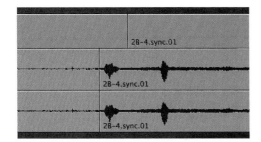

FIGURE 4.40 A J-cut split edit in Avid Media Composer

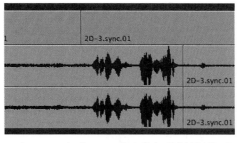

FIGURE 4.41 An L-cut split edit in Avid Media Composer

Advanced Trimming

The four basic trims will suit most of your trimming needs. Here are a few other advanced trims. These trims are most useful when you have locked down the duration of your clips and edits, such as when you are cutting to the rhythm in a music video or montage sequence.

- A **roll edit** (also called a **dual-roller trim**) is a trim that affects two adjoining clips simultaneously. If the A-side is lengthened, the B-side is shortened, and vice versa.

- The **slip trim** lets you change the content of a clip without changing the duration or location of the clip.

- The **slide trim** lets you move the location of the clip without changing the duration of the clip. Rather, the clip before it and the clip after it are shortened or lengthened, depending on the direction of the move.

End-of-Chapter Activities

REVIEW QUESTIONS

1. What is casting?

2. What is a casting breakdown?

3. Summarize the steps in the audition process.

4. What is source music?

5. List three types of microphones you could use for recording production sound. For each mic in your list, identify the pickup pattern and the audio cables and connectors it requires.

6. What is the difference between high definition and standard definition digital video platforms?

7. What are five responsibilities of a costume designer?

8. What is a cinematographer and what responsibilities are assigned to that position?

9. List at least five safety-related problems you might encounter while working on location and the steps you might take to avoid them.

10. What is trimming?

Review Project 1

With a partner, create a casting breakdown for a video project that has parts for at least five actors.

Review Project 2

Conduct the lighting experiment described on pages 155-157 to test the effects of different types of lighting on a subject. Capture the lighting effects using a video camera. Record narration or production sound explaining each effect. Discuss the results with a partner or as a class.

Review Project 3

With a partner, create a safety manual for use on a video set. Use the information in this chapter and research the topic for additional information, if necessary. Using a word-processing application, write the text for the manual, being sure to demonstrate use of content, technical concepts, and vocabulary. Describe possible safety issues and how to avoid them. Also include information on what to do if an accident or emergency occurs. When the copy is complete, ask a classmate to review it for spelling and grammatical errors, and to provide constructive criticism on how it could be improved. Use the feedback to correct and edit the copy. Format the text so it is easy to read and understand. With your teacher's permission, print the manual or post it online.

CHAPTER 4 – PORTFOLIO BUILDER

THE INTERROGATION

If you've watched enough television shows or movies, you're familiar with the interrogation scene. One room, one detective, one suspect, and many angles, both figuratively and literally. This project is adapted from one that vanguard media educator James Gleason has used for nearly three decades.

DEVELOPMENT

Start by writing a one-page script where the following events occur. You choose the names of the two characters.

1. A suspect sits alone in an interrogation room.

2. A detective walks into an interrogation room holding a piece of evidence.

3. Three questions are asked of the suspect. Each one plays off the answer to the previous question.

4. The suspect answers each question simply, quickly, and without hesitation.

5. Fit in a demand from either the detective or the suspect.

6. Allow the evidence the detective walked in with to be revealed in some way.

7. The shock of the reveal of the evidence silences the suspect.

8. Leave the scene with some ambiguity about the suspect's guilt or innocence.

PREPRODUCTION

With your script complete, it's time to cast your movie. It's easy to get a couple of friends to play the parts, but remember your friends may lose focus. You're better off using your newly learned casting skills to find some talent from a local drama class or theater troop.

Continue the process by following these steps:

1. Plan your shots with an overhead diagram, shot sheet, and storyboards.

2. Find a location that best suits the scene.

3. Sketch out how the location space could transform into a believable interrogation room.

4. Create breakdowns for props, set pieces, and wardrobe.

5. Put together a budget, a crew list, a gear list, a detailed schedule (shot by shot), and a call sheet. Don't forget to schedule in time for a lunch break!

6. Schedule and arrange an audition session. Invite members of local drama classes and theater troops as well as friends from class.

7. Once you've cast the parts, hold a rehearsal.

PRODUCTION

With this project being only a page long, you should expect the shoot to last about four to six hours. Follow your schedule as closely as you can. For a variety of coverage, shoot the actions of each entire scene in each angle. You might want to capture additional shots that come to mind during the shoot. Hold onto those ideas, but don't act on them until each scheduled shot is completed.

POSTPRODUCTION

Follow these steps to bring all the pieces together:

1. Assemble your rough cut.

2. Get feedback from your cast and crew.

3. Make your trims.

4. Sweeten the sound.

5. Post it online or screen it for a selected audience, such as the class.

Chapter 5

Authenticity and Professionalism

Chapter 5 Overview

One of the key quests in life is finding out what kind of work you like to do—some combination of an activity you enjoy, something you do well, and work that pays the bills. Those who enjoy video production, filmmaking, or media creation find satisfaction with the kind of work that leaves a record of its time, whatever the scope.

Whether they work in the camera department or in postproduction and whether they focus on fictional features, television, documentaries, infomercials, or wedding videos, filmmakers enjoy even the most difficult parts of their job: rising before dawn, putting in long hours, and constantly solving problems in order to produce work that is interesting, thought-provoking, and commercially viable.

In this chapter, you will look at some of the key strategies employed by media creators taking their first steps to employment and making a living in content creation, distribution, and exhibition.

The Professional World

Several key aspects of content creation have three parts. Screenplays and treatments consist of three acts, and the production cycle consists of three parts—preproduction, production, and postproduction. Likewise, industries involved in content creation can be divided into three categories, broken down as follows:

- *Production*: This includes everything involved in the creation of media, from the germination of the idea to filming to the final audio mix (see **FIGURE 5.1**). Examples of production companies include Pixar (*Toy Story*, 1995), Lightstorm Entertainment (*Avatar*, 2009), and Gracie Films (*The Simpsons*, 1989).

- *Distribution*: This accounts for the methods of getting the media to the audience. Distributors are the companies that can handle the logistical challenges of creating thousands of copies of film prints, flying them all over the world so a film can open in many countries on the same day, or broadcasting their content on television sets or the Internet around the globe. They have been the big guns of the media game and have reaped the lion's share of the profits. Examples of distributors include Paramount Pictures, 20th Century Fox, and NBC Universal.

- *Exhibition*: The companies that own and operate the spaces that show or exhibit media. Throughout history, these went from being part of a monopoly to being owned by the major studios to being broken off into independent theaters occasionally managed in chains. Exhibitors keep some of the profits from the viewing of media (ticket sales) but all of the profits from concession sales. Examples of exhibitors include Regal Entertainment Group, AMC Theatres, and Cinemark.

PHOTO BY ANTB, VIA SHUTTERSTOCK

FIGURE 5.1 Floor manager and presenter planning a television broadcast

How the Trend to Digital Affects Jobs

Every job in media relates to one of these stages, but the technical methods by which they occur have changed radically over the past 15 years, as most theaters have moved from exhibiting film prints to exhibiting digitally. Movies are hardly ever carried into theaters in film cans anymore; rather, they are transported on hard drives, beamed in over satellites, or transferred via broadband cables.

Broadcast media, such as television and Internet, have been produced and distributed digitally for quite a while, but as theaters have made the switch, it seems inevitable that within a short time frame, motion picture film itself—which debuted in 1888—may be going the way of the compact disc and the VHS cassette.

This is a source of great sadness for film enthusiasts who believe that digital cinema cameras, while getting better at approximating the texture, look, and feel of film, will never completely re-create the magical chaos of film and its ability to transport the viewer into a world of a dreams and nightmares, as masters of the filmmaking craft have done for more than a century.

A small band of influential film rebels is working to extend the timeframe wherein motion-picture film will continue to be developed, printed, and screened, but without a doubt, the digital tide has arrived.

This revolution has changed the way entertainment is distributed and exhibited from the ground up, and it has also changed the jobs available in the field. The process of digital distribution is much cheaper for studios and requires far fewer workers to execute.

It's difficult to predict how much this process will continue to evolve or how the job market will change as a result.

But other factors have a positive influence on industry hiring. People are more interested in audio and video experiences than ever before, due in large part to new media. For example, video gaming, virtual reality, and Internet-based video channels have opened the door to many new opportunities and careers.

Getting an Education

Education requirements for careers in audio/video production vary depending on the position. Although a rare few succeed based on talent alone, most people invest the time, effort, and money to learn from the best.

Top media schools such as the University of Southern California's School of Cinematic Arts (see **FIGURE 5.2**); the University of California, Los Angeles, School of Theater, Film and Television; the American Film Institute Conservatory; New York University's Tisch School of the Arts; and Columbia University's School of the Arts are only a few of the options available to anyone aspiring to a career in audio and video production. There are many media programs at private universities and community colleges that can help you take the next step to a career. Almost all of these programs include classes in business management, which demonstrates the importance of understanding business planning, sales, finance, and marketing in the audio/video production industry.

PHOTO BY ANGRY JULIE MONDAY VIA FLICKR CC BY 2.0

FIGURE 5.2 University of Southern California's School of Cinematic Arts

At these schools, you can get great training and experience and meet like-minded students to collaborate with. Director Albert Hughes graduated from Los Angeles City College. Tim Burton and John Lasseter went to California Institute of the Arts.

Not all employers require a college degree, but in general, film and video editors will be expected to have a four-year bachelor's degree in a related field. Many industry associations offer certificates, as well. For example, Adobe offers certifications for showing proficiency with Premiere Pro. Avid Technology, Inc. offers certification for showing proficiency with its non-linear digital editing system. Other certificates are offered by organizations such as the Society for Broadcast Engineers, the National Institute for Certification in Engineering Technologies, and the International Association of Lighting Management Companies.

Where Are the Jobs?

When deciding on what kind of job to get in the media and entertainment field, the first thing to do is to become familiar with the names of key jobs in audio/video production (refer to Chapter 1). Even with all of the innovations in the way media is distributed and exhibited, certain aspects of the main production jobs will not fundamentally change.

Unlike other fields where you are hired by an employer, work in media creation is often project to project. Each project enables you to add another **credit** to your resume, which in turn leads to you being hired for another project. Over time, you build a reputation so that clients come looking for you and you can pick and choose from a variety of projects to pursue. Or, you develop your own projects.

Some jobs may be done best by forming a company of your own or with partners, for instance, **above-the-line** jobs, which are for those people who have creative influence over the project, such as director and producer.

For **below-the-line** jobs, which are for those who do not have creative influence, such as a camera operator or sound recordist, it's more common to be a freelancer hired by the owner of a company or the producer of a project.

It is also a good idea to get experience in as great a variety of professional environments as possible through internships, volunteer work, or as a paid employee. So, where do you begin? Here are a couple ways to get started.

MAKE YOUR OWN PROJECT

Start recording. Get your smartphone, DSLR, or HD camcorder; make a plan and start showing the world what you've got. Every once in a while, a Vine or YouTube video by someone who has creative flair or has tapped into the spirit of the day will catapult its creator into the media stratosphere.

The main advantage here is you can just start filming, make your mistakes, get better, and find your own best path forward. Of course, you might have to wait tables or park cars to pay the bills while you wait to be noticed.

CONSIDER ALL OPTIONS

One of the best exercises for those interested in a career in media is to stick around for the credits after a film, television show, or video game. Here's where you will learn a crucial truth—media projects, particularly the big ones, have one (occasionally two) director, one (but occasionally 12) writer, and a gaggle of producers.

However, if you look at the nuts-and-bolts departments that audience members don't always know about as much—visual effects designers, sound department, grip and electrical, and other below-the-line jobs—you will learn that there are an enormous number of jobs that are statistically much more attainable than the boss-type positions but that are very rewarding and pay extremely well.

GET A FOOT IN THE DOOR

If you hear of a company that is doing good work and looking for an intern, apply. In this industry, getting a foot in the door is more important than what you are doing. It doesn't matter whether you're getting coffee or filing papers; you are doing two of the most important things you can do to improve your career—learning and meeting people.

For years, one of the most sought-after entry-level jobs in Hollywood was the Agent Trainee program at the William Morris Agency, known as the mailroom, because as the story goes, even new hires were able to look through the mail they were sorting and learn the ins and outs of deal making. Find a way in to wherever you want to be—a production office, a studio lot, or a television network. Once you are in the door, pay attention, make yourself useful, make friends, and learn.

It's Not All About Hollywood

Many types of productions are created on a small budget by a small crew. This work can actually pay very well, especially once you're established and if you can keep the costs of your overhead down. Here are some types of work that you might go after on your own or with a small company.

EVENT VIDEOS

There's definitely a growing market for event videography, such as at weddings, red carpets, company parties, and bachelor and bachelorette parties. Many businesses specialize in this type of production. If the company or entity is big enough, they may hire in-house content creators or they may hire freelancers (see **FIGURE 5.3**).

PHOTO FIRST DANCE BY ANGELO DESANTIS VIA FLIC<R CC BY 2.0

FIGURE 5.3 The wedding videographer

This type of production can usually be done by a one- or two-person crew and is often high paying. People in this field must work closely with the client in order to create a product that everyone likes. It requires meeting at least once prior to the event. At the event it means being unobtrusive so as not to disturb or otherwise impact the action. For these types of once-in-a-lifetime events, shooting with multiple cameras is a must. Using small cameras like DSLRs allows you to move around quickly to capture the coverage you need but still get a professional cinematic look. Drones are becoming a popular method for capturing the overall experience.

Here are some strategies to employ while shooting an event:

- Check the location before the shoot.

- Look at your angles and obstructions.

- Try to determine the weather and change of lighting over the course of the day.

- Know who matters so you include them in as much footage as possible. That means focusing on the bride and groom and their families, not the cute date of a distant cousin who no one will remember five years from now.

- Have backups for batteries, mics, cameras, and other key equipment.

CORPORATE TRAINING VIDEO

Every industry has a growing need for media to showcase what they do and what their business plan is for the future. This is not to say that you can bring in a two-person crew and film their commercials or high-end publicity right off the bat. But, as with any position in film, it's all about getting in the door, getting along, and trying to do business.

Corporate videos typically follow the model of the expositional documentary. That means it is well-planned, scripted, and visualized, usually by a team that includes the in-house marketing department and the content producer.

As with wedding video, in corporate video it is incumbent on the media creator to be clear about the goals and priorities of the client, which is the company hiring you to make the video. Be sure to ask your client what they want or don't want and what their goals are for the video. Your responsibility is to satisfy your client, which you can do only through clear planning, reliability, and quality work. For your protection, you need to be clear about exactly what you are providing and what your payment schedule will be.

MUSIC VIDEOS

You may not be able to walk in off the street and shoot the next Taylor Swift video, but a media creator can do well to collaborate with music producers or an artist by applying for a project and being hired by those musicians. Alternatively, you can go out of the way to collaborate with an artist you admire, who is herself looking for a break, and offer to produce a video for her.

The production of music videos has a lot in common with narrative films or documentaries. You need either a clear script or at least a treatment exploring the theme of the song or piece. It will usually parallel the story of the song, but many music videos focus on style instead of story.

A couple of the most inventive and successful music videos ever are Michael Jackson's tribute to horror movies, *Thriller* (dir. John Landis, 1983) and the Beastie Boys paean to cop thrillers, *Sabotage* (dir. Spike Jonze, 1994). Both of these examples used familiar genres (horror, cop action) with established visual parameters as their jumping-off point to engage the audience.

One difference in the production of a music video is that the visual elements need to be edited to the rhythm of the musical piece and build to a visual, and usually a narrative, climactic moment, as they would in the montage of a feature-length film.

PUBLIC SERVICE ANNOUNCEMENTS

Recall that a public service announcement (PSA) is a message distributed without charge to raise awareness or change attitudes towards a social issue. You can use your skill as a producer of media content to create unique products to deliver messages for public agencies and nonprofit organizations. There are many such organizations and agencies, and if you build a reputation with one, the experience will lead you to others. Or lead them to you. Just because the PSA is distributed without charge does not mean you won't get paid for creating it!

Or...Be Your Own Boss!

Do your friends call you a lone wolf? Do you like to go it alone? Perhaps the better option for you is to bypass all of that coffee-getting and take the entrepreneurial route. An **entrepreneur** is someone who starts his own company in order to create a product or provide a service. Being an entrepreneur takes hard work and dedication, but you get to be your own boss and follow your own vision.

It's understood that everyone who wants to work in media may not start their own business to do so. However, if you want to work for yourself and make money legally, these are the steps you should take.

BUILD YOUR BRAND

When you're your own boss, you sometimes have to get tough with yourself, never more so than when it comes time to promote your new company by doing the following:

- Creating a design or logo (see FIGURE 5.4)

- Designing stationery and business cards with your logo

- Starting a Web site and building a social media presence

- Keep your resume, portfolio, references, reel, and any other materials you're using to promote yourself up-to-date.

These are just a few ways to get your name, your reputation, and the type of work you do in front of your audience, which in this case includes anyone who might hire you. Advertise your business in local newspapers, gazettes, and on local Web sites.

CHECK YOUR COMPETITION

You need to research companies similar to yours. Find out "best practices" by learning what the market is for productions like the ones you are capable of making, what those projects typically cost, and what the pitfalls are for those types of productions. Develop sample budgets and pricing sheets for any services you might provide.

STARTUP COSTS

Many companies get underway with little more than a phone and a computer. Or just a smartphone, which is both. That said, you may find that once you have some of your promotional materials (business cards, letterhead paper, invoices, and so on) in place, moving forward with your venture gets a little easier.

It's in your interest to keep your startup costs as low as possible to make your company sustainable over the long haul. Some new companies make a lot of splashy purchases and bad investments right off the bat and have a hard time paying their bills after as little as six months.

Fake Productions
LOGO DESIGN BY ROMERO DESIGNS

FIGURE 5.4
A generic production company logo

Tip:

The value of listening during any job interview, even a casual one over the phone, cannot be overestimated. Job posters will often tell you what they are looking for and what their priorities are. Don't get so caught up in delivering your resume the way you want them to hear it that you don't listen to what they are telling you. Thinking on your feet and adjusting your pitch as you go can greatly improve your chances of making a solid connection with the interviewer and getting the job.

NOW HIRING!

You may find as your company grows that you need to hire someone to cover the areas outside your skill set, or when you can't be two places at once. One of the side benefits of developing good habits as a worker is that you know what you are looking for as a boss.

Reflexively, the qualities you know that you would look for in your own employees ("Be on time! Be polite! Work hard! Think ahead!") are the same qualities you should strive to represent as an employee or when looking for work.

Set up interviews in person or over the phone, check references, and find the help you need.

Networking

Networking means meeting and talking to as many people as possible. You never know who knows someone who knows someone who is looking to hire someone with your skill set. So, it's important to get out there and schmooze.

For any new company, the first gigs are the hardest to land, and identifying them may take some time. More than half of small companies fold within the first year, ironically, after making the kind of mistakes they probably needed to make and learn from in order to be successful.

You may need to drop your rates or even work for free in the beginning of your career to show what you can do, which you can then promote in order to get more work.

One of your best strategies for getting the word out about your company and the quality of your work will be *networking*, getting yourself out there to meet with professionals like yourself and possibly clients as well at conventions or social meetups. You can find these opportunities via searches on the Internet or social media.

As a student, you can find networking opportunities by joining a career and technical student organization (CTSO) such as SkillsUSA or Future Business Leaders of America (FBLA) and by using social media. Professionals also use social media as well as industry professional organizations.

Some major entertainment industry conventions where media pros get together and technical and organizational breakthroughs are reported and celebrated include the following:

- *Consumer Electronics Show (CES)*: Showcases new developments in professional and consumer entertainment technology and a great place to see the newest electronic gadgets

- *National Association of Broadcasters (NAB) conventions*: Features the latest in professional media production gear and an exhaustive array of workshops and presentations on video production technology and techniques

- *National Association of Television Programming Executives (NATPE)*: Focused on program development, acquisitions, and networking for media executives

- *Comic-Con*: For fans and creators of the ever-growing and intersecting worlds of fantasy, comic books, graphic novels, films, gaming, and other media (see **FIGURE 5.5**).

FIGURE 5.5 A cosplay extravaganza at Comic-Con 2013

This is just the tip of the tip of the iceberg. Wherever you live, your town probably has meetups for professionals, amateurs, and enthusiasts engaged in media creation.

Meetup.com is a good place to start looking for like-minded folks and learn where the jobs are. When exploring a new Web site for the latest information, do your best to validate the legitimacy of the Web site and any events listed therein before depending on any information you get from it. And never send anyone money!

Lots of jobs feature constancy and reliability. Once you have the job, you keep it until you decide to change it or are fired or laid off. Media work is different. When you are a media professional, your current job may be your last, unless you have something else lined up. Over time, you will build up a database of clients who will ideally rehire you or recommend you for future work, and you will develop a **client base**.

Writing a Business Proposal

A **business proposal** is a written document sent to a prospective client in order to obtain a job. When you write a proposal and pitch yourself or your company to produce a project for your client, you need to think about several things that will make your proposal more competitive.

FULFILL A NEED

You might feel there's a need for a food bank to feed the underprivileged in your community. You could contact a local outreach, propose the project, and help them create media to promote this mission.

Or maybe you are a skateboarder with an idea for an innovation to the board or the GoPro camera. Ronald Bennett of Bennett Trucks invented a skateboard truck that granted boarders more control turning. Could your innovation become the next campaign for a company you follow and admire? Why not? Familiarity is a sort of expertise. Use what you know.

BE BOLD

You need to have a point of view about the work you are planning to do. Playing it safe and saying as little as possible will probably land your proposal in the circular file, also known as the garbage can. Remember that when you write a proposal, both sides are looking for something. You are looking for a job, and your potential client is looking for a new, interesting, and exciting project.

A great example of this comes from an episode of the show *Mad Men* (2007). Ad man Don Draper is meeting with executives from Kodak Camera who are looking for the best way to market a new device they call "The Wheel," which rotates photographic slides on a circular tray so they can be projected against a wall.

Draper's proposal does not promote "The Wheel"; rather, he explains to the execs that the device they have created is a time machine families will use to revisit themselves at their best. He tells them that their device is not called "The Wheel"; it's called "The Carousel."

Once again, he doesn't ask his client, he tells them.

Needless to say, they accept his proposal based on the strength and clarity of his conviction. This may represent more confidence and will than you are comfortable demonstrating, but it speaks to a key dynamic in the relation-ship between the idea pitcher and the client.

The key to writing or delivering a successful proposal is salesmanship, and that comes from having a good project or a good idea and selling it well. This can require boldness and tenacity; in a competitive market, the strong thrive, and the timid change jobs.

BE CLEAR

You will need to develop a business plan for a promotional film, as well as a production plan. Your business plan must clarify your understanding for key aspects of your deliverables including deadlines and financial compensation, as well as covering all the legal responsibilities involved.

To do this, you will have to research the elements that should be included in your proposal. Simultaneously, you need to develop some script ideas for the project to give your potential client some choices.

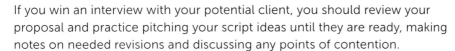
If you win an interview with your potential client, you should review your proposal and practice pitching your script ideas until they are ready, making notes on needed revisions and discussing any points of contention.

You will then make any needed adjustments based on a clarification of goals of the project, methodology, costs, scheduling, and so on, and return for client approval.

CONSIDER THE COMPETITION

Considering the competition has two meanings in regard to your project. First, you need to understand the market you are making a proposal regarding. You need to ask the following questions:

- Is your client the market leader?

- If not, who is, and why?

- What aspect of your client's product should your proposal focus on? Have they recently made a change they want your campaign to focus on?

- If your client has made a recent development to their product, why did they change it, and what sort of advance in the market would they like to see their development create? Are their expectations reasonable? How can you find out?

- What intelligence or reports are available to clarify the history of your client, the product in question, and the market? Does a quantitative (data-based) analysis of this information yield an understanding of how the client came to be where they are—market leader or also-ran—and how likely the current development might be to improve their market performance as much as they hope?

The second meaning asks you to consider your worldwide competition as a media creator. For your promotion to succeed, you need to keep your audience's attention. This is an increasingly difficult challenge in a world where millions of other images and sounds are vying for them.

Ask yourself what in your proposal is designed to do that. You should have a central idea, preferably visual, that you introduce, explore, and come back to throughout your video project.

Most importantly, your proposal should grab the audience and not let go. It should make them interested in what comes next.

HERE'S THE PITCH

You will need to prepare a pitch based on your potential client's perceived needs, as well as produce visual and written material to support the pitch. You should practice your presentation before others who will act as the client.

> **Tip:**
> Be certain that the promotional campaign you are coming up with for the client or producing based on the campaign of someone else is likely to achieve the desired effect for the client.

QUALITY IS KEY

High-end commercials cost more to produce per minute than feature films. Even though you may not be shooting at that top bracket, it will benefit you to make every image you record as visually stunning, well composed, and professional as it can be. It should look like it was shot for a million bucks even though you actually spent only five.

Cool locations, exciting costumes, funny script, and great videography add up to powerful promotions. Companies often hire stars for commercials (if they can afford them) because they have a proven track record of holding the audience's attention and their persona might improve the chances of convincing the audience to try the product.

WHERE ARE YOU SCREENING?

Success in promotions often depends on exposure—not the brightness of the image but the degree to which it reaches the largest possible audience and makes a good impression, engendering positive word-of-mouth. These days, YouTube, Facebook, and Instagram get the word out much more cheaply and sometimes more effectively than traditional broadcast and print media outlets.

The Interview

Interviewing is an important component of media production. Sometimes you are the interviewer, and sometimes you are the interviewee. Following are practices to help you participate successfully from both sides of an interview.

Interviewing Documentary Participants

If you've watched documentaries or television news shows, you've probably noticed that interviews, also called **talking heads**, are one of the cornerstones of that format, often dominating the content and driving the production of B-roll to support the topics introduced during the interview (see **FIGURE 5.6**).

Typically, the respondent replies to a series of questions posed by the interviewer, and the questioner is relegated to a disembodied voice or in many cases not heard from at all, having been removed via editing, to allow the viewer to focus on the response of the interviewee. Interviews are juxtaposed with B-roll, reenactments, freeze frames, graphics, and voiceover to create most of the content.

In the greatest interviews of all time, including that of President Richard Nixon by journalist David Frost, of actor Marlon Brando by author Truman Capote, and of political leader Malcolm X by writer Alex Haley, the subject was very comfortable engaging in an open exchange of ideas with the interviewer.

Remember to keep your goals for the interview in mind when conducting the interview. Sometimes the interviewer puts himself or his agenda before the goal of getting the subject to reveal something important on camera. This often leads to a "gotcha" moment instead of a true, well-developed dialogue with the subject.

FIGURE 5.6 Students shooting a standing interview

BEFORE THE INTERVIEW

The key to a successful interview is research. Knowing the truth, or at least as much of it as is available to you, may guide you to areas of significant investigation or epiphany.

Keep in mind that if you present as ignorant on the topic you are interviewing your subject about, you will immediately lose credibility with your subject as well as your audience. Practice adhering to the following guidelines:

- Unbiased news must be as faithful as possible to the facts of the account; however, facts need to be massaged out of interviewees by asking appropriate questions to the **main respondent**, supported by secondary interviews of **ancillary respondents**.

  In other words, if you are conducting an interview about climate change, activist and former Vice President Al Gore might be considered a main respondent, someone in a key position to make an educated statement on the topic at hand. Next might be inhabitants of areas immediately affected by climate change, such as the Maldives, Seychelles, and the Solomon Islands, or those who are fighting climate change in those affected areas.

- Consider the bigger picture or "big idea" underlying the topic of your interview. What will happen if the problem you are considering is left unchecked? What is the ultimate upside if the innovation you are discussing is supported and allowed to develop?

- Practice your interview with a friend or associate. Make sure you are comfortable with the topic, questions, and wording.

- Choose the location to make the subject most comfortable, whether their home office or a location key to the topic at hand.

DURING THE INTERVIEW

Having researched and prepared for the interview (see **FIGURE 5.7**), here are some tips and technical requirements to make sure your interview is successful at gathering footage and a method for further research:

- While your crew sets up camera and lights and "mics up" the subject, have a pre-interview with the interview subject.

  Be honest about the kinds of information you are hoping to collect on camera and share a few of the questions with the person you are going to interview. Remember, it's not an interrogation. If you do this right, the interview will flow more like a conversation, rather than an oral exam.

  Also, ask the subject to include the question you ask into their answer so that in case you ask a yes or no question, you have a better chance of capturing a useful sound bite.

FIGURE 5.7 A sit-down interview with Bill Pope, cinematographer of the *Matrix* trilogy

- Sit or stand as close to the lens as possible. The line of sight (eyeline) of your subject should be near the lens to allow the viewer to share in the participation of the conversation.

  Filmmaker Errol Morris, in a quest for the most intimate interviews, uses two teleprompters, in a configuration he calls the *interrotron*, to get the interview subject to look directly into the lens, while seeing the inter-viewer's face on the two-way mirror of a teleprompter.

- Start the interview by asking the subject to state his name and spell it on-camera. Spelling an interview subject's name incorrectly onscreen is not acceptable.

- Don't just wait to ask the next question; listen to what your subject is saying.

To ensure that you do just that, repeat and paraphrase a point the subject made, and ask a question that relates to what was said. For example, if he told you what he had for breakfast this morning, you can jump off of that by saying, "You mentioned you had cereal for breakfast; what is your favorite breakfast food?"

- Before ending the interview and thanking the interview subject, ask him whether there is any additional information he'd like to share. Sometimes there's great information available that you did not ask for.

Interviewing For Prospective Clients

The other type of interview you are likely to conduct in your career involves interviewing for a job after submitting your proposal. Once you get a callback, you may have to meet with the client to describe your vision.

Often, the interview is the last step before the hire. Recall the importance of vision and the value of research. These are the key strategies you can use to convince the client that you and only you can deliver the exact effect they are looking for.

The key to a good interview is having the information you need to convince your potential client you are the one for the job. This may be in the form of a written proposal, or it may simply come from you in the course of your meeting.

You should go into the meeting with a plan and specific goals or outcomes you want to achieve, but remain flexible and listen to what the client is telling you. Some interviewees hear every criticism as a rejection, but the most successful play the long game with potential clients and stay positive and focused on winning the work, either now or the next time. Many clients with experience can sense insincerity, so you will do well to scrutinize your delivery and choose the approach that works best for you and comes across as the most sincere.

First Impressions

Often, a job is won or lost and a project goes forward or doesn't based on what happens before anyone says a word. Here are a couple ways to make a great first impression on the client:

- Good grooming: Dress well, be clean, smell good.

- Breath mints: Enough said.

- A firm handshake: Not too hard, not too soft. And not wet. Keep a dry handkerchief or paper towel nearby.

- Eye contact: Make it, not creepy and intense but direct. Some interviewees go on autopilot when answering a question. Keep in touch with the interviewer during questioning. Confirm that your potential client is "getting" what you have to say.

A wise old salesman used to pitch 30 to 40 potential clients every day. After he made his pitch, he would wrap up by saying, "I hope I won your business today. If I didn't, please let me know what I could do to win it, and I assure you, I will do everything in my power to make you happy you chose my company."

He didn't win over all his potential clients on his first round of stops. But he kept up with them, reminded them of past meetings, asked after their families, and did his best to resolve their issues. Over time, his attitude and consistency won most of his clients from his competitors.

ASK QUESTIONS

You should definitely go into any interview situation with an attitude that's active as opposed to passive, and that means having questions for your potential client.

If they ask whether you have any questions for them and you say "I'm good," take a minute later and think about how your competitors answered that question—you know, the ones who got the job.

Or, just add to this list of starter questions:

- "First and foremost, I want you to be beyond thrilled with the media I create for you. What do you want this project to achieve for you, short-term and long-term?"

- "What aspects of your product are you keen to focus on, and what aspects do you want to deemphasize?" You may want to express to the client that the project can do even more for them than they are hoping. Most clients will be happy to learn that you are as ambitious or more ambitious about the goals of the project than they are. More generally, most people respond to or are turned on by vision, so long as yours does not directly contradict theirs and does not make them see you a direct competitor.

- "What aspects of your company's mission and vision should be evident in this media campaign?"

- "What are your must-haves for this project? How much leeway can you give me as to how I include them?"

- "What are your concerns about my ability to produce this project to your maximum level of satisfaction?"

Shooting with Multiple Cameras

There are many reasons a video production might require the use of multiple cameras. The most common is to be able to capture multiple angles of an event that is either difficult or impossible to re-create. Live events such as sports, concerts, and theatrical performances demand it.

In the early days of television, multiple cameras were required because the majority of programs were broadcast live because of the cost and time involved with producing work on film and the nonexistence of any other recording medium. The use of videotape as an affordable method to record and store video content did not become standard until the mid-1960s.

The three-camera **multicamera** sitcom that is credited with establishing the format is the 1950s classic *I Love Lucy*. The show is still remembered and celebrated today, not just because of the quality of the writing and the timeless talent of Lucille Ball and Desi Arnaz but also because of the choice to shoot on film instead of broadcasting video directly to the viewing audience. It survives today, unlike many programs that were not recorded on a permanent medium, because of how well the show's film elements could be (and were) preserved.

One holdover from the early days of television that still uses a multiple-camera, theatrically staged format is the **situation comedy**, or **sitcom**. Television comedy borrowed other forms from cinema with the single-camera format and a documentary approach known as the **mockumentary**.

Many shows are shot in a single-camera documentary style yet still use multiple cameras in production. This is because of contemporary documentaries' use of multiple cameras to capture once-in-a-lifetime moments in **cinema verité** style, as well as talking head interviews.

When editing single-camera talking head footage, the use of **B-roll** becomes a necessity not only to show what the subject is talking about but also to cover up jump cuts that occur when a portion of the interview is removed, such as a long pause, a flub, or redundant and unnecessary speech.

The advantage to shooting interviews with two cameras (see **FIGURE 5.8**) is the opportunity for B-roll to cover up those awkward cuts that are exposed when a transition from one shot at a certain size and angle to another with a different size and/or angle allows you to stay in the moment with the interview subject.

FIGURE 5.8 Doubling up on cameras on a student documentary shoot

Besides using the two shots to cover up edits in the interview, the choice of angle can be used creatively for emphasis. Start on a medium shot for the first part of a sound bite and then, just when an important moment occurs during the interview—bam!—punch in to the close-up.

Syncing

Professional studio cameras that are designed for multicamera shoots have the ability to use identical **timecodes**, coming from an external source to make **synchronizing**—or **syncing**—footage quick and easy.

There are a few considerations to make when shooting with multiple cameras if you don't have the kind of budget to get cameras and gear that are specifically designed for multicamera shooting. The syncing of multiple clips in editing can be difficult if these technical considerations are not made.

- Shoot with identical cameras if at all possible.

- Set the cameras to record in the same frame rate and format.

- Match the white balance, shutter speed, and gain settings on each camera.

- Set up each camera at an angle and focal length different enough that cutting between them does not look awkward like a jump cut.

- Record audio on each camera as a reference to aid in syncing.

- Assign one person (usually the assistant director) to be responsible for calling "Roll" and "Cut."

- With all cameras rolling, clap a slate (clapboard) to mark a slate to sync to.

- Once the cameras start rolling, they must stay rolling until "Cut" is called. Stops and starts can make syncing the angles difficult.

- Optionally, you can clap or slate at the end of the roll before cutting to have a backup sync point.

- Upon ingesting the footage, name each clip with an angle number or letter.

Most editing software requires you to place a mark—either an In point, an Out point, or a marker—on a clip to determine the point at which the clips of each angle are to be synchronized.

Synchronizing angles can be done automatically when using a third-party plug-in, such as Red Giant Plural Eyes, or when the editing software has an automatic clip syncing feature, such as Apple Final Cut Pro X.

Both of these options require reference audio on each clip that is analyzed to find matching indicators in the sound to sync the angles. This feature makes syncing clips much easier, even if most of the considerations mentioned were not made.

Note:

Timecode is an 8-digit addressing system based on the 24-hour clock that allows each frame to have its own address number. It is formatted as HH:MM:SS:FF (which stands for hours:minutes: seconds:frames).

Tip:

As an alternative to a slate, you can use a camera flash or a person clapping their hands.

Note:

You can also use the multi-camera syncing feature of your editing software to edit the various angles of projects that were not shot simultaneously, such as music videos.

Lighting an Interview

The lighting for a sit-down, talking-head interview for nonfiction takes its cues from portrait lighting in straightforward and classic approach. This style of lighting is called **three-point lighting**. The three points of light are the **key light**, the **fill light**, and the **back light** (see FIGURE 5.9).

FIGURE 5.9 A floor layout plan for a three-point lighting an interview

> **Tip:**
> Placing the key light slightly higher than eye level can help avoid the subject discomfort and squinting from the directness of the light angle. This also creates a triangle of light on the subject's cheek and is called the Rembrandt style of portrait lighting.

The key light is the main source of light in a shot. It is the brightest source and can also be used to light a larger area around the interview subject. It is placed at around a 45-degree angle from the camera to give a sense of depth and present detail of the subject.

A decision needs to be made as to whether the key light should be placed on the same side as the interview subject's line of sight (*eyeline*) or the opposite side (see FIGURE 5.10). Placing the key light on the same side as the subject's eyeline will allow more coverage of light on the subject's face (both eyes are lit). Placing the key light on the opposite side creates more shadow on the face (one eye is lit).

The transition from light to shadow is called **fall-off**. When using a direct source with no diffusion for the key light, a harder shadow appears on the face, which can also be described as a fast fall-off.

The fill light (see FIGURE 5.11) is used to *fill* in the shadow that is created by the key light. The fill should be a lower-intensity light and a much softer, or diffused, source of light. A fill does not have to be a direct source; it can be a light bounced off of a bounce board or foamcore card.

Because of the lower intensity of the light due to the diffusion or bounce, you may need to use a higher-intensity light or bring the light closer to the subject. Too close or too intense, and the effect of the shadow from the key will be lost, causing what is called **flat lighting**, like the look of flash photography.

FIGURE 5.10 The interview subject lit with only a key light

FIGURE 5.11 The interview subject lit with a key light and a fill light

The softer light used for fill (see **FIGURE 5.12**) has a longer transition from light to shadow, or a **slow fall-off**.

The third point of light, the back light (see **FIGURE 5.13**), is designed to separate the subject from the background by giving an outline around the head and shoulders or a halo effect. This type of back light is often called a **rim light** (see **FIGURE 5.14**) and is placed above the subject's head.

If the back light is not coming from directly behind the subject but from the side so that the light hits a bit of the side of the subject's face, it is called a **kicker**. The back light should be of a lower intensity than the key or the fill light.

FIGURE 5.12 The interview subject lit with only a fill light

FIGURE 5.13 The interview subject lit with a key light, a fill light, and a back light

FIGURE 5.14 The interview subject lit with only a back light (rim light)

If you are interested in creating a darker mood for the look of your interview, consider using only two points of light, but don't sacrifice the back light. Use the key light and a back light for a dramatic transition from light to dark (see **FIGURE 5.15**).

FIGURE 5.15 The interview subject lit with a key light and a back light

For a softer yet still moody look, go with a back light and what you would normally use as a fill, which would now be considered your key light (see **FIGURE 5.16**).

FIGURE 5.16 The interview subject lit with a soft key light (or fill) and a back light

The same approach can be made even outside of the studio environment. When out on location, indoors or outdoors, identify what the main source of light is—your key light—and place your subject, framing your shot with the direction of that light in mind. Use additional light sources or bounce boards and reflectors as your other points of light.

Tip:
Be aware that having a strong source of light such as the sun as your back light can make it a challenge to get an acceptable exposure on your subject if you are not adding enough light to balance it out. This is a common problem in amateur production.

Postproduction: Adding Titles and Graphics

To achieve a truly professional look and to provide information to your audience in an alternative manner to dialogue and images, you may want to consider using text onscreen.

Words onscreen, called **titles**, are most necessary to identify people and places. **Graphics**, such as photos, logos, and illustrations, are used to present and clarify information visually and can help brand your productions. Both titles and graphics should be used creatively yet thoughtfully to support the themes and styles of your video.

Placing Titles in the Zone

Before throwing a bunch of words onto the screen, you have to establish some boundaries so that everything is done safely. Those boundaries are called **action-safe** and **title-safe** zones (see **FIGURE 5.17**).

FIGURE 5.17 The overlays for action-safe and title-safe zones

Since not every video monitor, smartphone screen, and television is made the same, the safety zones were established to be a reference of the safe distances from the edge of the video frame that could be cropped by the **overscan** of most video displays. The standard overscan of 16:9 video is 5 percent. That means that 5 percent of each edge of the captured frame is cut off by most displays.

> **Note:**
> Video displayed on computer screens usually shows the entire uncropped frame.

Before high-definition digital displays, analog televisions were less precise about how much or how evenly the overscan was cropped. Therefore, it was possible for important text information at the edge of the action-safe zone to be cropped off on certain television sets.

For this reason, an even tighter zone is considered safe for text onscreen. The *title-safe* zone on a 16:9 image is 10 percent from each edge of the frame. Keeping all of your text within this zone ensures that no text or graphic placed in the area will be cropped off by a video display or television.

Unfortunately, there is no single standard tool that every media creator can learn to master the art of title creation. The closest thing is Adobe Photoshop.

Within Photoshop, there is a Film & Video preset you can select when creating a new file that allows you to choose the format of the video you are working in. Files created with this preset conveniently have guides set up for action- and title-safe zones.

Titles

Text onscreen comes in many forms. All forms of onscreen text are referred to as *titles*, even if the actual title of the show is shown only once. The most basic title is text that stays static onscreen and is called a *title card*.

Before electronic and digital technology could generate text on a screen, the text, such as the title of a program, would have to be painted or printed on a physical card; thus, the term *title card* remains.

Text that identifies a person who appears onscreen, such as in a **talking head shot**, is called a **lower-third** (see FIGURE 5.18), because the text is positioned on the lower horizontal third of the screen. Lower-thirds typically contain two lines of text—the top line for the name and the bottom line for the title—aligned to the left and frequently with a background bar.

FIGURE 5.18 A sample lower-third title card

Titles that scroll up from the bottom of the screen, most associated with the end credits of a feature film, are called a **title roll**. Lists of text in title rolls are formatted in two columns. The left column contains character roll or job title and is aligned right. The column on the right contains the full name of the credited cast or crew member and is aligned left, leaving a slight gap between the columns.

The Chyron Legacy

When electronic machines and computers started to be used to create titles, they were called *character generators* (CGs).

A popular brand of these machines was made by the Chyron Corporation. In television and video production, titles were often called *Chyrons* in the same way facial tissue is often called Kleenex and photocopies are called Xeroxes.

Title generators are built into most video-editing applications. Many have professionally designed templates to work from, which can be helpful. Some of the templates even have motion integrated into the title, making them quite impressive. But remember that the choices you make should serve your project. Sometimes a title card that flies into frame and then explodes away is not the best choice, if it is inconsistent with all the other design decisions you've made throughout your video.

Here are some suggestions when designing your titles, to maintain a professional look:

- Choose a typeface or font within a typeface family that is easily legible and appropriate for the tone and purpose of your program. Script fonts might be okay for a main title, depending on the tone of your project, but might not be a good choice for the rest of your credits.

- Certain fonts, such as **Comic Sans**, are avoided in professional design. It's also a good idea to avoid the default font on the title generator.

- Choose a style for your text, including choices such as color, size, and letter case (title case or uppercase), and stay consistent with your style choice throughout your project.

- Carefully check for spelling and grammatical errors on every title. Nothing makes you lose credibility faster than a misspelled word.

- Even worse than a misspelled word is a misspelled name. For many microbudget and student productions, the only payment a crew or cast member receives for their time is a credit. If their name is not spelled correctly, it's an insult.

- Add a **drop shadow** to add some depth and separation from the background.

> **Tip:**
> When creating a title or graphic with Photoshop that has a transparent background, make sure the video-editing software you use can accept PSD files. If not, save your titles in PNG format to keep the transparency data.

Graphics

There are many reasons to include graphics in your project. If you have designed a logo for your production company, the logo could be edited in at the top of the show, or you could place it as a **bug** on the bottom-right corner of the screen like most TV channels do. In many cases, there are photographs, graphs, and illustrations that can be used as B-roll to support an idea or provide visual evidence.

Photographs may make up the majority of your visual content in projects such as historical documentaries. Filmmaker Ken Burns is credited with having popularized the effect of panning and zooming into photographs with an animation camera in his documentaries. Although he is the first one to tell you that the technique had been used by other filmmakers before him, most refer to it as the *Ken Burns effect*.

Adding movement to graphics not only helps keep the attention of the viewer but allows you to help tell your story by calling attention to a detail on a photo. By using keyframes for scale and position, similarly to how they are used in automating audio levels, you can achieve the same effect that required filmmakers to use special equipment in the past.

Some third-party plug-ins, such as Noise Industries' free Pan and Zoom, and built-in features in video-editing applications can make it even easier to add movement to your still images.

In Final Cut Pro, Apple actually named the photo-animating feature the Ken Burns effect. It works quite easily. By placing a frame on a still (or video) for the start and end of the movement, you create the effect. The speed of the effect is based on the duration of the segment in your sequence.

End-of-Chapter Activities

REVIEW QUESTIONS

1. Explain how the trend to digital affects jobs in the audio and video production industry.

2. List at least three business classes you might take as part of a media program.

3. What is the difference between above-the-line and below-the-line jobs? Give an example of each.

4. Give four examples of event videos.

5. What is an entrepreneur?

6. What is networking and why is it important?

7. What is a business proposal?

8. Why is it important to conduct research to prepare for an interview?

9. What is the most common reason for shooting with multiple cameras?

10. What are two reasons for adding titles to a video?

Review Project 1

Use the information in this chapter and research you conduct online to learn about employment opportunities in entrepreneurship in the audio and video production industry. Use the information you find to select a business you might like to start, then deliver an informal presentation on the topic to a partner or to the class.

Review Project 2

Research Career and Technical Student Organizations for students interested in careers in audio and video production. Examine how these organizations provide opportunities for professional networking that may lead to employment. If your school has a chapter, join, and take an active role in networking opportunities such as meetings, conferences, and competitions. If your school does not have a chapter, take a leadership role to explore options for starting one.

Review Project 3

With a partner, prepare an interview. Each write questions you will ask the other. Then take turns setting up and recording your interview. Take care to use proper lighting. After you each have the opportunity to conduct and record the interview, work independently to edit and prepare a preview copy. Critique each other's work, then use the constructive criticism to make improvements. Share your finished work with the class, or, with your teacher's permission, post it online.

CHAPTER 5 – PORTFOLIO BUILDER

NONPROFIT PROMOTIONAL VIDEO

New media has evolved to the point where video content is as necessary to a Web site as photos and text. Big corporations and companies hire in-house production teams to create videos to promote products, support their customers, train their employees, and document company events.

The ease of creating acceptable, if not professional, video using mobile devices has made it possible for smaller companies to expect their employees to be able to create video, even without special training or equipment.

Entrepreneurs must create video pitch presentations to raise money on crowdfunding sites, such as Kickstarter and Indiegogo. Nonprofit organizations have a need to create promotional video for their Web sites to show supporters the work they do.

Nonprofit organizations function solely on the funds that are raised through donations and grants. To attract and maintain supporters, they create (or commission) promotional materials that present the goals and accomplishments of the organization.

DIRECTIONS

You will create a video for a company or organization in your community. If possible, use steps 1-6 to reach out and work with an actual organization. If that is not possible, work with school officials, or complete that project as if you have an actual client.

DEVELOPMENT

The first step is to identify the organizations in your area that are doing work that is charitable and beneficial to you and the people who live around you.

1. Establish a brand identity for yourself as a production company that includes an original name and a logo design.

2. Create a Web site and business cards. Having a social network presence is optional but effective in demonstrating your commitment to doing professional work.

3. Research the organizations you are targeting to understand the details of their goals. Be aware of existing promotional material they have made public.

4. Create a written proposal for the type of video you intend on making for the organizations you will pitch to. You might need to send this by e-mail, deliver it on paper in person, or both.

   Be clear in your proposal that you want the video to be used to help and support the organization in its goals.

5. Make some phone calls. Reaching out through e-mail can work, but it's much more effective to connect with others to make your pitch by telephone or in person.

6. Once you've made a contact with a member of the organization, schedule meetings so you can work together with them to develop your video idea. Make a list of what should be included in the promotional video, such as a message from organization leadership, past activities and accomplishments, or current and future goals.

7. Write an outline and a script for the video and then meet to have it approved by your contact. Remember that the video is for their purposes, so do your best to take their feedback positively and make changes according to their wishes.

8. Create a written agreement with your client, establishing criteria for what each of you is providing to complete the project, including time commitment, quality, and other processes.

PREPRODUCTION

The production phase on a promotional video has the same challenges as any other project, except now you have a client and building a good reputation is at stake, so plan your production meticulously.

1. Gather any previously created material from your client, such as video clips, slideshows, photos, and graphics.

2. Schedule your production to prioritize material that tells the story and fills the bulk of your project's duration, for example, interviews or voiceover narration.

3. Have a production meeting with your crew to inform them of all the major details of the video's purpose and what is expected of you and them during production.

PRODUCTION

Here are some production considerations for commissioned projects:

1. Before you begin to shoot, take extra care to ensure that all of your equipment is in working order. Production problems are bound to happen; just make sure they aren't the ones you could have prevented.

2. With a professional demeanor and a smile on your face, start shooting and check off each item on your shot list as you acquire them.

3. Leave the locations looking better than you found them.

POSTPRODUCTION

Your client is going to be eager to see what you put together, so waste no time if you intend to build a good reputation.

1. Ingest and organize your footage. There is a chance that your client will visit you or that you will bring the laptop you edit on with you to them. The organization of your project assets (bins, events, clip names) is a reflection on you and your professionalism. Use standard conventions of asset organization, or at the least, keep things neat.

2. After cutting your rough-cut assembly, continue the post process by adding B-roll, cutting in music, layering titles and graphics, and sweetening audio

3. For feedback, provide your client with a compressed export that cannot be mistaken for completed product. Add a low-opacity title card across the middle of the screen with your name or the words "NOT FOR DISTRIBUTION" on it. This watermark should protect you from the unfinished work being used, especially if it's a paying gig.

4. Make as many changes as you can within the agreed-upon time commitment.

5. Deliver the product on time and within budget.

Chapter 6

Delivering the Message

Chapter 6 Overview

- The World of Nonfiction Filmmaking
- Objectivity and Subjectivity
- Developing a Theme: Nonfiction
- Crew Positions: Nonfiction
- Postproduction: Color Correction and Grading
- Postproduction: Delivery and Exhibition
- Resume and Portfolio Development
- End-of-Chapter Review and Activities

How can you effect change in your society if you don't know the facts? How can you know the facts if media companies with means to report the facts do not cover the stories that are most relevant to your life?

This chapter provides some guidelines on how to approach making a documentary project, from the consideration of what topic would be the best candidate worthy of your time and effort to the steps you will need to take to execute your project so that it is entertaining, is informative, and has integrity.

The World of Nonfiction Filmmaking

Documentaries (or *docs*), more than any other type of media projects, are the inspirations or drivers for social change. It's amazing to think that the work of one person or a handful of people can instigate change in the policies of a major corporation and even cause new laws to be introduced on the floor of Congress. But that is exactly what happens.

- *The Thin Blue Line* (1988): This doc by Errol Morris investigated the life imprisonment of a man convicted of killing a police officer in Dallas, Texas. The man, Randall Adams, was freed because of the film, which also went deeper in its critique of the American legal system than simply targeting the officials who mishandled Adams' case.

- *Supersize Me* (2004): Because of this film, in which Morgan Spurlock showed how quickly eating McDonald's food can affect the health of an individual, the mega-restaurant chain discontinued its "supersize" option.

- *Bowling for Columbine* (2002): After this Michael Moore doc explored the relationship between the bloody killing spree at a school in Colorado and America's willingness to accept the world's highest degree of gun deaths in exchange for the freedom to own guns, K-Mart stopped selling bullets.

Documentaries

Documentaries tell the stories that most need to be told (see **FIGURE 6.1**). By definition, they are supposed to provide a factual record or report. There was a time when the majority of Americans turned to the evening news to stay informed and had confidence that the news was presented free of bias without an agenda beyond informing the general populace. As the relationship between corporations, politicians, and the American public changed, competitiveness, the need to improve viewership, and the fear of losing viewers have diminished that early mission.

PHOTO BY HAIDER Y. ABDULLA, SHUTTERSTOCK

FIGURE 6.1 An interview subject telling a story, with a camera capturing

So then, what is a documentary? Is it "the news" with a longer production schedule? Is it a story-based film with more talking heads? *Webster's Dictionary* defines a documentary as follows:

" of, relating to, or employing documentation in literature or art; *broadly*: factual, objective"

Even the casual audience member may realize that this is a very tall order. To re-create even one scene from reality, one would have to cast actors who seem like facsimiles of the original subjects; re-create their actions; get inside their minds to glean their intentions; use the original locations or re-create them; and choose or re-create the original clothing, props, and dialogue of the original scene.

That's not just tough; it's impossible. The best anyone can do is try to be true to the essence of the original events and portray them as close to reality as possible. Even that much is difficult, because most people interpret stories through the lens of their own experience, and try to make sense of the facts based on their own understanding of reality.

Film festivals, Netflix, and the Academy Awards would have everyone believe that "narrative" films and "documentary" films are two completely different genres, but documentary filmmakers or those who have worked in nonfiction media will tell you that these two types of projects have much more in common than many people think. Like fictional films, documentary films do the following:

- Shoot on an agreed-upon schedule

- Coordinate the efforts of a film crew that may be small or large, depending on the size of the production

- Have story arcs that feature rising action, falling action, twists and reversals, and a climactic (or anticlimactic) moment.

News, Entertainment, Propaganda...or All Three?

Who do *you* believe? Manipulation of the media to achieve certain results is a process that has exploded over the last century because of the worldwide distribution of mass media.

The question for today's media creators is, what is your main goal in creating your piece, and what questions does that goal suggest about the style or limits of your methodology?

NEWS

With news, the goal is to *report*, to make complicated stories involving multiple points of view easier for the general audience to understand, and to educate viewers about the facts of their world. The question is, *who* gives you the facts, and *which* facts do you report and which do you not?

ENTERTAINMENT

The goal of entertainment is to *amuse* the target audience, and perhaps others, with a successful project that earns money and respect. The question is, are you presenting the events in your piece as factual or "inspired by true events," and are you sacrificing either the details of the truth or the underlying truth to have a more entertaining and popular project?

PROPAGANDA

Recall that propaganda is information used out of context to try to mislead and influence thinking. In other words, the goal of propaganda is to *convince* the audience of something. However, are you limiting yourself to the truth to make your argument, or are you structuring a false argument based on mistruths or half-truths because the success of the campaign is more important than promoting the truth?

Any description of propaganda should begin with a mention of the Nazi-produced *Triumph of the Will* (1935), directed by Leni Riefenstahl. This observational doc celebrated the practices of the Third Reich with cinematic shots of cheering crowds and marching armies, which motivated the impoverished and disenfranchised German people to support the Reich. It is possibly the most effective media manipulation of all time.

In American politics, President Lyndon Johnson was a particularly colorful media manipulator. During his 1964 Presidential campaign, Johnson's campaign created a television commercial called "Daisy" (see **FIGURE 6.2**) where an adorable little girl picks flowers in a field. She hears a countdown, and then the camera zooms in on her eye as a nuclear blast destroys, presumably, everything around her. Johnson's reassuring voice plays over the blast, warning people to vote for him so that this terrible event does not happen. Though the ad ran only once, it was considered a key component of his landslide victory against the pro-nuclear Barry Goldwater.

A Quick History of News

"What's new?" or as the question was posed in antiquity, "What news?" has intrigued humankind for as long as there have been civilizations. Whether the news of the day was communicated in the agora, the square, the local lunchroom, or the pub, the public has always had a boundless desire to know what was going on. This has led to the development of news tellers and news organizations, which address this need using methods of increasing technical complexity. Here are a few highlights from this history:

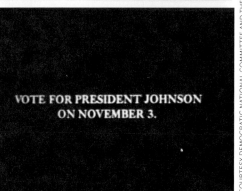

VOTE FOR PRESIDENT JOHNSON ON NOVEMBER 3.

COURTESY DEMOCRATIC NATIONAL COMMITTEE AND THE LYNDON BAINES JOHNSON PRESIDENTIAL LIBRARY

FIGURE 6.2 Three stills from Johnson's "Daisy" campaign ad

- Couriers (2400 BCE to 1700s) were sent around by pharaohs, Caesar, prime ministers, et al. Their goal was to disseminate the news as publicity for the government.

- Newspapers were introduced in Germany at the beginning of the 17th century, inspired by the pamphlets of Protestant Reformation thinker Martin Luther—specifically, the *95 Theses* in 1517. Luther was the social media superstar of his day, using the relatively recent technology of the printing press to distribute pamphlets to the masses and distributing his ideas much more widely than was previously possible.

- From the issuing of the first commercial radio licenses in the United States in 1921 up to the introduction of the television in the early 1950s, radio and newsreels that played before feature films in theaters delivered news in America and throughout Europe.

- Popularized in 1948, network television news took off with the presentation of the program *See It Now* in 1954 by journalist Edward R. Murrow (see **FIGURE 6.3**), who is best known for challenging the Communist-baiting tactics of Senator Joseph McCarthy. McCarthy retired in part because of the challenges posed by Murrow, the first major case of the influence of television journalism.

FIGURE 6.3 Publicity photo of Edward R. Murrow

Later, when Murrow saw the audience for his show diminished by the success of games shows like *The $64,000 Question*, he wondered how long television would be able to protect or promote the mission of honestly reporting the issues of the day in the face of competition from entertainment, which produced higher ratings and more advertising revenue to their networks.

Murrow prophetically realized that promoting the public interest was costly and challenging because networks needed to allow equal time to organizations that were criticized by their news department. Here is an excerpt from his famous "Wires & Lights" speech, delivered in 1958, about the responsibility of those working in such a powerful and influential medium as television:

" This instrument can teach, it can illuminate; yes, and it can even inspire. But it can do so only to the extent that humans are determined to use it to those ends. Otherwise it's nothing but wires and lights in a box. There is a great and perhaps decisive battle to be fought against ignorance, intolerance, and indifference. This weapon of television could be useful."

Even facing the challenges of entertainment television, television news expanded in its influence, and anchormen such as ABC's Harry Reasoner and NBC's Chet Huntley and David Brinkley became media stars as well as news reporters.

From 1962 through the early 1980s, CBS News remained the gold standard for presenting news that the nightly audience felt that they could believe in and that was relevant to their lives. CBS anchorman Walter Cronkite (see **FIGURE 6.4**) was "the most trusted man in America." Cronkite was followed by Dan Rather (1981–2005), who maintained the network's high level of integrity.

PHOTO BY ROB BOGAERTS / ANEFO / CC BY-SA 3.0 NL

FIGURE 6.4 Walter Cronkite

The 1980s saw the growth of cable television and the 24-hour news channel. The Cable News Network (CNN) was created in Atlanta in 1980 by Ted Turner. Events such as the Challenger disaster in 1986 and the Gulf War in 1991 spurred America's addiction to watching news as it unfolded.

During this time, criticism of television news (and newspapers, including the *New York Times*) by conservatives increased. Australian mogul Rupert Murdoch began broadcasting the Fox News Channel in 1996 in response to what some Republicans felt was the liberal bias in the major media outlets of the day. That network has remained the most-watched cable network in the United States for more than a decade. Even though it is often cited as intentionally disseminating mistruths in its reportage, Fox News maintains a stronghold on cable news over all other stations including CNN, ESPN, and MSNBC.

Rise of the Documentary

The documentary film was invented at the same time as motion pictures. **Actualities** were films produced between 1890 and 1905 in order to document something real and show it to the audience.

Interpretation, commentary, and, for that matter, editing would come later. These earliest films were travelogues, biographies, and popular filmed events, such as boxing matches. The **newsreel** developed during the 1910s as the main method of showing audiences the most exciting developments of the day, such as Sir Ernest Shackleton's Trans-Antarctic Expedition.

The different **genres** of documentary mostly derive from the philosophy used to gather the material. There is not absolute agreement even among documentary filmmakers as to the limits of these definitions, but there are several useful guidelines.

The **cinema vérité** style of documentary uses the camera to reveal unaltered truths, letting the camera be a fly on the wall, unobtrusive to the events it records. It was based on the earlier Russian concept of *Kino-Pravda* by Dziga Vertov, which, like *cinema vérité*, means *cinema truth*.

Vertov believed the truest goal and greatest power of filmmaking was to combine the *actualities* by editing strips of film together to get at a deeper truth than could be perceived with the eye.

Toward this end, vérité filmmakers would use techniques including the hidden camera to maximize the truthfulness of the recording and minimize the invasiveness of the camera as a participant in what is being recorded.

The goal of vérité cinema, to depict events as accurately as possible, is also the occasional goal of narrative feature films that are "inspired by true events." Paul Greengrass produced and directed *United 93* (2006) with a goal of faithfully and solemnly re-creating the experience of the passengers on that fateful flight on September 11, 2001, who overwhelmed terrorists and forced their flight to a crash landing before it reached its intended target, either the White House or the Capitol Building.

To achieve that goal, the film used real airline employees to portray their counterparts in the film, and the project utilized 110 minutes of screen time to depict 110 minutes of real time to maximize the loyalty to truthfulness of the storytelling.

Description, Styles, and Purposes of Documentaries

The structure and timetable of the production for a documentary will be based on the specific project. Documentary filmmakers usually say that the main difference in documentaries comes from the main purpose of the project.

Is the project attempting to *document* and explain the truth of something that is or will be readily available, such as the construction of a building or a high-school football game?

For a project such as this, the director, producer, and crew can agree upon what elements will be included in the shoot (interview, time-lapse videography, B-roll), schedule the shoot, and edit it together, a relatively

Tip:
Capture audio B-roll of background sounds (traffic, horns, helicopters) at your locations as well. This may help smooth out your transitions and fill empty areas of your soundtrack.

straightforward procedure. B-roll or **cutaways** are shots used to show something referenced by the interviewees while they are speaking. The term refers to older methods of editing motion pictures, where a shot of an interviewee (nicknamed *talking head*) would be on the *A-roll* of film and shots to overlay or cut away from would run parallel on the B-roll.

The following are two examples of this type of documentary:

- *Gimme Shelter* (1970): This is a visual account of the Rolling Stones 1969 tour and the tragic concert at Altamont Speedway in California in which a concertgoer was killed. The Maysles Brothers, wanting to create a true record of the events, made a point of minimizing the participation of the camera and not reframing reality through the editing process. Interestingly, Martin Scorsese and George Lucas both served as camera operators covering the concert for the Maysles.

- *The Civil War* (1990): Ken Burns breathed new life into the historical documentary with his juxtapositioning of period music, talking-head commentary, narration of period documents including personal letters, and reliance on period photos that he panned over and slowly zoomed into in a manner that has since been referred to as the *Ken Burns effect*.

An alternative style of documentary is the **investigative style**, in which a topic is chosen but the entire narrative of the piece, the individuals to be investigated and interviewed, and even the schedule of filming depend entirely on the day-to-day results of the filming.

This type of filmmaking, in which the camera and the crew may be much more active and involved (and can even change the direction of the story), can take a lot longer (and may therefore be more expensive) and is more likely to fizzle out if the story doesn't go anywhere interesting.

Many documentary filmmakers have tales of films they developed and worked on, only to walk away from the project when the investigation dried up or took an unpredicted turn.

The following are a couple of popular investigative documentaries from the last few years:

- *Super Size Me* (2004): Morgan Spurlock wondered whether eating fast food, particularly McDonald's, was really unhealthy, so he documented himself eating something from the McDonald's menu three meals a day for 30 days. As a participant rather than an observer, when his investigation/experimentation compromised his health, Spurlock had to visit his doctor, the result of which changed the course of his documentary.

- *Fahrenheit 9/11* (2004): This strong critique of the Bush administration's response to the terrorist attacks of September 11, 2001, produced and directed by Michael Moore, is the most commercially successful documentary of all time. Its release also highlights the challenge posed to filmmakers who speak truth to power. When the Walt Disney Company, the parent company of the production company that made the film, tried to block its release, the producers bought back the rights and released it independently. This film's road to release is representative of the trend that media critical of federal and state administrations has to be produced and distributed independently of either large corporations or corporate-owned news agencies.

- *Hoop Dreams* (1994): This doc directed by Steve James followed two high-school basketball players over several years, documenting their lives while investigating the many influences that direct young people toward success or failure and going with the two young men wherever life took them.

It is not uncommon for the producers of documentaries, especially the low-budget variety, to work on them for several years, particularly if the project is investigative in nature and takes any number of turns while filming.

An Ethical Impact

Documentaries, actually all audio and video products, demonstrate how the audio and video production industry has an **ethical** impact on society. Ethical means relating to moral principles or standard values of what is right and what is wrong. That impact can be positive or negative.

It is human nature to be influenced by things you see and hear. On the positive side, people can learn about things that might not have known before being exposed to the media product. They might be outraged by the same injustice that prompted the documentarian to create the film, or motivated to work harder or be stronger, or otherwise develop positive personal characteristics.

On the negative side, media content producers can use their skill with story telling, video capture, and editing to create a product that inspires hate or fear, or appeals to the basest human instincts.

Since the beginning, there have been people claiming that the audio and video production industry has a bad influence on society. They say music lyrics are hateful, racist, and misogynistic, and that video games are violent and encourage people to lose touch with reality.

In response to consumer concerns, both the motion picture and video gaming industries have rating systems to identify violent or adult content. There are also laws and regulations that control some content, such as the Communications Decency Act of 1996, which allows the Federal Communications Commission (FCC) to prohibit the broadcast of obscene or indecent language.

Still, media creators have great freedom to publish and distribute content of all types. The audience can choose what to watch, and should choose what to believe. Being aware of the ethical impact your projects might have is your responsibility.

Truth or Fiction?

Most people identify a documentary as something based on facts. They expect a documentarian will approach a subject *objectively*, which means without bias. In truth, many so-called documentary films and television shows play as fast and loose with the truth as their fictional cousins.

Sometimes, documentarians are subjective, which means influenced by pre-conceived ideas, values, or opinions. They rewrite or edit the "script" during the postproduction process, in order to achieve a desired effect or deliver a specific message.

In an early behind-the-scenes account of the MTV show *The Real World* (1992–present), before the rules of modern reality television were etched in stone, the producers were dismayed to find that the seven charismatic, multicultural young people they'd hired weren't doing much of anything while the cameras were rolling. They were just seven nice-looking diverse people from different parts of the country sitting around watching TV, which does not make for a very interesting hour of television.

One of the most successful early examples of combining documentary and fiction storytelling was Robert Flaherty's *Nanook of the North* (1922). In this filmed actuality, the lives of Inuit natives were staged by the filmmaker to re-create aspects of their indigenous ancestors' lives from centuries before, though the staging was not revealed to the audience (see **FIGURE 6.5**).

PHOTO BY ROBERT J. FLAHERTY, PUBLIC DOMAIN

FIGURE 6.5 Nanook, the Harpooner, subject of *Nanook of the North* (1922)

By making one of the seminal documentaries of the silent era of film, Flaherty also laid the groundwork for a new genre: the **docudrama**.

The other towering figure in the development of the documentary from this time is the Russian filmmaker Dziga Vertov, whose ground-breaking 1929 film *Man with a Movie Camera* (see **FIGURE 6.6**) showed as much innovation in the development of the documentary as Méliès and Porter had done years before with narrative—superimpositions, montages, freeze frames, and jump cuts. Much of what Vertov concocted for this and other films was considered **avant-garde,** or ahead of its time. His goal, and the goal of his filmmaking collective, the Kinoists, was to find new ways for film to show reality by getting rid of the elements—actors, sets, a script, even titles—that created the artificial world that distances the audience from most films.

FIGURE 6.6 Poster art for *Man with a Movie Camera* (1929)

Over the next 30 years, the documentary developed all over the world along the paradigms discussed earlier in this chapter—news, observational, and propaganda. The main aspects of documentaries that distinguished them from television and movies was their relatively low production costs.

As a result, their producers were not as beholden to corporate interests as their TV and feature-film counterparts. They could be more sophisticated and intellectual in the range of ideas they presented since they didn't need, as TV and movies typically did, to reach the whole available audience.

The next major development in documentary production came in the late 1950s as the result of a number of technical innovations. First was the introduction of new lightweight, handheld film cameras produced by the ARRI Group. These more compact cameras and the portable Nagra reel-to-reel audio tape, along with the crystal sync process that allowed the filmmakers to record sync sound without needing a cable between camera and recorder, made portable shooting much more doable.

This marked an exciting and empowering revolution in filmmaking that some would argue is comparable to the latest digital revolution.

The goals of the Direct Cinema movement, which started in Quebec around this time and expanded to the United States, were to use this new equipment to show real life, as opposed to what they saw as the artificiality of Hollywood and the increasing reluctance of television journalism to take on government and big business.

Filmmakers, including Drew Associates—a collective including Richard Drew, D.A. Pennebaker, and the Maysles Brothers—took the techniques they developed as journalists, engineers, and photographers and developed them into films such as *Yanqui, No!* (1960), *Primary* (1961), and *Salesman* (1969). These Drew Associates docs were sometimes critical of the U.S. government and culture and showed the audience the lives of those profiled in the film—salesmen, politicians, South American citizens with negative impressions of the United States—without commentary or editorial judgment.

For many, this approach represented a new independent vision and voice, an American version of *cinema vérité*. This was confirmed when Drew Associates as a journalistic enterprise was dropped by its corporate sponsors, Time-Life.

The opportunities for filmmakers with a passion for their topic and limited funding have exploded over the past 25 years. Throughout this chapter you will find lists of incredible films that celebrate what is good (*Spellbound*, 2002; *Wordplay*, 2006), criticize what is wrong (*Enron: The Smartest Guys in the Room* (2005); *Inside Job*, 2010), and make audiences wonder about life and the world they live in (*Koyaanisqatsi*, 1982; *Crumb*, 1994).

With the advent of smaller camcorders, phones, and mobile devices with built-in HD cameras, as well as social media, everyone is a potential documentarian. Not only can anyone broadcast content direct from their smartphones via sites such as Facebook, Twitter, and Instagram, but with Final Cut Pro, Adobe Photoshop, and Adobe After Effects, everyone can edit and produce quality video, as well. The following events are only a few that were documented by individuals who were in the right place at the right time and recorded footage that changed the world:

- The Los Angeles riots of 1992/the Rodney King beating (videotaped by George Holliday)

- The Arab Spring (2011), democratic revolutions in Egypt and elsewhere documented variously on Facebook, circumventing state media

- The death of Osama bin Laden (2011), posted on Twitter before it was carried by major news outlets

There are so many more ways to get a piece in front of an audience now than there were even ten years ago. Social media, including Twitter, YouTube, and Facebook, has risen up to provide powerful tools for circumventing the traditional channels of news delivery. The power to distribute news is no longer in the hands of the few. As a result, the challenge of controlling what the audience gets to see has become nearly impossible for major news corporations.

One key takeaway from the growth of **citizen journalism**, which is the collection, distribution, and analysis of news and information by the general public, is that it is more important than ever before for audiences and consumers of media to be aware of the content source. Is it news? Is it entertainment? Is it propaganda? The best approach is to check for accuracy and validity before trusting what you see and hear.

Docudrama: The Two-Headed Monster

It's not only the line between news and propaganda that has become blurry. The difference between documentary and fiction is less clear than even, mainly because of the development of the **docudrama**. A docudrama dramatizes real events and may juxtapose them with interviews and news reports to heighten the sense of reality and engagement with the audience.

There is a wide spectrum of media projects along which adherence to the truth may or may not be key to the production and goals of the project. Many of these projects are described as "inspired by true events" and "based on true events."

One example from the "fictional" world of docudrama, *Boys Don't Cry* (1999) documented the real-life story of Brandon Teena. Teena was a transgendered individual who was born biologically female but who chose to live as a man and was killed by acquaintances in Nebraska.

The film was inspired by an article in the *Village Voice* about Teena, who was born Teena Brandon. Filmmaker Kimberly Peirce read the story and connected deeply to Teena's life and plight. Her passion for the story inspired producers to develop and buy a script and produce a film.

The film was released to great acclaim. However, the real-life version of one of the characters objected to her portrayal in the film. She argued in a lawsuit that events dramatized in the film were depicted inaccurately.

So, did Peirce and her team, in an effort to maximize empathy for the character of Brandon Teena and perhaps encourage tolerance for the transgendered community, stray from the facts? Were the facts correct in ways that the real people involved did not want to acknowledge? Or was the truth somewhere in between?

Since there were no cameras on the original events, it is impossible to know how significant the difference is between reality and what was filmed. But the truth is, even if there were cameras rolling, it would be hard to know. The truth is a mystery, left to the interpretation of those with the will to create a media project "inspired by real events."

Everyone has biases, and everyone has their own set of priorities when they create a media piece. They decide just how much liberty they are willing to take with the objective details of the story itself in order to get at what they feel is an underlying, more important, or universal truth.

Transforming the Form

Over the past 100-plus years, some of the most interesting media projects have defied expectations of what a film is or what a documentary should be.

These works sometimes transcend the requirements of nonrealistic story styles such as **surrealism** and **expressionism** and can be described as **metafiction**, works that comment on, play with, or subvert the form or rules of narrative storytelling itself.

Don Quixote, the 1605 Spanish novel by Miguel de Cervantes, is most associated with the development of metafiction. In this book, a middle-aged gentlemen deludes himself that he is a knight and goes on a series of quests whose purpose is to revive chivalry.

Different readings of the text over the centuries interpreted *Don Quixote* (see FIGURE 6.7) as social commentary, farce, philosophical novel, or self-reflexive treatise on the relationship between life and fiction. It is considered the first modern novel, and so can be considered the father of the modern metafictional documentary or fiction film hybrid.

Besides the projects already discussed in this chapter and throughout this book, some of these historical paradigm busters are the following:

- *Cannibal Holocaust* (1980): This cheerfully titled fake horror doc gave birth to the whole **found footage** craze. In this genre, finished fictional works are purported to be real, mysteriously discovered documentaries in order to engage the audience on a deeper level, paving the way for *The Blair Witch Project* (1999), *Paranormal Activity* (2007), and *Chronicle* (2012).

- *Tarnation* (2003): This is a postmodern hybrid of documentary and home movie, created by Jonathan Caouette and edited from hundreds of hours of his family's home movie footage along with current interviews with his mother and other family members.

- *The Act of Killing* (2012): Directed by Josh Oppenhemier, this doc features reenactments of murders committed during the Indonesian purges of 1965–1966, performed by the leaders of the death squads that carried out the original murders. Some killings are staged in the style of a musical or other film genre to enhance the presentational approach of the filmmakers. In one scene, a real-life murderer plays his own victim and then breaks down talking about the experience.

FIGURE 6.7 Bronze statues of Don Quixote and Sancho Panza at the Plaza de España in Madrid, Spain

Developing a Theme: Nonfiction

There are three main steps that will help you develop a documentary that other people find interesting and worth watching.

1. Research media such as books, films, and television shows that are relevant to your topic. Look for those that might overlap with your project or have covered your material in a way that might make yours seem like a cliché, or at the very least creatively undernourished.

   If you make a project where you eat only Burger King for a month to see what happens to you, don't be surprised if folks say, "Oh, so it's like *Supersize Me*...but with Burger King instead of McDonald's." There may be a bit of disconnect between your drive to make that project and the world's enthusiasm to receive it.

2. Narrow your topic. Less is more. Or rather, more specific is more. Think about the length and other limits on your project and try to make sure the scope of your project matches this. For instance, *The History of Drug Abuse in America* is probably too ambitious for a 10-minute piece. But you could, with the proper access, profile someone struggling with drug addiction in that amount of time and, with a decent amount of research and visualization using your subject's pictures and home video, create a vivid and memorable portrayal of one person's struggle.

3. Present all sides of the argument in your doc. Minimize editorializing when you let the other side present their case. Providing an objective view will make your argument stronger.

In the Beginning

A nonfiction project or documentary is a perfect opportunity to examine real-world issues that relate to current topics, such as health care, government, business, or education. It gives you a chance to pick a topic that interests you, ask meaningful questions, and produce something that will encourage other people to become interested and ask meaningful questions, too.

Two ways to start developing your documentary are by choosing something you'd like to know more about and then investigating it, or by seeing something you think is wrong and trying to figure out why. Here are some other questions to ask:

- Is there a topic you feel strongly about that you think has not been adequately covered in the news, or where you feel the media's take on the subject doesn't get at the real story?

- Is there a story you've heard from a friend or family member that has stayed with you, that you want to learn more about, or that you thought others would be interested in hearing?

- Is there something happening in the world that touched your heart in such a way that you wanted to help and contribute to forming a solution to that problem?

This happens for a lot of young people, most prominently in 2012 when a video called *Kony 2012*, produced by a group called Invisible Children Inc., premiered on YouTube. It detailed the atrocities committed by African militia leader Joseph Kony, who commands a group that forces children into brutal service.

Demonstrating the massive potential of social media, within days *Kony 2012* was watched by approximately half of the young people in the United States and was declared the number-one viral video of all time. It generated national support for the "Stop Kony" cause and motivated the U.S. government to send troops to Africa in response.

- Is there an interesting family story you would like to document? These may be the most personal subjects, and also the easiest to access.

Planned Spontaneity: Structuring an Unscripted Project

Just as with a fiction film, the preproduction process for documentaries involves successfully completing several steps.

1. Select key crew members such as producer, director, camera operator, and sound recordist. Frequently, depending on the timeframe of shooting your project and your budget, the key production personnel (usually the director and producer) may need to draft available crew members as needed since the project may not be full-time.

   Additionally, even more so than in fiction films, it is normal for the key participants in documentary productions to "wear many hats," or serve in multiple positions, such as producer as director or director as producer.

2. Make sure the whole team is on the same page regarding the vision and goals of the project. Communication is key. Don't be afraid to rock the boat by getting your vision out there in front of your colleagues, but also listen to what they have to say. The more people talk, the more you will learn where any differences in opinion lie. This can save a lot of arguments later.

3. Script or outline as much as possible. Where will you film? What will you research? Who will you interview on camera? Depending on what type of doc you are making, you will be more or less able to prepare the majority of your filming beforehand. Even if there are surprises, or unexpected events, your organizational and proactive planning abilities will be paramount to your success.

4. Create as much of a budget and schedule as possible. This will allow you to maximize your results and manage expectations for your shooting.

5. Research thoroughly. Choose archived images and audio thoughtfully. In the place of fiction films' production design and costume design, your project may require substantial research until you find just the right historical information, images, and audio to support the subject of your project.

Once you find the material you need, make sure you have permisson to use it! The process of making sets and costumes is typically replaced by applying for the correct license to use whatever elements you want to the copyright holder.

6. Discuss the stylistic guidelines of your project with your team. If you are conducting interviews, will your subjects be seen on camera? Will subjects look into the camera to respond, or look off-camera? Will audio from your interview continue as you cut away to B-roll shots that complement or contrast what your interviewee is saying? It's helpful for the crew to know what you expect and need to achieve the product you want.

If you plan any sort of commercial release for your doc, you will have to obtain a license for the use of any music playing in the background of your shots. You may want to choose to shoot in places where music is not play-ing, or to turn off music that is playing, if that is an option. You will also need permission to use any other media—photos or video clips you use in your film—that you do not create yourself.

Also, just as in a fiction project, you will need *location releases* for any places you film and *consent forms* that state that anyone featured in your project agreed to be filmed. If you interview a subject younger than 18, the consent forms must be signed by a parent or legal guardian.

Choose the Right Gear

The proper equipment will allow you to maximize your results and man-age expectations for your shooting. This may include the following:

FIELD (PRODUCTION) SHOOTING

- Lightweight camera with stabilizer
- Reflector boards
- Radio microphone
- Boom microphone
- Tripod

INTERVIEWS

- Lightweight camera with stabilizer
- Basic three-point lighting kit
- Halogen lights
- China ball
- Gels
- Reflectors
- Extensions
- Clothes pins

Crew Positions: Nonfiction

How many crew members do you need to make your documentary? This depends on what it is and how much footage you need.

Although many crew positions have similar responsibilities to a fiction film, it's not uncommon to see documentaries conceived, produced, directed, and edited by one or two creators who wear various hats, meaning they perform many jobs, throughout the production process.

Especially at the low-to-medium end of the budget spectrum, the do-it-yourself (DIY) mentality and maverick style can be a good fit for documentarians.

However, for those who don't want to go it along, the most common crew list for documentary films includes the following positions/responsibilities:

- *Director/interviewer*: The creative boss of the project also typically asks the questions of subjects interviewed in the project.

- *Producer*: This role can be combined with the director; however, many project creators agree that two project leaders can be useful during production.

- *Camera operator/director of videography*: This role may be performed by a number of different crew members over the course of the shoot. The additional camera credits for a doc are typically long because any number of filming days and locations might necessitate adding on or substituting more crew members.

  However, unless your documentary involves producing reenactments or other dramatizations (approximating the requirements of a fiction film shoot), the doc's camera "crew" will frequently be one or two members at a time.

- *Sound mixer/recordist*: This role can be combined with the *camera operator* depending on crew availability and shooting logistics. For instance, will recording "clean" audio where you are filming require one crew member's undivided attention? If so, you will need someone dedicated to that job.

- *Editor*: As with a fiction film, the editor helps the director find the story in the footage, while adhering to whatever standard of journalistic integrity furthers the goals of the project.

- *Assistant director (AD)/production crew*: If scenes are dramatized for the doc production, then an AD plus production assistants, and a larger camera crew, grip, and electric crew and hair and makeup team may be required.

- *Production assistant (PA)*: The smaller the crew, the more responsibility each member will have. The PA on a doc might need to have even more hustle than his fiction-film counterpart.

Postproduction: Color Correction and Grading

Near the end of postproduction comes the time for **finishing**. In this context, finishing does not mean being done with the project. Rather, it means using **color correction** and **grading** techniques to apply the finishing touches to your work.

Color Correction and Grading

The processes of *color correction* and *grading* let you adjust the look of your shots to match other shots in a scene and to reflect your visual design and style.

There are two risks when starting this process. One, you could become overwhelmed with the number of controls that can be used to manipulate your images. Or, two, you could get carried away and make too many changes to your images, to the point where your shots are unrecognizable or look obviously over-manipulated.

With either occurrence, you can let time be on your side, rather than against you. Just like with preproduction, creating a clear plan of attack for the color correction of your project will keep you on track. A good way to plot your plan is a prioritized to-do list. It is easier to make such a list by knowing the types of corrections you can to make to your images.

CORRECTION FOR FORM AND STANDARDS

A video image needs to adhere to certain standards, especially if it is intended for broadcast. If you've been using your camera controls correctly and lighting aesthetically and effectively, you may think your shots don't need any correction. These shots are not high-priority items. The shots that are high-priority are the ones that you play back and say, "Whooooah, was the operator even looking at the viewfinder?"

Depending on shooting circumstances or the skill level of your camera operator, you might find some common errors in your image, such as the following:

- White-balance shift (cold or warm images)

- Overexposure or underexposure

- Excessive head space

- Excessive nose room or lead space

- Slanted horizon line (due to unbalanced tripod)

- Shakiness

While it is always best to avoid these problems from the beginning, they can be improved upon at this point in the process. Still, remember that there are limits to what every correction tool can accomplish.

GRADING FOR STYLE AND TONE

Beyond correcting a video image to meet basic image standards and balancing color, the same tools can allow you to enhance your image to meet a desired style or tone. If your project fits within a certain genre, you likely designed a look for the imagery during production through production design, lighting, and camera techniques.

To complete the look and make sure it's balanced throughout the program, **color grading** is necessary. The terms *color correction* and *color grading* are somewhat interchangeable. Correction implies there is a problem, whereas grading (also known as **color timing**, when referring to film) intends a deliberate artistic enhancement of the image.

Good, bad, or indifferent, a trend has emerged where certain genres have acquired a specific look or color palette. Here are some examples:

- Movies that take place in the past have an aged, warm, or **sepia** tone

- Horror movies have a cool, blue look

- Movies that take place after an apocalypse are washed out, **desaturated**, or lack color

- Sci-fi movies tend to have a specific *futuristic* color palette, sometimes layered over every shot, like the color green in *The Matrix* (1999)

- Blockbuster action movies have adopted the use of **complementary colors** such as orange and blue, which are opposite to one another on the **color wheel** and cancel each other out when combined

LUMINANCE, HUE, AND CHROMINANCE

Three properties that make up the image of a video signal are **luminance**, **hue**, and **chrominance** (see FIGURE 6.8). Understanding these three properties is essential to being able to correct or create the look of the images in your projects.

> **Note:**
> Hue control can also be done through a Color Board as in the Color Adjustment mode in Apple Final Cut Pro X. The rectangular shape allows you to add or remove a chosen hue vertically.

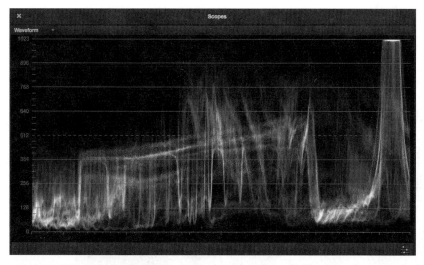

FIGURE 6.8 The waveform monitor in Blackmagic Design DaVinci Resolve color corrector

Luminance is the measurable intensity of light or brightness in an image. In video, luminance is measured by **IRE** (named for the Institute of Radio Engineers) units on a **waveform monitor** or scope; 0 IRE represents true black where 100 IRE represents pure white. Any parts of an image that are at or beyond either end of the spectrum lose all perceptible detail.

Hue is the specific value or color within the color wheel (see **FIGURE 6.9**). A hue is a pure color, not defined by brightness or vibrance of the color. The color wheel is the chart that shows the relationship between **primary colors**, **secondary colors**, and all colors in between.

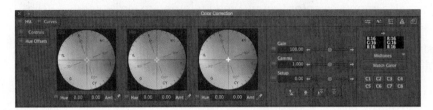

FIGURE 6.9 The color wheel controls in Avid Media Composer

If you've taken an art class, you learned that the primary colors are red, yellow, and blue. In painting, the **subtractive color** model is used, whereas video uses the **additive color** system in which the primary colors are red, green, and blue (see **FIGURE 6.10**).

Additive color works by combining two or more colors to create other colors. When an equal amount of red, green, and blue are added, you get white. Combining two of either primary colors creates secondary colors. Green and blue make cyan; blue and red make magenta; red and green make yellow.

Chrominance, or **saturation**, is the value of vibrancy of a color or hue. It can be described as how *much* color is in an image, or how colorful it is. An image with no chrominance would be considered **black and white** or **grayscale**.

Hue value and chrominance are measured on a *vectorscope monitor* (see **FIGURE 6.11**). The vectorscope uses the same shape and positions as the color wheel. The distance between **traces**, or pattern the chrominance signal draws on the vectorscope, and the center of the scope determines the image's chrominance or saturation.

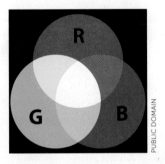

FIGURE 6.10 Additive color system

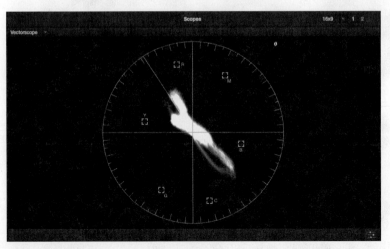

FIGURE 6.11 The vectorscope monitor in Blackmagic Design DaVinci Resolve

PRIMARY CORRECTION

Whether you are correcting an image for form or for style, the first step is primary color correction, which can be achieved in color correction software using your keyboard and mouse or using an external control surface (see **FIGURE 6.12**). In most video color correction tools, control is split between three parts of the image: **shadows**, **midtone**, and **highlights**. Shadows are the darker parts of the image that fall within the lower 30 percent of the waveform monitor. Highlights are the brighter parts of the image that fall within the upper 30 percent of the waveform monitor. Midtones, or *mids*, are what is in between.

FIGURE 6.12 The Tangent Wave color correction control surface

The Flesh-Tone Line

On a color correction vectorscope, a line runs between red and yellow. That is the **flesh-tone line**, representing the tone of human skin. The first question that commonly arises when learning this is, "Whose flesh tone? Certainly not everyone's."

Yes, everyone's. The flesh-tone line points to the hue of human skin with blood underneath it. Technically speaking, the difference of skin tone our eyes perceive from humans of various races and ethnicities is only a difference in how reflective the skin is (luminance) and the saturation (chrominance) of the flesh-tone hue. All human beings' skin is the same color. The vectorscope sees no race or ethnicity.

The controls of each of the three parts blend into the others, so there's no definite value in which shadows end and midtone begins. Within those three parts, you can control the luminance (also called **contrast control**) and hue. Saturation or chrominance controls commonly apply to the entire image.

To get started, turn on your scopes, particularly your waveform monitor and vectorscope. The first step in primary color correction is to fix the luminance using the contrast controls. If your image has a serious color shift that is really obvious, ignore the urge to adjust the color before you've adjusted the contrast.

1. Adjust the contrast control for the mids. Think of this as adjusting the exposure of your shot. Get the image in a range that you determine fits the desired tone for the shot.

2. Adjust the contrast control for the highlights to bring detail back to parts of the image that have gone beyond 100 IRE (brightness). Try to bring all the traces to stay no further than 90–100 IRE.

3. Adjust the contrast control for the shadows. Be careful; this control has more extreme results with the tiniest of adjustment.

Next, move on to adjusting color controls. If it's clear that there was an error in color correction, for instance if the image is too cold, first adjust only the color wheel on the highlights. You will be directing the image toward the desired hue, so if it is cool, move the color control away from cyan and blue and toward yellow and red. On the vectorscope, you should see the traces settle closer to the middle (see **FIGURE 6.13**).

If your image still has a slight shift in white balance, after adjusting the highlights color control, adjust the color control for the mids but only slightly. If there is a human face in the shot, especially a close-up, you might see the traces pointing toward the flesh-line (see **FIGURE 6.14**). Since human flesh tone falls mostly within the midtones of an image, the mids controls are where you want to adjust an image to get an accurate representation of color. Try to adjust control to get the traces to line up closely with the flesh-tone line.

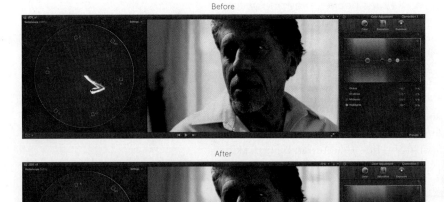

FIGURE 6.13 Before and after primary color correction

FIGURE 6.14 Traces on a vectorscope along the flesh-tone line

After contrast and hue adjustments, you might want to adjust the saturation. If your image was overexposed and you had to bring the contrast controls down to reduce brightness, your image may seem too saturated now. The opposite is true as well: an image that needed to have a boost in brightness because it was shot too dark will seem washed out and could use a slight lift in saturation.

SECONDARY CORRECTION

Once you have the overall image corrected through primary color correction, you might want to add another layer of correction to fix a specific part of the image. For example, if you wanted the sky to be more vibrant, adding saturation or adjusting the color in primary color correction can affect the rest of the image undesirably.

With secondary color correction, you can **mask** an area of your shot or key a specific value to change only what you need corrected (see FIGURE 6.15). With this method, you can change the color of an object or a piece of clothing. Try not to get too carried away because doing this can be time-consuming, so focus on making only changes that are essential to the story.

FIGURE 6.15 After secondary color correction

Other types of secondary correction can include adding a filter, such as fog or grain. You might also want to add a **vignette**, which is the darkening of the corners, to bring the audience's attention toward the center of the frame.

Postproduction: Delivery and Exhibition

Just when you think it's over, there's another phase in the postproduction process to pull you back in. You've gone through the marathon of completing a video project. If the project is personal, you might just export and upload it to a video-hosting service like YouTube or Vimeo. But, if the project is for broadcast or has to be delivered to a client, a contest, or a festival, there are some other considerations to make.

CREATE A MASTER

There are a growing number of exhibition platforms and opportunities for video projects, and they all have different requirements. Because of this, you will need to deliver your project in a variety of formats. If it has a long life and if interest in your project continues deep into the future, you may need to deliver your project in formats that don't exist today, for uses you didn't originally intend.

To prepare for the **delivery** and **archiving** of your project, you must first create a **master file**. A master file is the completed project in a high-quality format. Expect your master file to be hefty in size because high quality means low compression, and low compression means a large file size. All other copies you need to make, either for the Web, consumer disc formats, or specific exhibition requirements, will be based on this master file.

If you can afford to store a large file, either because you are rolling around in data storage space or because your project has a short running time, creating an uncompressed master file is an excellent choice to preserve the quality of your work. Alternatively, the *codec* or *compression format* that was chosen for editing is a safe choice of format for the creation of your master file. Codecs designed for editing, such as the Apple Pro Res and Avid DNxHD families, have a comfortable amount of compression. Although not **lossless**, a compression method that results in no loss of data or quality, mastering to the format the video was edited in does not cause any loss of quality, as would mastering to a format designed for web distribution, such as H.264.

QUALITY CONTROL, SPEC SHEETS, AND DELIVERABLES

Most projects have specific quality and technical criteria. These may be established by the client, by the outlet that will host the finished project, or by you, the content creator.

Quality control is a process you use to make sure your project meets the highest standards, or at least the standards you set for it. You start this in preproduction, and follow it through until the project is complete. The client may provide a quality control check list, itemizing the criteria to meet, or you can create one of your own. It will help you monitor the product quality throughout the project.

There is a document, called a **spec sheet**, that describes the technology specifications. The client or host will provide it, or you will create one for your own project. For example, festivals and competitions have specific technical requirements for submission (see **FIGURE 6.16**).

It is your responsibility to create a master file and other **deliverables** that meet these specifications. You do this beginning with preproduction, when you define the technology specifications for your project. What format will you use? What will the running time be? How many frames per second? This is the information found in a spec sheet.

LALIFF 2011
YOUTH FILMMAKERS' SHOWCASE
FILM SUBMISSION FORM

Submission deadline Must be received by your teacher/instructor by Thursday June 30th, 2011 by 5pm
Please print clearly. This form must be completed for <u>each</u> film submitted.

Title _____
Teacher(s) _____
Director(s) _____
Writer(s) _____
Logline (One sentence maximum)
_____

Film Synopsis (Three sentences maximum)
_____
_____
_____

Year of Completion _____ (film must have been completed within past school year)
Total Running Time _____ min
Language (If other than English) _____
English Subtitles? (circle one)   Yes   No
Submission Category/Genre (Check One)
○ Animation Narrative Newscast/Commercial Music Video
○ Documentary/Mockumentary Experimental Public Service Announcement
Will you permit the use of a 1 minute excerpt for television, website, or other promotional use? (circle one)   Yes   No

CHECK-OFF LIST
All following items must be included with each film submission.
○ Completed and signed Submission Form with each film entry
○ Film cover art (if any)
○ At least two (2) digital film stills (600 DPI) for program booklet
○ Labeled DVD with title, length, production date, director name, teacher email and phone

TERMS OF AGREEMENT
• I hold the Festival harmless from damage to or loss of the print (DVD/Mini-DV tape) en route or otherwise during the course of the Festival's possession of the film, and agree to provide the festival with a print of the film at my own risk.
• I agree that all materials will be submitted and understand that submissions will not be returned whether or not my film is selected.
• I understand that the number of screenings, days, and venue is at the sole discretion of the Los Angeles Latino International Film Festival (LALIFF)
• I understand that the festival does not pay rental fees. Once a film is submitted for entry, it may not be withdrawn from judging.
• I understand that if my project was exhibited at last year's Youth Filmmaker' Showcase, it will be disqualified from the competition this year.
• I understand that all incomplete Youth Filmmakers' Showcase submission forms will be disqualified.
• I agree that if I am selected as a finalist, I am required to attend the showcase on Sunday July 24th, 2011 from 10pm to 12pm for the showcase and 7 pm to receive my award.
High School films must be works shot, directed, and produced by high school or secondary school (pre-college) students. Adult supervision must be limited to advisory capacity.

Teacher Signature _____ **Date** _____
Teacher Name (Print) _____
Email _____ **Phone** _____
High School/Youth Center _____

FIGURE 6.16 Submission form for a student film showcase

The following items are what you might find in a spec sheet:

- Total running time (TRT) limit or range

- Tape format, if tape is required instead of a file

- Raster size or resolution (for example, 1920 x 1080)

- Aspect ratio

- Frame rate (for example, 23.98, 29.97, 59.94)

- Codec or compression type (for example, Apple Pro Res 422 HQ, Avid DNxHD, H.264)

- Video color space (for example, YUV [YCbCr], RGB)

- File bit rate, if compression is required

- Audio format (for example, two-channel stereo, 5.1 surround)

- Timecode

Tip:
Some networks and most video sharing Web sites publish their standards and spec sheets. The BBC has especially well-formatted, informative, and detailed standards documents.

Deliverables are items that you are required to deliver along with the video, including materials for print, publicity, or legal documentation. For example, you might be asked to deliver a compressed video file for Web viewing or previewing along with the high-quality video file. Projects that will have an international audience might require separate audio files containing the production audio (dialogue), music, and sound effects separated. These are called **audio stems**.

Other deliverables might include the following:

- Video files in different formats

- A transcript of all dialogue and audio for closed captioning

- Promotional photos or screengrabs

- A short synopsis of the project

- A credit list

- Copies of talent and crew release forms

- Copies of licensing agreements

Note:
U.S. law requires that all broadcast programs must contain closed captioning. Online video-hosting services also support closed captioning and contain tools to help you easily transcribe your videos, including automatic transcribing. Although not yet required by law, consider adding captions to all your online videos as to not limit your audience and exclude those who are hearing disabled.

To make sure your project meets all technical specifications and quality standards, you must monitor all processes from preproduction to postproduction, making sure that the established criteria are met.

Archiving Your Project

Preserving your master file is serious business. All physical media, including hard disks, optical media, tape media, or solid-state drives, wear out over time. Sometimes storage systems fail. Standards change, and the software and hardware in use now for reading and playing back files might not work, be available, or exist in the future. Even professionals with access to costly, state-of-the-art technology have to follow the same guidelines to archive and preserve media as everyone else.

The first line of defense against the march of time is having **duplicate copies** with **geographic separation**. The reason for duplicate copies is to ensure that the data still exists if either drive fails. The reason for geographic separation is to ensure the data still exists if there is theft or damage at the location of either copy.

Cloud storage is a convenient way to store and protect your data. It is also useful to be able to access your data from any location in the world with Internet access. Be careful as to which networks you choose to upload your valued data. Some cloud storage services have clauses in their terms and conditions that allow the service to claim ownership of the data you upload to their servers.

Your master is in two places, geographically separated, only on cloud services that allow you to retain ownership of your data. Does this mean you can sigh a breath of relief? Yes. But not for long. Data rots. Believe it or not, data sitting on a drive collecting dust can degrade over time. The reasons for **data degradation** (also known as **data rot**) depend on the kind of physical media used to store the data.

To battle this, keep your files moving. Set a reminder for every six to eight months to move your important data from one location to a new one. This is called **data migration**. All this moving around could cause some confusion as to where you left your files and which copy is the latest, so keep records of where your data is stored and backed up so that you can easily find it when you need it, and use a file naming scheme that identifies the content and the date. While following these measures may seem obsessive, you can rest easy knowing you don't have to do this to all your data, only the data you want to keep.

Resume and Portfolio Development

Developing professional habits is the best way to be treated as a professional. This includes having the information that every prospective client or employer will ask for ready when you are offered a gig or if you apply for a job. The two most requested items are a **resume** and a **showreel**.

Building a Resume

The writing of a resume focusing on entertainment industry jobs (see FIGURE 6.17) is similar to the writing of a traditional resume. Every resume is expected to have the following sections:

- Your contact information
- Your education
- Your experience
- Your awards, honors, and accomplishments
- Your skills

FIGURE 6.17 A standard business resume

You can find numerous examples of different styles and formatting of resumes online. The good thing about writing a resume for an industry job is that you can have fun and be creative with the design.

Other than starting with your contact information, the order of the rest of the resume is something you can play with until it looks good to you.

IT'S ALL ABOUT THE EXPERIENCE

The main difference between an industry resume and a traditional resume is that the experience and skills sections may be organized differently. Most resumes have experience listed in chronological order from latest job or gig to earliest. This works fine under two conditions: one, on all of the projects you've worked on, you performed the same job; or, two, on all of the projects you've worked on, you had multiple roles and responsibilities.

With each listing, you identify the project name if you worked freelance, or company name if you worked on a staff. Follow that with the timeframe of the work and the job title or titles you had within the listing. If you think your resume might be a little light, add a description of what your job responsibilities were on the show or company you listed. You can also list some details about what type of project it was and any awards or accolades the project received, even if you were not the recipient.

You should organize your experience section in subsections, if there are large differences in the type of work you did or if you had what might be considered a career or focus shift.

For example, if half of your listed experience was as an assistant editor and the other half was as an editor, that might warrant splitting it into two subsections, even if you went back and forth between job titles for a while.

> **Note:**
>
> When writing your resume, do your best to fit it onto one side of a single page. If your resume spills a little onto a second page, it's best to cut it down rather than stretch it to fit two pages.

SKILLS

For the skills section of your industry resume, it is a good idea to separate your skills into subsections. Devote one section to your technical skills that relate directly to the work you are trying to get. It can include specific tools and gear that you are experienced in using, and industry-specific software. Do not list any technical skills you are not yet supremely confident about.

The other subsection of your skills section can focus on basic career skills, such as office software proficiency and **soft skills**. Soft skills are personal traits and abilities that can't be proven by a certification, a credential, or a degree. Soft skills include the ability to communicate, manage time, be reliable, solve problems, work collaboratively, be confident and accountable for oneself, and bring a strong work ethic to a project.

Creating a Showreel

A *showreel*, also called a **demo reel** or just a **reel**, is a **portfolio** of samples of your best work. When putting your reel together, it's best to avoid creating a fast-cut montage for the whole duration. A short, quick montage is fine for the introduction with your name and title, but the purpose of the reel is to give the viewer a strong sense of what your work is like.

When cutting your reel, start by gathering the masters of each of your projects. If you can't obtain the masters, get the highest-quality versions possible. Once ingested and organized in a project or event, mark selects for each of the samples you plan on assembling. The duration of each sample should be long enough to give the viewer a sense of the tone and pace of the original material but not long enough to bore them. Aim for your samples to be around 30 seconds each.

If you don't have a clear idea about how to structure your reel, you can either assemble the samples in chronological order—beginning with your latest work and ending with your earliest—or start and end with the two strongest pieces that represent you best.

The complete duration of your reel should be somewhere between three and five minutes long. If it's not quite three minutes, there's nothing wrong with adding a second sample from a project you are most proud of. If it's longer than five minutes, lift out samples that are low in quality or don't show your best work.

Once you have the duration set, it's time to move some clips around. If you find that there is a clip somewhere in the middle of your assembly that is clearly the most impressive sample of your work, move it to the top of your sequence. Transitions from one sample to the next are important, too. Look for thematic connections if at all possible to create a flow for the viewer.

Laying out your samples from best to worst order is not necessarily the best approach. If it's clear to the viewer that as they watch the reel is worsening, there's no reason for them to keep watching. Keep a solid, fun, and/or powerful sample for the end of the reel to leave a good impression.

> **Note:**
> Even if you have worked only on student productions, don't be embarrassed about listing them in your resume. It's better to have those projects listed than to have an empty resume. As time goes on and you build a history of more professional-level experience, you will cut those earlier projects from your list.

Having formed the body of your reel, you can then have some fun and cut together a fast-paced, ten-second music montage to put at the top of your reel, acting as a grabber, and finish with your name and career title before going into your first sample of work. Use snippets of your work that were not in any part of the main assembly. Be creative and have fun with it because you are selling yourself and designing your brand. Slap on the same title after the last clip to bookend your reel.

Mix your audio so that the volume levels are consistent from one clip to the next. Cross-fade between samples to blend abrupt transitions. Use all the skills and knowledge you have acquired to make the best looking reel you can, including applying color-correcting and grading to improve your clips.

When the reel is complete, post it online, embed it in your personal Web site, and even burn it on a business card-shaped optical disc. The point is to get it into people's hands and in front of their eyes, so they know you are ready to work. You have messages to deliver and a professional career to build.

End-of-Chapter Activities

REVIEW QUESTIONS

1. What is a documentary?

2. What is the goal of a news video?

3. What is the goal of an entertainment video?

4. What is propaganda?

5. Give one positive and one negative example of the ethical impact of the audio and video production industry on society.

6. What is a master file and why is it important?

7. What is the purpose of color correction and grading?

8. List at least five items you might find on a spec sheet.

9. What is a resume and what information should you include on one?

10. What is a showreel and what information should you include in one?

Review Project 1

Develop a list of real-world issues relating to current topics that you would like to examine in more detail. For example, you might want to explore why health care costs are so high, why there are no term limits for U.S. Supreme Court Justices, how the stock market is influenced by emotion, or why charter schools cause conflict. Write a pitch for a documentary about each issue on your list.

Review Project 2

Using the information in this chapter and additional information you find through research, analyze the ethical impact of the audio and video production industry on society. Evaluate the content you find for accuracy and validity, and keep track of your sources so you can cite them properly. When your research is complete, use the information to create a poster illustrating something you have learned. Explain your poster to a partner or to the class.

Review Project 3

Find the technical specifications for a video sharing Web site or a student video competition. Create a video that meets the specifications.

Review Project 4

With a partner, develop technology specifications for an audio/video project. Trade your spec sheet with another team, and create a video that meets the specifications.

CHAPTER 6 – PORTFOLIO BUILDER

DOCUMENTARY

The documentary is nonfiction, but it is not unbiased like broadcast news and journalism should be. There's a great amount of freedom in creating a documentary, but without boundaries and limitations, it can be difficult to define and shape a story.

The audience is lenient in its expectations of production quality, with good reason, because there are no opportunities for multiple takes if anything goes wrong while acquiring footage. The documentary is designed to educate and motivate its audience to act, but is ultimately a form of entertainment. For these reasons, the creation of a documentary can be both an excruciating and exhilarating experience.

DIRECTIONS

This project is designed to culminate all the skills learned and practiced from each chapter of this book. The workflow cannot be rigidly defined because subject and topic choice, shooting circumstances, and the complexity of the form itself will require you to put into full gear your practice of critical thinking and problem-solving skills.

DEVELOPMENT

Unlike a scripted narrative film, a documentary has most of its writing and structure created during post-production. That doesn't mean you should just shoot whatever strikes you and see what you can slap together while editing. Start the process by meeting with your team to discuss the project, assign roles, and brainstorm topic ideas. Next, choose a topic and begin the research you will need to answer the following questions:

1. Who is your audience?

   Be specific. Just answering "Everybody" creates a problem. Programming created for a distinct audience requires specific considerations. For the success of your documentary, narrow your audience by demographic information such as age, gender, geographic location, languages known, education level, ethnicity, abilities, and now even species.

2. What do you want your audience to do after watching your documentary?

   Just like with a call to action in a public service announcement (PSA), having an expected outcome for the message you deliver will guide you in creating your story.

Continue to research your topic and keep up-to-date with any current events that are relevant to your story. Watch other documentaries on your topic. Rewatch your favorite documentaries to get inspiration for stylistic choices.

Write an outline of what you would like your story to look like. As you continue your research and gather footage (which is still a form of research), there will be changes to your outline.

PREPRODUCTION

The workflow of a documentary has much more flexibility than a scripted project, but planning, scheduling, and budgeting are still not only useful but requirements. Continue meeting regularly with your team to make sure you are all on the same page, working toward the same goal.

1. Establish technical and quality criteria for the projects. Create a spec sheet to list the technology specifications and a quality control sheet you can use to monitor the processes until the project is complete.

2. Create a list of the interview subjects you would like to have in your documentary.

   Go through the list and contact each one to make a pitch and schedule an interview.

3. Create a master schedule of all your shoots.

   Any original material you need to acquire for B-roll and montages needs to be scheduled like with any other shoot.

   When scheduling your interviews, allow time for the pre-interview to discuss your topic with your subjects before throwing them under lights and in front of the lens.

4. Create a budget. Shooting a documentary can mean more shoot days and a lot more travel to get from interview to interview. With a documentary where one subject is followed, or all events take place in a single location, meals for crew and talent, gas, equipment rental, and expendables must all be taken into consideration.

PRODUCTION

Follow your schedule as closely as you can, but expect frequent changes as your interview subjects request to reschedule. When shooting your documentary, keep an open mind about what you will learn from the people you interview and what you capture. It is inevitable that what you thought your documentary was going to look like and be about will be different when it's all put together. Continue to meet with your team to monitor progress, processes, and quality throughout.

POSTPRODUCTION

Stay flexible in anticipation of revelations about your story as you piece it together in editing.

If your shoot takes place over a long period of time, the post process should overlap with production. Documentaries will have more footage to manage than scripted narrative projects. Follow these steps to take control of the process:

1. Transcribe your interviews.

   Being able to see, as text, what was said during the interviews will make it much easier to narrow down the footage for the assembly. The process of transcribing will help you become more familiar with your footage.

2. Create a **paper cut**.

   To create a paper cut, mark down the numbers of the first and last frames of each shot and arrange into the order you want to use. Like choosing quotes when writing an essay, a paper cut is a script with the actual words from your footage that will allow you to get a better handle on the overall structure of your story before putting together your assembly.

3. Create bins or keyword tags for multiple subjects to keep your selected footage organized.

4. Mark your footage, based on your paper cut, and place it in the proper bins or mark it with the appropriate keywords.

5. Splice together only your interviews into the assembly based on the paper cut.

   Before adding B-roll or cutting together montages, feel free to reorder any interview segments if you discover that a different order works better than what you expected when you put it together on paper.

6. Add appropriate B-roll over your talking heads and cut together your planned montages.

   Allow at least four to five seconds somewhere within the first instance of a talking head shot uncovered by B-roll to establish who is speaking, and allow time enough to read any lower-third title cards.

7. Add title cards that are important to the story, such as lower-thirds or expository text.

8. Before spending any time on color correction or serious audio sweetening, show your assembly to your crew and trusted advisors to convey notes on improving the cut or make sure the story makes sense and the message is clear to others.

9. Duplicate your sequence to keep a record of the first cut and then make all suggested trims and changes.

10. Repeat steps 8 and 9 until you are sure that your message is ready for delivery.

11. Color correct, add graphics, and sweeten and mix your audio.

12. Create a master file.

13. Publish your final product according to the establish specifications.

14. Deliver your message.

Chapter 7

Getting Started with Adobe Premiere Pro

Chapter 7 Overview

- Exploring Nonlinear Editing in Premiere Pro

- Defining the Standard Digital Video Workflow

- Touring the Premiere Pro Workspace

- Customizing the Workspace

- Examining Tools for Working with Audio and Video

- Recording Quality Video

- Capturing Video for Editing in Premiere Pro

- Project Planning and Management

- Creating a Premiere Pro Project File

- Setting Up a Sequence

- Identifying Audio Track Types

- Importing Assets

- Using a Tapeless Workflow

- Finding Assets with the Media Browser

- Importing Images

- Recording a Scratch Narration Track

- Exploring the Project Panel

- Working with Bins

- End-of-Chapter Review and Activities

Adobe® Premiere Pro® is video editing software that supports the latest technology and cameras with powerful tools that are easy to use and that integrate with almost every type of media, as well as a wide range of third-party plug-ins and other post-production tools.

In this chapter you will gain hands-on experience working with Adobe Premiere Pro. You will learn about the main components in the Premiere Pro interface and how to use and customize them. You will explore methods for recording quality audio and video clips, then capturing and ingesting the clips so you can edit them with Premiere Pro. You will learn how to create a new project and choose sequence settings that control the way Premiere Pro plays your clips. Finally, you will import media assets into your projects and organize those assets within the Premiere Pro environment.

Exploring Nonlinear Editing in Premiere Pro

Recall that there are two basic types of video editing processes: linear and nonlinear. **Linear editing** was developed for working with video tape. It required selecting, arranging, and modifying images and sound in a predetermined, ordered sequence. Each desired video clip had to be isolated and recorded (or dubbed) onto a master tape. Linear editing is economical and has application to projects in which you simply want to add a video clip to the end of another. But today, the standard is nonlinear editing.

Premiere Pro is a **nonlinear editing system** (NLE). Like a word processor, Premiere Pro lets you place, replace, and move footage anywhere you want in your final edited video. You can also adjust any parts of the video clips you use at any time. You don't need to perform edits in a particular order, and you can make changes to any part of your video project at any time.

With Premiere Pro, you combine multiple clips to create a sequence that you can change simply by clicking and dragging with your mouse. You can edit any part of your sequence, in any order, and then change the contents, move clips so that they play earlier or later in the video, blend layers of video together, add special effects, and more.

You can even combine multiple sequences and jump to any moment in a video clip without needing to fast-forward or rewind. It's as easy to organize the clips you are working with as it is to organize files on your computer.

Premiere Pro supports both tape and tapeless media formats, including XDCAM EX, XDCAMHD 422, DPX, DVCProHD, AVCHD (including AVCCAM and NXCAM), AVC-Intra, and DSLR video. It also has native support for the latest in raw video formats, including media from RED, ARRI, and Blackmagic cameras.

Defining the Standard Digital Video Workflow

As you gain editing experience, you will develop your own preference for the order in which to work on the different aspects of your project. Each stage requires a particular kind of attention and different tools. Also, some projects call for more time spent on one stage than another.

Whether you skip through some stages with a quick mental check or spend hours (even days!) dedicated to perfecting an aspect of your project, you will work through the following steps:

1. Acquire the video. This can mean recording original footage or gathering assets for a project.

2. Capture (transfer or ingest) the video to your hard drive. With tape-based formats, Premiere Pro (with the appropriate hardware) can convert the video into digital files. With tapeless media, Premiere Pro can read the media directly, with no need for conversion. If you are working with tapeless media, be sure to back up your files to a second location because physical drives sometimes fail unexpectedly.

3. Organize your clips. There can be a lot of video content to choose from in your project. Spend the time to organize clips together into special folders (called bins) in your project. You can add color labels and other metadata (additional information about the clips) to help keep things organized.

4. Combine the parts of the video and audio clips you want as a sequence and add them to the Timeline.

5. Place special transition effects between clips, add video effects, and create combined visual effects by placing clips on multiple layers (tracks).

6. Create titles or graphics, and add them to your sequence in the same way you would add video clips.

7. Mix your audio tracks to get the combined level just right, and use transitions and effects on your audio clips to improve the sound.

8. Export your finished project to videotape, to a file for a computer or for Internet playback, to a mobile device, or to a DVD or Blu-ray Disc.

Premiere Pro supports each of these steps with industry-leading tools.

Touring the Premiere Pro Workspace

It's helpful to begin by getting familiar with the editing interface. To make it easier to configure the user interface, Premiere Pro offers workspaces. Workspaces quickly configure the various panels and tools onscreen in ways that are helpful for particular activities, such as editing, special effects work, or audio mixing.

Try It!

1. Launch Premiere Pro.

To Launch Premiere Pro CC on a Mac:

Do one of the following:

- On the startup drive, open the Applications > Adobe Premiere Pro CC folder, then double-click the Adobe Premiere Pro CC application icon. (The year of release will also be included after CC in the program name.)

- Click the Adobe Premiere Pro CC application icon in the Dock, if it is available.

- To launch Premiere Pro by opening a file, double-click an Adobe Premiere Pro CC file icon or drag an Adobe Premiere Pro CC file icon over the application icon in the Dock.

- Open Launchpad, then click the Premiere Pro CC application icon.

To Launch Premiere Pro in Windows:

Do one of the following:

- In Windows 8, display the Start screen, then click the tile for Adobe Premiere Pro CC.

- In Windows 10, click the Start button, choose All Apps, then click Adobe Premiere Pro CC.

On the Start screen of Premiere Pro, you can start a new project or open a saved one.

1. Click Open Project.

2. In the Open Project window, open **Ch07_01.prproj** from the data files for this chapter.

3. Save the file as **Ch07_01_xx.prproj** in the location where your teacher instructs you to store the files for this chapter, and leave the file open.

All Premiere Pro project files have a .prproj file extension

The Workspace Layout

Before you begin, make sure you are using the default Editing workspace.

Try It!

1. Choose Window > Workspaces > Editing.

2. Choose Window > Workspaces > Reset to Saved Layout.

3. In the Project panel, double-click the clip in the upper-left to display it in the Source Monitor panel (see **FIGURE 7.1**).

Although it might look confusing at first, the Premiere Pro interface is designed to make video editing easy. The principal elements are shown in **FIGURE 7.1**.

> **Note:**
> You may be prompted with a dialog box asking where a particular file is stored. This will happen when the original files are saved on a hard drive different from the one you are using. You will need to identify the storage location. Navigate to the asset files for this chapter and select the file to open. Premiere Pro will remember this location for the rest of the files.

> **Note:**
> To reset the workspace layout in a version of Premiere Pro prior to CC 2015:
> 1. Choose Window > Workspace > Editing.
> 2. Choose Window > Workspace > Reset Current Workspace.
> 3. Click Yes in the Reset Workspace dialog box.

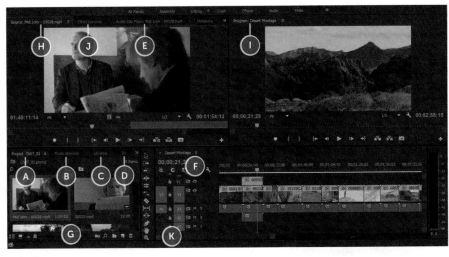

FIGURE 7.1

A. Project panel
B. Media Browser panel (hidden)
C. Info panel (hidden)
D. Effects panel (hidden)
E. Audio Clip Mixer (hidden)
F. Timeline panel
G. Clips
H. Source Monitor
I. Program Monitor
J. Effect Controls panel (hidden)
K. Tools panel

Tip:
Rest your mouse pointer on any icon in the Premiere Pro workspace to display a tooltip identifying the name and purpose of the icon.

Each workspace item appears in its own panel, and multiple panels can be combined into a single frame. Some items with common industry terms stand alone, such as Timeline, Audio Clip Mixer, and Program Monitor. The main user interface elements are as follows:

- **Timeline panel:** This is where you will do most of your actual editing. You view and work on sequences in the Timeline panel. One strength of sequences is that you can nest them (place sequences inside other sequences). In this way, you can break up a production into manageable chunks or create unique special effects.

- **Tracks:** You can layer—or *composite*—video clips, images, graphics, and titles on an unlimited number of tracks. Tracks in Premiere Pro are similar to layers in Photoshop and Flash. Video clips on upper video tracks cover whatever is directly below them on the Timeline. Therefore, you need to give clips on higher tracks some kind of transparency or reduce their size if you want clips on lower tracks to show through.

- **Monitor panels:** You use the Source Monitor (on the left) to view and select parts of clips (your original footage). To view a clip in the Source Monitor, double-click it in the Project panel. The Program Monitor (on the right) is for viewing your current sequence.

- **Project panel:** This is where you place links to your project's media files: video clips, audio files, graphics, still images, and sequences. You can use bins—similar to folders—to organize your assets.

- **Media Browser:** This panel allows you to browse your hard drive to find footage. It's especially useful for file-based camera media.

- **Effects panel (FIGURE 7.2):** This panel contains all the clip effects you will use in your sequences, including video filters, audio effects, and transitions. It's docked, in this workspace, with the Project panel. Effects are grouped by type to make them easier to find.

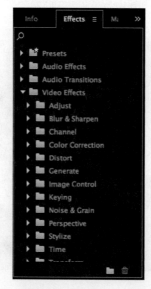

FIGURE 7.2

- **Info panel:** The Info panel (docked, by default, with the Project panel and Media Browser) presents useful information about any asset you select in the Project panel or any clip or transition selected in a sequence.

- **History panel:** This panel (docked, by default, with the Effects and Info panels) tracks the steps you take and lets you back up easily. It's a kind of visual Undo list. When you select a previous step, all steps that came after it are also undone.

- **Audio Clip Mixer** (FIGURE 7.3): This panel (docked, by default, with the Source, Metadata, and Effect Controls panels) is based on audio production studio hardware, with volume sliders and panning knobs. There is one set of controls for each audio track on the Timeline. The adjustments you make are applied to audio clips. There's also a dedicated Audio Track Mixer for applying audio adjustments to tracks.

FIGURE 7.3

- **Effect Controls panel** (FIGURE 7.4): This panel (docked, by default, with the Source, Audio Clip Mixer, and Metadata panels) displays the controls for any effects applied to a clip you select in a sequence. Motion, Opacity, and Time Remapping controls are always available for visual clips. Most effect parameters are adjustable over time.

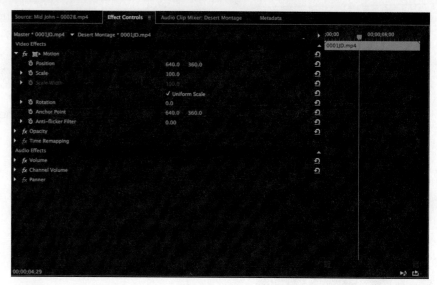

FIGURE 7.4

- **Tools panel** (FIGURE 7.5): Each icon in this panel represents a tool that performs a specific function, typically a type of edit in a sequence. The Selection tool is context-sensitive, which means it changes appearance to indicate the function that matches the positioning. If you find your pointer doesn't work as you expect, it might be because you have selected the wrong tool.

FIGURE 7.5

Customizing the Workspace

In addition to customizing the default workspaces (based on tasks), you can adjust the position and location of panels to create a workspace that works best for you. You can then store a workspace or even create multiple work-spaces for different tasks.

• As you change the size of a frame, other frames change size to compensate.

• All panels within frames are accessible via tabs.

• All panels are dockable—you can drag a panel from one frame to another.

• You can drag a panel out of a frame to become a separate floating panel.

In this exercise, you will try all these functions and save a customized workspace.

Try It!

1. Click the Source Monitor panel (selecting its tab if necessary), and then position your pointer on the vertical divider between the Source Monitor and the Program Monitor. Then, drag left and right to change the sizes of those frames. You can choose to have different sizes for your video displays.

2. Now place the pointer on the horizontal divider between the Source Monitor and the Timeline. Drag up and down to change the sizes of these frames.

3. Click the tab for the Effects panel (to the left of the name), and drag it to the middle of the Source Monitor to dock the Effects panel in that frame.

   When many panels are combined in a single frame, you may not be able to see all the tabs. If a panel contains hidden tabs, a horizontal double chevron appears at its upper-right corner. Click this to display a menu of all of the tabs in the panel. You can also display a panel by choosing it in the Window menu.

4. Drag the Effects tab to a point near the right of the Project panel to place it in its own frame within the panel (FIGURE 7.6).

> **Note:**
> As you move a panel, Premiere Pro displays a drop zone. If the panel is a rectangle, it will go into the selected frame as an additional tab. If it's a trapezoid, it will go into its own frame.

FIGURE 7.6

The drop zone is a trapezoid that covers the right portion of the Project panel. Release the mouse button, and the Project panel is now divided into two frames, one containing the Effects tab and the other containing the remaining tabs.

You can also pull a panel out into its own floating panel.

5. Click the Source Monitor's tab, and hold down the Ctrl (Windows) or Command (Mac) key while dragging it out of its frame.

6. Drop the Source Monitor anywhere, creating a floating panel. Resize it by dragging from a corner or a side like any other panel (**FIGURE 7.7**).

FIGURE 7.7

7. As you gain experience, you might want to create and save the layout of your panels as a customized workspace. To do so, choose Window > Workspaces > Save As New Workspace. Type a name, and click OK.

8. If you want to return a workspace to its default layout, choose Workspaces > Reset to Saved Layout. To return to a recognizable starting point, choose the preset Editing workspace and reset it now.

9. Save the changes to **Ch07_01_xx.prproj** and leave it open.

Exploring Preferences

The more you edit video, the more you will want to customize Premiere Pro to match your specific needs. There are several types of preferences, all grouped into one panel for easy access.

Try It!

1. Choose Edit > Preferences > Appearance (Windows) or Premiere Pro > Preferences > Appearance (Mac).

2. Drag the Brightness slider to the left or right to suit your needs (FIGURE 7.8). When you are done, click OK, or click Default to return to the default setting.

FIGURE 7.8

The default brightness is a neutral gray to help you see colors correctly.

3. Switch to the Auto Save preferences.

   Imagine if you had worked for hours and then there was a power cut. If you hadn't saved recently, you'd have lost a lot of work.

   Premiere Pro automatically saves a backup copy of your project file while you work, in case of system failure. Premiere Pro is integrated with Adobe Creative Cloud, so an additional backup project file can be saved to your Creative Cloud shared files folder if you check the box in this dialog box.

4. Click Cancel.

5. Reset the Editing Workspace to the saved layout, save the changes to **Ch07_01_xx.prproj**, and close the Premiere Pro project file.

Moving, Backing Up, and Syncing User Settings

User preferences include a number of important options. The defaults work well in most cases, but as you become more familiar with the editing process, it's likely you will want to make a few adjustments.

Premiere Pro includes the option to share your user preferences between multiple machines: When installing Premiere Pro, you will have entered your Adobe ID to confirm your software license. You can use the same ID to store your user preferences in Creative Cloud, allowing you to sync and update them from any installation of Premiere Pro.

You can sync your preferences on the Start screen by choosing Sync Settings Now, or you can sync your preferences while working with Premiere Pro by choosing File > Sync Settings and then choosing the *Adobe CC ID number* (Windows) or Premiere Pro > Sync Settings > *Adobe CC ID number*.

This option to sync preferences between multiple machines makes it easier than ever to move your creative work from one location to another.

Examining Tools for Working with Audio and Video

Audio (sound) and video (movies and animations) are essential components of multimedia. You will need these tools to work with multimedia.

- Video camera: Video cameras (also called video recorders) range widely in price and features. You can shoot quality video with a camera that has full manual image control and audio control and XLR audio inputs. Some of the more expensive cameras offer bigger imaging chips and interchangeable lenses.

- Tripod: A tripod is useful for not only recording video but also serves as a handy platform to put your camera on instead of laying it on the ground when you are not recording.

- Microphone(s): On-camera mics (the ones built into the video camera) can be useful for reference, but they capture all the sound in the environment and, if you are shooting from a distance, they might not pick up the audio you are hoping to record. There are several types of microphones available. These include handheld mics like those used in public address systems; shotgun mics which are placed on a boom pole to get the mic close to the sound source, while keeping it out of the camera frame; and lavalier microphones, or body mics that are clipped to clothing. If they are not built in, microphones are connected to a camera or audio recorder with cables. The most common cable used in professional audio recording is a cable that has XLR connectors with three pins at each end.

XLR connectors allow for a balanced audio connection and therefore longer-distance runs with less noise in the signal. Lavalier mics can be part of a wireless kit that consists of a transmitter, which stays with the "talent," and a receiver, which is connected to the audio or video recording device.

- Headphones: Over-ear headphones are more suitable than earbuds. Keep in mind that with a good pair of headphones, what you hear will sound good even at low volumes.

- Lights: Even if you are shooting outdoors or in a well-lit indoor location, lighting is important to the quality and ambience of your video. Incandescent and halogen lights are the most commonly used.

- Audio recorder (for recording audio only): Portable digital recorders come in the following formats: solid state, which use flash memory; hard disk drive, which record to an internal or external hard disk; CD, or compact disc, which record to CD-Rs; and direct-to-computer, which requires a computer with a microphone and analog-to-digital converter that sends the signal into the computer via FireWire or a USB connection.

- Sound card: A sound card is a special expansion board that allows the computer to input, edit, and output sounds. Audio—whether voices, music, or sound effects—is entered into the computer through the input jacks on the sound card. Once audio is captured on the computer's hard drive, you can edit and work with it. You can then play it through the computer's speakers or headphones, or save it to a disc. You can also send it to another audio device using the sound card's output jack. Full-featured cards even include optical inputs and outputs for digital sound and special software for mixing sound.

- Video capture board: Video signals, such as those from television programs or movies, have to be converted into a format that computers understand. This is done with a video capture board, a special card that plugs into a computer. You can transfer video to the capture board from video cameras, digital cameras, and other sources.

After video and audio are saved to the computer's hard drive, you can combine them in new ways. You do this work with a video editor program, such as Premiere Pro.

Safety Considerations

When working with audio- and video-recording equipment, keep these safety guidelines in mind:

- If the device feels hot or begins to smoke, discontinue use and turn it off immediately.

- If you are on rough or unstable terrain, use a tripod to avoid moving around and risking a slip or fall.

- Be careful when handling batteries, especially if you notice any leakage.

- Avoid taking the equipment apart and handling any of the electronic components, as they may cause an electrical shock.

- Do not use the equipment underwater unless it is made specifically for that use.

- Do not use the equipment in dangerous or threatening environments, such as fire scenes or in severe weather conditions, such as tornadoes and floods.

In addition, you must always be aware of ethical issues when recording audio and video. Some guidelines to consider include the following:

- Respect the privacy of others. Almost always, you should obtain permission and consent from the subjects involved in your recording. When the subject is a public figure, you may not need their permission to record.

- Do not record audio or video that harasses, bullies, or defames others.

- Do not portray others in a false or misleading way.

- Be sure to distinguish clearly between what is fact and what is your opinion.

- Adhere to copyright laws. Obtain permission and/or provide attribution for any work you use that was created by another individual.

- Comply with community guidelines posted by video-sharing Web sites.

Recording Quality Video

With your video recorder of choice in hand, it's time to venture out and shoot videos. The better the video segments you capture, the better the completed project will be. Following are some tips for shooting quality video.

Plan Your Shoot

When you consider a video project, plan what you need to shoot to tell the story. Videotaping a soccer championship match, a corporate backgrounder, or a medical procedure each require planning to ensure success. Know what you want your final video project to say, and think of what you need to videotape to tell that story.

Even the best-laid plans and most carefully scripted projects might need some adjusting once you start recording in the field. No matter how you envision the finished project, be willing to make changes as the situation warrants.

Get an Establishing Shot

An establishing shot sets a scene in one image (FIGURE 7.9). Although super wide shots work well (aerials in particular), consider other points of view: a shot from the cockpit of a race car, a close-up of a scalpel with light glinting off its surface, or a shot of paddles dipping frantically in roaring white water. Each grabs the viewer's attention and helps tell your story.

FIGURE 7.9

Shoot Plenty of Video

Videotape is cheap and expendable, and digital video is limited only by the amount of storage space you have. Shoot a lot more raw footage than you will put in your final production. Five times as much is not unusual. Giving yourself that latitude might help you grab shots you would have missed otherwise.

Adhere to the Rule of Thirds for Good Composition

It's called the rule of thirds, but it's more like the rule of four intersecting lines. When composing your shot, think of your viewfinder as being criss-crossed by two horizontal and two vertical lines. The center of interest should fall along those lines or near one of the four intersections, not the center of the image.

Consider all those family photos where the subject's eyes are smack dab in the center of the photo. Those are not examples of good composition.

Another way to follow the rule of thirds is to look around the viewfinder as you shoot, not just stare at its center. Check the edges to see whether you are filling the frame with interesting images. Avoid large areas of blank space.

Keep Your Shots Steady

You want to give viewers the sense they are looking through a window or, better yet, are there with your subjects on location. A shaky camera shatters that illusion.

When possible, use a tripod. The best "sticks" have fluid heads that enable you to make smooth pans or tilts.

If it's impractical to use a tripod, try to find some way to stabilize the shot: Lean against a wall, put your elbows on a table, or place the video recorder on a solid object.

Follow the Action

This might seem obvious, but keep your viewfinder on the ball (or sprinter, speeding police car, surfer, conveyor belt, and so on). Your viewers' eyes will want to follow the action, so give them what they want.

One nifty trick is to use directed movement as a pan motivator. That is, follow a leaf's progress as it floats down a stream, and then continue your camera motion past the leaf—panning—and widen out to show something unexpected: a waterfall, a huge industrial complex, or a fisherman.

Use Trucking Shots

Trucking or dolly shots move with the action. For example, hold the camera at arm's length right behind a toddler as she motors around the house, put the camera in a grocery cart as it winds through the aisles, or shoot out the window of a speeding train.

Find Unusual Angles

Getting your camera off your shoulder, away from eye level, leads to more interesting and enjoyable shots. Ground-level shots are great for frolicking lambs or cavorting puppies. Shoot up from a low angle and down from a high angle (**FIGURE 7.10**). Shoot through objects or people while keeping the focus on your subject.

FIGURE 7.10

Lean Forward or Backward

The zoom lens can be a crutch. A better way to move in close or away from a subject is simply to lean in or out. For example, start by leaning way in with a tight shot of someone's hands as he works on a wood carving; then, while still recording, lean way back (perhaps widening your zoom lens as well) to reveal that he is working in a sweatshop full of folks hunched over their handiwork.

Get Wide and Tight Shots

Grab wide shots and tight shots of your subjects. If practical, get close to your subject to get the tight shot rather than use the zoom lens (**FIGURE 7.11**). Not only does it look better than a medium-angle shot, but the proximity leads to clearer audio.

FIGURE 7.11

Shoot Matched Action

Consider a shot from behind a pitcher as he throws a fastball. He releases it, and then it smacks into the catcher's glove. Instead of a single shot, grab two shots: a medium shot from behind the pitcher showing the pitch and the ball's flight toward the catcher, and a tight shot of the catcher's glove. It's the same concept for an artist: get a wide shot of her applying a paint stroke to a canvas, and then move in for a close shot of the same action. You will edit them together to match the action.

> **Note:**
> Matched action keeps the story flowing smoothly while helping to illustrate a point.

Get Sequences

Shooting repetitive action in a sequence is another way to tell a story, build interest, or create suspense. A bowler wipes his hands on a rosin bag, dries them over a blower, wipes the ball with a towel, picks up the ball, fixes his gaze on the pins, steps forward, swings the ball back, releases it, slides to the foul line, watches the ball's trajectory, and then reacts to the shot.

Instead of simply capturing all this in one long shot, piecing these actions together in a sequence of edits is much more compelling. You can easily combine wide and tight shots, trucking moves, and matched action to turn repetitive material into attention-grabbing sequences.

Avoid Fast Pans and Snap Zooms

Fast pans and zooms fall into MTV and amateur video territory. Few circumstances call for such stomach-churning camera work. In general, it's best to minimize all pans and zooms. As with a shaky camera, they remind viewers they are watching TV.

If you do zoom or pan, do it for a purpose: to reveal something, to follow someone's gaze from his or her eyes to the subject of interest, or to continue the flow of action (as in the floating leaf example earlier). A slow zoom in, with only a minimal change to the focal length, can add drama to a sound bite. Again, do it sparingly.

Shoot Cutaways

Avoid jump cuts by shooting cutaways. A jump cut is an edit that creates a disconnect in the viewer's mind. A cutaway—literally, a shot that cuts away from the current shot—fixes jump cuts.

Cutaways are common in interviews where you might want to edit together two 10-second sound bites from the same person. Doing so would mean the interviewee would look like he suddenly moved. To avoid that jump cut—that sudden disconcerting shift—you make a cutaway of the interview. That could be a wide shot, a handshot, or a reverse-angle shot of the interviewer over the interviewee's shoulder. You then edit in the cutaway over the juncture of the two sound bites to cover the jump cut.

The same holds true for a soccer game. It can be disconcerting to simply cut from one wide shot of players on the field to another. If you shoot some crowd reactions or the scoreboard, you can use those cutaways to cover up what would have been jump cuts.

Use Lights

Lights add brilliance, dazzle, and depth to otherwise bland and flat scenes. Consider using an on-board camera fill light and, if you have the time, money, patience, or personnel, a full lighting kit with a few colored gels.

In a pinch, do whatever you can to increase available light. Open curtains, turn on all the lights, or bring a couple of desk lamps into the room. Keep in mind one caveat: Low-light situations can be dramatic, and flipping on a few desk lamps can destroy that mood in a moment.

Grab Good Sound Bites

Your narrator presents the facts. The people in your story present the emotions, feelings, and opinions. Don't rely on interview sound bites to tell the who, what, where, when, and how. Let those bites explain the why.

In a corporate backgrounder, have the narrator say what a product does, and let the employees or customers say how enthusiastic they are about that product.

Your narrator should be the one to say, "It was opening night, and this was her first solo." Let the singer, who is recalling this dramatic moment, say, "My throat was tight, and my stomach was tied in knots."

In general, even though your interviews might take forever, use only short sound bites in your final production. Use those bites as punctuation marks, not paragraphs.

Get Plenty of Natural Sound

Think beyond images. Sound is tremendously important. Listen for sounds you can use in your project. Even if the video quality is mediocre, grab that audio.

Your camera's on-board microphone is not much more than a fallback. Consider using additional microphones: shotgun mics to narrow the focus of your sound and avoid extraneous noise, lavalieres tucked out of sight for interviews, and wireless mics when your camera can't be close enough to get just what you need.

Capturing Video for Editing in Premiere Pro

In order to edit video that is not already stored in a file format, you must capture or digitize it. (In some programs, capture is synonymous with ingest.)

Capturing is used with live video or video on tape. Premiere Pro saves captured footage to a storage device as files, and imports the files into projects as clips.

Digitizing is used to convert analog video into a digital form so it can be saved as a file.

All that Adobe Premiere Pro does during digital video (DV) capture is to place the video data in a movie file "wrapper" without changing the original DV data.

The capture process in the analog world takes several steps: transfer, conversion, compression, and wrapping. Your camera transfers the video and audio as analog data to a video capture card. That card's built-in hardware converts the waveform signal to a digital form, compresses it using a codec (compression/decompression) process, and then wraps it in the AVI file format on Windows systems or in the QuickTime format for users working on a Mac.

Three DV-Capturing Scenarios

Premiere Pro offers tools to take some of the manual labor out of the capturing process. Three basic approaches exist:

- Capture your entire videotape as one long clip.

- Log each clip's In and Out points for automated batch capturing.

- Use the scene detection feature in Premiere Pro to automatically create separate clips whenever you press the Pause/Record button on your video camera.

To do this exercise, you will need a DV camcorder. You can work with HDV or with a professional-level camcorder with a Serial Digital Interface (SDI) connector and a specialized video capture card.

> **Note:**
> Before beginning the next section you will need to record some footage on a tape-based video camera (camcorder).

Premiere Pro handles HDV and SDI capture with the same kind of software device controls used with a standard DV camcorder. SDI requires an extra setup procedure.

If you have an analog camcorder, you need a video capture card that supports S-Video or composite video connectors. The only option with most analog camcorders is to manually start and stop recording. Most analog capture cards do not work with remote device control or have timecode readout, so you can't log tapes, do batch capture, or use the scene detection feature.

Capturing an Entire Tape

To capture an entire tape, follow these steps.

Try It!

> **Note:**
> When you power up, Windows might display a Digital Video Device connection message. Mac OS may start a default associated application, such as iMovie.

1. Connect the camcorder to your computer.

2. Turn on your camcorder and set it to playback mode: VTR or VCR. Do not set it to camera mode.

Project Settings for SDI or HDV

This chapter assumes you are recording from a DV camcorder: standard 4:3 format or widescreen anamorphic 16:9 screen ratio. If you are working with SDI or HDV, you need to start Premiere Pro, click New Project, and select the preset project settings that match your camcorder.

Try It!

> **Tip:**
> When capturing video, power your camcorder from its AC adapter, not its battery. When using a battery, camcorders can go into sleep mode, and the battery will often run out before you have completed your shoot.

1. Start Premiere Pro and click New Project. Save the file as **Ch07_02_xx.prproj** to the location where your teacher instructs you to store your files for this chapter, and leave it open.

2. Connect your camcorder to your computer using the FireWire or USB connector cables that came with the camera.

3. Choose File > Capture to open the Capture panel.

4. Insert a tape into your camcorder. You will be prompted to give the tape a name.

5. Type a name for your tape in the text box. Be sure not to give two tapes the same name; Premiere Pro remembers clip in/out data based on tape names.

> **Note:**
> To help you identify buttons, in the Capture panel move the pointer over them to see tool tips.

6. Use the VCR-style device controls in the Capture panel to play, fast-forward, rewind, pause, and stop your tape.

7. Try some of the other VCR-style buttons:

   - Shuttle (the slider toward the bottom) enables you to move slowly or zip quickly—depending on how far you move the slider off center—forward or backward through your tape.

   - Single-frame Jog control (below the shuttle slider)

   - Step Forward and Step Back, one frame at a time

   - Slow Reverse and Slow Play

8. Rewind the tape to its beginning or to wherever you want to start recording.

9. In the Setup area of the Logging tab, note that Audio and Video is the default setting. If you want to capture only audio or only video, change that setting.

10. Click the Tape button in the Capture area of the Logging tab or the Record button in the Capture panel to start recording.

    You will see (and hear) the video in the Capture panel and on your camcorder. Since there is a slight delay during capture, you will hear what sounds like an echo. Feel free to turn down the speaker on either your camcorder or your computer.

11. Click the red Record button or the black Stop button when you want to stop recording.

    The Save Captured Clip dialog box appears.

12. Give your clip a name (add descriptive information if you want) and click OK.

    Adobe Premiere Pro stores all the clips you capture in the folder where you save your project.

    You can change the default location by choosing File > Project Settings > Scratch Disks (Windows) or File > Project Settings > Scratch Disks (Mac).

13. Save the **Ch07_02_xx.prproj** file and leave it open.

Using Batch Capture and Scene Detection

When you perform a batch capture, you log the In and Out points of a number of clips and then have Premiere Pro automatically transfer them to your computer.

Use the logging process to critically view your raw footage. You want to look for "keeper" video, the best interview sound bites, and any natural sound that will enhance your production.

The purpose of using a batch capture is threefold: to better manage your media assets, to speed up the video capture process, and to save hard disk space (one hour of DV consumes roughly 13 GB). If you batch capture all your clips, you may use the combination of the Premiere Pro project file (which is relatively small) and the MiniDV tapes as a backup of your project. To re-edit the project, simply open the project file and recapture the clips.

Using a Clip-Naming Convention

Think through how you are going to name your clips. You might end up with dozens of clips, and if you don't give them descriptive names, it'll slow down editing.

You might use a naming convention for sound bites such as "Bite-1," "Bite-2," and so forth. Adding a brief descriptive comment, such as "Bite-1 Laugh," will help.

Here are the steps to follow.

Try It!

Note:

Handles are extra frames at the beginning and end of a clip. For example, adding 30 frames as handles would add 1 second of video to the start and end of your clips. This can be useful for transitions.

1. In the Capture panel, click the Logging tab.

2. Change the Handles setting (at the bottom of the Logging tab) to 30 frames.

   This adds 1 second to the start and finish of each captured clip, which will give you enough head and tail frames to add transitions without covering up important elements of the clip.

   When changing the Handles value, you can click the current number and type a new figure, or you can simply position your pointer over the Handles number and drag left or right to lower or raise the value. This method of changing a numeric value works throughout Premiere Pro.

3. In the Clip Data area of the Logging tab, give your tape a unique name.

4. Log your tape by rewinding and then playing it.

5. When you see the start of a segment you want to transfer to your computer, stop the tape, rewind to that spot, and click the Set In button in the Timecode area of the Logging tab.

6. When you get to the end of that segment (you can use Fast Forward or simply Play to get there), click Set Out. The in/out times and the clip length will appear.

7. Click Log Clip to open the Log Clip dialog box.

8. Change the clip name, if needed, and add appropriate notes if you want; then click OK.

   That adds this clip's name with its in/out times and tape name information to the Project panel (with the word "Offline" next to it). You will go there later to do the actual capture.

9. Log clips for the rest of your tape using the same method.

   Each time you click Log Clip, Premiere Pro automatically adds a number to the end of your previous clip's name. You can accept or override this automated naming feature.

10. When you've finished logging your clips, close the Capture panel.

    All your logged clips will be in the Project panel, with the offline icon next to each.

11. In the Project panel, select all the clips you want to capture.

12. Choose File > Batch Capture.

    A very simple Batch Capture dialog box opens, allowing you to override the camcorder settings or add more handle frames.

13. Leave the Batch Capture options unselected and click OK.

    The Capture panel opens, as does another little dialog box telling you to insert the proper tape (in this case, it's probably still in the camcorder).

14. Insert the tape and click OK.

    Premiere Pro now takes control of your camcorder, cues up the tape to the first clip, and transfers that clip and all other clips to your hard drive.

15. When the process is complete, take a look at your Project panel to see the results. The offline icon is now a movie icon, and your footage is ready to be edited.

16. Save the **Ch07_02_xx.prproj** file and leave it open.

Using Scene Detection

Instead of manually logging In and Out points, you might want to use the scene detection feature. Scene detection analyzes your tape's time/date stamp, looking for breaks such as those caused when you press the camcorder's Pause button while recording.

When scene detection is on and you perform a capture, Premiere Pro automatically captures a separate file at each scene break it detects. Scene detection works whether you are capturing an entire tape or just a section between specific In and Out points.

To turn on scene detection, do either of the following:

- Click the Scene Detect button (below the Record button in the Capture panel).

- Select the Scene Detect option in the Capture area of the Logging tab.

Then you can either set In and Out points and click Record or cue your tape to wherever you want to start capturing and click Record. In the latter case, click Stop when done.

Your clips will show up in the Project panel. You don't need to batch capture them—Adobe Premiere Pro captures each clip on the fly. Adobe Premiere Pro then names the first captured clip by putting a "01" after the name you put in the Clip Name box and increments the number in each new clip name by one.

> **Note:**
> Scene detection works for DV, HDV 1080i, and HDV 720p footage.

Tackling Manual Analog Movie Capture

If you need to transfer analog video—consumer-level VHS, SVHS, Hi-8, or professional-grade video such as Beta SP—you need a video capture card with analog inputs. Most analog capture cards have consumer-quality composite connectors as well as S-Video and sometimes top-of-the-line component connections.

Check your card's documentation for setup and compatibility issues.

With analog video, you have only one capture option—to do it manually.

Try It!

1. Open the Capture panel (File > Capture).

2. Use the controls on the camcorder to move the videotape to a point several seconds before the frame you want to begin capturing.

3. Press the Play button on the camcorder and then click the red Record button in the Capture panel.

4. When your clip has been captured, click the Stop button in the Capture panel and on the camcorder. Your clip will show up in the Project panel.

5. Save the **Ch07_02_xx.prproj** file and then close it.

Capturing HDV and HD Video

You can capture HDV video in the same way as DV video: by connecting the HDV camcorder or deck to your computer via IEEE 1394. When you start a new HDV project, select the appropriate HDV project preset and capture as described for DV video.

HD video requires an SDI card in your computer to connect the coaxial interface from the HD camcorder to your computer. The vendor that supplies the SDI card will typically install additional HD presets into Adobe Premiere Pro as part of its installation.

If you have ventured into tapeless camcorders such as the Panasonic P2 or Sony XDCAMs, the capture process is eliminated altogether.

> **Note:**
> If you are using a Mac to capture HDV, you will have to use the camera's viewfinder or an external TV monitor to preview your footage during the capture process. The preview pane in the Capture panel displays the message: *Previewing on Camera* to let you know that you are actively playing footage.

Project Planning and Management

By now, you've probably realized that creating a digital media project, such as a video, requires a lot of planning, organization, and management. A good manager uses a four-step process to make thoughts and ideas become reality:

1. First, you figure out what needs to be done. You identify the purpose of the project and who it is for, or its audience. This may involve a series of meetings with a client or other stakeholders in which you assess problems that might arise and set goals. Based on the information you gather, you develop a proposal or concept that outlines the scope of the project and identifies the budget, length, and delivery format.

2. Then you develop an action plan with a timeline for completing key parts of the project. You identify and acquire resources, assign responsibilities, and set milestones. You develop the story in the form of a script or screenplay and further define the audience needs. You might flesh out the story in the form of storyboards. You might also need to identify audio needs and requirements.

3. Next, you put the plan into action and execute tasks according to its timeline. You create script breakdowns, if necessary, to detail each task. You monitor the plan to make sure it is going the way you expect. You might even need to make revisions and changes along the way.

4. Finally, you look back to assess and evaluate. Did the plan work the way you expected? Did you achieve your goal? What lessons did you learn?

Capture Format Settings

It's most common to record video as data files you can work with immediately. However, if you are working with archival material, you might need to capture from videotape.

The Capture Format settings menu tells Premiere Pro what tape format you are using when capturing video to your hard drive through your computer's FireWire port.

DV and HDV Capture

Premiere Pro can capture from DV and HDV cameras using the FireWire connection on your computer, if it has one. FireWire is also known as IEEE 1394 and i.LINK.

FireWire is a convenient connection for tape-based media because it uses one cable to transmit video and sound, device control, and time-code information.

Third-party Hardware Capture

Not all video decks use a FireWire connection, so you may need additional third-party hardware installed to be able to connect your video deck for capture.

If you have additional hardware, you should follow the directions provided by the manufacturer to install it. Most likely you will install software supplied with your hardware, and this will discover that Premiere Pro is installed on your computer, automatically adding extra options to this menu and other menus.

Creating a Premiere Pro Project File

A Premiere Pro project file stores links to all the video and sound files—aka clips—used in your Premiere Pro project. A project file also has at least one sequence—that is, a series of clips that play, one after another, with special effects, titles, and sound, to form your completed creative work. You will choose which parts of your clips to use and in which order they'll play. The beauty of editing with Premiere Pro is that you can change your mind about almost anything.

Starting a new Premiere Pro project is simple. You create a new project file, choose a sequence preset, and get on with editing.

The sequence settings control the way Premiere Pro plays your video and audio clips. To speed things up, you can use a built-in preset to choose sequence settings and then make adjustments if you need to (**FIGURE 7.12**).

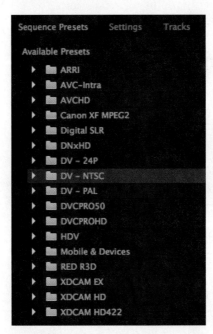

FIGURE 7.12

You need to know the kind of video and audio your camera records, because your sequence settings will usually be based on your original source footage. To make it easier for you to choose the right settings, Premiere Pro sequence presets are named after different camera recording formats. If you know which video format your camera records, you will know what to choose.

Setting Up a Project

You start by creating a new project.

Try It!

1. Launch Premiere Pro. The Start screen displays. There are several options available:

   • **New Project:** Opens the New Project dialog box.

   • **Open Project:** Lets you browse to an existing project file and open it to continue working on it.

   • **Sync Settings:** Allows you to synchronize your user preferences with those you store in Creative Cloud. This makes it easy to move from one editing system to another.

2. Click New Project to open the New Project dialog box (**FIGURE 7.13**).

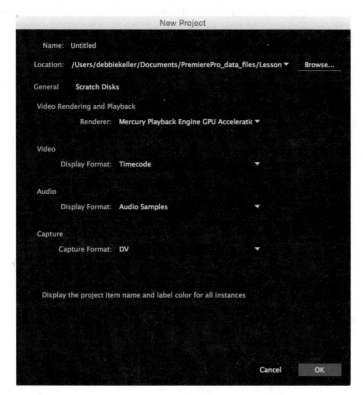

FIGURE 7.13

This dialog box has two tabs: General and Scratch Disks. All of the settings in this dialog box can be changed later. In most cases, you will want to leave them as they are. Let's take a look at two useful areas of the New Project dialog box:

Video Display Format

There are four options for Video Display Format. The correct choice for a given project largely depends on whether you are working with video or film as your source material.

When a camera records video, it captures a series of still images of the action. If there are enough images captured each second, it looks like moving video when played back. Each picture is called a frame, and the number of frames each second is usually called frames per second (fps).

The fps will vary depending on your camera/video format and settings. It could be any number, including 23.976, 24, 25, 29.97, 50, or 59.94 fps. Some cameras allow you to choose between more than one frame rate, with different options for accompanying frame sizes.

The choices are as follows:

- **Timecode:** This is the default option. Timecode is a universal standard for counting hours, minutes, seconds, and individual frames of video. The same system is used by cameras, professional video recorders, and nonlinear editing systems all around the world.

- **Feet + Frames 16mm or Feet + Frames 35mm:** If your source files are captured from film and you intend to give your editing decisions to a lab so they can cut the original negative to produce a finished film, you may want to use this standard method of measuring time. Rather than measuring time, this is the number of feet plus the number of frames since the last foot. It's a bit like feet and inches but with frames rather than inches. Because 16mm film and 35mm film have different frame sizes (and so different numbers of frames per foot), there's an option for each.

- **Frames:** This option simply counts the number of frames of video, starting at 0. This is sometimes used for animation projects and is another way that labs like to receive information about edits for film-based projects.

Scratch Disks Tab

Whenever Premiere Pro captures (records) from tape or renders effects, new media files are created on your hard drive. Scratch disks is the term for the places where these files are stored. Use the Scratch Disks tab in the New Project dialog box to choose the location of these files.

In addition to choosing where new media files are created, you can also choose the location for storing Auto Save files. These are copies of your project file, created automatically while you work. If you need to go back to an earlier version of your project, you can open one of these copies. If you store your Auto Save files in a different location than your project file, they serve as a useful backup in case of system failure. The default location for both Scratch Disks and Auto Save files is Same as Project. (**FIGURE 7.14**).

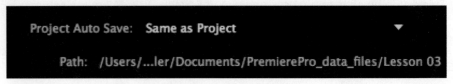

FIGURE 7.14

Try It!

1. Click in the Name box and name your new project **Ch07_03_xx**.

2. Click the Browse button; then choose the location where your teacher instructs you to store the files for this chapter.

> **Note:**
> You'll notice that tabbed panels and dialog boxes appear a lot in Premiere Pro. They are a useful way of packing extra options into a smaller space.

> **Note:**
> The speed of your scratch disks can have quite an impact on playback performance.

3. If your project is set up correctly, the General (**FIGURE 7.15**) and Scratch Disks (**FIGURE 7.16**) tabs in your New Project window should look identical to the screens shown here. If the settings match, click OK to create the project file. If not, go back and make the necessary changes and then click OK.

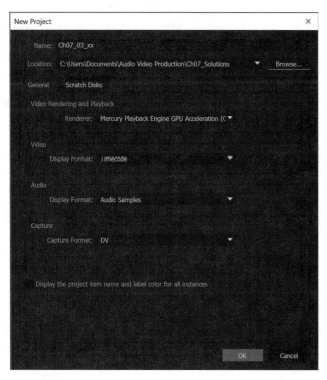

FIGURE 7.15

FIGURE 7.16

Setting Up a Sequence

In your Premiere Pro projects you will create sequences, into which you will place video clips, audio clips, and graphics. If necessary, Premiere Pro adapts video and audio clips that you put into a sequence so they match the settings for that sequence. Each sequence in your project can have different settings, and you will want to choose settings that match your original media as precisely as possible. Doing so reduces the work your system must do to play back your clips, improves real-time performance, and maximizes quality.

If you are editing a mixed-media format project, you may have to make careful choices about which format to match with your sequence settings. You can mix formats easily, but playback performance is best when the sequence settings match.

Creating a Sequence that Automatically Matches Your Source

If you are not sure what sequence settings you should choose, don't worry. Premiere Pro has a special shortcut to create a sequence based on your original media.

At the bottom of the Project panel, there is a New Item menu. You can use this menu to create new items, such as sequences and titles.

To automatically create a sequence that matches your media, drag and drop any clip (or multiple clips) in the Project panel onto this New Item menu button. Premiere Pro creates a new sequence with the same name as the clip and a matching frame size and frame rate. Now, you are ready to start editing, and you can be confident your sequence settings will work with your media.

If the Timeline panel is empty, you also can drag a clip (or multiple clips) into it to create a sequence automatically.

Choosing the Correct Preset

Premiere Pro can play back and work with a very wide range of video and audio formats and will often play back mismatched formats smoothly.

However, when Premiere Pro has to adjust video for playback because of mismatched sequence settings, your editing system must work harder to play the video, and this will impact real-time performance. It's worth taking the time before you start editing to make sure you have sequence settings that closely match your original media files.

The essential factors are always the same: the number of frames per second, the frame size (the number of pixels in the picture), and the audio format. If you turn your sequence into a file, then the frame rate, frame size, and audio format will match the settings you choose here. When you output to a file, you can choose to convert your sequence to any format you like.

If you know exactly which settings you need, Premiere Pro gives you access to all the options to configure a sequence. If you are not so sure, you can choose from a list of presets. To open the New Sequence dialog box, you click the New Item menu button on the Project panel, and choose Sequence.

The New Sequence dialog box has three tabs: Sequence Presets, Settings, and Tracks.

The Sequence Presets tab (**FIGURE 7.17**) makes setting up a new sequence much easier. When you choose a preset, Premiere Pro chooses settings for your sequence that closely match a particular video and audio format. After choosing a preset, you can tweak these settings on the Settings tab.

You will find a wide range of preset configuration options for the most commonly used and supported media types. These settings are organized based on camera formats (with specific settings inside a folder named after the recording format).

You can click the disclosure triangle to see specific settings in a group. These settings are typically designed around frame rates and frame sizes.

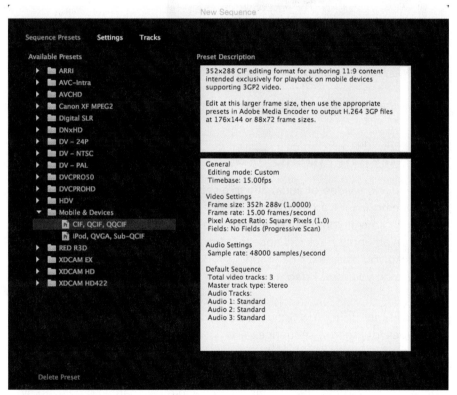

FIGURE 7.17

Try It!

1. Click the New Item button in the Project panel and select Sequence.

2. Click the disclosure triangle next to the group AVCHD.

   You can now see three subfolders, based on frame sizes and interlacing methods. Remember that video cameras can often shoot video using resolutions of HD, as well as different frame rates and recording methods. The media used for the next exercise will be AVCHD at 720p and a frame rate of 25fps.

Note:
If the first clip you add to a sequence does not match the playback settings of your sequence, Premiere Pro asks if you would like to change the sequence settings automatically to fit.

3. Click the disclosure triangle next to the 720p subgroup (**FIGURE 7.18**).

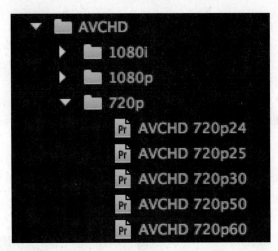

FIGURE 7.18

4. Choose the AVCHD 720p25 preset by clicking its name. Click OK.

5. Save the **Ch07_03_xx.prprog** file and close the project file.

Identifying Audio Track Types

When you add a video or audio clip to a sequence, you will put it on a **track**. Tracks are horizontal areas in the sequence that hold clips in a particular position in time. If you have more than one video track, any video clips placed on an upper track will appear in front of clips on a lower track. For example, if you have text or a graphic on your second video track and a video clip on your first video track, you will see the text or graphic in front of the video.

The Tracks tab of the New Sequence dialog box allows you to preselect the track types for the new sequence.

All audio tracks are played at the same time, creating a complete audio mix. To create the mix, position your audio clips on different tracks, lined up in time. Narration, sound bites, sound effects, and music can be organized by putting them on different tracks. You can easily rename tracks, making it easier to find your way around your sequence. Premiere Pro lets you specify how many video and audio tracks will be added when the sequence is created. You can add and remove audio or video tracks later, but you can't change your Audio Master setting.

You can choose from several audio track types. Each track type is designed for specific types of audio. When you choose a particular track type, Premiere Pro gives you the right controls to make adjustments to the sound, based on the number of audio channels. For example, Stereo clips need different controls than 5.1 Surround clips.

When you add a clip to a sequence that has both video and audio, Premiere Pro makes sure the audio part goes to the right kind of track. You can't accidentally put an audio clip on the wrong kind of track; Premiere Pro will automatically create the right kind of track if one doesn't exist.

Audio Tracks

Audio tracks are the horizontal areas where you will put your audio clips. The types of audio tracks available in Premiere Pro are as follows:

- **Standard:** These tracks are for both mono and stereo audio clips.

- **5.1:** These tracks are for audio clips with 5.1 audio (the kind used for surround sound mixes).

- **Adaptive:** Adaptive tracks are for both mono and stereo audio and give you precise control over the output routing for each audio channel. For example, you could decide the track audio channel 3 should be output to your mix in channel 5. This workflow is commonly used for multilingual broadcast TV.

- **Mono:** This track type will accept only mono audio clips.

Importing Assets

When you import items into a Premiere Pro project, you are creating a link from the original media file to a pointer that lives inside your project. This means you are not actually modifying the original files; you are just manipulating them in a nondestructive manner. For example, if you choose to edit only part of a clip into your sequence, you're not deleting the unused media.

You will import media into Premiere Pro in two principal ways:

- Standard importing by choosing File > Import

- Using the Media Browser panel

When to Use the Import Command

Using the Import command is straightforward (and may match what you are used to from other applications). To import any file, just choose File > Import.

You can also use the keyboard shortcut Ctrl+I (Windows) or Command+I (Mac) to open the standard Import dialog box.

This method works best for self-contained assets such as graphics and audio, especially if you know exactly where those assets are stored and you want to quickly navigate to them. This importing method is not ideal for file-based camera footage, which often uses complex folder structures with separate files for audio, video, and important additional data. For camera-originated media, you will use the Media Browser, instead.

> **Note:**
> Another way to open the Import dialog box is to simply double-click an empty area of the Project panel.

When to Use the Media Browser

The Media Browser (**FIGURE 7.19**) is a robust tool for reviewing your media assets and then importing them into Premiere Pro. The Media Browser shows the fragmented files you might get from a digital video camera as whole clips; you will see each recording as a single clip, with the video and audio combined, regardless of the recording format.

This means you can avoid dealing with complex camera folder structures and instead work with easy-to-browse icons and metadata. Being able to see this metadata (which contains important information, such as clip duration, recording date, and file type) makes it easier to select the correct clip from a long list.

Note:

If you need to use assets from another Premiere Pro project, you can import that project into your current one. Just use the Media Browser to locate it; once you double-click a project, Premiere Pro will reveal all of its assets and its bin structure. You can then navigate through it to select individual clips and sequences or drag the whole project into your current project.

FIGURE 7.19

By default, you will find the Media Browser in the lower-left corner of your Premiere Pro workspace (if your workspace is set to Editing). It's docked in the same frame as the Project panel. You can also quickly access the Media Browser by pressing Shift+8.

You can position the Media Browser elsewhere onscreen by dragging it, or you can undock it and make it a floating panel by clicking the panel menu on the right side of the panel's tab and choosing Undock Panel.

You will find that working in the Media Browser is not significantly different from browsing using your computer's file management program. There are a series of navigation folders on the left side and buttons to navigate forward and backward at the top. You can use the Up Arrow and Down Arrow keys to select items within a list and the Left Arrow and Right Arrow keys to move further along a file directory path (such as stepping into a folder to examine its contents).

The major benefits of the Media Browser include the following:

- Narrowing the display to a specific file type, such as JPEG, Photoshop, XML, or AAF.

- Autosensing camera data—AVCHD, Canon XF, P2, RED, ARRIRAW, Sony HDV, or XDCAM (EX and HD)—to correctly display the clips.

- Viewing and customizing the kinds of metadata to display.

- Correctly displaying media that has spanned clips across multiple camera media cards. This is common in professional cameras, and Premiere Pro will import the files as a single clip even if a longer video file filled one card and continued on a second one.

Using a Tapeless Workflow

A **tapeless workflow** (also known as a file-based workflow) is simply the process of importing video from a tapeless camera, editing it, and exporting it. Premiere Pro CC makes this especially easy because it does not require the media from these tapeless formats to be converted before editing. Premiere Pro can edit tapeless formats (such as P2, XDCAM, AVCHD, and even formats from DSLRs that shoot video) natively with no conversion.

For best results when working with your own camera media, follow these guidelines:

- Create a new folder for each project.

- Copy the camera media to your editing hard drive with the existing folder structure intact. Be sure to transfer the complete data folder directly from the root directory of the card. For best results, you can use the transfer application that is often included by the camera manufacturer for moving your video clips. Visually inspect it to ensure that all media files have been copied and that the card and new copied folder sizes match.

- Clearly label the copied folder of the media with the camera information, including card number and date of shoot.

- Create a second copy of the cards on a physically separate, second drive.

- Ideally, create a long-term archive using another backup method, such as Blu-ray disc, LTO tape, and so on.

Finding Assets with the Media Browser

Using the Media Browser is an easy way to locate and import assets in Premiere Pro.

Try It!

1. Open Premiere Pro, and open **Ch07_04.prproj** from the data files for this chapter.

2. Choose File > Save As.

3. Rename the file **Ch07_04_xx.prproj**, save it in the location where your teacher instructs you to store the files for this chapter, and leave it open.

4. Choose Window > Workspaces > Editing. Then choose Window > Workspaces > Reset to Saved Layout.

5. Click the Media Browser (it should be docked with the Project panel by default). Make it larger by dragging its right edge to the right.

6. To make the Media Browser easier to see, place your mouse pointer over the panel and then press the ` (grave) key (it is often in the upper-left corner of a keyboard).

   The Media Browser panel should now fill the screen. You may need to adjust the width of columns to make it easier to see items.

7. Using the Media Browser, navigate to the folder for the data files for this chapter. You will see individual project files as well as the Ch07_assets folder. The Ch07_assets folder contains several subfolders, which you can open by double-clicking. Double-click the Video and Audio Files folder, then double-click the Theft Unexpected folder.

8. Drag the resize slider at the bottom of the Media Browser to enlarge the thumbnails of the clips (**FIGURE 7.20**). You can use any size you like.

> **Note:**
>
> Filter the assets you're looking for by using the File Types Displayed menu in the Media Browser.
>
> The Media Browser filters out non-media files, making it easier to browse for video or audio assets.

FIGURE 7.20

9. Click the Theft Unexpected folder, and then click any clip in the folder to select it.

   You can now preview the clip using keyboard shortcuts.

10. Press the L key to play a clip.

11. To stop playback, press the K key (**FIGURE 7.21**).

Mid John – 0...   00:03:05:16

FIGURE 7.21

12. To play backwards, press the J key. Press K to stop.

13. Experiment with playing back other clips. If the volume of your computer is turned up, you should be able to hear the audio playback clearly.

    You can press the J or L keys multiple times to increase the playback rate for fast previews. Use the K key or the spacebar to pause.

14. Now you will import all of these clips into your project. Press Ctrl+A (Windows) or Command+A (Mac) to select all of the clips.

15. Right-click one of the selected clips and choose Import (**FIGURE 7.22**).

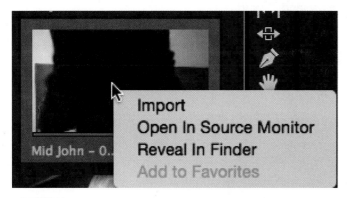

Import
Open In Source Monitor
Reveal In Finder
Add to Favorites

Mid John – 0...

FIGURE 7.22

Alternatively, you can drag all of the selected clips onto the Project panel's tab and then down into the empty area to import the clips.

16. When the import has finished, press the ` (grave) key to restore the Media Browser to its original size. Then switch to the Project panel.

17. Save the project and leave it open.

Importing Images

A multimedia project includes graphics as well as sound and video (and may also include animation). Graphics have become an integral part of the modern video edit. People expect graphics to both convey information and add to the visual style of a final edit. Fortunately, Premiere Pro can import just about any image and graphic file type. Support is especially excellent when you use the native file formats created by Adobe's leading graphic tools, Adobe Photoshop and Adobe Illustrator.

Importing Flattened Adobe Photoshop Files

Anyone who works with print graphics or does photo retouching has probably used Adobe Photoshop. It's the workhorse of the graphic design industry. Adobe Photoshop is a powerful tool with great depth and versatility, and it's becoming an increasingly important part of the video production world. Let's explore how to properly import two files from Adobe Photoshop.

To start, you will import a basic Adobe Photoshop graphic.

Try It!

1. Click the Project panel to select it.

2. Choose File > Import, or press Ctrl+I (Windows) or Command+I (Mac).

3. Navigate to the data files for this chapter.

4. Select the file **Theft_Unexpected.psd** (it should be stored in a folder named Graphics), and click Import.

   The graphic is a simple logo file and imports into the Premiere Pro project.

5. Save the project and leave it open.

Importing Layered Adobe Photoshop Files

Adobe Photoshop can also create graphics using multiple layers. Layers are similar to tracks in your Timeline and allow for separation between elements. You can import Photoshop layers into Premiere Pro individually to allow for isolation or animation.

Try It!

1. Double-click an empty area of the Project panel to open the Import dialog box.

2. Navigate to the data files for this chapter.

3. Select the file **Theft_Unexpected_Layered.psd** (again, in the Graphics folder), and click Import.

4. A new dialog box opens, giving you a choice of how to interpret the layered file (**FIGURE 7.23**). There are four ways to import the file, controlled by a pop-up menu in the Import Layered File dialog box:

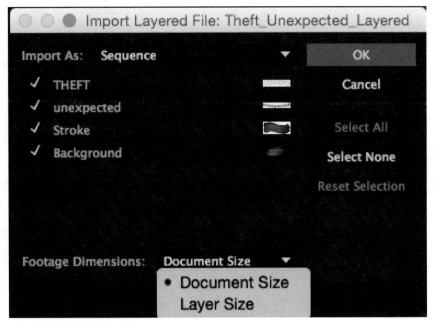

FIGURE 7.23

- **Merge All Layers:** Merges all layers, importing the file into Premiere Pro as a single, flattened clip.
- **Merged Layers:** Merges only the layers you select into a single, flattened clip.
- **Individual Layers:** Imports only the layers you select, with each layer becoming a separate clip in a bin.
- **Sequence:** Imports only the layers you select, each as a single clip. Premiere Pro also then creates a new sequence (with its frame size based on the imported document) containing each layer on a separate track (that matches the original stacking order).

  Choosing Sequence or Individual Layers allows you to select one of the following options from the Footage Dimensions menu:

- **Document Size:** Brings the selected layer in at the size of the original Photoshop document.
- **Layer Size:** Matches the frame size of the clips to the frame size of their content in the original Photoshop file. Layers that do not fill the entire canvas will be cropped tightly, as transparent areas are removed. They'll also be centered in the frame, losing their original relative positioning.

5. Click the Import As drop-down arrow and choose Sequence. Keep the Document Size option. Click OK.

6. Looking in the Project panel, locate the new bin Theft_Unexpected_ Layered. Double-click it to open it and reveal its contents.

Note:

The controls for choosing List view or Icon view are in the lower-left corner of the Project panel.

7. Switch to List view in the Project panel then double-click the sequence Theft_Unexpected_Layered to load it.

8. Zoom in to examine the sequence in the Timeline panel (**FIGURE 7.24**). Try turning the visibility icons off and on for each track to see how the layers are isolated.

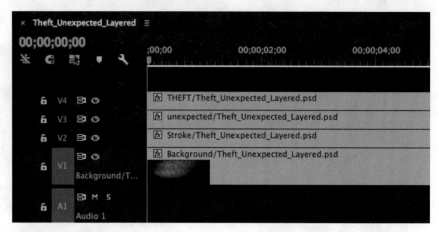

FIGURE 7.24

9. Save the project and leave it open.

Recording a Scratch Narration Track

Many times, you may be working with a video project that has a narration track. While most choose to eventually get these recorded by professionals (or at least recorded in a location quieter than their desks), you can record temporary audio, called a scratch track, right into Premiere Pro.

This can be helpful if you need something to edit your video to, especially as it will give you a sense of timing for your edits.

Here's how to go about recording a scratch audio track.

Try It!

1. You will need something to read for your recording. Keep it short—only a few sentences will be necessary to demonstrate how to capture the audio. If you are not using a built-in microphone, make sure your external microphone is properly connected to your computer. You may need to see the documentation for your computer or sound card.

2. Choose Edit > Preferences > Audio Hardware (Windows) or Premiere Pro > Preferences > Audio Hardware (Mac) to properly configure your microphone so Premiere Pro can use it (**FIGURE 7.25**). Use one of the choices from the Default Device pop-up menu, such as System Default Input/Output or Built-in Microphone/Built-in Output, and click OK.

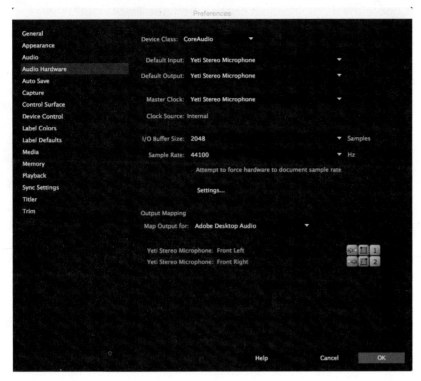

FIGURE 7.25

3. Turn down the speakers on your computer to prevent feedback or echo.

4. Open a sequence, and select an empty track in the Timeline by clicking its name.

5. Choose Window > Audio Track Mixer (which is likely to be docked in the same frame as your Source Monitor).

6. In the Audio Track Mixer, click the Enable Track For Recording icon (R) for the track you have chosen (**FIGURE 7.26**).

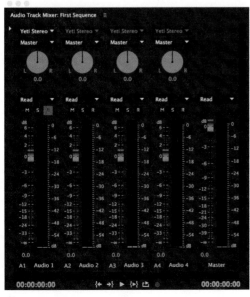

FIGURE 7.26

7. Choose the recording input channel from the Track Input Channel menu, at the top of the Audio Track Mixer.

8. Click the Record button at the bottom of the Audio Track Mixer to enter Record mode (**FIGURE 7.27**).

FIGURE 7.27

9. Click the Play button to start recording. Read the passage you selected.

10. If the levels are too loud or too quiet, you can adjust the track volume fader up (louder) or down (quieter) as you record. If you see the red indicators at the top of the VU meters light up, you likely have distortion. A good target to aim for is loud audio registering near 0 dB and quiet audio registering around –18 dB.

11. Click the Stop icon to stop recording.

12. Locate both instances of the recorded audio. The newly recorded audio appears both on the audio track in the Timeline and as a clip in the Project panel. You can select the clip in the Project panel and rename it or delete it from your project.

13. Save **Ch07_04_xx.prproj** and leave it open.

Exploring the Project Panel

Anything you import into your Premiere Pro project will appear in the Project panel (**FIGURE 7.28**). As well as giving you excellent tools for browsing your clips and working with their metadata, the Project panel has special folders called bins that you can use to organize everything.

> **Note:**
>
> Premiere Pro CC allows you to customize the Timeline by adding and removing buttons on the track headers (the far left of the Timeline panel). You can add a Voice-over Record button that begins recording audio immediately.

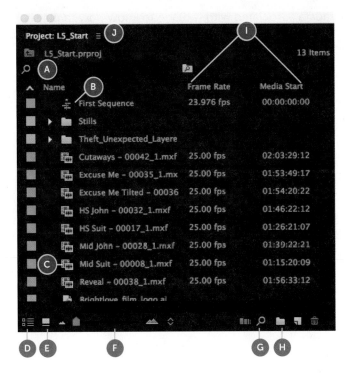

A. Filter Bin Content field

B. Sequence

C. Clip

D. List View

E. Icon View

F. Zoom

G. Find

H. New bin

I. Headings

J. Panel menu

FIGURE 7.28

Everything that appears in a sequence must be in the Project panel. If you delete a clip in the Project panel that is already used in a sequence, the clip will automatically be removed from the sequence. Premiere Pro will warn you if deleting a clip will affect an existing sequence.

Before you begin, make sure you are using the default Editing workspace.

Try It!

1. Choose Window > Workspaces > Editing.

2. Choose Window > Workspaces > Reset to Saved Layout.

3. Choose File > Save As.

4. Rename the file **Ch07_05_xx.prproj**.

5. Save the project file in the location where your teacher instructs you to store the files for this chapter, and leave it open.

As well as acting as the repository for all of your clips, the Project panel gives you important options for interpreting media. All of your footage will have a frame rate (frames per second, or fps) and a pixel aspect ratio (pixel shape), for example. You may want to change these settings for creative reasons.

You could, for example, interpret video recorded at 60fps as 30fps to achieve a 50% slow-motion effect. You might also receive a video file that has the wrong pixel aspect ratio setting.

Premiere Pro uses metadata associated with footage to know how to play it back. If you want to change the clip metadata, you can do so in the Project panel.

Working with Bins

Bins allow you to organize clips by dividing them into groups.

Just like folders on your hard drive, you can have multiple bins inside other bins, creating a folder structure as comprehensive as your project requires.

There's an important difference between bins and folders on your hard drive: Bins exist only inside your Premiere Pro project file to organize your media within your project. You won't find individual folders representing project bins on your hard drive.

Creating Bins

Try It!

1. Click the New Bin button at the bottom of the Project panel.
   Premiere Pro creates a new bin and automatically highlights the name, ready for you to rename it. It's a good habit to name bins as soon as you create them.

2. We have already imported some clips from a film, so let's give them a bin. Name the new bin **Theft Unexpected**.
   You can also create a bin using the File menu.

3. Make sure the Project panel is active and that your new bin (Theft Unexpected) is not selected. Choose File > New > Bin, and name the new bin **PSD Files**.
   You can also make a new bin by using a shortcut menu.

4. Right-click a blank area in the Project panel and choose New Bin. Name the new bin **Illustrator Files**.
   Finally, you can use shortcut keystrokes.

5. Make sure the Project panel is active but no existing bins are selected. Press the keyboard shortcut Ctrl+B (Windows) or Command+B (Mac) to make another bin. Name the bin **Sequences**.

6. Save the changes to **Ch07_05_xx.prproj**, and leave it open.

Using Bins

If your Project panel is set to List view, bins are displayed in name order among the clips.

Try It!

1. Import the clip **Brightlove_film_logo.ai** from the data files (see the Graphics folder) into the Illustrator Files bin.

2. Drag **Theft_Unexpected.psd** from the list of data files into the PSD Files bin.

3. In the Project panel, drag the sequence named **First Sequence** into the Sequences bin.

4. Drag all of the remaining clips into the Theft Unexpected bin.

   You should now have a nicely organized Project panel, with each kind of clip in its own bin (**FIGURE 7.29**).

5. Save the changes to **Ch07_05_xx.prproj**, and leave it open.

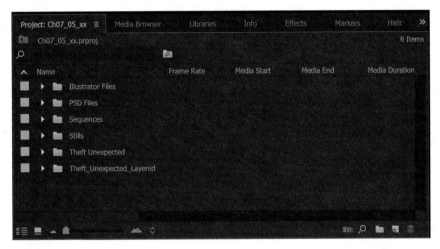

FIGURE 7.29

Copying a Clip to a Bin

Notice that you can also copy and paste clips to make extra copies if this suits your organizational system. You have a Photoshop document that might be useful for the Theft Unexpected content. Make an extra copy.

Try It!

1. Click the disclosure triangle for the PSD Files bin to display the contents.

2. Right-click the **Theft_Unexpected.psd** clip, and choose Copy.

3. Click the disclosure triangle for the Theft Unexpected bin to display the contents.

4. Right-click the Theft Unexpected bin, and choose Paste.

   Premiere Pro places a copy of the clip in the Theft Unexpected bin.

5. Save the changes to **Ch07_05_xx.prproj**, and close Premiere Pro.

End-of-Chapter Activities

REVIEW QUESTIONS

1. Why is Premiere Pro considered a nonlinear editor?

2. Summarize the eight steps in the digital editing workflow.

3. What is the Media Browser used for?

4. List at least five basic tools you will need for shooting and capturing a video.

5. Summarize safety procedures you should follow while using digital audio and video equipment.

6. Describe eight different tips for shooting quality video.

7. What is one advantage of using the Media Browser rather than the File > Import method to import tapeless media?

8. What is a bin?

9. What is timecode?

10. Describe how to capture video from tape with no additional third-party hardware.

Review Project 1

With a partner, write a script for a video in which a reporter interviews an "expert" on proper ethics in recording and capturing video. With your teacher's permission, record the interview, then capture or ingest it, and edit it using Premiere Pro.

Review Project 2

Make a three-column chart listing video tape, tapeless, and file formats. Include the format name, a description, and its usage. Explain your chart to a partner or to the class.

Review Project 3

With a partner or small team, plan a video to provide a tour of a historic or notable location in your community. Follow the workflow for planning, preproduction, production, and postproduction, including creating all necessary documents and spec sheets, writing scripts, and preparing storyboards. Plan the shoot using at least five of the technques for recording quality video that are covered in this chapter. Practice effective planning and time-management skills to complete your tasks and make use of technology to enhance your productivity. After recording all video and capturing or ingesting it into Premiere Pro, record a scratch narration track.

Preview the video for other students and use their feedback to make improvements. When the project is complete, make it available online.

CHAPTER 7 – PORTFOLIO BUILDER

PRODUCE AN ADVERTISEMENT

An advertisement is media content that promotes a product, service, or event. The point of the ad is to convince the target audience of something–for example, to buy the product, use the service, or attend the event. In this project, work in small teams to create a 30-second advertisement from concept to completion. Then screen the ad for your classmates and evaluate its effectiveness.

DIRECTIONS

1. Start by researching advertising techniques. Then, meet with your team to select the item you are going to promote with your ad, and your target audience. Have the selection approved by your teacher.

2. Assign roles to each team member, allowing each person the opportunity to lead one aspect of the project.

3. Use technology applications to set up a project schedule that you can use for planning and time-management.

4. Write the screenplay or script for your advertisement. Remember that the goal is to convince your target audience of something.

5. Walk through the script and analyze it for errors and places where it can be improved, and then revise it.

6. When the script is final, create all the other documents you will need for the workflow process, such as a shot list, script breakdown, and budget.

7. Have a production meeting to review the project and make sure everyone understands his or her responsibilities and the schedule.

8. Collect resources you want to import for use in the advertisement, such as music and graphics. Secure permission to use all media that you do not create yourself.

9. Record the video clips you will need for your advertisement. Use the techniques for recording quality video described in this chapter and throughout this book.

10. Capture or ingest the footage and organize it within Premiere Pro.

11. Use Premiere Pro to edit the video, including music, narration, and graphics, as necessary.

12. Preview the advertisement as a team and analyze it for ways you can improve it.

13. Revise and improve the video. When you are satisfied with the product, export it in a format of your choice that allows you to share it with your class.

14. As a class, develop a rubric that you can use to evaluate the advertisements for quality, effectiveness and other benchmarks that you set.

15. Screen the advertisements for the class, and use the rubric to evaluate each one. Use the information you learn about your project to improve your future media creation content and processes.

Chapter 8

Editing with Adobe Premiere Pro and Adobe Audition

Chapter 8 Overview

- Using the Source Monitor
- Adjusting Audio Channels
- Navigating the Timeline
- Creating a Sequence
- Splitting a Clip
- Moving Clips
- Extracting and Deleting Segments
- Exploring the Use of Transitions
- Adding Video Transitions

- Working with Text
- Creating Titles from Scratch
- Sharing Your Project
- Working with Adobe Media Encoder
- Capturing and Working with Audio
- Configuring Audition
- Navigating in the Audition Workspace
- Editing Audio Files
- End-of-Chapter Review and Activities

This chapter will teach you the core editing skills you will use again and again when creating sequences with Premiere Pro, and provide an introduction to editing audio with Adobe® Audition®.

You will choose your cuts precisely, placing clips in sequences at exactly the right point in time and on the track you want (to create layered effects), adding new clips to existing sequences, and removing old ones. You will also learn how transitions can help create a seamless flow between two video or audio clips. Video transitions are often used to signify a change in time or location. Audio transitions provide a useful way to avoid abrupt edits that jar the listener.

The Premiere Pro CC Titler is a powerful tool set for text and shape creation. These objects can be placed above video or used as stand-alone clips to convey information to an audience.

One of the best things about editing video is the feeling you have when you can finally share it with your audience. Premiere Pro offers a wide range of export options to record your projects to tape or convert them to digital files. Within those formats you have dozens of options and can also export in batches.

Adobe Audition is a digital audio editing program that you can use to record, edit, mix, and restore audio files. Audition provides all the tools you need to mix multiple tracks of narration, dialogue, music, and sound effects to create professional-grade audio compositions. In addition to its editing functionality, Audition integrates smoothly with Premiere Pro, so you can edit audio within your video projects.

Using the Source Monitor

The Source Monitor is the main place you will go when you want to check your assets before including them in a sequence.

When you view video clips in the Source Monitor (FIGURE 8.1), you watch them in their original format. They will play back with their frame rate, frame size, field order, audio sample rate, and audio bit depth exactly as they were recorded.

When you add a clip to a sequence, Premiere Pro conforms it to the sequence settings. This means the frame rate and audio type might be adjusted so that all the clips in the sequence play back the same way.

FIGURE 8.1

As well as being a viewer for multiple file types, the Source Monitor provides important additional functions. You can use two special kinds of markers, called In points and Out points, to select part of a clip for inclusion in a sequence. You can also add comments in the form of markers that you can refer to later or use to remind yourself about important facts relating to a clip. You might include a note about part of a shot you don't have permission to use, for example.

Before you begin, make sure you are using the default Editing workspace.

Try It!

1. Start Premiere Pro if necessary and open **Ch08_01.prproj** from the location where the data files for this chapter are stored.

2. Choose Window > Workspaces > Editing.

3. Choose Window > Workspaces > Reset to Saved Layout.

4. Choose File > Save As.

5. Rename the file **Ch08_01_xx.prproj**. Save the project in the location where your teacher instructs you to store the files for this chapter, and leave it open.

Timecode Information

At the bottom left of the Source Monitor, a timecode display shows the current position of the playhead in hours, minutes, seconds, and frames (00:00:00:00).

For example, 00:15:10:01 would be 0 hours, 15 minutes, 10 seconds, and 1 frame.

Note that this is based on the original timecode for the clip, which probably does not begin at 00:00:00:00.

At the bottom right of the Source Monitor, a timecode display shows the duration of your clip. By default, this shows the whole clip duration, but later you will be adding special marks to make a partial selection.

Loading a Clip

To load a clip, do the following.

Try It!

1. In the Project panel, hold down the Ctrl (Windows) or Command (Mac) key and double-click the Theft Unexpected bin icon. To navigate back to the Project panel contents, click the Navigate Up icon beside the project name.

2. Double-click a video clip, or drag and drop a clip into the Source Monitor.

   Premiere Pro displays the clip in the Source Monitor, ready for you to watch it and add markers.

3. Position your mouse pointer so that it is over the Source Monitor, and press the ` (grave) key. The panel fills the Premiere Pro application frame, giving you a larger view of the video clip. Press the ` (grave) key again to restore the Source Monitor to its original size.

4. Save the changes to **Ch08_01_xx.prproj**, and leave it open.

Loading Multiple Clips

Next you will create a selection of clips to work with in the Source Monitor.

Try It!

1. Click the Recent Items menu at the top left of the Source Monitor, and choose Close All (FIGURE 8.2).

FIGURE 8.2

Safe Margins

Old-style CRT monitors crop the edges of the picture to achieve a clean edge. If you're producing video for a CRT monitor, click the Settings (wrench icon) button at the bottom of the Source Monitor and choose Safe Margins. Premiere Pro displays white outlines over the image (**FIGURE 8.3**).

The outer box is the action-safe zone. Aim to keep important action inside this box so that when the picture is displayed, edge cropping does not hide what is going on.

The inner box is the title-safe zone. Keep titles and graphics inside this box so that even on a badly calibrated display, your audience will be able to read the words.

FIGURE 8.3

Click the Settings button at the bottom of the Source Monitor and choose Safe Margins to turn them off.

2. Click the List View button on the Theft Unexpected bin, and make sure the clips are displayed in alphabetical order by clicking the Name heading.

3. Select the first clip, Cutaways, and then hold down the Shift key and click the clip Mid John - 00028.

 This makes a selection of multiple clips in the bin.

4. Drag the clips from the bin to the Source Monitor.

 Now the clips selected will be displayed in the Source Monitor Recent Items menu. You can use the menu to choose which clip to view.

5. Save the changes to **Ch08_01_xx.prproj**., and leave it open.

Essential Playback Controls

Take a look at the playback controls (FIGURE 8.4).

A. Navigator
B. Playhead
C. Time ruler
D. Step Back 1 Frame
E. Step Forward 1 Frame
F. Play-Stop toggle
G. Zoom Level

FIGURE 8.4

Try It!

1. Double-click the shot Excuse Me in the Theft Unexpected bin to open it in the Source Monitor.

2. At the bottom of the Source Monitor, there's a blue playhead marker. Drag it along the bottom of the panel to view different parts of the clip. You can also click wherever you want the playhead to go, and it will jump to that spot.

3. Use the Select Zoom Level drop-down menu to zoom in on the clip.

4. Click the Play-Stop button to play the clip. Click it again to stop playback. You can also use the spacebar to play and stop playback.

5. Click the Step Back 1 Frame and Step Forward 1 Frame buttons to move through the clip one frame at a time. You can also use the Left Arrow and Right Arrow keys on your keyboard.

6. Try using the J, K, and L keys to play your clip.

7. Save the changes to **Ch08_01_xx.prproj**., and leave it open.

Source Monitor Controls

As well as playback controls, there are some important additional buttons in the Source Monitor (FIGURE 8.5).

FIGURE 8.5

A. Mark In

B. Go to In

C. Go to Out

D. Overwrite

E. Add Marker

F. Mark Out

G. Insert

- **Add Marker:** Adds a marker to the clip at the location of the playhead. Markers can provide a simple visual reference or store comments.

- **Mark In:** Sets the beginning of the part of the clip you intend to use in a sequence. You can have only one In point. A new In point will automatically replace the existing one.

- **Mark Out:** Sets the end of the part of the clip you intend to use in a sequence. You can have only one Out point. A new Out point will automatically replace the existing one.

- **Go to In:** Moves the playhead to the clip In point.

- **Go to Out:** Moves the playhead to the clip Out point.

- **Insert:** Adds the clip to the sequence currently displayed in the Timeline panel using the insert edit method.

- **Overwrite:** Adds the clip to the sequence currently displayed in the Timeline panel using the overwrite edit method.

Adjusting Audio Channels

Premiere Pro has advanced audio management features. You can create complex sound mixes and selectively target output audio channels with original clip audio. You can produce mono, stereo, 5.1, and even 32-channel sequences with precise control over the routing of audio channels.

If you are just starting out, you will probably want to produce sequences mastered in stereo using stereo clips. In this case, the default settings are most likely exactly what you need.

When recording audio with a professional camera, it's common to have one microphone record onto one audio channel and a different microphone record onto another audio channel. These are the same audio channels that would be used for regular stereo audio, but they now contain completely separate sound.

Your camera adds metadata to the audio to tell Premiere Pro whether the sound is meant to be mono (separate audio channels) or stereo (channel 1 audio and channel 2 audio combined to produce the complete stereo sound).

You can tell Premiere Pro how to interpret audio channels when new media files are imported by going to Edit > Preferences > Audio (Windows) or Premiere Pro > Preferences > Audio (Mac).

If the setting was wrong when you imported your clips, it's easy to tell Premiere Pro how to correctly interpret the audio channels.

Try It!

1. Right-click the Reveal clip in the Theft Unexpected bin, and choose Modify > Audio Channels (**FIGURE 8.6**).

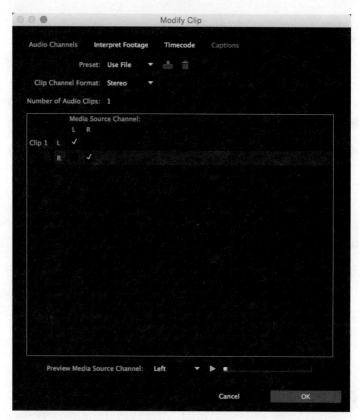

FIGURE 8.6

2. This clip is set to use the file's metadata to identify the channel format for the audio. Click the Preset menu, and change it to Mono (**FIGURE 8.7**).

   Premiere Pro switches the Channel Format menu to Mono. You will see that the Left and Right source channels are now linked to tracks Audio 1 and Audio 2. This means that when you add the clip to a sequence, each audio channel will go on a separate track, allowing you to work on them independently.

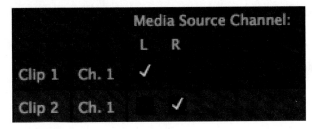

FIGURE 8.7

3. Click OK.

4. Save the changes to **Ch08_01_xx.prproj**., and leave it open.

Navigating the Timeline

The Timeline panel in Premiere Pro is the canvas on which you develop your video content (**FIGURE 8.8**). The Timeline is where you will add clips to your sequences, make editorial changes to them, add visual and audio special effects, mix soundtracks, and add titles and graphics.

Here are a few facts about the Timeline panel:

- You view and edit sequences in the Timeline panel.

- You can open multiple sequences at the same time, and each will be displayed in its own Timeline panel.

- The terms sequence and Timeline are often used interchangeably, as in "in the sequence" or "on the Timeline."

- You can create an unlimited number of video tracks; however, the complexity of the project and computer hardware may affect the number of tracks you can reasonably work with at a given time. Upper video tracks play "in front" of lower ones, so you would normally place graphics clips on tracks above background video clips.

- You can create an unlimited number of audio tracks that all play at the same time to create an audio mix. Audio tracks can be mono (1 channel), stereo (2 channels), 5.1 (6 channels), or adaptive—with up to 32 channels.

- You can change the height of Timeline tracks to gain access to additional controls and thumbnails on your video clips.

- Each track has a set of controls, shown on a track header, that change the way it functions.

- Time always moves from left to right on the Timeline.

- The Program Monitor shows you the contents of the currently displayed sequence at the position of the playhead.

- For most operations on the Timeline, you will use the standard Selection tool. However, there are several other tools that serve different purposes, and each tool has a keyboard shortcut. If in doubt, press the V key. This is the keyboard shortcut for the Selection tool.

- You can zoom in and out of the Timeline using the + and − keys at the top of your keyboard to get a better view of your clips. If you press the \ key, Premiere Pro toggles the zoom level between your current setting and showing your whole sequence. You can also double-click the navigator at the bottom of the Timeline panel to view the whole timeline.

A. Timecode

B. Track selection

C. Track lock

D. Source tracks

E. Time ruler

F. Clip video

G. Playhead

H. Clip audio

I. Track

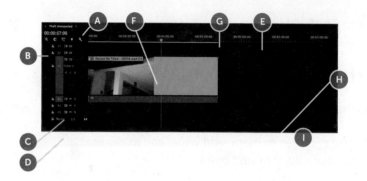

FIGURE 8.8

Creating a Sequence

A sequence is a series of clips that play, one after another—sometimes with multiple blended layers, and often with special effects, titles, and audio—making a complete film.

You can have as many sequences as you like in a project. Sequences are stored in the Project panel, just like clips. They have their own icon.

Make a new sequence for the Theft Unexpected drama.

Try It!

1. In the Theft Unexpected bin, drag the clip Excuse Me (not Excuse Me Tilted) onto the New Item button at the bottom of the panel.

   This is a shortcut to make a sequence that perfectly matches your media. Premiere Pro creates a new sequence and automatically names it after the clip you selected.

   The sequence is highlighted in the bin, and it is a good idea to rename it right away.

2. Right-click the sequence in the bin, and choose Rename. Name the sequence **Theft Unexpected** (FIGURE 8.9).

FIGURE 8.9

The sequence is automatically open, and it contains the clip you used to create it. If you had used a random clip to perform this shortcut, you might choose to select it in the sequence and delete it now (by pressing the Delete key).

3. Close the sequence by clicking the **x** on its name tab in the Timeline panel. Save the changes to **Ch08_01_xx.prproj.**, and close the project.

Using Thumbnails to Create a Storyboard

The term **storyboard** usually describes a series of drawings that show the intended camera angles and action for a film. Storyboards are often quite similar to comic strips, though they usually include technical information, such as intended camera moves, lines of dialogue, and sound effects.

You can use clip thumbnails in a bin as storyboard images. Arrange the thumbnails by dragging and dropping them in the order in which you would like the clips to appear in your sequence, from left to right and from top to bottom. Then drag and drop them into your sequence, or use a special automated edit feature to add them to your sequence with transition effects.

Splitting a Clip

It's also common to add a clip to a sequence and then realize you need it in two parts. Perhaps you want to take just a section of a clip and use it as a cutaway, or maybe you want to separate the beginning and the end to make space for new clips.

You can split clips in several ways:

- Use the Razor tool, with the keyboard shortcut C. If you hold the Shift key while clicking with the Razor tool, you will add an edit to clips on every track.

- Make sure the Timeline panel is selected, go to the Sequence menu, and choose Add Edit. Premiere Pro adds an edit, at the location of your playhead, to clips on any tracks that are turned on. If you have selected clips, Premiere Pro adds the edit only to the selected clips.

- If you go to the Sequence menu and choose Add Edit to All Tracks, Premiere Pro adds an edit to clips on all tracks, regardless of whether they are turned on.

- Use the Add Edit keyboard shortcuts. Press Ctrl+K (Windows) or Command+K (Mac) to add an edit to selected tracks or clips, or press Shift+Ctrl+K (Windows) or Shift+Command+K (Mac) to add an edit to all tracks regardless of selection.

Clips that were originally continuous will play back seamlessly unless you move them or make separate adjustments to different parts.

Moving Clips

Insert edits and overwrite edits add new clips to sequences in dramatically different ways. Insert edits push existing clips out of the way, whereas over-write edits simply replace them.

When moving clips using the Insert mode, you may want to ensure you have the sync locks on for your tracks to avoid any possible loss of sync.

Try a few techniques.

Dragging Clips

At the top left of the Timeline panel, you will see the Snap button. When snapping is enabled, clip segments snap automatically to each other's edges. This simple but useful feature will help you position clip segments accurately.

Try It!

1. Start Premiere Pro, and open **Ch08_02.prproj** from the data files for this chapter.

2. Save the file as **Ch08_02_xx.prproj** in the location where your teacher instructs you to store the files for this chapter.

3. Click the last clip on the Timeline, HS Suit, and drag it a little to the right (**FIGURE 8.10**).

   Because there are no clips after this one, you simply introduce a gap before the clip. No other clips are affected.

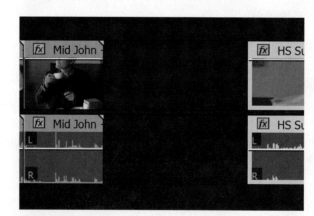

FIGURE 8.10

4. Drag the clip back to its original position. If you move the mouse slowly and if Snap mode is on, you will notice that the clip segment slightly jumps into position. When this happens, you can be confident it is perfectly positioned.

Note:

If you do not see thumbnails on the clips in the Timeline, click the Timeline Display Settings icon in the upper-left of the panel and click Expand All Tracks.

Note:

When you open a project file and Premiere Pro can't find its linked files, the Link Media dialog box will open. Select a clip in the Missing Media list and click the Locate button. The Media Browser will open. Using the folder tree at the left, navigate to the folder where you have stored the data files for this book and click Search. To speed your search, select the option Display Only Exact Name Matches. When you have found one file, select it and click OK. The rest should relink automatically.

Tip:

Click the Snap icon in the upper-left of the Timeline panel to toggle Snap off and on. When the icon is blue, Snap is on.

5. Drag the clip to the left so it's positioned earlier in the Timeline. Slowly drag the clip until it snaps to the end of the Excuse Me clip. When you release the mouse button, HS Suit replaces the Mid John clip.

   When you drag and drop clips, the default mode is Overwrite.

6. Undo to restore the clip to its original position.

7. Save the changes to **Ch08_02_xx.prproj**, and leave it open.

Nudging Clips

Many editors prefer to use the keyboard as much as possible, minimizing the use of the mouse. Working with the keyboard is often faster.

It's common to move clip segments inside a sequence by using the arrow keys in combination with a modifier key, nudging the selected items left and right in time, or up and down between tracks.

You won't be able to nudge linked video and audio clips on V1 and A1 up and down until you separate them, or unlink them, because the separator between the video and audio tracks blocks the movement.

Premiere Pro includes many keyboard shortcut options, some of which are available, but not yet assigned keys. You can set these up, prioritizing the use of available keys to suit your workflow.

Rearranging Clips in a Sequence

If you hold the Ctrl (Windows) or Command (Mac) key while you drag clips on the Timeline, Premiere Pro uses Insert mode instead of Overwrite mode.

The HS Suit shot around 00:00:20:00 might work well if it appeared before the previous shot—and it might help hide the poor continuity between the two shots of John.

Try It!

1. Verify the Theft Unexpected sequence is active in the Timeline panel.

2. Start to drag the Mid John clip to the left. As you drag, press and hold the Ctrl key (Windows) or the Command key (Mac). When the left edge of the Mid John clip lines up with the right edge of the Mid Suit clip (**FIGURE 8.11**), release the mouse button and then release the modifier key.

   Once you have begun dragging, hold the Ctrl key (Windows) or Command key (Mac). Release the key after you've dropped the clip.

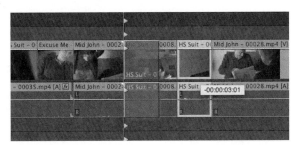

FIGURE 8.11

3. Play the result. This creates the edit you want, but it introduces a gap where the Mid John clip used to be (FIGURE 8.12).

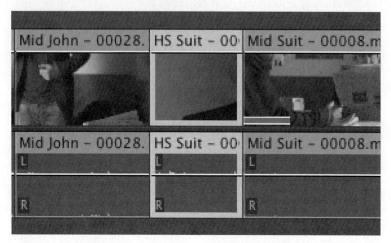

FIGURE 8.12

Try that again with an additional modifier key.

4. Use the Undo command to restore the clips to their original positions.

5. Holding Ctrl+Alt (Windows) or Command+Option (Mac), drag and drop the Mid John clip between the Mid Suit and Excuse Me clips again. This time there is no gap in the sequence (FIGURE 8.13).

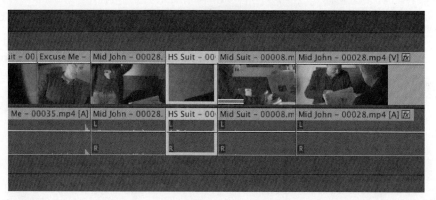

FIGURE 8.13

6. Play through the edit to see the result.

7. Save the changes to **Ch08_02_xx.prproj**, and leave it open.

Using the Clipboard

You can copy and paste clip segments on the Timeline just as you might copy and paste text in a word processor.

Try It!

1. In a sequence, select any clip segment (or segments) you want to copy, and then press Ctrl+C (Windows) or Command+C (Mac) to add them to the clipboard.

2. Position your playhead where you would like to paste the clips you copied, and press Ctrl+V (Windows) or Command+V (Mac).

3. Save the changes to **Ch08_02_xx.prproj**, and leave it open.

Premiere Pro adds copies of the clips to your sequence based on the tracks you enable. The lowest enabled track receives the clip (or clips).

Extracting and Deleting Segments

Now that you know how to add clips to a sequence and how to move them around, all that remains is to learn how to remove them. Once again, you will be operating in Insert or Overwrite mode.

There are two ways of selecting parts of a sequence you want to remove. You can use In and Out points combined with track selections, or you can select clip segments. If you use In and Out points, selecting clips overrides selecting tracks, so you can ignore track selection if you make careful clip selections.

You will still be working with a selected amount of time, but selecting clips can be quicker than selecting tracks.

Lift

A lift edit will remove the selected part of a sequence, leaving blank space. It's similar to an overwrite edit but in reverse.

You will need to set In and Out points on the Timeline to select the part that will be removed. You can do this by positioning the playhead and pressing I or O. You can also use a handy shortcut.

Try It!

1. Open the sequence Theft Unexpected 02 in the Sequences bin. This sequence has some unwanted extra clips. They have different label colors to make them easier to identify.

2. Position the playhead so that it's somewhere over the first additional clip, Excuse Me Tilted.

3. Make sure the Video 1 track header is turned on, and press X.

   Premiere Pro automatically adds an In point and an Out point that match the beginning and end of the clip. You will see a highlight that shows the selected part of the sequence.

   The correct tracks are already selected, so there's no need to do anything else to prepare for the lift edit. In fact, because you have selected a clip, the track selection has no effect anyway. The edit you are about to perform will apply to the selected clip.

4. Click the Lift button at the bottom of the Program Monitor, or press the ; key (**FIGURE 8.14**).

FIGURE 8.14

Premiere Pro removes the part of the sequence you selected, leaving a gap behind. This might be fine on another occasion, but in this instance you don't want the gap. You could right-click inside the gap and choose Ripple Delete, but for this exercise you will use an extract edit.

5. Save the changes to **Ch08_02_xx.prproj**, and leave it open.

Extract

An extract edit removes the selected part of your sequence and does not leave a gap. It's similar to an insert edit, but in reverse.

Try It!

1. Undo the last edit.

2. Click the Extract button at the bottom of the Program Monitor (next to the Lift button) (**FIGURE 8.15**), or press the ' (apostrophe) key.

   This time, Premiere Pro removes the selected part of the sequence and doesn't leave a gap.

3. Save the changes to **Ch08_02_xx.prproj**, and leave it open.

There are also two ways of removing clips by selecting segments: Delete and Ripple Delete.

4. Click the second unwanted clip, Cutaways, and try these two options:

   - Pressing the Delete key removes the selected clip (or clips), leaving a gap behind. This is the same as a lift edit.

   - Pressing Shift I Delete (Windows) or Option+Delete (Mac) removes the selected clip (or clips) without leaving a gap behind. This is the same as an extract edit.

   The result seems similar to what is achieved using In and Out points because you used the In and Out points to select a whole clip. You can use In and Out points to choose any parts of clips, while selecting clip segments and pressing Delete will remove whole clips.

5. Save the changes to **Ch08_02_xx.prproj**, and then close it.

Exploring the Use of Transitions

Adobe Premiere Pro offers several special effects and preset animations to help you bridge neighboring clips in the Timeline. These transitions—such as dissolves, page wipes, dips to color, and so on—provide a way to ease viewers from one scene to the next. Occasionally, a **transition** can also be used to grab viewers' attention to signify a major jump in the story (**FIGURE 8.15**).

FIGURE 8.15

Adding transitions to your project is an art. Applying them starts simply enough; it's a mere drag-and-drop process. The skill comes in their placement, length, and parameters, such as direction, motion, and start/end locations.

Most transition work takes place in the Effect Controls panel (**FIGURE 8.16**). In addition to the various options unique to each transition, the Effect Controls panel displays an A/B timeline. This feature makes it easy to move transitions relative to the edit point, change the transition duration, and apply transitions to clips that don't have sufficient head or tail frames (additional content to provide an overlap). You can also apply a transition to a group of clips.

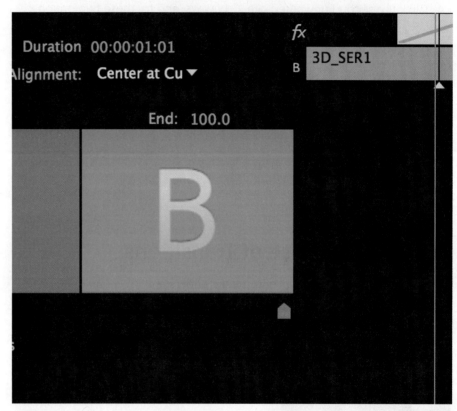

FIGURE 8.16

When to Use Transitions

Transitions are most effective when you have no options other than making a distracting edit that makes your sequence appear jarring when viewed. For example, you may switch from indoors to outdoors in a video, or you may jump forward in time by several hours. An animated transition or a dissolve helps the viewer understand that time has passed or that the location has changed.

Transitions are a standard storytelling tool in video editing. For many years, viewers have become used to seeing transitions applied in standard ways, such as the changing of one section to another in a video or the slow fade to black at the end of a scene. The key with transitions is to use restraint.

Best Practices with Transitions

Many editors have a tendency to overuse transitions. Some come to rely on them as a crutch and think that they add visual interest. But that can be a mistake.

Think of transitions as seasoning or spice. When added in small amounts and at the right time, they can make a meal tastier and more enjoyable. When overdone, they can quickly ruin that meal. Keep this in mind when you are applying transitions to your projects.

Watch some TV news stories. Most use cuts-only edits. You will rarely see any transitions. Why? The principal reason for the lack of transitions is that they can be distracting. If a TV news editor uses one, it's for a purpose. Their most frequent use in newsroom editing bays is to take what would have been a jarring or abrupt edit—often called a **jump cut**—and make it more palatable.

That's not to say transitions don't have their place in carefully planned stories. They do smooth the change between scenes, and they can send a clear message to the audience.

Adding Video Transitions

Premiere Pro contains several video transitions (plus three audio transitions). You will find two types of video transitions inside Premiere Pro. The most commonly used transitions are those in the Video Transitions group. These are organized into seven categories based on style. You will also find additional transitions in the Video Effects group in the Effects panel. These are meant to be applied to an entire clip and can be used to reveal the footage (typically between its start and end frame). This second category works well for superimposing text or graphics.

Applying a Single-Sided Transition

The easiest transition to understand is one that applies to just one end of a single clip. This could be a fade from black on the first clip in a sequence or a dissolve into an animated graphic that leaves the screen on its own.

Try It!

1. Start Adobe Premiere Pro CC, and open the project **Ch08_03.prproj** from the data files for this chapter.

2. Save the file as **Ch08_03_xx.prproj** in the location where your teacher instructs you to store the files for this chapter, and leave it open.

3. Choose Window > Workspaces > Effects.

   This changes the workspace to the preset that was created to make it easier to work with transitions and effects.

4. If necessary, click the Effects panel to make it active.

5. Make sure the sequence 01 Transitions is open. This sequence has four video clips. The clips have long enough handles for transitions to be applied.

6. In the Effects panel, open the Video Transitions > Dissolve bin. Find the Film Dissolve effect.

    You can use the Search field, at the top of the panel, to locate the effect by name, or you can manually open the folders of effects.

7. Drag and drop the effect onto the start of the first video clip. You can set the effect only to Start at Cut for the first clip (FIGURE 8.17).

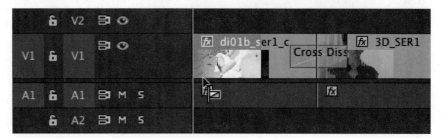

FIGURE 8.17

8. Drag the Film Dissolve effect onto the end of the last video clip (FIGURE 8.18).

    The Dissolve icon shows that the effect will start before the end of the clip and complete by the time it reaches the clip's end.

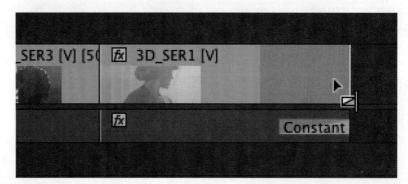

FIGURE 8.18

Because you are applying the Film Dissolve transition onto the ends of clips, where there is no connected clip, the picture dissolves into the background of the Timeline (which happens to be black).

Transitions of this kind don't extend the clip (using the handle) because the transition doesn't reach past the end of the clip.

9. Play the sequence to see the result.

    You should see a fade from black at the start of the sequence and a fade to black at the end.

10. Save the changes to **Ch08_03_xx.prproj**, and leave it open.

Applying a Transition between Two Clips

Now apply transitions between several clips. For the purposes of exploration, break the rules and try a few different options.

Try It!

1. In the 01 Transitions sequence, move the playhead to the edit point between clip 1 and clip 2 on the Timeline, and then press the equal sign (=) three times to zoom in fairly close.

2. Drag the Dip to White transition from the Dissolve category onto the edit point between clip 1 and clip 2 (FIGURE 8.19).

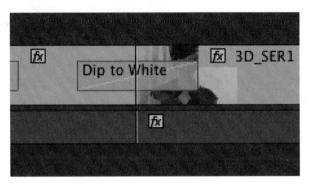

FIGURE 8.19

3. Next, drag the Push transition from the Slide category onto the edit point between clip 2 and clip 3.

4. Click the Push transition effect on the Timeline and go to the Effect Controls panel. Change the direction of the clip from West to East to East to West (FIGURE 8.20).

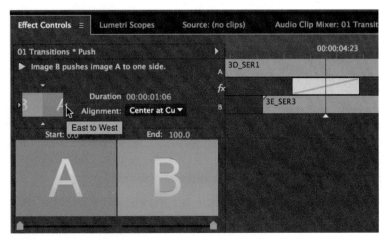

FIGURE 8.20

5. Drag the Flip Over transition from the 3D Motion category onto the edit point between clip 3 and clip 4.

6. Review the sequence by playing it from beginning to end.

   Having watched this sequence, you can probably see why it's a good idea to use transitions with restraint.

   Try replacing an existing effect.

7. Drag the Split transition from the Slide category onto the existing effect between clip 2 and clip 3. The new transition replaces the old one.

8. Select the Split transition on the Timeline. In the Effect Controls panel, set Border Width to 7 and Anti-aliasing Quality to Medium to create a thin black border at the edge of the wipe.

   The anti-aliasing effect reduces potential flicker when the line animates.

9. Watch the sequence to see the new transition.

   Transitions have a default duration, which is measured in frames, not seconds. This means the frame rate of your sequence will change the time it will take to play a transition. The default transition duration can be changed to match your sequence settings in the General tab of the Preferences panel.

10. Choose Edit > Preferences > General (Windows) or Premiere Pro CC > Preferences > General (Mac).

11. This is a 24-frames-per-second sequence, so enter a value of 24 frames for Video Transition Default Duration and click OK. Because this matches the frame rate of the sequence, the default duration is now 1 second.

12. Save the changes to **Ch08_03_xx.prproj**, and close it.

    The existing transitions stay the same, but any future ones you add will have the new duration. Be sure to update this value to match your specific needs if you are using 25, 30, or 60 fps sequence settings, keeping in mind that few transitions employed by professional editors are actually a full second in duration.

Working with Text

Text is very effective when you need to convey information quickly to your audience. For example, you can identify a speaker in your video by superimposing their name and title during the interview (often called a **lower-third**). You may also use text to identify sections of a longer video (often called **bumpers**) or to acknowledge the cast and crew (with credits).

Text, properly used, is clearer than a narrator and allows for information to be presented in the middle of dialogue. Text can be used to reinforce key information.

Premiere Pro has a versatile Titler tool. It offers you a range of text editing and shape creation tools that you can use to design effective titles. You can use the fonts loaded on your computer.

You can also control opacity and color and insert graphic elements or logos created using other Adobe applications, such as Adobe Photoshop or Adobe Illustrator.

Exploring the Titler Window

Starting with some preformatted text and modifying it is a good way to get an overview of the powerful features of the Premiere Pro Tiller. Later in this chapter, you will build titles from scratch.

Try It!

1. Open the **Ch08_04.prproj** from the data files for this chapter.

   The sequence 01 Seattle should already be open. If not, open it now.

2. Save the file as **Ch08_04_xx.prproj** in the location where your teacher instructs you to store the files for this chapter.

3. Go to Window > Workspaces > Effects.

4. Choose Window > Workspaces > Reset to Saved Layout.

5. Double-click the clip Title Start, in the Project panel.

   This is a Premiere Pro title, so it opens in the Titler, with the title displayed over the current frame in the Program Monitor (**FIGURE 8.21**). The text object should be selected by default; if not, click once to choose it.

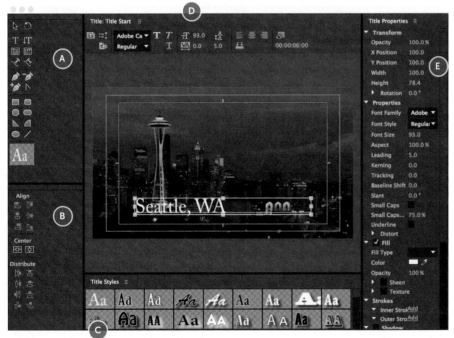

A. Title Tools panel
B. Title Actions panel
C. Title Styles panel
D. Title Designer panel
E. Title Properties panel

FIGURE 8.21

Note:

If the Title Styles panel is hidden, drag the horizontal border between it and the main area of the Titler up.

Here's a quick rundown of the Titler's panels:

- **Title Tools panel:** These tools select objects, set text position, define text boundaries, set text paths, and select geometric shapes.
- **Title Designer panel:** This is where you build and view text and graphics.
- **Title Properties panel:** Here you will find text and graphic options, including font characteristics and effects.
- **Title Actions panel:** You will use these to align, center, or distribute text and groups of objects.
- **Title Styles panel:** Here you will find preset text styles.

6. Click a few thumbnails in the Styles panel to acquaint yourself with the default styles available (**FIGURE 8.22**).

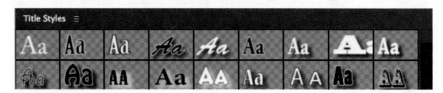

FIGURE 8.22

Each time you click a style, Premiere Pro changes the selected text object to that style. Some of the styles are so large that some of the text disappears off-screen; you will adjust these settings shortly.

7. Choose the style Adobe Garamond White 90, the seventh from the left in the top row. This style works with the background.

8. Click the text object, then click the Font Browser menu at the top of the Titler. This is a duplicate of the Font Browser menu in the Properties panel (**FIGURE 8.23**).

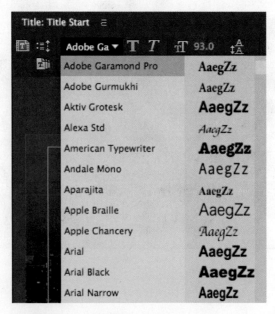

FIGURE 8.23

9. Scroll through the fonts. Each time you choose a new font, the text updates. If you click into the menu without using the dropdown option, you can use the Up Arrow and Down Arrow keys on your keyboard to choose different fonts.

10. Click the Font Family menu in the Title Properties panel, on the right side of the Titler. This is another way to change fonts. Experiment with changing the font through this panel. You can also experiment with the Font Style menu.

11. When you've finished experimenting, choose Adobe Caslon Pro (or a similar-looking font) from the Font Family menu. Choose Bold from the Font Style menu to make the text easier to read.

12. Change the font size to 140 by typing 140 into the Font Size field or by dragging the Size number until it reaches 140. When you do this, it's likely the text will be hidden. This is because it no longer fits inside the text box.

13. Resize the text box by dragging the top handle of the bounding box with the Selection tool (**FIGURE 8.24**).

FIGURE 8.24

14. In the Title Designer panel, click the Center button to center the text.

15. In the Title Properties panel, change Tracking to 3.0. Tracking changes the spacing between the characters.

    Now, make the drop shadow more pronounced and easier to read.

16. In the Title Properties panel, select the Shadow option. Change Shadow Distance to 10, Shadow Size to 15, and Shadow Spread to 45 (**FIGURE 8.25**). You can enter numbers into each field or drag the numbers to scrub their values.

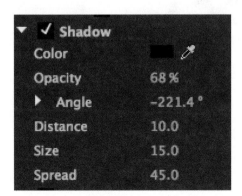

FIGURE 8.25

17. In the Title Actions panel in the Center section, click the Horizontal Center and Vertical Center buttons to align the text object to the absolute center of the screen.

    Your screen should look like this (**FIGURE 8.26**).

FIGURE 8.26

18. Drag the Titler floating window to the right—far enough to be able to see the Project panel.

19. In the Project panel, double-click Title Finished to load it in the Titler.

20. Your text should look similar to the Title Finished text.

21. Close the Titler by clicking the x in the upper-right corner (Windows) or the Close button in the upper-left corner (Mac).

22. Drag the Title Start clip from the Project panel to the Video 2 track on the Timeline, stretch it so it matches the length of the video clip, and drag the playhead through it to see how it looks over that video clip (**FIGURE 8.27**).

FIGURE 8.27

23. Save the changes to **Ch08_04_xx.prproj**, and leave it open.

Safe Title Margin

When you are designing in the Titler, you will see a series of two nested boxes. The first box shows you 90 percent of the viewable area, which is considered the **action-safe margin**. Things that fall outside this box may get cut off when the video signal is viewed on a CRT television monitor. Be sure to place all critical elements that are meant to be seen (like a logo) in this region.

The second box, which is 80 percent of the viewable area, is called the **title-safe zone.** Just as this text you are reading has margins to keep the text from getting too close to the edge, it's a good idea to keep text inside the innermost, or title-safe, zone. This will make it easier for your audience to read the information.

Creating Titles from Scratch

When you create a title, you will need to make some choices about how the text is displayed. The Titler panel offers three approaches to creating text, each offering both horizontal and vertical text-direction options (**FIGURE 8.28**):

FIGURE 8.28

- Point text: This approach builds a text bounding box as you type. The text runs on one line until you press Enter (Windows) or Return (Mac) or until you choose Title > Word Wrap. Changing the shape and size of the box changes the shape and size of the text.

- Paragraph (area) text: You set the size and shape of the text box before entering text. Changing the box size later displays more or less text but does not change the shape or size of the text.

- Text on a path: You build a path for the text to follow by clicking points in the text screen to create curves and then adjusting the shape and direction of those curves using the handles.

In the Title Tools panel, you can select a tool from the left or right column. This determines whether the text will appear horizontally or vertically.

Adding Point Text

Now that you have a basic understanding of how to modify and design a title, you can build one from scratch, working with a new sequence.

You will create a new title to help promote a tourist destination.

Try It!

1. If the Title panel is open, close it and then open the sequence 02 Cliff.

2. Open the New Title dialog box by choosing File > New > Title or by pressing Ctrl+T (Windows) or Command+T (Mac).

3. Type The Dead Sea in the Name box (**FIGURE 8.29**), and click OK.

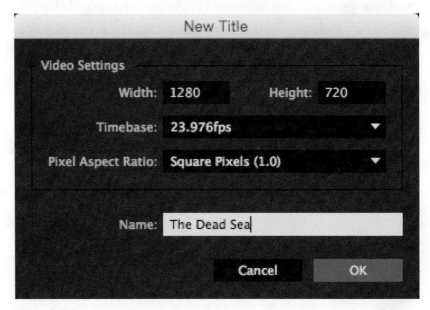

FIGURE 8.29

Try changing the background video frame by dragging the timecode next to the Show Background Video button. You can also move the Timeline playhead to change the background image in the Titler, but it may be hidden by the Titler frame.

4. Click the Show Background Video button to hide the video clip.

The background now shows a grayscale checkerboard, which represents transparency. If you reduce the opacity of text or graphics, you will see some of the background show through.

5. Click the Myriad Pro White 25 style, highlighted here (**FIGURE 8.30**).

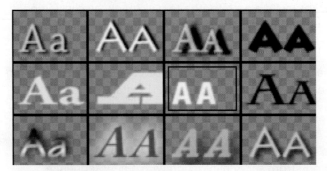

FIGURE 8.30

6. Click the Type tool (shortcut T), and click anywhere in the Title Designer.

   The Type tool creates point text.

7. Type THE DEAD SEA to match the text in the figure (**FIGURE 8.31**).

FIGURE 8.31

8. Click the Selection tool, in the upper-left corner of the Title Tools panel. Handles appear on the text bounding box.

   You won't be able to use a keyboard shortcut for the Selection tool, because you are typing into a text bounding box.

9. Drag the corners and edges of the text bounding box. Notice that the settings for Font Size, Width, and Height change as you do. Hold the Shift key to constrain the text so it scales uniformly.

10. Hover the pointer just outside a corner of the text box until a curved pointer appears. This allows you to rotate the text box. Drag to rotate the bounding box off its horizontal orientation.

11. With the Selection tool still active, click anywhere in the bounding box and drag the text and its bounding box somewhere else in the Title Designer.

    Adjust the size, rotation, and position of the text using the techniques you've learned so far.

12. Click the Show Background Video button to redisplay the background video. Close the Titler window if necessary.

13. Drag The Dead Sea clip from the Project panel to the Video 2 track on the Timeline, stretch it so it matches the length of the video clip, and drag the playhead through it to see how it looks over that video clip.

14. Save the changes to **Ch08_04_xx.prproj**, and close it.

Sharing Your Project

How you share or deliver your project to your client or audience depends on the how you intend to distribute it. Some video-editing applications have direct upload options to online video-hosting services such as YouTube or Vimeo.

Just like with the process of transcoding media for editing, conversion to a more compressed codec for Internet delivery such as H.264, called **encoding**, is needed to keep file size down for quick transfer. Because of the nature of the encoding process, compressing media into a smaller file size while maintaining an acceptable quality can be time-consuming, especially if you have a long program.

Once compressed, you will have a single file, containing all the edited clips, titles, graphics, effects, and audio in one neat compact stream, ready to be delivered through the Internet, stored on the cloud, or copied onto a flash drive or external hard drive.

Nowadays, the primary form of media distribution is digital files. To create these files, you can use Adobe Media Encoder. Adobe Media Encoder is a stand-alone application that handles file exports in batches, so you can export in several formats simultaneously and process in the background while you work in other applications, including Premiere Pro and Adobe After Effects.

Examining Export Options

Whether you've completed a project or you just want to share an in-progress review, you have a number of export options:

- You can select a whole sequence as a single file to post to the Internet or burn to a disk.

- You can export a single frame or a series of frames to post to the Internet or attach to an email.

- You can choose audio-only, video-only, or full audio/video output.

- Exported clips or stills can be reimported back into the project automatically for easy reuse.

- You can play out directly to videotape.

Beyond choosing an export format, you can set several other parameters as well:

- You can choose to create files in a similar format, and at the same visual quality and data rate as your original media, or you can compress them to a smaller size for distribution on disk or the Internet.

- You can transcode your media from one format to another to make it easier to exchange with other people involved in the post-production process.

- You can customize the frame size, frame rate, data rate, or audio and video compression techniques if a particular preset doesn't fit your needs.

You can use exported files for further editing, in presentations, as streaming media, or as sequences of images to create animations.

Working with Adobe Media Encoder

Adobe Media Encoder is a stand-alone application that can be run independently or launched from inside Premiere Pro. One advantage of using Adobe Media Encoder is that you can send an encoding job directly from Premiere Pro and then continue working on your edit as the encoding is processed. If your client asks to see your work before you finish editing, Adobe Media Encoder can produce the file without interrupting your flow.

Choosing a File Format for Export

It can be a challenge to know how to deliver your finished work. Ultimately, choosing delivery formats is a process of planning backwards; find out how the file will be presented, and it's usually straightforward to identify the best file type for the purpose.

Very often, clients will have a delivery specification you must follow, making it easy to select the right options for encoding.

Premiere Pro and Adobe Media Encoder can export to many formats. Following is a list of some of those formats and when you should use them.

- **AAC Audio:** The Advanced Audio Coding format is the audio-only format that is most often used with H.264 encoding.

- **AIFF:** The Audio Interchange File Format is an audio-only file format popular on the Mac.

- **AS-11:** This format is based on MXF (see below), with precise configuration for broadcast television delivery. If you are producing content for TV, you might be asked to deliver in this format.

- **DNxHD MXF OP1a:** This format is included primarily for providing compatibility with Avid editing systems. It is, however, a high-quality, cross-platform file format for professional editing.

- **DPX:** DPX (Digital Picture Exchange) is a high-end image sequence format for digital intermediate and special effects work.

- **H.264:** This is the most flexible and widely used format today, with many presets for devices such as the iPod and Apple TV and TiVo Series3 SD and HD, and for services such as YouTube and Vimeo. H.264 files can be played on smartphones or used as high-quality, high-bit-rate intermediate files for work in other video editors.

- **JPEG:** This setting creates a sequential series of still images.

- **MP3:** This compressed audio format is popular because it produces a relatively small file that still sounds good to the ear.

- **MPEG2:** This older file format is primarily used for DVDs and Blu-ray Discs. Presets in this group allow you to produce files that can be distributed for playback on your own or other computers. Many broadcasters use MPEG2 as a format for digital delivery.

- **MPEG2-DVD:** This creates a DVD-compliant MPEG2 video and audio file for standard-definition discs.

- **MPEG4:** This produces lower-quality H.263 3GP files for playback on older cellphones.

- **QuickTime:** This container format can store media using one of several codecs. QuickTime files use the .mov extension, regardless of the codec. It is the preferred format for use on Macintosh computers.

- **Waveform Audio:** This uncompressed audio file format is popular on Windows computers using the .wav formats.

The following formats are available only in Windows:

- **AVI:** Like QuickTime files, this "container format" can store files using one of several codecs. While not officially supported by Microsoft for a number of years, AVI files are still in widespread use.

- **Windows BMP:** This is an uncompressed, rarely used still-image format.

- **Animated GIF and GIF:** These compressed still-image and animated formats are used primarily on the Internet. They are available only on the Windows version of Premiere Pro.

- **Uncompressed Microsoft AVI:** This is a very high-bit-rate intermediate format that is not widely used and is available only on the Windows version of Premiere Pro.

- **Windows Media:** This produces WMV files for playback using the Windows Media Player, and is ideal for Microsoft Silverlight applications (Windows only).

Configuring the Export

To export from Premiere Pro with Adobe Media Encoder, you will need to queue the project. The first step is to use the Export Settings dialog box to make choices about the file you are going to export.

Try It!

1. Start Premiere Pro, and open **Ch08_05.prproj** from the data files for this chapter.

2. Save the file as **Ch08_05_xx.prproj** in the location where your teacher instructs you to store the files for this chapter.

3. Make sure the Review Copy sequence is open, select it in either the Project panel or the Timeline panel, and go to File > Export > Media.

It's best to work through the Export Settings dialog box from the top down. Choose your format and presets first, then pick the output, and finally decide whether you'd like to export audio, video, or both.

4. Choose H.264 from the Format menu. This is a popular choice for files you will upload to online video Web sites.

5. In the Preset menu, choose Vimeo 720p HD (**FIGURE 8.32**).

These settings match the frame size and frame rate of the sequence. The codec and data rate match the requirements for the Vimeo.com Web site.

Tip:
If the Media option is not available, make sure you have the sequence selected.

FIGURE 8.32

6. Click the output name (the blue text), and rename the file **Review Copy 03** (the program adds the .mp4 file extension by default). Save it to the same destination where you are saving the files for this chapter.

7. Examine the Summary information text to check your choices.

8. Click Export.

Here's an overview of the various tabs displayed under Summary:

- **Effects:** You can add a number of useful effects and overlays as you output your media.

- **Video:** The Video tab allows you to adjust the frame size, frame rate, field order, and profile. The default settings are based on the preset you chose, but you can change them to anything you like.

- **Audio:** The Audio tab allows you to adjust the bit rate of the audio and, for some formats, the codec. The default settings are based on the preset you chose, but you can change them to anything you like.

- **Multiplexer:** These controls let you determine whether the encoding method is optimized for compatibility with a specific device (like an iPod or PlayStation Portable). This can also control if the video and audio are combined or delivered as separate files.

- **FTP:** This tab lets you to enter the details of an FTP server to which to automatically upload the new video file when it has finished encoding.

- **Use Maximum Render Quality:** Consider enabling this setting when scaling from larger image sizes to smaller image sizes. This option requires more RAM, which can dramatically slow down the output.

- **Use Previews:** When you render special effects, preview files are produced that look like your original footage combined with the effects. If you enable this option, the preview files will be used as the source for the new export.

- **Queue:** Click the Queue button to send the file to Adobe Media Encoder.

- **Export:** Select this option to export directly from the Export Settings dialog box. You won't be able to edit in Premiere Pro until the export is complete.

9. Click the Queue button to send the file to Adobe Media Encoder, which starts up automatically.

10. Save the changes to **Ch08 _05_xx.prproj**, and close Premiere Pro.

Capturing and Working with Audio

As early as the 1860s, analog audio was recorded on mechanical devices, using media that included glass, paper, and wax cylinders. The technology progressed to tape, including reel-to-reel (introduced in the 1930s) and tape cartridges (late 1950s). The shift to digital that started in the mid-1970s now means tape is rarely, if ever used, as most audio recordings are digital and stored on media such as hard disks, flash drives, or CDs.

You can record audio with a camcorder at the same time that you record video, or you can record it separately using an audio recorder or a device such as a computer or smartphone. Tapeless devices store the sound on a hard drive in digital format. Some devices store audio on flash memory cards or CDs. There are still some that use cassette tapes, which store audio formats such as digital audio tape (DAT) or even older media such as analog minicassette (analog, 1/8-inch wide), and microcassette (analog 1/8-inch wide).

Capturing audio to a computer requires converting audio signals into digital data that your computer and your audio-editing program can recognize. Similarly, playback requires converting that digital data back to analog audio so you can hear it. The device that performs these conversions is usually called a **sound card** when it's built into the computer or an **audio interface** if it's an external piece of hardware. Both include analog to digital (A/D) and digital to analog (D/A) converters. In addition, software **drivers** handle communications between your computer and audio hardware.

You can capture audio sound bites in much the same manner as you capture video.

- Connect the audio source, such as a portable audio recorder or microphone, to the computer's audio input jack using the cables that were bundled with the source. These are typically either USB or FireWire (IEEE 1394) cables.

- If you are not using internal speakers, plug headphones (or earbuds) into the computer's line-level output.

- Open your digital audio-editing program, such as Adobe Audition. Configure the program settings according to the equipment you are using. Set the latency and sample rate values. Latency determines the delay that audio experiences as it passes through the computer. Low values result in less delay through the system, whereas high values increase stability. Sample rate refers to the number of samples or "snapshots" taken of the signal and is measured in hertz/second. The higher the sample rate, the better the sound will be. A value of 44,100 is the sample rate for CDs and most consumer digital audio.

- Arrange frames and panels in your workspace as you do with video capture and editing.

- Open the audio files you want to edit, and use the tools for editing as desired. When you are done working with a file, you can save it in various formats for use on various delivery platforms. Common formats are MP3, which is suitable for the Web or portable media players; Wave PCM (shortened to WAV), which is the audio format on Windows; WMA (Windows Media Audio), which stores compressed audio and is more common for today's devices; AIFF, which is the standard audio format on Mac OS; Monkey's Audio, which compresses files to roughly half their original size; and MP2, which is popular in radio broadcasting.

Configuring Audition

The following exercises assume you are working in Adobe Audition CC, Adobe's digital audio editing program. Before you start, you should configure your system's audio inputs and outputs according to the hardware you are using. You will also need to set preferences and configure settings in Audition as well. These include the device class (usually MME), the default input and output devices, the latency value (200ms for most computers), the sample rate (44100 is standard), and channel mapping.

Testing Inputs and Outputs

Connect your audio source to your computer. If you are not using speakers, plug the earbuds/headphones into the computer's line-level output. Test these connections to ensure that the inputs and outputs are set up properly.

Try It!

1. Start Audition.

2. Choose File > New > Audio File to create a new file. A dialog box appears (**FIGURE 8.33**).

FIGURE 8.33

3. Name the file **In-OutTestFile**. Leave the sample rate set to default value.

4. Set Channels to Stereo. The Channels inputs will default to what you specify in Preferences. If you choose Mono, only the first channel of the input channel pair will be recorded.

   The bit depth represents the project's internal bit depth, not the bit resolution of your interface's converters. This resolution will be used to calculate changes in volume, effects, and the like. If it did not default to the highest resolution, which is 32 (float), change it, now.

5. Click OK to close the dialog box. The new file is displayed in the Waveform Editor, which is used for editing individual audio files.

6. In the transport controls beneath the Waveform Editor window, click the red Record button, and then start playback from your audio source. If all connections are defined and all levels are set properly, you will see a waveform being drawn in the Waveform Editor window. Record several seconds of audio, then press the Record button to stop.

7. Click the Move Playhead to Previous button in the Transport panel, or drag the playhead (also called the current time indicator [CTI]) back to the beginning of the file. Click Play, and you should hear what you recorded in your chosen output device (internal speakers, earbuds, or headphones). Click the Stop button to end playback.

8. Now test recording and playback in the Multitrack Editor. Choose File > New > Multitrack session. A dialog box appears (**FIGURE 8.34**).

FIGURE 8.34

9. Name the file **In-Out Test Session**. For template, choose None. The sample rate should default to the value you selected in Preferences.

10. As with the Waveform Editor, choose the highest resolution of 32 (float), and then choose the number of output channels (Stereo) for the Master Track.

11. Click OK to close the dialog box.

12. Arm a track by clicking the R (Record) button. Start playing your audio source; the channel's meter should indicate a signal. Note that the input will connect automatically to the default input; however, if you click the input field's right arrow, you can choose just one input for mono tracks (**FIGURE 8.35**) or you can open the hardware section under Preferences if you have a multi-input audio interface and want to choose an input other than the default.

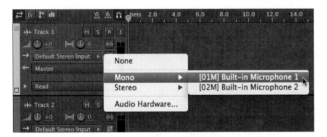

FIGURE 8.35

13. Click the Record button in the Transport panel. If all connections are defined and all levels are set properly, you will see a waveform being drawn in the Multitrack Editor window. Record several seconds of audio.

14. Click the Move Playhead to Previous button in the Transport panel, or drag the playhead back to the beginning of the file. Click Play, and you should hear what you recorded in your chosen output device (internal speakers, earbuds, headphones, or monitoring system). Click the Stop button to end playback.

15. Click File > Close All. If you are asked if you want to save the files, click No To All. Leave Audition open for the next exercise.

The Audition Workspace

Audition's workspace has the same look and functionality as Premiere Pro and other Adobe graphics applications. It consists of frames and panels that you can arrange and customize to suit your needs. You can also choose various ways to navigate through Audition's Waveform Editor and Multitrack Editor.

Audition's Dual Personality

A unique aspect of Audition is that it combines the functionality of two programs within a single piece of software:

- A Waveform Editor that can perform highly detailed and sophisticated editing

- A Multitrack Editor for creating multitrack music productions

The two sections are interrelated in that audio can move freely between the two environments. Audio in the Multitrack Editor can be transferred to the Waveform Editor for detailed editing and then transferred back. Files brought into the Waveform Editor can be tweaked prior to making them the basis of a multitrack project.

Both editors have highly customizable workspaces that you can optimize for any of Audition's uses—not just editing or multitrack productions, but also audio for video, sound library development, audio restoration, sound effects creation, and even forensics. This chapter concentrates on the Waveform Editor, but operations in the Multitrack Editor are similar, and in many cases identical.

Try It!

1. With Audition open, click File > Open. Navigate to the data files for this chapter, and open the file **Ch08_06.aif**.

2. Choose Window > Workspace > Classic.

3. To make sure the workspace uses the stored version, choose Window > Workspace > Reset to Saved Layout.

4. Click on the waveform, which is within the waveform's Editor panel.

5. If you want to see more of the waveform's Editor panel, click the panel's left border, and drag to the left to widen the panel.

6. Increase the panel's height by clicking the panel's lower line and dragging down. Return the panel's lower line to its original location.

7. The Selection/View panel toward the lower right probably isn't needed right now, so choose Close Panel from the panel menu to free up some more space. Note how the Zoom panel expands to take up the space.

   As you have seen, every panel has a tab at the top. Click the panel menu to the right of the tab name, and choose Close Panel to hide the panel. (You can always reopen a panel from the Window menu if you need it later.) Every panel is housed in a frame. You can save space by grouping several panels into the same frame to create a collection of panels that has tabs across the top.

8. Click a panel tab to select the panel. You can drag a selected panel to a different location in the window. Click the Time panel's tab and drag it to the right of the Zoom panel's tab. A strip containing this tab turns blue to indicate it is a "drop zone" where a panel can be dropped.

9. Release the mouse button; the Time and Zoom panels are now within a tabbed frame.

10. Click the Transport panel's tab (the section where you can click and drag a panel to move it), and drag it into the blue drop zone strip that already has the Zoom and Time tabs (**FIGURE 8.36**). Now the Zoom, Transport, and Time panels are all within a tabbed frame.

FIGURE 8.36

11. Click the Zoom tab, then the Time tab, and then the Transport tab. Note that the original double rows of Transport buttons are now arranged as a single row, which allows more space for increasing the Editor panel's height.

12. With the Transport tab showing, click in the Editor panel. Click its lower border and drag down until the Transport panel is just high enough to show all the Transport buttons. Click the Time tab and then the Zoom tab, and note that they've also been resized to fit.

13. To create even more space, move the Levels panel to the left of the Audition Workspace. Click the Levels panel gripper, and drag it to the Audition Workspace's left edge, to the left of the waveform's Editor. Now you can drag the bottom of the Editor panel down even further.

14. Choose File > Close. If you are asked if you want to save changes, click No. Leave Audition open for the next exercise.

Navigating in the Audition Workspace

There are three main elements to navigation in the Audition Workspace:

- Navigating to desired files and projects so you can open them, typically using Audition's Media Browser

- Navigation related to playing back and recording audio within the Waveform Editor and Multitrack Editor

- Navigating visually within the Waveform Editor and Multitrack Editor (zooming in and out to specific parts of the file)

Navigating to Files and Projects

For Mac and Windows, Audition adopts standard navigation menu protocols (such as Open and Open Recent) for navigating within your computer's file system to find specific files and projects.

Try It!

1. If necessary, open Audition, and choose Window > Workspace > Reset to Saved Layout. Navigate to the data files for this chapter, and open the file **Ch08_06.aif**. Or as a shortcut, choose File > Open Recent > **Ch08_06aif**.

2. Choose File > Open Append > To Current.

3. Navigate to the data files for this chapter, choose **String_Harp.wav**, and click Open.

4. The file you selected is appended to the end of the current waveform in the Waveform Editor (**FIGURE 8.37**).

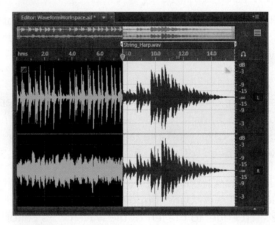

FIGURE 8.37

5. Choose File > Open Append > To New.

6. Navigate to the data files for this chapter, choose **String_Harp.wav**, and then click Open.

7. The file you selected opens in a new Waveform Editor view. It does not replace the previously loaded file, and you can select either one using the Editor panel menu.

8. Choose File > Close All, and then select No To All in the dialog box. Leave Audition open for the next exercise.

Navigating with the Media Browser

The Media Browser is an enhanced version of the browsing options offered on the Windows and Macintosh operating systems. You should be familiar with it from working in Premiere Pro.

Once you locate a file, you can drag it into the Waveform Editor or Multitrack Editor window.

Try It!

1. Choose Window > Workspace > Default.

2. Choose Window > Workspace > Reset to Saved Layout.

3. Click the Media Browser panel tab, press Ctrl (Windows) or Command (Mac), and choose Undock Panel from the panel menu to float it. This isn't necessary but makes it easy to extend the size to see all the available options in the Media Browser.

4. The left Media Browser column shows the drives mounted to your computer. Clicking any of these drives displays its contents in the right column. You can also click a drive's disclosure triangle to reveal its contents.

5. In the left column, navigate to the data files for this chapter. Click its disclosure triangle to expand it, and then click the Moebius_120BPM_F# folder.

   The folder's audio files are shown in the right column (**FIGURE 8.38**). Note how additional subcolumns show file attributes, such as duration, sample rate, channels, and more.

FIGURE 8.38

6. You can change subcolumn widths. Click the divider line between two subcolumns, and drag left or right to change the width.

7. You can rearrange the order of subcolumns. Click a column name, like Media Type. Drag it left or right to position it. This feature is helpful because you can drag the columns containing the information you need the most to the left side, so the data is visible even if the window isn't fully extended to the right.

8. Another Media Browser feature is that you can listen to the files as you browse, thanks to the Preview Transport. If it's not visible, choose Show Preview Transport from the drop-down menu in the Media Browser panel menu. Click the Auto-Play button with the speaker icon; you will then be able to hear a file play when you click it. Click the Stop button to stop the playback.

9. Choose Window > Workspace > Reset to Saved Layout. Leave Audition open for the next exercise.

Navigating within Files and Sessions

Once you are in the Waveform Editor or Multitrack Editor, you will want to be able to navigate within the Editor to locate or edit specific sections. Audition has several tools you can use to do this.

Try It!

1. Using the File > Open command or the Media Browser, navigate to the data files for this chapter, and open the file **Ch08_06.aif**.

2. Drag the left border of the Editor window so you can see all the Transport and Zoom buttons at the bottom.

3. Click about a third of the way into the waveform and drag to about two-thirds of the way through the waveform to create a selection. Notice the playhead at the top at the beginning of the selection (**FIGURE 8.39**).

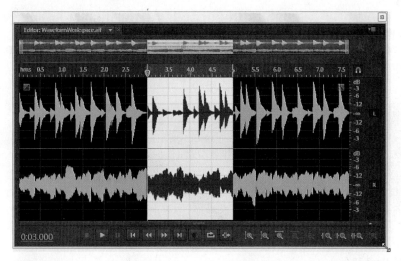

FIGURE 8.39

4. Click anywhere in the waveform to deselect the selection. Leave the file open for the next exercise.

Navigation with Markers

You can place markers (also called cues) within the Waveform Editor and Multitrack Editor to indicate specific places you want to navigate to immediately. For example, in a Multitrack project, you might place markers before a verse and chorus so you can jump back and forth between them. In the Waveform Editor, you might place markers to indicate places where edits are required.

1. Choose Window > Markers to open the Markers panel.

2. Click in the waveform toward the beginning, around 1.0 second.

3. Press M to add a marker at the playhead location and add the marker to the list of markers in the marker window.

4. Now click in the waveform at around 3.0 seconds. As an alternate way to add a marker, click the Add Cue Marker button in the Markers panel (**FIGURE 8.40**).

FIGURE 8.40

5. You can also mark a selection. Click around 5.0 and continue to drag right to 6.0 to create a selection. Press M to mark the selection. Note that the Markers panel shows a different symbol to indicate that this Range marker is marking a selection.

6. You can also convert the Range marker to an individual marker at the selection start. Right-click (Control-click) on either the start or end of the Range marker in the Editor panel, and then choose Convert to Point. You will then see a single marker around 5.0.

7. There are several ways to navigate among markers. Double-click any marker in the Markers panel list, and the playhead will jump to that marker. With Range markers, the playhead will jump to the marker at the range's beginning. Leave the file open for the next exercise.

Navigation with the Transport

The Transport controls offer several navigation options, including navigation using markers.

Try It!

1. In the Markers panel, double-click Marker 03 to move the playhead to that marker. Then, in the Editor panel, click the Move Playhead to Previous button (**FIGURE 8.41**). The playhead moves to Marker 2.

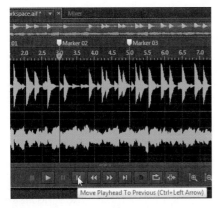

FIGURE 8.41

2. Click the Move Playhead to Previous button again. The playhead moves to Marker 1. Click the Move Playhead to Previous button once more, and the playhead moves to the beginning of the file.

3. Click the Move Playhead to Next button (the button to the left of the Record button with the red dot) four times. The playhead steps to each marker until it reaches the end of the file.

4. To move the playhead backward in the file without dragging the play-head or using markers, click and hold the Rewind button in the Transport until the playhead is in the desired location. You will hear audio during the scrolling process. Rewind back to the beginning.

5. Click the Play button (the second Transport button from the left with the right arrow). Playback begins.

6. As soon as the playhead passes the first marker, click the Move Playhead To Next button. The playhead jumps to the second marker. Click the Move Playhead To Next button again, and the playhead jumps to the third marker.

7. Right-click (Control-click) the Transport Play button and choose Return Playhead to Start Position on Stop (**FIGURE 8.42**). With this option selected, clicking Stop will return the playhead to where it started. With this option deselected, the playhead will stop at the position it had when you clicked the Stop button.

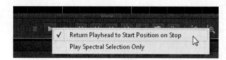

FIGURE 8.42

8. Click File > Close to close the **Ch08_06.aif** file. Click No when you are asked if you want to save changes. Leave Audition open for the next exercise.

Editing Audio Files

Audition makes it easy to cut, paste, copy, trim, fade, and apply other edits to audio files. You can also zoom in to make extremely precise edits while seeing a zoomed-out version in the overview window at the top.

You can open multiple files in Adobe Audition, which are stacked behind each other in the main Waveform view. Individual files are selected via the Editor panel drop-down menu for file selection.

Try It!

1. With Audition open, in the Files panel, click the Open file button (**FIGURE 8.43**). Navigate to the data files for this chapter, select the file **Narration01**, and then click Open.

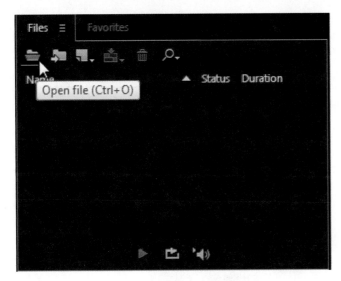

FIGURE 8.43

2. To open multiple files simultaneously, choose File > Open, and navigate to the data files for this chapter. Select **Narration02**, and then Shift-click on **Narration05**. Four files are selected. (To select noncontiguous files, press Ctrl+Click [Command+Click] on each file you want to load.)

3. Click Open. Audition loads the selected files and displays the list of files in the Files panel.

4. In the Files panel, double-click one of the Narration files to display it in the Waveform Editor. Click the Play button to listen to the recording.

5. Click the Editor panel menu to see a list of the files you loaded. Click on any of these files to select it and open it in the Waveform view.

6. Open the file **Finish Soft.wav** from the data files for this chapter. Leave Audition open for the next exercise.

Selecting a Region for Editing and Changing its Level

To begin editing your audio, you need to start by choosing a file and specifying which parts of that file you want to edit.

Try It!

1. If **Finish Soft.wav** isn't the currently loaded waveform, click on the Editor panel menu to see a list of recent files loaded into Audition. Select Finish Soft.wav, and it will load into the Editor panel.

2. Click the Play button to hear the file play from start to finish.

   Note how the words "to finish" are softer than the other words. Sometimes when you are recording narration, a drop in volume can occur at the end of phrases. You can fix this in Audition.

3. Click at the beginning of the words **"to finish,"** and then drag to the end (or click at the end and drag to the beginning). You've now selected those words for editing, as indicated by a white background. You can fine-tune the selection by clicking on the region's right or left border, either in the Waveform view or timeline, and dragging. Note that upon selecting a region, a heads-up display (HUD) with a small volume control appears automatically.

4. Click on the HUD's volume control and drag upward to increase the volume level to +6dB. To preview this change, click Play (**FIGURE 8.44**). Then click anywhere in the waveform to deselect the selection, move the playhead to the beginning, and click Play to hear the change in context.

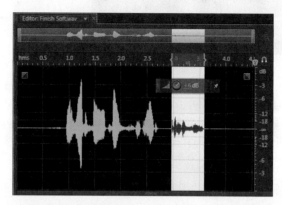

FIGURE 8.44

5. If the level is good, you are done. If not, choose Edit > Undo Amplify, or press Ctrl+Z (Command+Z). Then you can vary the level and audition the results again, as you did in the previous step.

6. When you are satisfied with the level, click anywhere in the waveform to deselect the region. Audition will retain any volume changes, because they occur as soon as you change the level, and they will be retained unless you undo the edit.

7. Make sure the **Finish Soft.wav** clip is selected in the Files panel. Click File > Save As. In the Save As dialog box, rename the file **Finish Soft_xx.wav**, and navigate to the location where your teacher instructs you to save files for this chapter. Click OK. Leave Audition open for the next exercise.

Cutting, Deleting, and Pasting Audio Regions

Cutting, deleting, and pasting audio regions is particularly useful with narration audio files because you can remove unwanted sounds from your narration, like coughs or "umms," lighten up spaces, increase spaces between words and phrases, and even rearrange the dialogue if needed. In this next exercise, you will edit the narration file Narration05.wav so it flows logically and doesn't have unwanted sounds. Here's what the narration says:

"First, once the files are loaded, select the file you, uh, want to edit from the drop-down menu. Well actually, you need to go to the File menu first, select open; then choose the file you want to edit. Remember; you can (clears throat) open up, uh, multiple files at once."

You will get rid of the uhs and throat clearing, and rearrange the narration to say:

"Go to the File menu first; select open; then choose the file you want to edit. Remember: you can open up multiple files at once. Once the files are loaded, select the file you want to edit from the drop-down menu."

Try It!

1. In the Files panel, double-click the file **Narration05.wav** to open it in the Waveform Editor.

2. Click File > Save As. In the Save As dialog box, rename the file **Narration05_xx.wav** in the location where your teacher instructs you to save files for this chapter. Click OK.

3. Play the file until you reach the first "uh" (around 3.5). Stop the Transport, and click and drag across the "uh" to select it.

   To hear what the file will sound like after you delete the "uh," click in the timeline several seconds prior to the region, and then click Skip Selection (the rightmost Transport button (**FIGURE 8.45**)). Click the Transport Play button; the file will play up to the region start, and then seamlessly skip to the region end and resume playback.

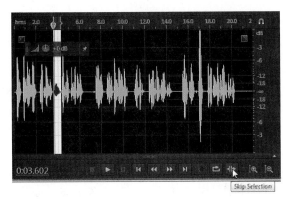

FIGURE 8.45

4. Choose Edit > Delete to delete the **"uh."**

   When you invoke this command (Delete), you may not see any visual difference when zoomed out, because the adjustments are often very minor. However, Audition is indeed moving the region boundaries as defined by the command; you can verify this by zooming in to the waveform so you can see the results with more accuracy.

5. Play the recording from the beginning and listen for the unwanted throat clearing (around 16.0). Drag to select the throat clearing section and slightly after it. Click the Skip Selection button and then replay the section. When you are satisfied with the edit, press the Del [Delete] key on your keyboard as a shortcut.

6. Now delete the second "uh" that's in the audio. This occurs after the throat clearing noise you just removed. You may need to zoom in to be more precise in your editing.

   Notice that deleting this "uh" results in too tight a transition between the words before and after the "uh" (you also have to be careful not to cut off too much of the beginning of the word "multiple").

7. Undo your last cut (press Ctrl+Z [Command+Z]). Instead of deleting the "uh," you will insert silence to produce a better result. To do this, select the "uh" and choose Edit > Insert > Silence. A dialog box appears denoting the length of the silence, which will equal the region length you defined (**FIGURE 8.46**). You could edit this, but simply click OK.

FIGURE 8.46

8. If the silent gap is too long or too short, redefine it. You may have to test and redefine several times to get it right. When you are satisfied with the edit, choose Edit > Delete. The gap is now shorter.

9. Save the **Narration05_xx.wav** file and leave Audition open for the next exercise.

Now that you've fixed some of the verbal glitches, change the sentence structure into a more coherent narration.

Cutting and Pasting with Multiple Clipboards

You are probably familiar with the computer's clipboard. In a word processing program, you typically copy a sentence to the clipboard and then paste it from the clipboard to somewhere else in the text. Audition's clipboard feature works similarly but it has five clipboards so you can temporarily store up to five different pieces of audio for pasting later. You will put that feature to good use when making additional edits to the Narration05 file.

Try It!

1. Select the part of the file that says, **"Once the files are loaded, select the file you want to edit from the drop-down menu."**

2. Choose Edit > Set Current Clipboard and select Clipboard 1 (it will likely already be selected). You can also select this clipboard by pressing Ctrl+1 (Command+1).

3. To remove the phrase and store it in Clipboard 1, choose Edit > Cut, or press Ctrl+X (Command+X) to place the phrase in Clipboard 1. The word (Empty) will no longer appear next to the Clipboard 1 name.

4. Select the part of the file that says, **"Go to the file menu first; select open; then choose the file you want to edit."** You might find it helpful to mark beginning and end points with markers.

5. Press Ctrl+2 (Command+2) to make Clipboard 2 the current clipboard (you could also choose Edit > Set Current Clipboard and select Clipboard 2).

6. Choose Edit > Cut to place the phrase in Clipboard 2.

7. Select the part of the file that says, **"Remember; you can open up multiple files at once."**

8. Press Ctrl+3 (Command+3) to make Clipboard 3 the current clipboard.

9. Choose Edit > Cut to place the phrase in Clipboard 3.

10. Save the **Narration05_xx** file and leave it open for the next exercise.

Now you have a separate clip for each phrase, which will make it easy to place the phrases in a different order. The goal is to end up with "Go to the file menu first; select open; then choose the file you want to edit. Remember; you can open up multiple files at once. Once the files are loaded, select the file you want to edit from the drop-down menu."

Try It!

1. Select all the leftover bits of audio in the Narration05 file (or simply press Ctrl+A [Command+A]), and press the Delete key. This clears all the audio and places the playhead at the file's beginning.

2. Clipboard 2 contains the introduction you want. Press Ctrl+2 (Command+2) to select that clipboard, and then choose Edit > Paste or press Ctrl+V (Command+V).

3. Disable Skip Selection, return the playhead to the beginning of the file, and then click Play to confirm you have the desired audio.

4. Click within the Waveform view to deselect the pasted audio. Otherwise, subsequent pasting will replace the selected region.

5. Click where you want to insert the next phrase.

   For this Try It, you will place it at the end of the existing audio.

6. Clipboard 3 has the desired middle section for this project. Press Ctrl+3 (Command+3), and then press Ctrl+V (Command+V).

7. Repeat steps 4 and 5.

8. Clipboard 1 has the desired ending for this project. Press Ctrl+1 (Command+1), and then press Ctrl+V (Command+V).

Play the file to hear the rearranged audio. For further practice, you can do the following:

- Tighten up spaces between words by selecting a region and pressing Ctrl+X (Command+X) or Delete, or choosing Edit > Cut.

- Add more space between words by placing the playhead where you want to insert silence (don't drag; just click on the desired point in the timeline) and choosing Edit > Insert > Silence. When a dialog box appears, enter the desired duration of silence in the format minutes:seconds.hundredths of a second.

9. Click File > Close All > Yes To All. Close Audition.

Elements of an Audio Script

Audio scripts are written for different purposes, such as a podcast, a radio news program, or a voice over narration for a video. But, all types generally have some common key elements. They should start with an introduction and end with a closing. They should be written in language and cadence used for speaking. The body of the script may include narration, interviews, or a combination of both. It is important to distinguish between the two, usually by labeling interview segments, called actualities, with the text ACT, the name of the speaker, and the duration. Format actualities in bold. Label narration with TRX or TRK and the duration. Identify ambience sound with AMB.

Finally, it is a good idea to provide the phonetic spelling of words and names that may be difficult to pronounce, and to write out numbers and abbreviations so they are easier to read.

End-of-Chapter Activities

REVIEW QUESTIONS

1. When dragging clips into the Source Monitor, what modifier key (Control/Command, Shift, or Alt) should you use to make an insert edit rather than an overwrite edit?

2. In which panel do you view and edit sequences?

3. What is a jump cut?

4. What is a transition?

5. What are the three types of titles you can create with the Titler?

6. What Internet-ready export options are available in Adobe Media Encoder?

7. What encoding format should you use when exporting to most mobile devices?

8. What is the function of a sound card?

9. Summarize the key elements required in an audio script.

10. In which formats can you save an audio file for exporting? When would you use each?

11. Identify at least three audio tape formats.

Review Project 1

In teams of four or five, work together to plan, develop, and create a video that identifies and promotes a club or organization at your school. Target the video to an audience of middle school students who will be attending your school in the future. Assign each team member the responsibility to lead and manage one aspect of the project. Collaborate as a team to plan the schedule, develop the script, shoot the video, and acquire necessary media resources. Then, organize the oral, written, and graphic information you have collected for use in the project. Compile and edit the content to create your final project. Then, modify the script language and the project design so that you can use the video for a different audience, such as parents.

As you work through the project development process, use critical thinking to solve problems and inter-personal skills to resolve conflict. At key points of the process, ask another team to review and evaluate your work. Use their advice to improve your work. Present your video to the class.

Review Project 2

Use the Internet to research various audio tape, tapeless, and file formats. Make a three column chart listing the items, their features, and when you might use each one. Share it with a partner or with the class.

Review Project 3

Create a "how-to" audio clip, similar to the one you worked on in this chapter. Think of something you know how to do that you could teach others how to do; for example, how to use a template to create a resume, or how to open a savings account, or even how to make salsa. Prepare an instructional audio script, including all key elements such as an introduction, body, and closing. Using a microphone or other device, record your instructions. If necessary, capture the audio clip to your computer. Open and edit the clip in Audition. When you are finished, save and export it in a format of your choice and share it with the class.

CHAPTER 8 – PORTFOLIO BUILDER

Complete the following steps to begin editing a Premiere Pro project. The project file has been started for you and all the assets organized in bins.

DIRECTIONS

1. Launch Adobe Premiere Pro and open **PB08.prproj** from the data files for this chapter.

2. Save your project as **PB08_xx.prproj** and save in the location where your teacher instructs you to store the files for this chapter.

3. Choose Window > Workspaces > Editing, then choose Window > Workspaces > Reset to Saved Layout.

4. Double-click the **Promo Edit 01** sequence to load it in the Timeline, if it is not already loaded. In the Interview bin, select the clips **Interview_03.mp4** through **Interview_08.mp4**.

5. Click and drag the selected clips into the sequence, directly to the right of the existing clip.

6. Make sure the edge of the new clips snaps to the edge of the existing clip.

7. Drag the playhead to the beginning of the sequence, or press the Home key.

8. Press the spacebar to begin playback, and then stop playback after the first clip.

9. Park the playhead at 00:00:05:00.

10. Zoom in on your Timeline by pressing the equal (=) key on your main keyboard (not the numeric keypad) three times.

11. Drag the playhead to the right and then back to the left again, so you can hear where he says the word and.

12. If the waveform is not displayed in the Audio 1 track, hover your pointer over the divider line between the track headers of Audio 1 (or A1) and Audio 2 (or A2) until it changes shape, and then drag downward to stretch Audio 1 vertically in the Timeline.

13. Drag the playhead back and forth over the word and so you can identify it in the audio waveform.

14. Park the playhead at 05:17.

15. In the Program Monitor, click the Mark In button.

16. Park the playhead at 06:11.

17. In the Program Monitor, click the Mark Out button.

18. Now remove the video and audio from this region of time. Click the Extract button.

19. Drag the playhead to the beginning of the sequence, or press the Home key.

20. Make sure that the Zoom level in the Program Monitor is set to Fit, showing the entire frame.

21. Press the spacebar to play back the first 15 seconds of the edit, and then stop playback.

22. Press the backslash (\) key to zoom the sequence to fit the Timeline panel.

23. In the Project panel, double-click the **Live** bin to open it.

24. Select **Live_01.mp4**. Hold down the Shift key and select **Live_25-60.mp4**. This will select all clips in between.

25. Click the Toggle Track Output button for Video 2 to make it invisible.

26. Click the Toggle Track Output button for Video 2 again to make it visible.

27. Close the Live bin by selecting it and pressing Ctrl+W/Command+W.

28. Press the backslash (\) key to zoom your sequence to fit the Timeline panel.

29. Click the last clip on the Timeline in Video 2, **Live_25-60.mp4**, to select it.

30. Click and drag the clip to the beginning of Video 2.

31. Choose Edit > Undo to undo your Overwrite edit.

32. Click **Live_25-60.mp4**, to select it again.

33. While holding down the Ctrl (Command) key, click and drag the clip to the beginning of Video 2. Notice how the pointer changes while you do this.

34. Choose Edit > Undo to undo your Insert edit.

35. Toggle on the Lock button on both Video 1 and Audio 1.

36. Click the last clip on the Timeline in Video 2, **Live_25-60.mp4**, to select it.

37. While holding down the Ctrl (Command) key, click and drag the clip to the beginning of Video 2.

38. Click the next-to-last clip on Video 2, **Live_23-60.mp4**.

39. While holding down the Ctrl (Command) key, click and drag the clip so it lines up with the beginning of the **Live_01.mp4** clip on Video 2.

40. Release the mouse button.

41. Select the **Live_02.mp4** clip on your Timeline, and while holding down the Ctrl (Command) key, drag it to the beginning of the **Live_01.mp4** clip and drop it there.

42. Move the playhead to the beginning of the sequence, and start playback to review your changes.

43. Stop playback.

44. Press the backslash key (\) to show your entire sequence.

45. Select the clip at the end, **Live_24-60.mp4**.

46. Press the Delete key. The clip is deleted from your sequence.

47. Find what is now the second-to-last clip in Video 2, **Live_21.mp4**, and select it.

48. Press the Delete key.

49. Zoom in to your Timeline by pressing the equal (=) key.

50. Click on the gap between **Live_20.mp4** and **Live_22.mp4**.

51. Right-click on this selection and choose Ripple Delete. **Live_22.mp4** automatically moves to the left and fills in the gap.

52. Select the **Live_01.mp4** clip on your Timeline.

53. Right-click on the clip and choose Ripple Delete.

54. In the Project panel, twirl open the Audio bin.

55. Double-click the file **Can't_Listen_Edited_Even.aif** to load it into the Source Monitor.

56. Press the spacebar to preview the audio file.

57. In the Source Monitor, click and drag the Drag Audio Only button to the Audio 2 track on your Timeline.

58. Make sure the beginning of the audio file lines up with the beginning of the sequence, and then release your mouse button.

59. Adjust the playhead to the beginning of your sequence. Press the spacebar to preview the sequence with the new audio added. Stop playback when you have finished previewing.

60. Choose Window > Audio Track Mixer > **Promo Edit 01**. The Audio Track Mixer panel appears.

61. With the sequence playing back, click and drag down the volume fader for Audio 2 in the Audio Mixer until the volume is low enough so you can hear Joey's voice clearly. This will be in the area of −12dB.

62. Press the spacebar to stop playback.

63. Press Command+S (Ctrl+S) to save your project and then close Premiere Pro.

Chapter 9

Skills for
Professional Success

Chapter 9 Overview

- Making Decisions
- Setting Goals
- Solving Problems
- Developing Time Management Skills
- Thinking Critically
- Communicating Effectively

- Developing Teamwork and Leadership
- Making the Most of Constructive Criticism
- Developing Personal and Professional Qualities
- Using Technology
- End-of-Chapter Review and Activities

We live in an exciting, fast-paced, complex world. As the future leaders of our families, communities, government, and workforce, it is critical that you acquire the skills you need to succeed in school, work, and life. In addition to specific skills for using technology and applications, and for achieving in the specific field you choose to pursue, you will benefit from learning transferable skills that will help you no matter what life path you follow.

In this chapter you will explore key transferable skills you can use to succeed, including making decisions, settings goals, and solving problems. You will consider how to develop time management skills, think critically, and communicate effectively. You will also learn about teamwork and leadership, how to take and give constructive criticism, and how to develop qualities that will help you succeed personally and professionally. Finally, you will learn how using technology can help you succeed in school and in your career.

Making Decisions

Any time you make up your mind about something or choose one option over another, you are making a **decision**. Some decisions are simple—what time will I leave for school? Some are more difficult—what should I study in college? The results—or **consequences**—of your decisions affect you in big and small ways.

- If the consequences of a decision are positive and contribute to your well-being, it means you made a healthy—or good—choice.

- If the consequences are negative and interfere with your well-being, that means you made an unhealthy—or poor—choice.

You can turn decision making into a process. A process is a series of steps that leads to a conclusion.

1. Identify the decision to be made.

2. Consider all possible options.

3. Identify the consequences of each option.

4. Select the best option.

5. Make and implement a plan of action.

6. Evaluate the decision, process, and outcome. After you have acted on your decision, you can look back and evaluate it based on your values and standards.

Making Thoughtful and Ethical Decisions

Everyone makes poor choices some of the time. Usually, it doesn't matter too much. If you cut your hair too short, it will grow back. Sometimes, though, we must live with the consequences of our actions for a long time—maybe even our whole lives.

Thoughtful and ethical decision-making means considering how your decisions will affect other people, your community, and even your environment. Considering these questions when you are evaluating your options can help you make thoughtful and ethical decisions:

- Is it hurtful to me?

- Is it hurtful to someone else?

- Is it fair?

- Is it honest?

- Is it legal?

- Is it practical?

Setting Goals

A **goal** is something you are trying to achieve. Goals help direct your actions and guide your decision-making because they give you something to work toward. They help give your life meaning, because you know that there is a purpose in what you do. When you achieve a goal, you can be proud and express satisfaction.

If all you do is think about a goal, it's just a dream. You make goals real by deciding what you want to achieve and then planning how to get there. While you should set goals that are within reach, there is nothing wrong with challenging yourself to push harder.

There's a process you can use to help identify, assess, and set goals:

1. Identify the goal.

2. Assess whether the goal is something you really want.

3. Make a plan for achieving the goal.

4. Write down your action plan for achieving the goal, being as specific as possible.

5. Every once in a while, reevaluate your goals.

Developing Measurable Goals

A **measurable goal** is one that includes clear milestones for tracking success. You know you are moving toward your goal because you achieve each milestone. When you want to achieve something quickly, you set **short-term goals**. You can accomplish short-term goals in the near future. For example, meeting a deadline for a project at work is a short-term goal.

It is usually easy to define short-term goals because they are specific and not very complicated. If you keep a to-do list, it is full of short-term goals. You can measure your success each time you cross an item off the list.

FIGURE 9.1

A **long-term goal** is something you want to achieve in the more distant future —maybe a year from now, or maybe even more distant than that. Right now, graduating from college is a long-term goal (see **FIGURE 9.1**). So is buying your own home. Defining long-term goals may be more difficult than defining measurable, short-term goals. You might know you want to travel someday, but you don't know where or how. Breaking a long-term goal down into a series of measurable short-term goals—or milestones—makes it easier to stay on track and measure your success.

Becoming a cinematographer might be a long-term professional goal. The goal is measurable because you will be hired for the position, and work on films. Along the way, you can develop short-term measurable goals of:

- Working as an intern for a video production company

- Taking video production classes

- Producing student films

- Entering competitions

- Graduating from high school

- Attending college

Solving Problems

Any barrier or obstacle between you and a goal is a **problem**. Problems pop up all the time. Mostly, we come up with a **solution** without thinking too hard. You may want to go to the movies Saturday night, but your mother says you can't go out until you clean your room.

- The problem: Your messy room is an obstacle between you and the movies.

- The solution: You clean your room.

Problems occur at work, too, and knowing how to solve them is a valuable skill. Employers like to hire problem-solvers. Clients and co-workers respect problem-solvers.

One way to solve a problem is to use the decision-making process to figure out the best solution:

1. Identify the problem.

2. Consider all possible solutions.

3. Identify the consequences of each solution.

4. Select the best solution.

5. Make and implement a plan of action.

6. Evaluate the solution, process, and outcome.

Developing Time Management Skills

Planning and **time management** are critical skills for succeeding at work. Time management means organizing your schedule so you have time to complete tasks and meet your responsibilities.

To achieve your career goals, you will have to manage your time effectively and prioritize tasks—decide which tasks must be completed first.

Time management techniques include figuring out exactly how you currently spend your time, creating a schedule, making to-do lists, and ranking list items in order of importance.

You can create a time log to figure out how you are currently spending your time. Simply track how much time you spend each day on specific tasks. The log will help you identify how you can use your time more effectively.

Scheduling helps you plan ahead because you know when you will do something and you can be ready for it. You can schedule by any time period, but the most useful are by month, week, and day. For example, a monthly schedule can help you plan a project. You can schedule the time you need to meet with your team, conduct research, and complete your work. If you don't have a schedule, you might find yourself in the stressful situation of trying to complete the whole project in just a few days.

Making a to-do list every morning can help you plan your time for that day. **Prioritize** the items on the list by ranking them in order of importance so you know what you should do first. If something doesn't get done, put it at the top of the to-do list for the next day.

Using Technology to Improve Productivity

You can make use of technology tools to automate some of your time management tasks and increase your **productivity**, which is the amount of work you accomplish. Computer programs can help you organize and meet your responsibilities.

Make use of the calendar program on your computer or mobile device. You can enter schedules, phone calls, and appointments. Use the tasks list feature to record and prioritize the things you need to accomplish. Set the program to display a message or make a sound to remind you of deadlines.

Application programs can also help you complete the tasks on your to-do list. The more skilled you are at using applications, the faster and more efficient you will be at completing everyday tasks such as writing documents and reports, preparing budgets, sending and receiving email, and, of course, creating and editing media. Some programs such as Microsoft Excel even include templates for tracking projects, or creating a to-do list or schedule.

Project Management

Employers value employees who know how to use planning and project management skills to make sure work is completed on time. **Project management** is a process used to take a project from conception to completion.

It helps you design and implement procedures to track trends, set timelines, and evaluate progress for continual improvement in process and product. There are four basic parts to the project management process:

- Identifying measurable objectives. An **objective** is a short-term goal used to keep a project on track for completion. A measurable objective can be evaluated by specific standards.

- Identifying deliverables. A **deliverable** is a product, or segment of a product, that can be provided to an employer, client, or the public.

- Setting a schedule. The schedule should include a timeline with a final deadline, as well as milestones for each achieving each objective. It sets **priorities**—which means deciding which tasks must be completed first.

- Developing supporting plans. Supporting plans usually specify things like how to allocate resources such as funds and technology, how to identify and manage risk, methods for communication.

Many companies have project management software for scheduling, organizing, coordinating, and tracking project tasks. You can find basic project management templates in programs such as Microsoft Excel. There are also specific tools for project management, such as a **Gantt chart**, which is a horizontal bar chart developed by Henry L. Gantt in 1917, that shows a graphical illustration of a schedule (see FIGURE 9.2), and a **PERT chart** (Program Evaluation Review Technique), developed by U.S. Navy in the 1950s, which shows project tasks, the order in which they must be completed, and the time requirements.

These applications help you and your clients evaluate a project's success by tracking both the process and the product under development, based on established criteria, such as deadlines.

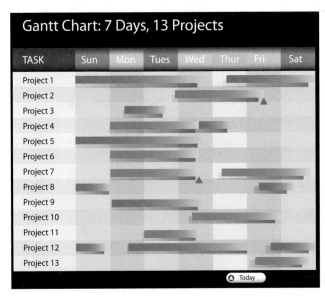

FIGURE 9.2

Goals and Time Management

Combining goal-setting with time management is a very effective way to make sure you get things done. Set realistic and attainable goals using daily, weekly, and monthly schedules. Different schedules can help you identify tasks that must be accomplished within a specific timeframe. For example, you may have to meet with a client today, but you may have to submit a progress report sometime this week. You may have to request vacation time before the 1st of next month, and you may have to attend a safety training session before Wednesday.

Setting specific goals also helps you know how much time you should schedule. For example, setting a goal to meet with team members is not very specific. You don't know how much time you will need. You could meet for ten minutes or for two hours. Setting a goal to meet with team members to brainstorm story ideas, or to review a script is more specific.

Respecting Time at Work

Employers and co-workers expect you to honor and respect time in the workplace. You can expect the same thing from them. That means:

- Showing up on time. No one ever likes waiting for someone who is late (see **FIGURE 9.3**).

- Showing up every day—except vacations and holidays.

- Leaving for lunch and breaks at the scheduled time—not before—and returning promptly—not late.

- Staying until the end of the work day.

- Meeting your deadlines, which means completing all work before it is due.

- Taking care of personal business on your own time, not during work hours.

Respecting time at work shows that you respect your co-workers. It demonstrates to your supervisor that you take your responsibilities seriously. It is one way you prove you are ready for new challenges such as those that might come from a promotion.

FIGURE 9.3

Tips for Managing Time at Work

- Learn to say no. Some people may ask for too much of your time. They may expect you to take on more responsibility than you can handle. It is OK to say no. Be polite and respectful, but explain that your schedule is full.

- Ask for help. If you are having trouble completing tasks that are part of your assigned responsibilities, you will need to find a way to get them done. Ask your supervisor, a co-worker, or someone in human resources to help you learn how to organize your time, or find ways to be more efficient so you can get more work done.

- Notify your supervisor if you are late. Most people try to be punctual—on time. They don't intend to be late for work or meetings. But things come up to delay them. If you are gone without an explanation, you appear disorganized, irresponsible, and unreliable.

- Do not procrastinate, which means putting off the things you need to do.

- Avoid interruptions, which means do not let someone or something distract you from what you need to do.

- Prioritize! Know what to do first helps you accomplish the important tasks so you can move on to the next item on your list.

Managing Resources

Keeping your time and to-do list organized is critical, but if the **resources** you need are not organized, you will not succeed at the task at hand. For example, if you complete the research for a project on time but cannot find it in order to write a script, you will be unable to complete the project. Set up a system of folders—both on your computer and, if you deal with paper, in a filing cabinet—that you keep organized so that you can always find the resources that you need.

One important resource you need to manage is money. Many people track finances by creating a spreadsheet of the **income** they earn and the **expenses** they spend. There are also financial and banking apps that you can use.

Keeping track of finances helps you plan a budget and make sure you are not spending more than you are earning. It also helps you understand where and how to spend your money. Budgeting shows you how much you should allocate, or put aside, for necessities like housing and food. Then, you will see how much you have left over to spend on other things, like entertainment. It is also important to remember a portion of your earned income is taxed by the government. This money must be deducted from your budget. Finally, a frugal money manager saves and invests. You need savings for emergencies and eventually for retirement.

Thinking Critically

Critical thinking can help you evaluate your options in many situations. You can use it when you are making decisions, setting goals, and solving problems, both individually and when you are working with a team. When you think critically, you are honest, rational, and open-minded about your options. You consider all possibilities before rushing to judgment.

- Being honest means acknowledging selfish feelings and preexisting opinions.

- Being rational means relying on reason and thought instead of on emotion or impulse.

- Being open-minded means being willing to evaluate all possible options—even those that are unpopular.

You can think critically about a lot of things, not just decisions and problems. You don't have to believe everything you hear or read. You can question a news report, look deeper into the meaning of a magazine article, or investigate the truth behind a rumor.

When you think critically, you consider all possible options and other points of view. You look objectively at information. Objective means fairly, without emotion or prejudice. Then, you use your values, standards, and ethics to interpret the information subjectively. Subjective means affected by existing opinions, feelings, and beliefs. Looking at things both objectively and subjectively can help you make choices that are right for you.

Communicating Effectively

Communicating is how people connect with others. Communication prevents misunderstandings. It gives you a way to share ideas. It even makes it easier for you to appreciate and respect other people's opinions.

At its most basic, communication is an exchange between a sender and a receiver. The sender transmits the message with a specific intent. The receiver interprets the message and responds.

- **Effective communication** is when the receiver interprets the message the way the sender intended.

- **Ineffective communication** is when the receiver misinterprets the message.

You can communicate effectively by using a six-step process:

1. **Be clear.** The receiver is more likely to get your message if you deliver it in a way he or she can understand. Speak slowly. Consider who you are talking to. You probably use different language when you talk to a client than when you talk to a friend.

2. **Be personal.** Use the other person's name or title so there's no doubt who you are talking to. Use an "I" statement—a statement that starts with the word "I"—to frame the statement in terms of you and your goals. An "I" statement indicates that you are taking responsibility for your thoughts and feelings. It helps the receiver understand your point of view and respond to you.

3. **Be positive.** Phrase your message in positive terms. Say what you want, not what you don't want. For example, say, "I want to start shooting at 9:30," instead of saying, "I don't want to start later than 9:30."

4. **Get to the point.** Follow the "I" statement with an explanation of the message you are sending. Explain how or why you feel a certain way, or how or why you think a certain thing. For example, say, "I want to start shooting at 9:30. I think that will give us enough time to get everything done without having to rush."

5. **Listen to the response.** Pay attention and use active listening techniques to make sure you hear the response.

6. **Think before you respond.** Make sure you understand the message. Repeat it, if necessary, and ask questions for clarification. Use critical thinking to make sure you are not letting emotions and preconceived ideas get in the way.

Ways to Communicate

Verbal, or **oral**, **communication** is the exchange of messages by speaking or writing. Talking is usually a very effective form of verbal communication. When you speak clearly and use language the receiver understands, he or she almost always gets the message the way you intend it. Clear, concise writing is also an effective form of verbal communication, whether it is in a letter, report, email, or text message. However, sometimes the context can be lost through writing, because the receiver cannot hear the sender's tone of voice or see the sender's facial expression.

Nonverbal communication helps put words into context. This form of communication includes visual messages that the receiver can see, such as a smile when you are talking. It also includes physical messages, such as a pat on the back.

Active listening is an important part of effective communication. When you are an active listener, you mindfully pay attention to the speaker, and make sure you hear and understand the message. Active listening is a sign of respect. It shows you are willing to communicate and that you care about the speaker and the message. When you listen actively, the other person is more likely to listen when you speak, too.

Communicating at Work

Just as you use different types of verbal communication when speaking to your friends and your parents, you use different types of verbal communication when speaking to people with whom you relate on the job, such as your boss, your co-workers, your clients, and your **subordinates**—the people you supervise.

- Your boss has a higher rank than you do and has control over your job. When communicating with a boss, you usually use a formal style of verbal communication. You show deference—courteous regard or respect—by using her title and refraining from jokes or casual remarks you might use with a friend. You must also recognize that your boss has the final say on most matters, and so you must know when to agree with her decisions, even if you disagree with them personally.

- Your co-workers, or colleagues, have the same rank in the company that you do. This does not mean that you should joke around with them as you do with your friends. It also does not mean you should use the same style of verbal communication you would use with your boss. You can speak to them more casually.

- Your clients are the source of your business. When communicating with clients, remember the old saying, "the customer is always right." This means that in order to be successful, you must respect your clients and speak with them positively (see **FIGURE 9.4**).

- If you supervise others in the company, you communicate with them using the respect that is due to any worker. You can also use an assertive or positive style of verbal communication, so that they know exactly what is expected of them.

FIGURE 9.4

Not only is what you say important, but so is how you say it. In addition to the different ways you can verbally communicate with others in the workplace, you can use different tones to make your meaning clear. These include:

- Assertive speech, which includes action verbs such as "should," "does," and "will."

- Aggressive speech, which you should avoid in the workplace, since it can lead to arguments or hurt feelings. An example of aggressive speech would be, "You better help me now!"

- Passive speech, which is usually best to use when you also want to show respect or deference. Examples of passive speech include words such as "can," "might," and "could."

Professional Communications Strategies

In a career in audio/video production, you will be expected to use professional communications strategies such as the following:

- Adapting your language for different audiences, purposes, situations, and intents

- Organizing oral, written, and graphic information to best convey your message

- Interpreting and communicating information, data, and observations

- Delivering formal and informal presentations

- Applying active-listening skills to obtain and clarify information

- Developing and interpreting tables, charts, and figures to support written and oral communications

- Listening to and speaking with diverse individuals

- Exhibiting **public relations** skills, which means developing and maintaining satisfactory company relationships internally with its employees and externally with its clients. This may include writing press releases, meeting with the public to discuss projects, and delivering presentations to local government officials or business leaders.

Developing Teamwork and Leadership

A **team** is a group of two or more people who work together to achieve a common goal. When you are part of a team, you have access to all the knowledge, experience, and abilities of your teammates. Together you can have more ideas, achieve more goals, and solve more problems.

A successful team relationship depends on all team members working together. They depend on each other. They trust one another. If one team member does not do his or her share, the entire team suffers. The challenges of a team relationship come from having different people working together. Even if everyone agrees on a common goal, they may not agree on how to achieve that goal.

Many professionals in the Arts, Audio/Video Technology, and Communications cluster work in teams (see **FIGURE 9.5**). For example, audio and video technicians must work with the entire production team to produce a product. Team members meet frequently to brainstorm, plan, check the status of the project, and make sure everyone is on track for achieving goals.

Members of an effective team:

- Listen to each other

- Respect each other's opinions

- Recognize each other's skills and abilities

- Share the work load

- Share responsibility

FIGURE 9.5

Developing Leadership Characteristics

Even when all members of a team have an equal role in making decisions and solving problems, it is important to have a leader. A **leader** is a type of manager who knows how to use available resources to help others achieve their goals.

Leaders exhibit positive qualities that other people respect, such as self-confidence, honesty, effective listening and speaking skills, decisiveness, respect for others, and open-mindedness. They are organized and supportive of the other team members. Being the leader does not mean you are always right.

The leader's opinion does not count more than the opinions of the other team members. An effective leader keeps the team on track and focused on achieving its goals.

Although you might have heard that someone is a "born leader," that's not usually the case. Becoming a leader takes time and patience. Leaders have to prove that they can make decisions, set goals, and solve problems. You can develop leadership characteristics by recognizing and modeling positive leadership qualities. One way to do this is by participating in student leadership and professional development opportunities. For example, you can join clubs and activities such as your school newspaper, yearbook, drama club, or audio-visual club, and volunteer for leadership roles. You might also join a career technical student organization (CTSO) such as SkillsUSA. CTSOs offers members a range of individual and group programs, activities, and competitions designed to build professional skills as well as leadership qualities.

Qualities of an Effective Team Member

While a strong leader is important to the success of a team, team members must also be committed to the group's success. An effective team member helps teammates if they need help, does not blame teammates for problems or mistakes, and offers ideas and suggestions instead of criticism. Effective team members use critical-thinking skills and interpersonal skills to identify and solve problems, overcome conflict, and achieve their goals.

You are a good team member if you are:

- Open-minded

- Willing to compromise

- Cooperative

- Friendly

- Trustworthy

Conflict Management

Conflict is a disagreement between two or more people who have different ideas. Conflict occurs in all areas of your life and can cause stress and interfere with your well-being if it is not resolved. Conflict at work can interfere with your career goals. It can make you angry and cause you to resent the other people at work. If it is left unresolved, conflict can make it difficult or even impossible to successfully complete your tasks and responsibilities (see **FIGURE 9.6**).

- Some workplace conflicts are small, such as a disagreement about who will drive the equipment van to the shoot.

- Some workplace conflicts are more significant, such as a disagreement over who will get the producer credit on a project.

Managing workplace conflict does not always mean eliminating the conflict completely. It means that you are able to recognize what is causing the conflict, and that you can cope with it in an honest and respectful way.

FIGURE 9.6

Coping with Conflict

Knowing how to use communication skills to manage workplace conflict will help you earn the respect of your supervisor and co-workers. It will make you a valuable member of your work team.

Knowing how to value diversity will also help you manage workplace conflict. You will encounter people with different backgrounds and experiences in your workplace. You are also likely to encounter people from different cultures. Sometimes, these differences can cause conflict.

- You might think the food a co-worker eats at lunch stinks, even though it is common in her native country.

- You might be frustrated trying to understand a client who speaks English as a second language.

- You might become impatient waiting for a disabled co-worker to complete a task you know you could do faster.

Understanding the differences between people makes it easier to communicate. Take the time to listen to and speak with diverse individuals. Focusing on the common goals you and your teammates share will help you see past the differences to resolve conflicts.

Coping with Workplace Barriers

Barriers in the workplace are obstacles that interfere with your ability to achieve your goals. Barriers often cause conflict, but they may be caused by conflict, too.

- You might not understand your responsibilities.

- You might find your supervisor is not helpful or supportive.

- You might not feel that you have received adequate training.

- You might think a co-worker is not pulling his or her weight on the job.

You can knock down a lot of barriers by maintaining a positive attitude. A negative attitude can quickly cause conflict and result in the loss of respect and support from the rest of your team.

Effective communication is one of the best ways to avoid barriers at work. Be respectful and polite. Show that you value the opinions of others, and present your point of view in a clear and positive way.

Making the Most of Constructive Criticism

Criticism is an analysis and judgment of the positive and negative aspects of something, such as a product, design, work of art, or project. **Constructive criticism** is when the judgment is delivered in a positive way, and includes advice for how to make improvements or solve problems (see **FIGURE 9.7**).

In any career, it is important to know how to accept constructive criticism and how to deliver it. Both of these require effective communications skills:

- When you offer constructive criticism it is important that you deliver your message in a positive, friendly way so the recipient recognizes the value in your advice.

- When you receive constructive criticism it is important that you listen carefully and consider the message as it is intended—to provide positive feedback to help you improve.

FIGURE 9.7

Judging Artistic Decisions

Many, if not most, careers in audio/video production involve creating or judging works of art. You are likely to find yourself evaluating your own work, and the work of others. For example, you might have to choose between two music selections, or approve a script for a video.

Specifically, you may be called on to interpret, evaluate, and justify your own **artistic decisions** and the artistic decisions of others.

- Interpreting artistic decisions involves analyzing the piece and determining the artist's intentions.

- Evaluating artistic decisions requires judging the piece and the artist's intentions in order to identify the positive and negative effects of those decisions.

- Justifying artistic decisions involves explaining how the decisions enable the artist achieve his or her intentions.

You can use critical thinking skills to make informed judgements about your own work and the work of others. This means considering the qualities of the piece carefully and objectively before making any evaluations or forming any conclusions. Things to consider include:

- the technical, or formal, qualities of the piece.

- the historical context of the piece.

- the cultural content of the piece.

- the artist's intent.

- the meaning.

Once you have taken the time to analyze the work, you can offer an informed judgement in writing or verbally. Remember to be respectful when delivering an evaluation and to point out positive as well as negative qualities.

Developing Positive Work Behaviors and Personal Qualities

Personal qualities are the traits that make you unique. You demonstrate your personal qualities by the way you act and the things you say. These qualities influence the way other people see you and the way you see yourself.

Professionalism, or **work ethic**, is the ability to show respect to everyone around you while you perform your responsibilities as best you can. It includes a basic set of positive qualities and work behaviors that make an employee successful. These qualities include:

- Integrity
- Courtesy
- Honesty
- Dependability
- Punctuality
- Responsibility
- Cooperative
- Positive
- Open-minded
- Flexibility

Professionalism also means you demonstrate professional standards and positive work behaviors, such as regular attendance. A professional also maintains a clean and safe work environment, performs tasks effectively, shows initiative, and takes pride in his or her work accomplishments (see **FIGURE 9.8**). These behaviors lead to advancement at work, in school, and in everyday life.

Most people have both positive and not-so-positive personal qualities. It is the positive personal qualities that will help you build relationships with others and succeed in your career. That's because the qualities that make you successful in other areas of your life make you successful at work, too. Employers look to hire people who exhibit both positive personal qualities and professional qualities.

FIGURE 9.8

Some positive qualities you can develop and demonstrate include the following:

- Flexibility, which is a willingness to compromise or adapt.

- Open-mindedness, which is a willingness to try new things or to hear and consider new ideas.

- Initiative, which is a willingness to take charge or to act in order to accomplish a goal.

- Active listening skills, which means that you listen attentively to speakers to make sure you hear and understand the message they are sending.

- A willingness to learn new knowledge and skills, which shows others that you are helpful, curious, and interested in expanding your abilities.

- Pride in quality work, which shows others that you recognize the importance of performing to a high level are willing to put in the effort to do so.

- Strong oral and written communications skills, which means you have the ability to speak and write effectively in order to get your message across to others.

- Interpersonal skills, which means the ability to communicate and relate to other people in a positive way.

- Leadership, which is the ability to take charge and encourage others to work together to achieve goals.

- Teamwork, which is the ability to cooperate and work with others to achieve goals.

- Appreciation for diversity, which is the ability to understand and respect people from different cultures and backgrounds as well as those who have different values and opinions.

- Ability to manage conflict, which means you can help yourself and others recognize disagreements and cope with them in a respectful and honest way.

- Customer service skills, which means the ability to assist and advise customers and clients in a positive, helpful way.

- Work ethic, which is behavior that shows you respect your employer, your co-workers, your clients, and your responsibilities.

- Adaptability, which is the ability to change in order to function more effectively in a particular situation or environment.

You are not stuck with the same personal qualities for your whole life. You can work to build positive qualities and eliminate the negative ones.

Using Technology

Today, A/V jobs involve working with computer equipment to digitally transmit, record, and play back communication messages. Video and audio editors, technicians that set up and maintain communications systems, print and broadcast journalists, and many other professionals are expected to know how to work with computer hardware and software.

Computers have also affected the way creative artists produce their artwork, from scriptwriting to video and audio editing and even special effects.

Technology is a varied resource that impacts all areas of your life. It makes everyday life easier, more fun, and more rewarding. As with any resource, knowing when and how to use technology can help you be more productive. Using technology just because it's there might be fun; it can also end up wasting other resources, such as time, energy, or money.

For example, the Internet is a technology we use all the time. It can provide many benefits when you use it wisely. You can find information to research a project, watch other people's clips, or to communicate with clients and co-workers (see **FIGURE 9.9**). If you don't use the Internet wisely, you might waste time looking at Web sites that provide incorrect or misleading information.

You might spend so much time online that you put your real-life relationships at risk. Or, you might accidentally send personal information to identity thieves.

Critical thinking can help you recognize how best to use technology in your own life. You can decide whether technology will be a resource you use to achieve your goals, or if it will cause new problems.

As an audio/video production professional you will use a variety of technology applications to communicate your message and deliver your projects. When used properly, these applications will enhance your productivity by enabling you create documents, store data, and manage projects.

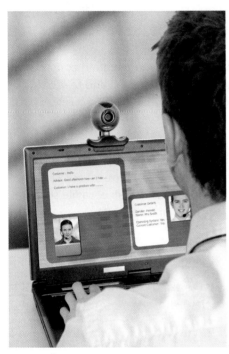

FIGURE 9.9

Social media, such as Facebook, Twitter, LinkedIn, and Vines let you communicate with others, stay up to date with current trends in the industry, and provide outlets for you to share your projects. They also provide opportunities for networking and learning about job openings.

Email lets you communicate with clients, co-workers, and others. While texting is gaining in popularity for immediate communication, email allows for longer, more thoughtful messages. It also facilitates the transfer of documents quickly and easily. All professionals should have an email address that can be included with their contact information on resumes, business cards, and other career-related documents.

Browsing the Internet is a skill all audio/video production professionals should possess. Knowing how to find information when you need it and how to evaluate it for accuracy and validity are important for success in a career.

Basic word-processing skills come in handy for preparing a resume, writing a letter, writing a script, taking notes, and preparing other useful documents.

Knowing how to use a desktop publishing application lets you create publications such as promotional flyers, invitations to screenings, and business cards.

Preparing and delivering presentations is common in the workplace. You may be asked to give a presentation about yourself at a job interview or about a project to a client. Skill with a program such as PowerPoint will help you be prepared for formal and information presentations.

Spreadsheet programs such as Excel let you store and analyze numeric information. They are useful for preparing invoices and budgets, creating charts and graphs, and tracking schedules and progress.

Database applications such as Access let you store all kinds of data and then manipulate the data into reports. You can maintain a database of clients, projects, crew members, and even talent.

Personal information management applications let you maintain contact lists and calendars. Some, such as Outlook, also have email and to-do list features. There are mobile personal information management apps that you can use right on your smartphone.

When you use technology applications, you store information in files. One of the most important skills you can develop is file management. If you cannot find a file, it does you no good. Key file management skills include organizing files in folders, copying and moving files, making files available via file sharing for teammates and clients, and creating backups and versions.

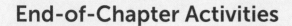

End-of-Chapter Activities

REVIEW QUESTIONS

1. Summarize the six steps in the decision-making process.

2. What is ethical decision making?

3. What are three technology tools you can use for project management? How do they help you evaluate a project's success?

4. What is the difference between effective and ineffective communication?

5. What is a team?

6. Explain conflict and conflict management.

7. What is the difference between criticism and constructive criticism?

8. What is professionalism?

9. List at least ten positive work behaviors and qualities you can develop.

10. How might word-processing skills help someone in an audio/video production career?

Review Project 1

Working with a partner, develop a list of 10 examples of slang in your own language that would probably be misinterpreted or misunderstood during a business conversation with someone from another culture who speaks a different language. Next to each example, suggest other words you might use to convey the same message. Do the alternatives mean exactly the same as the original slang or idiom? Summarize your findings in an email message or post for a class blog.

Review Project 2

In small groups, develop a simple survey about how your classmates use mobile devices to communicate, then use the survey to collect the information. Enter the information into a spreadsheet or table and use it to create a chart to visually communicate the survey results. Prepare and deliver a formal presentation to show your chart to the class and explain and interpret the data. Discuss how having a visual aid affects the communication process.

Review Project 3

Explore the schedule and to-do list templates available in a spreadsheet program, such as Excel. Select one and use it to practice time management skills for a week. At the end of the week, deliver an informal presentation to a partner or to the class explaining how using technology affected your productivity for the week.

Review Project 4

Use a database program such as Access to create a database of creative work you have completed for this course. Include fields for Title, Media Type, Date Created, and Artistic Decisions. Enter the information to complete the table. In the Artistic Decisions field, explain, interpret, evaluate, and justify the artistic decisions you made while creating the item. With your teacher's permission, print a report based on the table and share it informally with the class.

Review Project 5

In small groups, brainstorm a pitch for a 30 to 60 second video demonstrating how a public relations professional might communicate bad news in a way that maintains internal and external customer/client satisfaction. For example, the news might involve the discovery that client or employee information was hacked, or that profits are down and layoffs are imminent. Have the pitch approved by your teacher, and then plan the production. Assume roles that allow each team member to lead at least one aspect of the production. Use technology applications for tasks such as project management, script development, and organization, and to monitor and evaluate the process and the product for success based on established criteria, such as deadlines. When you have recorded the video and sound, use an editing program such as Premiere Pro to produce the final product. Post the video online.

CHAPTER 9 – PORTFOLIO BUILDER

DECISIONS, DECISIONS

How interesting is decision-making? In this project, you will imagine a situation in which someone has to make a decision, and then you will turn it into an engaging, funny, or thought-provoking video. You will work in teams to develop a pitch, and then to plan and produce the video. How much time to you need to deliver your message? The length will be up to you and your teammates.

This project will provide you with the opportunity to practice and demonstrate positive work behaviors and personal qualities that you need to be employable. You will use decision-making and problem-solving skills, as well as critical thinking, active listening, and effective communications.

DIRECTIONS

1. Start by meeting with your team to develop the idea for your video. Use the skills covered in this chapter to work together cooperatively, including effective communication skills, conflict resolution, and teamwork.

2. When you have your idea, pitch it to your teacher for approval.

3. Assign roles to each team member, allowing each person the opportunity to lead one aspect of the project.

4. Use technology applications to set up a project schedule that you can use for planning and time-management. You should be able to evaluate your progress based on criteria that you establish, such as deadlines and deliverables. For example, at what point will the script be complete? When will the storyboard be finished?

5. Write the screenplay or script for your video. Remember that message you want to deliver and the mood you want to create.

6. Walk through the script and analyze it for errors and places where it can be improved, and then revise it.

7. When the script is final, create all the other documents you will need for the workflow process, such as a shot list, script breakdown, and budget. Use technology applications that will help improve your productivity, such as a word processor or a spreadsheet. Keep your digital files organized and available for all team members to access or share.

8. Have a production meeting to review the project and make sure everyone understands his or her responsibilities and the schedule. Evaluate the progress of your process and the product using the criteria you established at the beginning.

9. Audition and cast the project.

10. Collect resources you want to use for the video, such as music and graphics. Secure permission to use all media that you do not create yourself.

11. Record the video clips you will need for your video. Use the techniques for recording quality video described throughout this book.

12. Capture or ingest the footage and organize it within Premiere Pro.

13. Use Premiere Pro to edit the video, including music, narration, and graphics, as necessary.

14. Preview the video as a team and analyze it for ways you can improve it.

15. Revise and improve the video. When you are satisfied with the product, export it in a format of your choice that allows you to share it with your class and others.

16. As a team, take the time to evaluate your work, including both the process and the product. Did your team function professionally? Did you meet your goals? Compile a list of ways you were successful and ways you could improve.

Chapter 10

Career Management

Chapter 10 Overview

- Exploring Careers in Audio/Video Technology
- Academic Planning
- Developing Employability Skills
- Creating Career Search Documents
- Analyzing Job Search Resources
- Ethics at Work
- Developing New Skills
- Applying Professional Communications Strategies
- End-of-Chapter Review and Activities

The field of audio and video technology is filled with exciting and interesting careers. In this chapter you will explore the trends, job outlooks, and educational requirements for these jobs. You will also learn about how to use academic planning to prepare for your career and how to develop employability skills.

Next, you will review how to prepare career search documents, including resumes, cover letters, and thank-you notes, and you will be introduced to the process of applying for a job, including how to find job opportunities, how to fill out an application, and how to prepare for a job interview.

Finally, you explore how to be ethical at work, develop new skills, and apply professional communications strategies on the job.

Exploring Careers in Audio/ Video Technology

The **career** you choose has a major impact on the kind of life you will lead. It determines the type of training and education you will need. It might impact where you live, and the type of lifestyle you achieve.

The U.S. Department of Education organizes careers into 16 **clusters**. Career clusters help you sort career possibilities into 16 manageable groups. The Arts, Audio/Visual Technology, and Communications career cluster prepares you for careers that generate, enable, or facilitate communication between people or businesses. That includes designing, producing, exhibiting, performing, writing, and publishing multimedia content. Audio/Video Technology is one of the pathways in the Arts, Audio/Visual Technology, and Communications career cluster.

The audio/video technology **pathway** prepares you for careers in fields that manufacture, sell, rent, design, install, integrate, operate, and repair the equipment of audio-visual communications. It includes the presentation of sound, video, and data in such venues as offices, convention centers, class-rooms, theme parks, and stadiums, as well as workers who record and edit film and video.

People who find satisfaction working in audio and video technology careers are usually creative, comfortable with technology, and have artistic vision. They must have effective communications skills, the ability to work inde-pendently as well as in teams, and be able to solve problems. Developing these qualities and skills will help you succeed in an audio and video pro-duction career.

Some typical job titles include motion picture projectionists, film and video editors, sound engineering technicians, camera operators, and audio and video equipment technicians.

Will there be jobs for camera operators when I get out of school? Will Texas be hiring video producers? Is the salary for sound engineers increasing or decreasing? One way to learn the answers to these questions is to look at **employment trends**. Sometimes trends in a specific field or industry are called the **job outlook**, which is a forecast or prediction about trends affecting that job. Analyzing employment trends can help you compare and evaluate job opportunities.

The job outlook in this pathway is very strong. According to the BLS, employment of audio/video technology workers is expected to grow by up to 35% through 2020. You can learn more on the BLS Web site, bls.gov.

Education requirements vary depending on the position. For example, pro-jectionists may only need a high school diploma or GED while film and video editors require a four-year bachelor's degree in a related field. According to the Bureau of Labor Statistics (BLS), the annual median salary for broadcast and sound engineers is about $41,000. For film and video editors it is about $57,000.

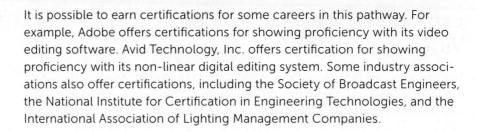

It is possible to earn certifications for some careers in this pathway. For example, Adobe offers certifications for showing proficiency with its video editing software. Avid Technology, Inc. offers certification for showing proficiency with its non-linear digital editing system. Some industry associations also offer certifications, including the Society of Broadcast Engineers, the National Institute for Certification in Engineering Technologies, and the International Association of Lighting Management Companies.

Careers in Audio and Video Technology and Film

- Audio and Video Equipment Technicians

- Broadcast Technicians

- Camera and Photographic Equipment Repairers

- Camera Operators for Television, Video, and Motion Pictures

- Electronics Engineering Technicians

- Film and Video Editors

- Graphic Designers

- Multi-Media Artists and Animators

- Photographers

- Photographic Process Workers and Processing Machine Operators

- Program Directors

- Radio Mechanics

- Riggers

- Set and Exhibit Designers

- Sound Engineering Technicians

- Technical Directors/Managers

Academic Planning

Can you name one thing you can do to increase the amount of money you will earn in your lifetime? How about graduating from high school? Even better, graduating from college!

Graduates are more likely to be hired than non-graduates. They earn more money, are healthier, and live better lifestyles. Completing your education is one of the best things you can do for yourself and your career. Academic planning can help you reach that goal.

School also provides an opportunity to prepare for a career (see **FIGURE 10.1**). Core subjects such as reading, writing, and math are vital for the career-search process. Science, social studies, music, art, technology, family and consumer sciences, and sports all help you gain knowledge and build skills you will need to succeed at work, such as teamwork, leadership, and problem solving. School clubs and organizations also help you build skills for future success.

FIGURE 10.1

How Education Affects Employment

Education teaches you skills and information you need to get and keep a job. Most companies will not hire an employee who has not graduated from high school. Some will not hire an employee who has not graduated from college. If a company does hire dropouts, it usually pays them less than it pays graduates.

Employers assume that graduates have certain characteristics that dropouts don't have. If a graduate and a dropout apply for the same job, the employer thinks that the graduate:

- Knows how to read and write

- Understands basic math

- Can communicate with others

- Knows how to solve problems

- Has a good work ethic

- Has a positive attitude

- Is self-disciplined

- Is motivated to succeed

Developing Communications Skills

Almost every employer wants workers who can read, write, and speak effectively. As an audio/video production professional, you might need to write and edit documents and copy, such as scripts, captions, schedules, reports, and manuals. You may be called on to pitch a project to a producer, read narration, or lead a preproduction team meeting. In all these situations you will be expected to demonstrate the use of content, technical concepts, and vocabulary, and to use correct grammar, punctuation, and terminology.

In school, Language Arts classes help you develop communications skills. You learn to organize written information, understand the things you read, and speak out loud in front of an audience. Clubs and organizations also help you build communications skills. You can join the debate team to learn how to argue politely and effectively. You can write for the school newspaper or Web site. You can perform with the drama club.

Building Math Skills

Basic math skills such as addition, subtraction, multiplication, and division are vital for success in all careers, including audio/video production. For example, you will have to apply mathematics knowledge and skill when you prepare budgets and invoices. You may have to call on math skills such as arithmetic operations for solving problems, such as measuring the size of a set for blocking and lighting, and to correctly position cameras and microphones. You may use time-based mathematics to calculate the number of hours you worked and how much you should be paid, sync audio and video tracks, and write a script that meets the technical specifications for length.

Many audio/video production professionals are self-employed. They benefit from a business math class that covers topics such as accounting, tax management, reading and creating charts and graphs, and personal finance. Many also use highly technical equipment, and would also benefit from advanced math classes, covering topics such as advanced algebra, calculus, and trigonometry.

Study Strategies for Success in School

People who do well in school usually work very hard. They know how to use study **strategies**—careful plans and methods—that improve their ability to remember new things. You can make study strategies part of your academic plan.

- **General strategies.** Sit near the front of the class so you pay attention; take notes; set a daily study goal, such as completing your homework.

- **Strategies for memory.** Study your notes soon after class; make flash cards with a key idea on one side and a definition or explanation on the other side.

- **Strategies for listening and note-taking.** Listen for clues that the speaker is giving a key point; underline or star the main points; use abbreviations for commonly used words.

- **Strategies for planning and organization.** Keep a calendar, schedule, or to-do list; write assignments and due dates in an assignment notebook and on a calendar; prioritize your responsibilities and tasks; break a large project into smaller steps, and set a deadline for each step.

- **Strategies for tests.** Ask your teacher what the test will cover and what type of questions it will include; don't wait until the night before to study—study a little bit each evening in the days leading up to the test; read test directions carefully; check your answers; skip questions you are unsure of and go back to them after you have completed the others.

Setting Goals for Postsecondary Education

Is a high school diploma enough education to land you the career of your choice? If not, you will want to start thinking about **postsecondary education**, or school after high school (see **FIGURE 10.2**). For most people, postsecondary education means college, but it can also include military training and apprenticeships.

FIGURE 10.2

You may enroll in a program to earn a professional certificate for a career such as camera operator. Many careers require a minimum of an associate's degree—two years after high school—and many require a bachelor's degree—four years post high school. Professions such as doctor, lawyer, and teacher require additional education. Planning for postsecondary education involves:

- Selecting a school or program

- Making sure you have the necessary qualifications

- Applying for admission

- Obtaining financial aid

Goal-setting skills can help you manage the process from start to finish. It can help you stay focused on the educational objectives that you need to achieve your career goals.

Researching Colleges

You can find information about different postsecondary opportunities online, in your school guidance center, and at the library. As you research the programs, ask yourself the following:

- Does it offer a degree in my field of interest?

- Where is it located? Will I live at home or on campus? Is it in a city or a small town?

- How many students are there? Will I be more comfortable in a small school or a large school?

- How much does it cost? What is the annual **tuition**—cost of education? How much is **room and board**—the cost of a dorm room and meals? Are there additional fees?

- Am I qualified for admission? Does my grade point average meet the school standards? Are my ACT or SAT scores high enough? Do I have the right extracurricular activities?

Things You Need to Apply to College

A college application form asks for information about yourself and your family. It has space for listing your extracurricular activities and for a personal essay that tells the college about you, your goals, and your abilities. In addition to the application form, you will also need:

- An official **transcript**, which is a record of the courses you took in high school and the grades you earned

- An official score report, which gives the results of the standard college entrance exam, such as the Scholastic Aptitude Test (SAT) or American College Test (ACT)

- Recommendations, which are forms that you ask one teacher and one counselor to fill out, describing your qualities as a student and a person

- Financial aid forms, which provide information about your ability to pay

Developing Employability Skills

You might graduate from college with a bachelor's degree in video production, but if clients think you are unfriendly, or if they question your confidence, they are unlikely to hire you. Attitude and confidence are part of employability. **Employability** means having and using your life skills and abilities to be hired and stay hired. It is more than just meeting the qualifications for a position. It also means knowing how to:

- Present your positive qualities to an employer

- Communicate effectively with employers, co-workers, and customers

- Meet your responsibilities at work

Having employability skills will give you an advantage when you are ready to apply and interview for a position, no matter what career you choose.

Employability skills can generally be placed into two groups: **hard skills** and **transferable skills**. Employers often look for people with hard skills to fill specific jobs. For example, a video producer looks to hire people skilled at operating a camera, mixing sound, or editing clips.

Transferable skills can be used on almost any job. They are called transferable skills because you can transfer them from one situation or career to another. The foundation skills you use to succeed in other areas of your life, such as decision-making and problem-solving, are transferable skills. You can practice and develop these skills in school and at home.

Some computer skills are also transferable. There are very few jobs today that do not require basic computer use. If you have these basic skills, you can take them wherever you go:

- Turn a computer on and start a program.
- Type on a computer keyboard without making many mistakes.
- Access the Internet and navigate from one location to another.
- Use a search engine to do basic Internet research.
- Write and send e-mail.

Professional Appearance

Dress standards vary depending on the career that you choose. For example, you wouldn't expect a boom operator to be wearing a suit and tie, and you wouldn't want a business manager to be wearing grease-covered clothing. However, good grooming habits are required in all professions. The following are recommendations for maintaining a well-groomed, professional appearance:

- Wear clothes that are clean, neat, and in good repair.
- Wear clean and appropriate shoes.
- Keep your hair neat and clean.
- Brush your teeth at least twice a day.
- Floss daily.
- Use mouthwash or breath mints.
- Bathe daily.
- Use unscented deodorant.
- Keep makeup light and neutral.
- Keep jewelry to a minimum.
- Do not use perfume or cologne.
- Keep nails clean.

Part of your responsibility as a worker is to make sure that you keep your work environment safe for yourself and for others. You can practice this at school and at home. You have to take some responsibility for your own safety. That means using equipment properly, according to instructions, and being aware of safety hazards.

Creating Career Search Documents

As part of a career search, you will need to prepare and organize the materials you will need for a job search. Every job search requires the following:

- A **resume**, which is a written summary of your work-related skills, experience, and education. It introduces you to the prospective employer by presenting a snapshot of your qualifications. It should be brief and to the point, printed on white paper, true and accurate and have no typographical, grammatical, or spelling errors. A good resume attracts the interest of the reader so he or she wants to learn more about you (see **FIGURE 10.3**).

- A **cover letter**, or letter of interest, which is a letter of introduction that you send with a resume.

- A list of **references** that includes the names and contact information of people who know you and your qualifications and who are willing to speak about you to potential employers.

- A **thank-you letter** that you send to the employer after an interview to show your interest in the position.

In addition, careers in audio/video production often require a **portfolio** and/or **showreel**, which is a collection of your best work that you can show a potential employer.

A cover letter is a strong and succinct way to introduce yourself to a potential client or employer. It also helps convince employers to review your resume by focusing attention on specific resume information, for example, credentials, skills, or specific projects in your portfolio of design work. The letter should be concise and well written, with no grammar or spelling mistakes. The cover letter is your first point of contact, so craft one that makes an excellent impression.

FIGURE 10.3

A resume, which summarizes your training and experience, is absolutely necessary when searching for a job, especially because employers will usually want to review all resumes and portfolios before inviting an applicant for an interview. Employers often have to sort through large numbers of resumes, so make yours informative, easy to read, and concise. A resume should list your education, experience, and skills but should never exceed two pages.

Here are some general best practice guidelines for a professional resume:

- Include a list of schools you attended, with dates and degrees you have earned.

- Include your work history, including internships and volunteer work. Emphasize jobs where you gained relevant experience, summarizing your responsibilities and skills with bullet lists.

- List all licenses and certifications you have earned.

- List relevant work samples, and/or provide links to an online portfolio where employers can view digital versions of your work.

- Make it easy to read. Leave space between lines so it is not crowded or overloaded.

- Use one, easy-to-read font, and apply different font styles and sizes for emphasis.

- Bullets are effective for making lines of text stand out.

- Employ proper spelling, punctuation, grammar, and use of any technical terms.

- Keep it to one page, if possible; two pages at the most. (If you use two pages, be sure to put your name in the header or footer on page 2, in case it becomes separated from page 1.)

- If you are printing the document, use plain white paper.

Filling out a Job Application

A **job application** is a standard form you will fill out when you apply for a job. You might fill it out in person when you visit a potential employer, or you might fill it out online. It requires a lot of the same information that you put on your resume, such as your contact information, as well as details about your education and work experience. It may ask for your Social Security number.

Filling out an application form may seem simple, but a lot of people make mistakes or forget important information. A messy or incomplete job application will not make a positive impression on the employer (see **FIGURE 10.4**).

- Read the form before you start filling it out.

- Follow all instructions.

- Be truthful and accurate.

- Write neatly.

- Enter N/A for not applicable if there is a question that does not apply to you.

- Check your spelling and grammar.

- If you make a mistake, ask for a new form and start again.

FIGURE 10.4

You might find it helpful to bring a personal information card with you when you apply for a job. A personal information card is an index card on which you write the information you might need, such as your Social Security number and the contact information for your past employers.

Preparing for a Job Interview

If an employer thinks you have the qualifications for the job, you will be invited for a **job interview**. A job interview is a meeting between a job seeker and a potential employer—the interviewer. A preliminary interview may be by phone, but almost all employers will expect a face-to-face meeting. The interview is an opportunity for you and the interviewer to ask questions and decide if the position is right for you. Of course, for some audio/video careers, you may have to audition, so be prepared.

Use these four steps to prepare for a job interview.

1. Research the company or organization where you are going for the interview. Talk to someone who works there. Visit the company's Web site.

2. Make a list of questions an interviewer might ask you. Common questions include, "Tell me about yourself.", "Why do you want to work here?", "Do you have the skills to get the work done?", and "Why should I hire you?".

3. Prepare answers to the questions. Be specific. Emphasize your strengths, skills, and abilities. Explain how you solved a problem, made an important decision, or showed responsibility. Mention your goals and how you plan to achieve them.

4. Make a list of five to ten questions you can ask the interviewer. Ask about the company, the work environment, and the position. Common questions include "What kinds of projects or tasks will I be responsible for?", "Is there opportunity for advancement?", "What are the hours?", "What is the salary range?", and "When will you make a hiring decision?".

PRACTICING FOR A JOB INTERVIEW

A job interview is stressful. You are trying to make a good impression. You want to look and sound your best. You want the interviewer to like you and to respect you. Practicing for the interview by rehearsing your behavior and answers to questions helps give you confidence.

Working with a partner is probably the best way to practice. You can take turns being the interviewer and the job seeker. If you are alone, practice in front of a mirror. If possible, record your practice so you can watch yourself.

- Be truthful.

- Pronounce your words in a strong, clear voice.

- Keep your answers brief and to the point.

- Use positive nonverbal communication, such as eye contact, relaxed arms, and good posture.

- Dress as you would for an actual interview.

- Avoid fidgeting or playing with your hair.

- Ask someone to critique your interviewing skills, and use their comments to improve your technique.

MAKING THE MOST OF THE JOB INTERVIEW

Many interviews are 10–15 minutes long. How can you best use that time to get a job offer?

- Dress neatly and professionally. Your clothes should be clean and appropriate for the workplace.

- Be clean. Comb your hair, brush your teeth, and wear deodorant. Avoid using body products that have a strong odor.

- Arrive ten minutes early.

- Be polite and respectful to everyone you meet.

- Shake hands with your interviewer.

- Listen carefully, using positive body language. For example, smile and lean forward slightly when the interviewer is talking.

- Use proper English when you speak; no slang.

- Avoid chewing gum, cell phone calls, and texting.

- At the end of the interview, shake hands again, and thank the interviewer.

After the interview, you should write a thank-you note. A thank-you note reminds the interviewer that you are serious about wanting the job. You use a thank-you note to restate your interest in the job and your qualifications and to thank the interviewer for spending time with you. Refer to something specific that you discussed during the interview. Address the note to the person who interviewed you. It may be acceptable to send a thank-you note by e-mail, but mailing an actual printed letter will make a positive impression.

Analyzing Job Search Resources

The first step in applying for a job is finding out what jobs are available. How can you find opportunities that meet your needs and fit your strengths? You can use **job search resources**—tools designed to help you find **job leads**—to identify opportunities for employment.

You can use a variety of resources to identify available jobs. You will probably need to use more than one of the following resources.

- Networking uses people you know to help you find opportunities.

- Online resources let you access information and job listings on the Internet.

- Career counselors help you identify jobs that match your skills, interests, and abilities.

- Employment agencies work to match employers with employees.

- Job fairs provide an opportunity to introduce yourself to many different employers.

Knowing how to make the most out of available job search resources is critical for finding a job.

What Is Networking?

Some studies show that nearly 80 percent of all job openings are never advertised. How can you find out about a job if it isn't advertised? Network! **Networking** in a job search means sharing information about yourself and your career goals with personal contacts—people you know already, or new people you meet in any area of your life. Hopefully, one of the contacts works for a company that is hiring, or knows someone at a company that is hiring. The contact recommends you for the position. Employers like to hire people who come with a recommendation from someone they know and trust.

How Do I Network?

The first step in networking is to tell everyone you know that you are looking for work. Be specific about your career goals. Tell your family, friends, classmates, and teachers. If you volunteer, tell the people at the volunteer organization. If you are a member of a club or organization, tell the other members. Stay in touch with your contacts through regular calls or e-mails.

Set up a networking file to keep track of each contact. Set up the file using index cards or a computer program. In the file, include:

- The name, occupation, mailing address, phone number, and e-mail address of each contact.

- A reminder of how you know the contact. Is it a personal friend? Did you meet through someone else? Did you meet through a club or organization?

- Notes about each time you communicate with the contact. The first time you call a contact, explain who you are and why you are calling.

Do not ask for a job. Instead, ask for:

- Job leads

- Information about occupations and companies, such as what trends are affecting a certain industry

- Introductions to people who might become part of your network

Remember to give the contact your phone number and e-mail address so he or she can reach you. Always be polite, speak clearly, and say thank you.

Using Online Resources

The Internet is a great tool for finding career prospects and job leads. You can even use it to make contacts for networking. Some of the more effective online resources include:

- **Company Web sites.** You can learn a lot about a company from its Web site, including what they do, the backgrounds of the people who work there, and who to contact in each department. Most sites also have a page listing job openings, with information on how to apply. Even if there are no openings that interest you, you can contact the human resources department to try to set up an informational interview.

- **Government sites.** Like corporations, government agencies list information and job openings. There are also government Web sites that provide job listings.

- **Industry sites.** Many industries and industry associations have Web sites that list job opportunities. This is particularly true for audio/video production jobs.

- **Social networking sites.** You can use social networking sites such as Facebook or LinkedIn to meet contacts and learn about jobs. There are groups for people in certain careers, or who work for specific companies. Employers join these sites, as well. They look for potential employees based on the personal profile you create.

Using a Career Center

A career center is an excellent place to start a job search. Your school might have a career center that you can use free of charge. Career centers have job listings, research resources, and counselors who will help you identify jobs that match your skills and interests. They can also introduce you to former students who are now employed—giving you more opportunities for networking.

Employment offices are similar to career centers. Some are sponsored by the state or local government. They provide job search resources and assistance free of charge.

Private employment agencies charge a fee to match employees with employers. Sometimes you pay the fee, and sometimes the employer pays the fee. Sometimes you pay even if you don't find a job. They all have different policies, so be sure to ask before you sign a contract.

Managing Your Job Search Resources

Keeping your job search resources organized will help you follow up on every possibility. When you are actively looking for work at many companies, it is easy to forget who you spoke to and even what you spoke about. An employer might not look favorably on someone who repeats the same conversation, or cannot remember who referred her in the first place.

- Keep a to-do list of tasks you want to accomplish each day, such as people you want to contact, resumes you have to send out, and thank-you notes to write. Cross off each item you complete, and add new items as they come up.

- Contact some people in your network every day. Make brief phone calls, or send brief e-mail messages to let them know you are looking for work, and to ask for assistance finding job opportunities.

- Follow up on all leads. Keep a record of the people you contact, including phone numbers, e-mail addresses, and mailing addresses. Include the dates and times, the method of communication, and the result. Did they invite you in for an interview? Did they refer you to someone else?

Most job seekers these days don't send resumes or cover letters via snail mail. Almost all initial communication is done by e-mail, so all job data (resumes, cover letters, etc.) should be in computer files, not paper files. Set up computer folders for storing document files that relate to your job search. Use the folders to keep track of information you send to each contact or potential employer, and the response you get back. The folder might include copies of the cover letter and work samples (in PDF format, perhaps) that you sent. It might also include notes you took during a phone call or interview, a brochure about the company, and copies of e-mails you received.

Comparing Job Opportunities

What happens if you are offered a job? A job offer is good news. But, before you accept the offer, make sure you have the information you need to make the best decision. You should evaluate and compare every opportunity to make sure the position is right for you. Things to consider include:

- What are the responsibilities?

- What is the salary?

- What is the work environment?

- Are there benefits, such as health insurance and vacation time?

- When does the job start, and, for a contract or project-based position, when does it end?

- What are the hours?

When you have all the information you need, use the decision-making process to decide whether to accept the position or not. If you accept the offer, thank the employer and ask when and where you should report to work. You may have to sign a formal letter of acceptance, sign a contract, or write a letter of intent, which states that you are accepting the position.

If you reject the offer, you should still write a letter of intent, thanking the employer and stating that you are not accepting the position.

Ethics at Work

Recall that ethics are a set of beliefs about what is right and what is wrong. Work ethics are beliefs and behaviors about what is right and wrong in a work environment. Ethical behavior includes treating people with respect and also following the law. For example, taking credit for someone else's ideas is not ethical, and taking home office supplies is not ethical—it's stealing. Ethical employees make ethical decisions, which means they consider how their decisions will impact others, including their employer. Ethical employees respect confidentiality. They do not share client information or sensitive company content with unauthorized individuals. Employers value employees who behave ethically at work. It shows that you are honest and respectful, so others will trust and respect you in return.

Behaving ethically at work also means following the company rules, regulations, and processes. Usually, when you start a new job you are given an employee handbook. An employee handbook describes company policies and procedures, such as how to request vacation time, and the different benefits that are available. It should also list all rules and policies that you are expected to obey. These might include:

- Maintaining confidentiality of information.

- Respecting copyrights and patents.

- Respecting co-workers' and customers' rights.

Ethics extends beyond the actions and behaviors of individual workers. It also applies to companies and organizations as a whole. A company that ignores the safety of workers, or hides information customers need to make an informed purchasing decision, is not behaving ethically. Sometimes an employee becomes aware that the employer is behaving in an unethical manner. In that case, the employee might be faced with a difficult decision about how to proceed. Options include speaking up in order to try to change the behavior or resigning. In some cases, it may include contacting the police or other law-enforcement agency to report illegal activity.

Using Technology Ethically

How people use technology, including computers, smartphones, networks and e-mail, can affect other people. People who practice ethics behave morally. Ethical computer users respect others, and make sure their actions do not harm anyone.

USING SOFTWARE LEGALLY

Buying proprietary, copyrighted software comes with a software license, which allows the buyer to use and install the program, and sometimes entitles the buyer to receive free or reduced cost support and updates. Individuals might buy a single-user license for one copy of the program, or a single-seat license to install the program on a single computer. Organizations such as schools or businesses usually buy a volume or site license, which lets them install on multiple systems or a network for multiple users. Network licensing generally costs less per user and allows users to share resources.

SOFTWARE PIRACY

People who copy copyrighted software to install on other computers, give away, or sell are guilty of violating federal copyright laws and stealing, called software **piracy**. Violating a copyright and pirating software are both morally wrong and illegal. These activities discourage the authors of good software from writing new and better programs because they may not get paid for their work. Pirated software cannot be registered, so users do not get the support services they may need.

ACCEPTABLE USE POLICIES

One way you can act ethically is to follow your school district's **acceptable use policy**, or AUP. These policies identify the responsibilities of Internet use. They spell out certain rules of behavior and explain the consequences of breaking those rules. Many businesses use AUPs, too, to govern the way workers use company-owned computers. An AUP may include the following ethical guidelines:

- Do not visit Web sites that contain content that does not meet community standards.

- Do not use language that is profane, abusive, or impolite.

- Do not copy copyrighted material or damage computer equipment belonging to the school.

- Do respect the privacy of other people.

Schools and businesses may restrict the content that users can access from internal computers. For example, they may censor, or block, specific sites that they determine are inappropriate.

They may also use a filter to block access to sites. Disabling the filters or otherwise accessing blocked sites is considered breaking the AUP and may result in punishment.

People who do not follow these rules may face consequences. They might lose privileges or be suspended from school activities. Very serious violations, such as using a school computer to threaten someone, may require police involvement.

PRACTICING NETIQUETTE

E-mail and other forms of digital communication sometimes feel anon-ymous, which might make you think you do not have to be polite and respectful. Personal communication with family and friends may be more informal than communicating for school or business, but in both cases it is important to follow basic rules of **netiquette**, or online behavior. As an ethical user of technology, you have a responsibility to use netiquette at all times. Some ways to practice netiquette include:

- Use correct spelling. Proofread before sending to make sure there are no errors.

- Using all capital letters is considered to be shouting. Be sure to use proper capitalization.

- Don't forward or send unwanted messages or spam.

- Don't flame, or insult, anyone, even as a joke. Sometimes written com-munication is misinterpreted as being serious, even when if you said it out loud it might be considered funny.

- Don't be a cyberbully. Using electronic communication to hurt, scare, intimidate, or otherwise bully others is a crime.

- Don't make false statements that might hurt someone's reputation. It's called libel, or slander, and it's illegal.

- Send e-mails only to people who really need to see a message.

- Keep e-mail messages short.

- Avoid sending extremely large files via e-mail.

- Do not use impolite or rude language when communicating online.

- Do not pretend to be someone else when communicating online.

- Do not use someone else's work without citing the source.

- Do not share files illegally.

PERSONAL SECURITY GUIDELINES

In addition to being an ethical user of technology, it is important that you protect your personal security online. Following are some guidelines for maintaining your security and privacy:

- Set your Internet browser to the highest level for security and privacy.

- Delete e-mail from unknown senders without opening it.

- Do business online only with established companies that you know and trust.

- Never send your user name, password, account information, or social security number over the Internet.

- Never reveal financial or other personal information over the Internet.

Personal security also includes following safety rules and emergency procedures in your classroom. Read all posted safety and emergency information and follow all procedures during drills so you are prepared if an actual emergency occurs.

MANAGING YOUR ONLINE IDENTITY

Online, people learn about you by what you post and what sites you frequent. You can use your online profile to both promote a positive image, or **brand**, of yourself, and to protect your identity. Building your brand means making sure everything you post or display online supports the reputation and character you want people to associate with you.

You can protect your identity by making sure you effectively manage all of your online profiles, including on gaming sites and on social networking sites such as Twitter, LinkedIn, and Facebook. Be sure to set privacy settings and to never give out your personal information in your profiles. You might also maintain both a professional and a personal identity. For example, you might have two e-mail accounts; one you use for professional and business communication such as a job search, and one you use for personal communication with your friends and family.

Exploring Laws Regarding the Use of Technology

As you create and use digital information for the use in arts, audio/video technology, and communications studies and careers, it is important that you comply with relevant laws. You have already explored ethical use of technology and copyright laws. Other regulations for compliance issues relevant to this cluster include:

- The First Amendment to the U.S. Constitution

- Federal Communications Commission regulations

- The Freedom of Information Act

- Liability Laws

THE FIRST AMENDMENT

The First Amendment to the Constitution guarantees rights to certain freedoms, including freedom of speech and freedom of the press. That means that the government cannot persecute individuals or organizations who express their opinions.

Of course, when the Constitution was written, this amendment applied to speech, writing, and print, as there was no digital information. Now, the U.S. Supreme Court has expanded its interpretation to include broadcasting, the Internet, and other digital forms of expression.

There are some instances, however, where freedom of speech is not protected. They include defamation, which is when you make false statements that damage another person's reputation; true threats, which is when you threaten to commit a crime; face-to-face personal insults deliberately used to provoke a fight; obscenity; child pornography; and misleading commercial advertising.

FEDERAL COMMUNICATIONS COMMISSION REGULATIONS

The Federal Communications Commission (FCC) is a U.S. government agency that regulates the radio, television, and telephone industries, including communications by radio, television, wire, satellite, and cable. This includes Internet and smartphone communications. Among other things, the FCC issues operating licenses for radio and television stations and enforces decency standards under the Communications Decency Act (CDA) of 1996.

Two key features of FCC regulations include:

- The FCC cannot censor broadcast stations

- The FCC can punish, usually by fine, a broadcast station if someone transmits obscene or indecent language

In early 2015, the FCC adopted the Open Internet rule, which prohibits Internet access providers from blocking, impairing, or impeding access to lawful content online. It reinforces the concept of Net Neutrality, which means that you can develop products and services for the Internet without having to ask someone else for permission.

THE FREEDOM OF INFORMATION ACT

The Freedom of Information Act (FOIA) is a U.S. law that gives you the right to request access to records from any federal agency. According to the law, federal agencies must disclose information unless it falls into one of nine categories that protect specific interests, such as personal privacy, national security, and law enforcement.

The Office of Information Policy at the Department of Justice is responsible for monitoring compliance with the FOIA .

LIABILITY LAW

Liability means being legally responsible for something. Liability laws are the laws that determine who is responsible or at fault when something goes wrong. Much of liability law has to do with personal injury, such as when someone rear-ends your car or falls in your driveway. Other liability laws concern products. Product liability laws are the legal rules concerning who is responsible for defective or dangerous products. Most liability laws are set at the state level and vary depending on the state you are in.

There is an area of liability law that covers publishers and distributors of information, including broadcasters, printers, and Internet providers. It involves determining if these publishers or distributors are protected by the First Amendment or if they are liable under the FCCs decency standards. For example, a Web site publisher may be liable for posting defamatory information. However, an Internet service provider might not be liable for hosting a forum where users post defamatory comments.

OTHER RELEVANT REGULATIONS

Most of the industries in the Arts, Audio/Video Technology, and Communications cluster are regulated by the above laws and agencies. In other words, they are protected by the First Amendment and liable under the CDA. In response to consumer concerns, many have adopted self-regulating policies. Self-regulation is when an industry sets regulations for itself rather than waiting for the government to do so. For example, both the motion picture and video gaming industries have ratings systems to identify violent or adult content. In addition, the video gaming industry has a code of marketing that regulates how they advertise and market games to children.

Communication is the process of transferring information and meaning between senders and receivers, using one or more print, oral, visual, or digital media. Effective communication strengthens the connections between a company, its customers, employees, shareholders, suppliers, neighbors, the community, the nation, and the world as a whole. As someone interested in a career in the Arts, Audio/Video Technology, and Communications cluster, you will need to employ professional communications strategies when you are applying for jobs, and while working.

Developing New Skills

There are many ways to develop new skills. Once you have a job, co-workers and supervisors often provide on-the-job training simply by showing you how to improve the way you do your regular tasks, or teaching you new skills.

Your company might also offer other opportunities for education and training, including:

- Specialized courses, such as a seminar on how to use Web-based storage for data management employees. You may receive certification after completing some of these courses.

- Professional development, which is training in your chosen career. Teachers are usually required to participate in professional development to learn about new trends in education and advancements in their area of expertise, or to prepare for certification exams.

- Tuition reimbursement programs, which means that if you take a class your company will pay the tuition costs. You can take classes at a local college on nights or weekends to earn a degree or certification, or simply to learn material that might help you advance.

Developing new skills and receiving additional education, licensure, and certificates prepares you for new responsibilities and helps you achieve career, academic, and life goals. It makes you a more valuable worker and helps you grow as a person.

Finding a Mentor

One of the best ways to develop your skills is to find a **mentor**. A mentor is someone knowledgeable and experienced in your field who is willing to teach you, advise you, and help you achieve your goals. While all mentors are teachers of sorts, not all teachers are mentors. A mentor is someone who is willing to give you extra individual attention, to guide you along your career path, and to pass along what he or she has already learned.

Finding a mentor at work can be as easy as asking someone you know and respect to train you or help you learn new skills. Consider these other tips when finding and choosing a mentor:

Know what you want. Are you looking for someone to teach you specific skills, to help you make important career decisions, or to just be a sounding board for when you are facing challenges? Know what you'd like your mentor to do for you and be clear about this up front.

Explore your network. Your mentor doesn't have to be your supervisor or another member of your work team or department, though that is often the case. He or she may be a teacher or a counselor, a coach, or even a family member.

Show your gratitude. Most mentors will help you because they honestly want to see you succeed. However, it doesn't hurt to thank them for their efforts and to help them out if ever the occasion arises.

Becoming a Lifelong Learner

Lifelong learning means continually acquiring new knowledge and skills throughout the course of your life. While this might sound like a given, it actually goes against traditional thinking that education ends the moment you graduate from high school or college. The truth is you never stop learning. It's just that nowadays people are making a more concentrated effort to keep learning, and it's not just because their careers demand it.

Education and training are not limited to learning new skills for the workplace. There are plenty of educational opportunities to enrich your life at home, with friends, and in your community. Studies have shown that people who continue to take an active role in their learning lead happier, even healthier, lives.

Applying Professional Communications Strategies

Recall that effective communication is a process that involves an exchange of information between a sender and a recipient. The sender transmits the message with a specific intent. The recipient interprets the message and responds.

To make your communication efforts as effective as possible, focus on making them practical, factual, concise, clear, and persuasive:

- Provide practical information. Give recipients useful information, whether it's to help them perform a desired action or understand a new company policy.

- Give facts rather than vague impressions. Use concrete language, specific detail, and information that is clear, convincing, accurate, and ethical. Even when an opinion is called for, present compelling evidence to support your conclusion. Present information in a concise, efficient manner. Concise messages show respect for people's time, and they increase the chances of a positive response.

- Clarify expectations and responsibilities. Craft messages to generate a specific response from a specific audience. When appropriate, clearly state what you expect from audience members or what you can do for them.

- Offer compelling, persuasive arguments and recommendations. Show your readers precisely how they will benefit by responding the way you want them to respond to your message.

Once you master the communication process, you will be able to use it effectively for verbal communication, which includes speaking or writing; nonverbal communication, which includes visual messages that help put words into context, such as a smile or the tone of your voice, as well as visual aids such as slides, tables, charts, images, and graphs (see **FIGURE 10.5**); and active listening, which is when you give the message sender your full attention and consideration.

FIGURE 10.5

Understanding What Employers Expect from You

Given the importance of communication in business, employers expect you to be competent at a wide range of communication tasks:

- Recognizing information needs, using efficient search techniques to locate reliable sources of information, and using gathered information ethically; this collection of skills is often referred to as **digital information fluency**.

- Organizing ideas and information logically and completely.

- Expressing ideas and information coherently and persuasively.

- Actively listening to others.

- Communicating effectively with people from diverse backgrounds and experiences.

- Using communication technologies effectively and efficiently.

- Following accepted standards of grammar, spelling, and other aspects of high-quality writing and speaking.

- Communicating in a civilized manner that reflects contemporary expectations of business etiquette, even when dealing with indifferent or hostile audiences.

- Communicating ethically, even when choices aren't crystal clear.

- Managing your time wisely and using resources efficiently.

Using an Audience-Centered Approach

Successful business professionals take an **audience-centered approach** to their communication, meaning that they focus on understanding and meeting the needs of their viewers, readers, and listeners. Providing the information your audience needs is obviously an important part of this approach, but it also involves such elements as your ability to listen, your style of writing and speaking, and your ability to maintain positive working relationships. You may find that you can tailor your projects for different audiences. For example, if you are writing a script for an automobile safety video, you might use different language for a version that will be shown to high school students than you use for a version that will be shown to senior citizens.

In recent years, a variety of technologies have enabled and inspired a new approach to business communication. In contrast to the publishing mindset, this social communication model is interactive, conversational, and usually open to all who wish to participate. Audience members are no longer passive recipients of messages but active participants in a conversation. Social media have given customers and other stakeholders a voice they did not have in the past. And businesses are listening to that voice. In fact, one of the most common uses of social media among U.S. businesses is monitoring online discussions about a company and its brands. Inside companies, social media make it easier for employees to voice concerns and frustrations, increasing the changes that managers will address problems that are getting in the way of people doing their jobs.

Instead of transmitting a fixed message, a sender in a social media environment initiates a conversation by sharing valuable information. This information is often revised and reshaped by the web of participants as they share it and comment on it. People can add to it or take pieces from it, depending on their needs and interests.

As much of a game-changer as social media have been, some experts predict that mobile communication will change the nature of business and business communication even more.

Market Research and Promotions

As an audio/video production professional, you may be responsible for marketing and promoting your projects. You can use marketing to communicate the value of your product to your audience. You can use promotion to influence people to watch, listen to, or purchase your product. Well-thoughtout marketing and promotion can be the difference between a film no one has ever heard of and a wildly successful smash hit (see **FIGURE 10.6**).

FIGURE 10.6

Promotion means taking action to raise awareness of your product. It includes strategies for capturing the attention of your target audience, holding their interest, and making the product appealing. Some common elements of a successful promotional strategy include:

- Advertising, which is a public promotional message that you pay for, such as printed ads, direct mailings, broadcast ads on radio or television, online advertisements, and outdoor advertisements such as billboards.

- Visual merchandising which is when you use artistic displays to promote products inside a store.

- Public relations, which are activities or events that encourage customers to have a positive attitude about a product.

Market research is when you identify and analyze current trends that will affect the success of your project. It helps you understand your audience, the competition, and the current business environment so you can determine the best methods for promote your project. It also helps identify problems and challenges so you can avoid costly mistakes. Finally, it arms you with the information you need to convince others to invest in your projects. You collect data for market research using surveys and by analyzing existing data. You can turn the information into charts, graphs, and tables that help you interpret it, and communicate it with others (see **FIGURE 10.7**).

FIGURE 10.7

Some of the information you can collect using market research includes:

- Market share, which is the percentage of total sales captured by a product or a business in a particular market.

- Audience-measurement rating, which is the percentage of a total audience watching or listening to a particular program or show.

- Sweeps periods, which are time periods during which a measurement agency collects demographic information about television and radio viewing habits. Typically, these are February, May, July, and November.

- Distribution, which is the way products are made available to an audience. This may include online, on network television, on a streaming service, in theaters, or on video disk.

- Product release dates, which are the dates on which products are released to an audience. Certain times may affect the success of a project. For example, blockbuster films are generally released in the summer or around Christmas. Films hoping for Academy Award nominations are often released in the fall.

- **Demographics** are facts about the population such as age, gender, education, and ethnic background.

- **Target audience**, which is the group of people most likely to buy your product.

- Advertising rates, which is the cost of advertising your product.

- Advertising revenue, which is the amount of money you earn because of advertising.

How Mobile Technologies Are Changing Business Communication

The rise of mobile communication has some obvious implications, such as the need for Web sites to be mobile friendly. If you've ever tried to browse a conventional Web site on a tiny screen or fill in complicated online forms using the keypad on your phone, you know how frustrating the experience can be.

Increasingly, users expect Web sites to be mobile friendly, and they are likely to avoid sites that aren't optimized for mobile. As mobile access overtakes computer-based access, some companies now take a mobile-first approach, in which Web sites are designed for optimum viewing on smart phones and tablets. Another successful approach is creating mobile apps that offer a more interactive and mobile-friendly experience than a conventional Web site can offer.

However, device size and portability are only the most obvious changes. Just as with social media, the changes brought about by mobile go far deeper than the technology itself. Mobile changes the way people communicate, which has profound implications for virtually every aspect of business communication.

Here are the most significant ways mobile technology is changing the practice of business communication:

- Constant connectivity is a mixed blessing. Like social media, mobile connectivity can blur the boundaries of personal and professional time and space, preventing people from fully disengaging from work during personal and family time. On the other hand, it can give employees more flexibility to meet their personal and professional obligations. In this regard, mobile plays an important role in efforts to reduce operating costs through telecommuting and other nontraditional work models.

- Mobile form factors present challenges for creating and consuming content, whether it's typing an email message or watching a video. For example, videos must be formatted differently to make them easier to view on mobile devices.

- Mobile users are often multitasking, so they can't give full attention to the information on their screens. Moreover, mobile use often occurs in environments with multiple distractions and barriers to successful communication.

Collaborating with Others

Thanks to advances in mobile and distributed communication, today's professionals work on the move while staying in close contact with colleagues, customers, and suppliers. These technologies are also redefining the very nature of some companies, as they replace traditional hierarchies with highly adaptable, virtual networks. The technologies highlighted below help businesses redefine the office, collaborate and share information, connect with stakeholders, and build communities of people with shared interests and needs.

WEB-BASED MEETINGS

Web-based meetings allow team members from all over the world to interact in real time. Meetings can also be recorded for later playback and review. Various systems support instant messaging, video, collaborative editing tools, and more.

VIDEOCONFERENCING AND TELEPRESENCE

Videoconferencing provides many of the benefits of in-person meetings at a fraction of the cost. Advanced systems feature telepresence, in which the video images of meeting participants are life-sized and extremely realistic.

Videoconferencing provides many of the benefits of in-person meetings at a fraction of the cost. Advanced systems feature telepresence, in which the video images of meeting participants are life-sized and extremely realistic.

WIKIS

Wikis promote collaboration by simplifying the process of creating and editing online content. Anyone with access (some wikis are private; some are public) can add and modify pages as new information becomes available.

CROWDSOURCING AND COLLABORATION PLATFORMS

Crowdsourcing, inviting input from groups of people inside or outside the organization, can give companies access to a much wider range of ideas, solutions to problems, and insights into market trends.

BLOGGING

Blogs let companies connect with customers and other audiences in a fast and informal way. Commenting features let readers participate in the conversation, too.

PODCASTING

With the portability and convenience of downloadable audio and video recordings, podcasts have become a popular means of delivering everything from college lectures to marketing messages. Podcasts are also used for internal communication, replacing conference calls, newsletters, and other media.

SOCIAL NETWORKING

Businesses use a variety of social networks as specialized channels to engage customers, find new employees, attract investors, and share ideas and challenges with peers.

REMOTE WORKFORCE MANAGEMENT TOOLS

Dispersed workforces also present a variety of supervision and management difficulties. Mobile workforce management apps can solve many of these, from basic functions such as ensuring that workers show up on time at remote job sites to rescheduling customer appointments on the fly to collecting information to share with technical support staff. Sales managers can give just-in-time coaching and encouragement to representatives who are about to call potential customers. Some systems can even embed information on best practices from experienced workers and deliver virtual coaching to less experienced workers in the field.

PROJECT MANAGEMENT TOOLS

Work teams are often dispersed over wide geographic ranges and frequently on the move, so mobile communication is an essential element of contemporary project management. Instant access to task status and other vital information helps project managers stay on top of rapidly moving projects and helps team members communicate efficiently.

Communicating in a World of Diversity

Throughout your career, you will interact with people from a variety of cultures, people who differ in race, age, gender, sexual orientation, national and regional attitudes and beliefs, family structure, religion, native language, physical and cognitive abilities, life experience, and educational background.

Although the concept is often narrowly framed in terms of ethnic background, a broader and more useful definition of diversity would include all the characteristics and experiences that define people as individuals. This might include things like military experience, parental status, marital status, and thinking style.

THE ADVANTAGES AND CHALLENGES OF A DIVERSE WORKFORCE

Smart business leaders recognize the competitive advantages of a diverse workforce that offers a broader spectrum of viewpoints and ideas, helps companies understand and identify with diverse markets, and enables companies to benefit from a wider range of employee talents.

For all their benefits, diverse workforces and markets do present some communication challenges, and understanding the effect of culture on communication is essential. Culture is a shared system of symbols, beliefs, attitudes, values, expectations, and norms for behavior. You are a member of several cultures, in fact, based on your national origin, religious beliefs, age, and other factors.

Culture influences the way people perceive the world and respond to others, which naturally affects the way they communicate as both senders and receivers. These influences operate on such a fundamental level that people often don't even recognize the influence of culture on their beliefs and behaviors.

Using Technology to Improve Professional Communication

Today's businesses rely heavily on technology to facilitate the communication process. In fact, many of the technologies you might use in your personal life, from Facebook to Twitter to video games, are also used in business.

In addition, business applications can help you interpret and communicate data, observations, and information.

- Word-processing programs let you create documents for communication such as letters, memos, and reports.

- Presentations programs let you create slide shows for communicating. They are used daily in most businesses for a wide range of purposes, including product demonstrations, training, marketing, and more. Presentations can be formal, which means they are planned, rehearsed, and scheduled, or informal, which means they are more casual and delivered on a moment notice without advance planning.

- Spreadsheets let you store and analyze information, and then generate charts and graphs to use as visual aids for reinforcing your message.

- Database programs let you store data and generate reports you can use to communicate information about the data.

To communicate effectively, you need to keep technology in perspective, use technological tools productively, guard against information overload, and disengage from the computer frequently to communicate in person.

KEEPING TECHNOLOGY IN PERSPECTIVE

Remember that technology is an aid to communication, not a replacement for it. Technology can't think for you, make up for a lack of essential skills, or ensure that communication really happens. For example, you might have a presence on every new social media platform that comes along, but if the messages you are sending are confusing or self-serving, none of that technology will help.

USING TOOLS PRODUCTIVELY

You don't have to become an expert to use most communication technologies effectively, but to work efficiently you do need to be familiar with basic features and functions.

The overuse or misuse of communication technology can lead to information overload, in which people receive more information than they can effectively process. Information overload makes it difficult to discriminate between useful and useless information, inhibits the ability to think deeply about complex situations, lowers productivity, and amplifies employee stress both on the job and at home—even to the point of causing health and relationship problems.

As a sender, make sure every message you send is meaningful and important to your receivers. As a recipient, take steps to control the number and types of messages you receive. Use the filtering features of your communication systems to isolate high-priority messages that deserve your attention. Also, be wary of following too many blogs, Twitter accounts, and social networking feeds, and other sources of recurring messages. Focus on the information you truly need to do your job.

RECONNECTING WITH PEOPLE FREQUENTLY

Even the best technologies can hinder communication if they are overused. For instance, a common complaint among employees is that managers rely too heavily on email and don't communicate face-to-face often enough. Speaking with people over the phone or in person can take more time and effort, and can sometimes force you to confront unpleasant situations directly, but it is often essential for solving tough problems and maintaining productive relationships.

Moreover, even the best communication technologies can't show people who you really are. Remember to step out from behind the technology frequently to learn more about the people you work with—and to let them learn more about you.

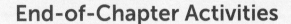

End-of-Chapter Activities

REVIEW QUESTIONS

1. List at least three audio/video technology industry associations that offer work-related certifications.

2. Define employability.

3. List and define at least four career search documents.

4. How can you prepare for a job interview?

5. What are six questions you should ask when evaluating and comparing job opportunities?

6. How can you behave ethically at work?

7. What are three ways an employer might provide an opportunity for you to develop new skills?

8. What is an audience-centered approach to communication?

9. What is market research and how can you use it to successfully promote a product?

10. What are four ways you can use business applications to interpret and communicate data, observations, and information?

Review Project 1

Review rules your school district may have for technology use as part of its acceptable use policy. Categorize policies based on appropriate use, vandalism or destruction, and consequences of violations. As a class, debate the benefits and drawbacks of items in the policy, such as censorship and filtering.

Review Project 2

In small groups, write a script for a skit that demonstrates ethical conduct related to interacting with others at work, such as client confidentiality, privacy of sensitive content, use of network resources, and providing proper credit for ideas. Perform your skit for the class.

Review Project 3

As a class, discuss personal security guidelines and safety rules and regulations. Plan and practice a safety drill to demonstrate the rules, following all emergency procedures, as needed.

Review Project 4

Look online for at least two job openings that require skill using Premiere Pro. Evaluate and compare the opportunities and select the one you think would be best. Using correct grammar, punctuation, and terminology, create a resume for someone qualified for the position. Include education, work history, and relevant licenses or certifications. Write a cover letter to go with the resume, and a thank-you letter to send after an interview. Exchange documents with a classmate and edit your partner's for correct grammar, punctuation, and terminology.

Review Project 5

You have just completed working on a two-day shoot as a boom operator. You worked from 7 a.m. until 8 p.m. on the first day, with one hour off for lunch. You worked from 7 a.m. until 1 p.m. on the second day, without a lunch break. Your wages are $24 per hour. Using a spreadsheet, word-processor, or a printed form, create an invoice for the job. Calculate the total number of hours you worked, and the total wages you earned. When the first invoice is complete, create another one that factors in a 5% discount if payment is made within 14 days.

Review Project 6

Create a career portfolio to document work experiences, licenses, certifications, and work samples. Share your portfolio with a partner or with the class.

Review Project 7

With a partner, write a pitch for a 30 to 60 second video on the topic of your choice. Have the topic approved by your teacher. Research the best method for promoting the video by using market research strategies. When your research is complete, write a marketing and promotion plan for the video based on the market research. Share the plan with the class.

Review Project 8

Conduct research about mentoring programs in audio/video production in your area. Contact a program to inquire about connecting with a mentor. If you cannot find a program, talk to your teacher or another person you think could act as your mentor about setting up a formal mentoring arrangement. This might include meeting once a month to discuss your progress, or communicating via email or text. After four months, write a personal essay about the mentoring experience.

CHAPTER 10 – PORTFOLIO BUILDER

CREATING A SHOWREEL

Recall that a showreel is a compilation of your best audio and video clips that you make available to prospective clients and employers. In this project, you will create a showreel.

DIRECTIONS

Throughout this book you have been creating audio and video projects. Now, use the skills you have learned working with Premiere Pro, and the knowledge you have acquired about developing quality products, to compile clips from your projects into a showreel that highlights your accomplishments. Use music and titles, obtaining permission as necessary. As you work, ask your classmates and teachers to review the project and offer advice on how to improve it. When you are satisfied with the end result, output it in a format suitable for posting online.

Glossary

Glossary

18% gray card
A card placed in front of a camera by the camera assistant to set a standard middle range of exposure and white balance for the shot.

180° rule
A rule that states that once the stageline is set, all shots must be taken from the same side of the line unless the line is legitimately crossed.

3/4 shot
A shot that is slightly closer than a full shot.

Above-the-line
Jobs in audio and video production for people who have creative influence over the project.

Acceptable use policy (AUP)
A policy published by an organization or entity that identifies rules of behavior that must be followed by anyone using that organization's telecommunications equipment, computers, network, or Internet connection.

Action cameras
Consumer-level cameras that specialize in capturing high frame rates that make movement look clearer and sharper with clear slow motion playback.

Action-safe zone
The area in the frame where all essential action should be contained. Usually 5% in from each edge of the frame.

Active listening
Mindfully paying attention to a speaker in order to hear and understand the message.

Actor release
A legal agreement or consent form that an actor signs allowing their performance and likeness to be recorded for a media project.

Actors
Performers who appear onscreen or whose voices are recorded in association with a media project. Also called talent.

Actualities
Early films that recorded moments from everyday life or news events.

Additive color
A color model or system used in video, in which all colors begin with black and colors are added to achieve white.

Ally
A friend. In a narrative, a second hero who wants the same goal as the protagonist, but often for different reasons.

Ambient sounds
The sound in the background of recorded dialogue that can be added to the sound mix to smooth over the difference in background sounds of different shots.

Analog
A device or system that represents changing values as continuously variable physical quantities.

Ancillary respondents
Additional subjects in an interview.

Antagonist
The character who opposes and tries to thwart the protagonist.

Anti-hero
In a narrative, a villain who inspires audience support.

Aperture
The size of the hole in the iris; making it larger allows more light to strike the lens and brightens the image.

Archiving
Storing a completed version of your project for safekeeping.

Art director
The crew member who oversees the art department on a media project under the direction of the production designer.

Artistic decisions
The choices an artist makes when creating a work of art in order to achieve a desired results.

A-side
In editing, the last frame of an outgoing clip. Also called the end, tail, or out-point.

Assembly
The rough cut of a project before all the fine tuning of each scene begins.

Assistant editor
The crew member who logs and organizes all the media recorded for the project, helps the editor, and may cut scenes.

Assumption
Something that is accepted as true even if there is no factual proof.

Atmospheric sounds
Background sounds such as fluorescent lights or computer hum.

Audience-centered approach
An approach that makes the audience's needs a top priority.

Audio inputs
Ports on a camera or other device which connect to audio devices such as microphones to allow the input of audio.

Audio interface
External piece of hardware used to convert audio.

Audio stems
Distinct separated tracks of audio that can be remixed.

Audio tracks
Individual channels of sound, broken down by categories, including production track, music, sound effects, ADR, and ambience. Also called audio channels.

Audition
The process by which the casting director chooses actors for the roles in a media project. Also, to try out for a role.

Avant-garde
New and experimental work that challenges the status quo or the way things are done.

Axis
An invisible line through the main axis of the action in a scene that provides the main orientation for the viewer. Also called the stageline or the 180°.

Back focus
An adjustable control on certain lenses that keeps sharp focus consistent at different focal lengths.

Back light
A lighting style designed to separate the subject from the background by giving an outline around the head and shoulders.

Backlit
A lighting situation in which the contrast between a brightly lit background and shadowy foreground is too high to allow for a balance of both areas in the shot.

Backstory
The life of a character that occurred before a narrative begins.

Balanced audio connection
A connection such as an XLR that allows for less noise added to the signal along the length of the cable.

Below-the-line
Jobs in audio and video production for people who do not have creative influence over the project.

Best boy
The chief assistant of the key group and underboss of the grip department.

Bins
An organizational unit in nonlinear editing (NLE) systems for storing a group of clips from the same scene or project.

Black and white
An image with no chrominance, or saturation, thereby displaying only shades of black and white.

Blade tool
The tool used to cut a clip in an NLE system.

Blocking
The movement of actors or the camera during a scene.

Blown out
A scene that is recorded too bright, or sound that is recorded too loud.

Body mic
A microphone, generally wireless, placed on the body of the actor or media subject.

Boom
An extension arm or rod to which a microphone is attached so it can be moved and repositioned during the shoot.

Boom operator
The sound technician who holds the boom microphone on a boom pole over the performers or subject, and is responsible for getting a high-quality recording of the dialogue during production.

Boom pole
The pole to which the microphone is attached.

Bounce board
Usually a white or silver board used to reflect sunlight in order to add or fill in light or shadow to create a pleasing contrast of light on the subject. Also called foamcore.

Brand
An image developed to support and promote a product's or individual's identity and reputation.

Broadcast camera
A large camera used for television production. Also called a studio camera.

Broadcast rights
The right to broadcast work that is copyrighted by someone else.

B-roll
Extra footage shot to support an existing scene.

B-side
In editing, the first frame of an incoming clip. Also called the start, head, or in-point.

Bug
A company logo that appears at the bottom-right side of the screen.

Bumpers
Text used to identify sections of longer videos.

Bureaucrat
In a narrative, a character who represents the status quo and opposes the protagonist, but is more of an obstacle than an antagonist.

Business proposal
A written document sent to a prospective client in order to obtain a job.

Call sheet
A form filled out daily that lists all the key information for the cast and crew, including the location, call time, required cast and crew, and contact information for key personnel.

Call time
The time each cast and crew member must be on set.

Callbacks
A second or third audition for a role by an actor.

Camcorder
A video recorder that can be held in the hand.

Camera assistants
The crew members responsible for various jobs associated with the camera, including changing rolls of film, marking or swapping tapes or memory cards, changing focus during a shot, and slating.

Camera obscura
A sealed box with a hole in one side; an early precursor to the camera.

Camera operator
The crew member responsible for operating the camera and recording the shot exactly as designed by the director.

Capturing
Ingesting footage from tape into a computer or NLE system.

Career
A chosen field of work in which you try to advance over time by gaining responsibility and earning more money.

Cassette tapes
Electronic media used for recording audiovisual signals in analog format.

Cast
To hire actors. Also, the group of actors portraying the characters in a media project.

Casting breakdown
A list and description of each role in a project to be cast.

Casting director
The crew member who finds the best actors for each role in a media project.

Character arc
The overall change in the main character from the beginning to the end of the story as a result of the action in the story.

Charge-coupled device (CCD)
A circuit developed for video cameras that allowed for higher-quality image capturing and smaller cameras.

Checkerboarding
A technique involving alternating audio tracks in order to minimize the abrupt, audible sound that may occur when two clips are placed together.

Chrominance
The level of intensity or brightness of a color; the less intensity, the grayer the color will appear. Also called saturation.

Cinema vérité
A media style that attempts to portray real life as it is and minimize the artificiality of the recording process

Cinematographer
The crew member in charge of the look and lighting of the media project. Also called a director of photography.

Cinematography
The art and craft of lighting a media project.

Citizen journalism
The collection, dissemination, and analysis of news and information by the general public, especially by means of the Internet.

Clapboard
A board held in front of the camera before each take containing all the key information about the scene, shot, and take. Also called a slate.

Client base
Customers, past customers, and potential customers.

Climactic scene
A scene in a narrative project that leads to a major resolution. Also called a showdown.

Clip
A piece of audiovisual media.

Close-up
A shot where the face of an actor fills the frame.

Cloud storage
Storage space for files on a network or Internet server.

Cluster
A group of similar things.

Codec
A device or program that compresses data to enable faster transmission and then decompresses the data for use.

Color correction
Adjusting the color scheme of certain clips to match other clips from the same scene.

Color grading
A subtle adjustment in the color of a clip. Also called grading or color timing.

Color timing
A subtle adjustment in the color of a clip. Also called color grading or grading.

Color wheel
A circular illustration of the relationships between different colors.

Complementary colors
Colors that, when combined, make black, or cancel each other out. For example, red and green.

Complementary metal-oxide semiconductor (CMOS)
A sensor that captures images with a very high dynamic range or differential between light and dark areas.

Composer
The writer of the original music in a media project.

Compression type
The format used to compress data, such as digital audio and video files.

Condenser
A category of microphones which require power to operate.

Conflict
A disagreement between two or more people who have different ideas.

Consequences
The results of a decision or other action.

Constructive criticism
Judgment delivered in a positive way, including advice for how to make improvements and solve problems.

Consumer-level A/V equipment
Inexpensive audio/visual equipment designed for the mass market.

Continuity
The flow throughout clips of a scene in a media project as if there were no break in time or space.

Continuity supervisor
The person responsible for making sure that a script is filmed in its entirety. Also called a script supervisor.

Contrast
The ratio between the lightest and darkest portions of a scene.

Contrast control
The control that lets you adjust the ratio between the lightest and darkest portions of a scene.

Contrasts
A storytelling technique in which the audience is steered to realization by focusing on the opposite.

Copyright law
The laws that govern who has control over how a creative work is seen, heard, used, or delivered.

Costume designer
The crew member who oversees the design and creation of all costumes in the production.

Cover letter
A letter to a potential employer you send with a resume to introduce yourself, express interest in the position, and highlight key information.

Crane shot
A shot in which the camera is positioned on a crane high above the scene, shooting down.

Creative Commons license
A license to make one's creative work available to others for reuse or redistribution.

Credit
Information about a production on which an actor or crew member worked, such as the title, position (or role), director, year, and location.

Credits
A list of the cast and crew positions in a media piece and who filled those roles.

Critical thinking
The ability to think in an honest, rational, and open-minded way.

Criticism
An analysis and judgment of the positive and negative aspects of something, such as a product, design, work of art, or project.

Cue
Audio elements such as music or sound FX, or a list of them showing where they occur on the soundtrack.

Cue sheet
Audio elements such as music or sound FX, or a list of them showing where they occur on the soundtrack.

Cut point
A frame (still image) in which to cut out of Shot A and another frame to cut into Shot B that will hide the edit and maintain the action with no break in time. Also called the edit point.

Cutaway
A shot other than the main action that is inserted into a scene.

Data degradation
The disintegration of stored data over time. Also called data rot.

Data migration
Transferring the location of archived media files in order to avoid data rot.

Data rot
The disintegration of stored data over time. Also called data degradation.

Decision
The process of choosing one option over one or more alternative options.

Deliverable
A product, or segment of a product, that can be provided to an employer, client, or the public, usually as specified by a contract. Typically, the finished version of the project.

Delivery
Releasing a completed version of your project.

Demo reel
A portfolio of audiovisual samples of one's best work. Also called showreel or reel.

Demographics
Facts about a population, such as age, gender, education, and ethnic background.

Denouement
In a narrative, the wrap-up at the end that clarifies the resolution.

Depth of field
The distance between the nearest object in focus and the farthest object in focus within a shot.

Derivative
A new creation that includes previously published work.

Desaturated
Lacking in color.

Digital
A device or system that represents information as a series of the digits 1 and 0.

Digital cinema cameras
Digital cameras that shoot in a progressive mode at the same frame rate as film with a large sensor that simulates the high contrast ratio of film, such as the RED or Blackmagic Cinema Camera.

Digital information fluency
Effectiveness in retrieving and understanding digital information and using it ethically.

Digital single-lens reflex (DSLR)
A camera that combines the single-lens reflex mechanism common to film cameras with a digital sensor.

Director
The creative manager of a media project through whom the creativity of the rest of the cast and crew flows.

Director of photography (DP)
The crew member in charge of the look and lighting of the media project. Also called a cinematographer.

Docudrama
A fictionalized version of a supposedly true story that may adhere to the stylistic parameters of a documentary.

Documentaries
Media projects such as movies or television shows that provide a factual record or report.

Dolly

A cart the camera travels on to create a smooth-moving shot.

Dolly zoom

A shot in which the camera is placed on a dolly and pulled away from the subject while zooming in, or pushed toward the subject while zooming out.

Dramatic irony

In a narrative, irony that the audience is aware of that the characters are not.

Driver

Software that manages the communication between a computer and connected hardware devices.

Drop shadow

A visual effect consisting of a drawing element which looks like the shadow of an object, giving the impression that the object is raised above the objects behind it.

Dual-roller trim

A trim that affects two adjoining clips simultaneously. If the A-side is lengthened, the B-side is shortened. Also called a roll edit.

Dual-system sound

Independent recording of audio as is done with film and that requires picture and sound to be synced.

Duplex cable

A sound cable that sends the audio signal simultaneously to the boom operator's headset and the recording device.

Duplicate copies

Copies, backups, or versions of a file or project.

Dynamic

A category of microphone that does not require power to deliver sound to the recording device.

Dynamic range

The range in f-stops between light and dark areas that a camera can record faithfully.

Edit point

A frame (still image) in which to cut out of Shot A and another frame to cut into Shot B that will hide the edit and maintain the action with no break in time. Also called the cut point.

Editor

The crew member primarily in charge of cutting the media project together, finding the best takes in the footage, creating cohesive and coherent scenes, and creating rhythm as needed.

Effective communication
Communication in which the receiver interprets the message the way the sender intended.

Electronic news gathering (ENG) camera
A camera used for news and many other forms of video production; among the earliest video cameras designed for portability.

Empathy
The ability to understand and share the feelings of another.

Employability
Having and using life skills and abilities to be hired and stay hired.

Employment trend
One way the job market changes over time.

Encoding
Compressing an audiovisual file for easy transfer.

End
In editing, the last frame of an outgoing clip. Also called the out-point, tail, or A-side.

Entrepreneur
Someone who starts a company or business in order to create a product or provide a service.

Establishing shot
A shot on a wide-angle lens designed to show or establish what the location of the scene is. Also called an extreme wide shot.

Ethical
Relating to moral principles or standard values of what is right and what is wrong.

Executive producer
The overseer of a production, who is responsible for deciding if the project is made, and hires the key personnel.

Expenses
How money is spent.

Exposure
The brightness of a recorded image.

Expressionism
A style of media creation that attempts to reflect how the world feels more than to document it realistically.

Extract
A type of edit that allows the user to trim a clip without leaving gaps with the previous clip. Also called a ripple delete.

Extreme close-up
A shot that shows something closer than the audience would ever see it in real life.

Extreme wide shot
A shot on a wide-angle lens designed to show or establish what the location of the scene is. Also called an establishing shot.

Eye-level
A shot at a neutral camera height that may appear to be a point-of-view (POV) shot.

Eyeline
The angle at which a character looks at another character who is off-screen.

Fair dealing
An exception from copyright law, allowing work to be distributed or exhibited. Also called fair use.

Fair use
An exception from copyright law, allowing work to be distributed or exhibited. Also called fair dealing.

Fall-off
The transition from light to shadow in a shot, which may be described as fast or slow.

Fast-motion
Shooting fewer frames per second and playing back at standard speed (24 fps) to achieve a fast-motion effect. Also called undercranking.

Feedback
Criticism, comments, or analysis of a project delivered by someone such as a client, friend, or mentor to the project creator, for the purpose of learning and improving.

Festival rights
Limited exhibition rights, typically granted in a music license to be used in arts festivals only.

Fill light
In studio lighting, a light that fills in the shadow created by the key light and lowers the contrast ratio on the subject.

Film budget
A document or spreadsheet that lists the cost of all expenses and items in a media project.

Film cameras
A camera that exposes photographic film to light in order to record an image.

Filter
A device attached to a lens to restrict, reduce, or change the quality of light striking the lens.

Final cut
The completely picture-edited version of a media project on which sound and effects work proceed, or the right to say when a media project has completed picture editing.

Finishing
Using color correction and grading techniques to apply the finishing touches to a project.

First act break
The moment in the first act of a three-act structured narrative when the protagonist accepts the challenge of achieving the goal.

First assistant director (1st AD)
The crew member who runs the set, maintains the schedule, and writes up the call sheets.

Fishpole
An extending pole used to hold a boom microphone over the head of performers for maximum audio recording.

Flashbacks
A storytelling technique in which a moment or scene from an earlier time is shown to establish something that happened in the past.

Flat lighting
A lighting style with no or little shadows or contrast.

F-number
The aperture setting on the lens that determines how much light will strike the lens. Also called f-stop

Foamcore
Usually a white or silver board used to reflect sunlight in order to add or fill in light or shadow to create a pleasing contrast of light on the subject. Also called bounce board

Focal length
The number of millimeters from the optical center of a lens to the sensor when the lens is focused at infinity.

Focal plane
The element of the lens where light comes into focus.

Focus
The adjustment used to control the clarity of an image. Also, to create a clear image.

Footcandles
The measurement of light falling on an object.

Found footage
Finished fictional works that are presented as if documentaries.

Frames per second (fps)
The number of individual images recorded each second by the camera.

Freeze frames
Playing the same frame continuously.

F-stop
The aperture setting on the lens that determines how much light will strike the lens. Also called f-number.

Full shot
A shot that give a full-body view of the subject.

Gaffer
The head electrician of a production.

Gaffer tape
Cloth tape used in lighting.

Gain
The electronic amplification of a video signal.

Gantt chart
A horizontal bar chart developed by Henry L. Gantt in 1917, that shows a graphical illustration of a schedule.

Gel
A piece of colored plastic placed in front of a light to change the color of a scene.

Genre
A category of film or other media with its own specific tropes, conventions, or storylines, such as westerns, historical epics, and science fiction.

Geographic separation
Physical distance between one thing, such as a version of a media project, and another.

Gimbal-based device
A device to steady a camera, such as a Steadicam.

Goal
Something you are trying to achieve. In a story, something the protagonist is trying to achieve.

Grading
A subtle adjustment in the color of a clip. Also called color grading or color timing.

Graphics
Art such as images, photos, logos, and illustrations.

Grayscale
A range of gray shades from black to white.

Green-lighted
Given permission or authorization.

Hair stylist
The crew member who oversees hair design.

Handheld mic
A dynamic microphone used by PA systems or during a musical performance.

Hard skills
Skills that are specific to a particular task or job.

Hard sound effects
Specific, isolated sound effects on the soundtrack of a media project.

Head
In editing, the first frame of an incoming clip. Also called the start, in-point, or B-side.

Henchman
In a narrative, an ally of the antagonist.

Hieroglyphs
A stylized picture of an object representing a word, syllable, or sound, as found in ancient Egyptian and other writing systems.

High frame rate (HFR)
A recording format of more than 24 fps.

High key lighting
A style of lighting that is very bright, without much contrast.

High-angle shot
A shot in which the camera is above the subject.

High-definition video (HD)
A video format that has a higher resolution, larger aspect ratio, and faster scanning and frame rates than standard video.

Highlights
The brightest parts of an image.

Hue
The quality or variance of a color away from a primary color.

Image noise
The graininess of a recorded image.

Image plane
The electronic sensor of a camera.

Image sensor
The electronic sensor of a camera.

Image stabilizer
Any device such as a tripod or feature on a digital camera that enables a still, clear composition. Also called camera stabilization.

Improvisation
Acting spontaneously in character without a script.

Incident meter
A device that measures the light falling on a subject.

Income
Earned money.

Ineffective communication
Communication in which the receiver misinterprets the message.

Ingesting
The process of importing any form of media into an editing system.

In-point
In editing, the first frame of an incoming clip. Also called the start, head, or B-side.

Inset shot
A close-up of a specific detail in a scene.

Intellectual property
An individual's original, creative work, which they have exclusive rights to exploit and distribute.

Interview shot
A medium shot or MCU in which the subject looks slightly off-axis to the camera. Usually used for interviews. Also called a talking head shot.

Investigative style
A style of documentary filmmaking where the structure of the project depends on the truths unearthed by it.

IRE
A scale that rates from 1 to 10 the values on the camera's 1:32 contrast range.

Iris
A ring of metal leaves on a lens which draws open or closed to create the aperture or hole that allows light into the lens.

Irony
The subversion of what is expected into something unexpected.

ISO
The speed of a film stock, its sensitivity to light, or how much light it needs to expose properly; a higher number reflects more sensitivity to light.

J-cuts
A cut in which the audio transition occurs before the video transition.

Job application
A standard form that is filled out when applying for a job.

Job interview
A meeting between a job seeker and a potential employer.

Job leads
Opportunities for employment.

Job outlook
A forecast or prediction about trends affecting a job.

Job search resources
Tools designed to help you find job leads.

Jump cut
A jarring or abrupt edit. Usually, a cut from shot A to shot B within a scene that creates an ellipsis, or a break in the time continuum either forward or backward.

Key grip
Manager of the grips, which is the team that builds up or breaks down the lighting rigs on a production.

Key light
The main light illuminating a scene.

Keyframes
Frames in an audio or video clip where an action occurs.

Kicker
A back light that hits a bit of the side of the subject's face.

Kuleshov effect
The phenomenon that two images, having no intentional connection or relation to one another, will create new meaning when seen sequentially.

Labor union
An organized association of workers, often in a trade or profession, formed to protect and further their rights and interests.

Lavalier
A wireless body mic that can be clipped directly on the talent.

LCD viewfinder
A liquid crystal display (LCD) viewfinder.

L-cuts
An edit where the video transition occurs before the audio transition.

Leader
A type of manager who knows how to use available resources to help others achieve their goals.

Leitmotif
A recurring theme or visual element in a media production, often varying throughout the narrative to reflect developments in the story.

Licensing agreement
A contract to license certain rights to copyrighted work under agreed-upon terms and conditions.

Lift
In editing, the removal of media from the middle of a clip that may leave a gap.

Light meters
A device that records either light falling upon an object or light reflecting off the subject in order to achieve proper exposure.

Linear editing
A method of editing video and audio using at least two videotape recorders to copy each shot from the camera source to the program tape one by one, sequentially, in a predetermined, ordered sequence.

Location permit
A legal agreement under which a property owner or legal representative allows a media crew use of a property for recording purposes under agreed-upon terms. Also called a location release.

Location release
A legal agreement under which a property owner or legal representative allows a media crew use of a property for recording purposes under agreed-upon terms. Also called a location permit.

Long lens
A lens with a longer focal length than a normal lens and a narrower angle of view, which compresses space and makes objects appear closer. Also called a telephoto lens.

Long shot
A shot where the subject is at a distance from the camera.

Long-term goal
A goal that is accomplished in the distant future.

Lossless
A method of compressing files in which the file can be returned to its original state without losing any data.

Love interest
In a narrative, a character who is or becomes romantically involved with the protagonist.

Low key lighting
A lighting style that uses shadow areas and low light to dominate the frame.

Low-angle shot
A shot in which the camera is angled up at a subject.

Lower-third
Name and title displayed on the lower portion of the viewable region of a clip.

Luminance
The measurable intensity of light or brightness in an image.

Macro lens
A lens used to magnify something in an extreme close-up shot.

Main character
The principal character in a story. Also called the protagonist.

Main respondent
The primary subject in an interview.

Make-up artist
The member of the crew in charge of designing and applying make-up, from everyday and stage make-up to prosthetic effect make-up.

Manual focus
The control on the camera that allows the user to control the focus.

Market research
Steps used to identify and analyze current trends that affect the success of a product or service.

Mask
To cover or affect a specific area of a clip as with color correction during post production.

Master file
A completed project in a high-quality format.

Master schedule
The overall schedule of production, identifying which scenes are going to be shot where, on which day, and starting when. Also called a shooting schedule.

Master shot
The main shot of a scene.

Master use synchronization rights
A type of licensing agreement that allows full use of a copyrighted musical work to be synchronized with another creator's project. Also known as synchronization rights agreements;

Measurable goal
A goal that includes clear milestones for tracking success

Medium
The format a media content creator uses to tell a story.

Medium close-up
A shot that is tighter on the subject than a medium shot and allows visual variety without cutting to a close-up.

Medium shot
A head and upper-body shot.

Megapixels
A million pixels, or individual picture elements. Used to measure the quality of a visual image.

Memory cards
Media used for storing data, such as audio and video, in digital format.

Mentor
Someone knowledgeable and experienced in your field who is willing to teach you, advise you, and help you reach your goals. In a narrative, the character who offers advice, experience, or training to the protagonist.

Message
The story a media content creator wants to tell.

Metafiction
Fiction that is self-reflexive, commenting on its own existence, or where characters seem aware they are in a movie or book.

Midtone
The middle third of the exposure range on an image; see also highlights, shadows.

Mini TRS connector
A mini-connector with a stereo output.

Mirror
In a narrative, a character similar to the protagonist in many respects who may show the audience an alternative conclusion.

Misdirection
A storytelling technique employed by media creators to fashion a false impression in the mind of the audience.

Mixer
The crew member responsible for recording the audio.

Mockumentary
A narrative comedy project in the style of a false or faux documentary crafted with a tongue-in-cheek style of humor.

Monologue
A speech delivered by a character in a media project.

Monopod
A one-legged stand for a camera.

Montage
A series of related clips that may show a sequence or compress a progression of time.

Multicamera
Recording a program using several cameras at different angles that are synchronized to each other.

Music supervisor
The crew member who helps the director choose prerecorded music that matches the feeling of the scene or comments on it.

Musical theme
A musical phrase that repeats and is usually associated with a character, place, or a time in a narrative.

Netiquette
Proper online behavior.

Networking
Socializing with other professionals and possibly clients to create future opportunities for employment.

Neutral density (ND)
A filter that cuts the amount of light striking the lens to help the operator control the exposure or brightness of the image.

Newsreel
Short motion pictures depicting topical news stories that played in theaters before feature films.

Nonlinear editing (NLE)
An editing system that allows the editor to move shots or clips around in any order without losing any previous work.

Nonverbal communication
Visual messages transmitted from a sender to a receiver, such as facial expressions.

Normal lens
A lens with a focal length causing its representation of a scene to approximate the perspective of human sight.

Objective
A short-term goal used to keep a project on track for completion. Also, fairly, without emotion or prejudice.

Oblique shot
A shot that is rotated left or right with a tilted horizon to give the audience a sense of disorientation.

Obstacle
Something that comes between a protagonist and a goal.

Omnidirectional
A type of microphone with a pickup pattern or polar pattern that allows the mic to pick up sound evenly in all directions.

Optical reflex viewfinder
A type of viewfinder on a film camera that shows the camera operator almost exactly what is being recorded on to the film negative.

Oral communication
The exchange of messages by speaking or writing. Also called verbal communication.

Orientation
The viewer's understanding of where the various characters and other elements in a scene are relative to one another, as clarified by the director's choice of shots to cover the scene.

Out-point
In editing, the last frame of an outgoing clip. Also called the end, tail, or A-side.

Over/under cable wrapping method
A method of wrapping cables in even and consistent loops, avoiding any figure-eight shapes, knots, or bending.

Overcranking
Shooting twice as many frames or more per second and then playing back at normal speed.

Overheads
Overhead depictions of the whole set showing where the camera, actors, and key props will be located.

Overscan
The amount of each captured image cut off by most displays; the standard overscan of 16:9 video is 5 percent.

Over-the-shoulder
A two-shot across one character's shoulder focusing on a second character.

Pan
The horizontal movement of a camera from a stationary point.

Paper cut
In editing, marking down the numbers of the first and last frames of each shot and arranging them before actually editing them together.

Pathway
A group of jobs within a career cluster.

Payoff
In a narrative, giving the audience a clue as to what will happen later. Also called planting.

Pedestal
A camera support that uses air or hydraulic pressure to allow the camera to move easily up and down.

Personal qualities
The traits that make each person unique.

PERT chart (Program Evaluation Review Technique)
A chart developed by the U.S. Navy in the 1950s, which shows project tasks, the order in which they must be completed, and the time requirements.

Phantom power
The direct current (DC) voltage sent through a microphone cable to power a microphone or associated device.

Pickup pattern
The pattern in which a microphone picks up or records the clearest sound quality. Also called polar pattern.

Pickups
Shots recorded after principal photography is complete.

Picture lock
Editing term referring to the end of changes to the visual elements in a media project.

Piracy
Copying copyrighted software, films, videos, or music to use, give away, or sell.

Pitch
A summary of the most original or exciting aspects of a project, designed to excite potential participants or investors to become part of the production.

Planting
In a narrative, giving the audience a clue as to what will happen later. Also called payoff.

Point-of-view (POV) shot
A shot where the camera shows what a character is seeing.

Polar pattern
The pattern in which a microphone picks up or records the clearest sound quality. Also called pickup pattern.

Portfolio
A collection of information and documents, such as samples of work.

Postproduction
The third and final stage in the production workflow, during which everything that must be done to complete a project is performed, including picture and sound editing, visual effects work, scoring, and pickups.

Postsecondary education
School after high school.

Practical light sources
Lights that illuminate a scene which are actually in the shot as part of the scene. Also called practicals.

Practicals
Lights that illuminate a scene which are actually in the shot as part of the scene. Also called practical light sources.

Preproduction
The first stage in the production workflow, including choosing the script, budgeting, casting, hiring crew members, scheduling, and choosing locations, costumes, and props for production.

Primary colors
In the additive system used by video, primary colors are red, blue, and green.

Prime lens
A lens that has a single fixed focal length, either wide, normal, or telephoto.

Principal photography
Also known as production, when the bulk of the recording takes place.

Prioritize
Organize tasks in the order in which they should be completed.

Problem
A difficulty or challenge that must be overcome in order to make progress or achieve a goal.

Process
A series of steps that leads to a conclusion.

Producer
The day-to-day manager of a media production, responsible for making sure everyone else is doing their job.

Production
A media project. Also, the second stage in the production workflow, when audio and video are recorded.

Production assistant
An all-purpose utility crew member who may be called on to help out with any job that needs doing on a production.

Production designer
The crew member who determines, along with the director and producers, the particular aesthetic or look of a media project.

Production sound
Audio recorded along with the picture during principal photography.

Production sound mixer
The crew member in charge of recording clear audio on the set, typically focusing on the voices of the actors.

Productivity
The amount of work someone accomplishes.

Professional camcorders
Camcorders with many controls that record audio using professional audio inputs.

Professionalism
The ability to show respect to everyone around you while you perform your responsibilities as best you can. Also called work ethic.

Professional-level A/V equipment
High end audio/visual equipment used for large-budget feature and television work.

Project management
A process used to take a project from concept to completion.

Promotion
Taking action to raise awareness of a product or service.

Prop master
The crew member who designs or procures objects seen onscreen, as indicated by the script or otherwise appropriate for the production.

Propaganda
Information used out of context to try to mislead and influence thinking.

Prosumer-level A/V equipment
Audio/visual equipment designed, priced, and marketed for the consumer market but with some higher-level controls as on professional-level gear.

Protagonist
The principle character in a story. Also called the main character.

Protocol
A standard process or order.

Public domain
The state of being available to the public and not subject to copyright law.

Public relations
Developing and maintaining satisfactory company relationships internally with employees and externally with clients.

Publicist
The crew member who determines the best strategy for getting the word out about any screenings or exhibition of a finished media piece.

Pulling out
Physically moving the camera away to change the image size during a shot.

Pushing in
Physically moving the camera closer to change the image size during a shot.

Quality control
A process for making sure a project meets the highest standards.

Rack focus
To change focus during a shot. Also called pulling focus.

Radio edit
A dialogue edit that is done without watching the video track.

Reaction shot
A shot whose purpose is to show a character's reaction to the action in a scene.

Receiver
Device that receives an audio signal from a wireless transmitter attached to a lavaliere microphone.

Reel
A portfolio of audiovisual samples of one's best work. Also called showreel or demoreel.

References
People who know you and your personal and work-related qualities and will speak on your behalf to potential employers.

Reflectance meters
A type of light meter that measures the light in footcandles coming off the subject.

Release
Legal consent that provides authorization. For example, a release to take someone's picture and use the image in a video.

Repetition
A recurring theme or visual element in a media production, often varying throughout the narrative to reflect developments in the story. The leitmotif.

Reshoots
During postproduction, the reshooting of a scene when some fundamental element does not work.

Resolution
A result. In a narrative, it is usually the achievement of the goal.

Resources
Things used to obtain something else.

Resume
A document that lists work experience, education, skills, awards, and other relevant information for a prospective employer.

Reverse angle
A shot recorded from the opposite angle as its matching shot.

Revision
A new draft or version of a project that incorporate changes, particularly after receiving feedback.

Rim light
A type of back light that separates the subject from the background by giving an outline around the head and shoulders.

Ripple delete
A type of edit that allows the user to trim a clip without leaving gaps with the previous clip. Also called an extract.

Rocker switch
A control on a zoom lens used to change from wide-angle to telephoto.

Roll edit

A trim that affects two adjoining clips simultaneously. If the A-side is lengthened, the B-side is shortened. Also called a dual-roller trim.

Room and board

The cost of lodging and meals.

Room tone

The background sound of the environment, which may be recorded during shooting. Also called ambiance or ambient sound.

Royalty-free

Creative work that can be used in a commercial media production without need of compensation.

Safety

An extra take recorded after an acceptable take, just in case it is needed.

Saturation

The level of intensity or brightness of a color; the less intensity, the grayer the color will appear. Also called chrominance.

Scene

A unit of action in one location and time.

Score

Music written for a media project to synchronize with the visuals and the soundtrack.

Screen direction

The specific orientation of the viewer tracking objects moving left, right, up, and down onscreen consistently throughout the piece.

Screenplay

A script or written version of a film, video, audio, animation, or television show that explains what will be seen and heard.

Scrim

A piece of fabric hung in front of a light to diminish its intensity.

Script breakdown

A marked-up script detailing everything that is necessary and accountable for each day of shooting, including cast, crew, and objects.

Script supervisor

The person responsible for making sure that a script is filmed in its entirety. Also called a continuity supervisor.

Seamless cut

A smooth cut between scenes. Also called transparent continuity.

Second act break
The moment in the second act of a three-act structured narrative when the protagonist defeats the antagonist or resolves the conflict.

Secondary colors
In the additive system used by video, secondary colors are yellow, cyan, and magenta.

Sepia
A color grading, filter, or effect that lends a project an aged feeling.

Sequence
An edited video segment or entire project that you are working on.

Set decorator
The crew member who decides what needs to be bought and what needs to be built for the sets in a media production.

Set piece
An elaborate and well-thought out scene, or piece of stage scenery.

Shadows
An area of the frame where light strikes the subject minimally or not at all.

Sharp
A high degree of clarity of a recorded image.

Shock mounts
A microphone holder that secures the mic with elastic suspension to keep vibrations on the boom or stand from creating unwanted noise.

Shooting schedule
A schedule of production, identifying which scenes are going to be shot where, on which day, and starting when. Also called a master schedule.

Short
An accidental path in an electrical circuit that can result in a loss of power and damage to equipment.

Short-term goal
A goal that can be accomplished in the near future.

Shot
A camera angle.

Shot list
A document prepared by the director that details which shots will be recorded on a shooting day.

Shotgun mic
A microphone with a long, cylindrical shape that is placed on a mount with a handle similar to that of a firearm.

Shoulder mount
A device that holds a camera steady on an operator's shoulders.

Showreel
A portfolio of audiovisual samples of one's best work. Also called demo reel or reel.

Shutter
The mechanical device on a camera that allows light to travel from the lens to the image sensor for a specified amount of time.

Shutter speed
The amount of time per second that the shutter is open to expose an image, letting in more or less light.

Side
Page from a script read during an audition.

Sidekick
In a narrative, an ally who frequently contributes humor or a sense of lightness.

Situation comedy (sitcom)
A genre of television programming that is humorous in nature and typically centered around a household or workplace.

Slate
A board held in front of the camera before each take containing all the key information about the scene, shot, and take. Also called clapboard.

Slide trim
A type of edit that lets the user move the location of the clip, without changing the duration of the clip.

Slip trim
A type of edit that lets the user change the content of a clip without changing the duration or location of the clip.

Slow disclosure
A type of tracking or moving shot that communicates more information to the audience throughout the shot. Also called a slow reveal.

Slow reveal
A type of tracking or moving shot that communicates more information to the audience throughout the shot. Also called a slow disclosure.

Slugline
A capitalized heading that comes before each new scene in a screenplay, identifying when and where the scene takes place.

Soft
A low degree of clarity or sharpness of a recorded image.

Soft skills
Personal traits that are key to success, such as communication skills, time management, reliability, accountability, problem-solving, collaborative capacity, and work ethic.

Solution
The action that will resolve a problem.

Sound card
Device use to convert audio signals into digital data that your computer and audio editing software can recognize.

Sound design
The overarching design of all the various audio elements in a media project including dialogue, ADR, music, sound effects, and room tone or ambience.

Sound editor
The crew member who cuts the music, sound effects, and rerecorded (or "looped") dialogue (ADR) into the film.

Sound effect
Sounds that are added to a media project, often designed by the sound designer and edited onto the soundtrack by a sound effects editor.

Soundtrack
Prerecorded songs used in a motion picture.

Source music
Music that would authentically be playing where a scene in a media production takes place.

Spec sheet
A list of technical specifications and standards that a project must meet.

Split edit
An edit where the audio and video are cut at different, or discrete, points. Also called L-cuts or J-cuts because of the shape the clips resemble after the trim is made.

Sports cameras
Consumer-level cameras that specialize in capturing high frame rates that make movement look clearer and sharper with clear slow motion playback.

Spotting
Identifying audio cues, listing how many cues are needed, and writing a description and purpose for each cue.

Stageline
An invisible line through the main axis of the action in a scene that provides the main orientation for the viewer. Also called the axis or the 180°.

Standard-definition video
A video format that has a lower resolution, smaller aspect ratio, and slower scanning and frame rates than high definition.

Start
In editing, the first frame of an incoming clip. Also called the in-point, head, or B-side.

Storyboards
A comic book-style depiction of a media project, used to detail the entire script shot by shot and scene by scene.

Strategies
Careful plans and methods.

Studio camera
Large camera used for television production. Also called a broadcast camera.

Studio lighting
Lighting style with a moderate contrast without domination by dark or light areas of the frame.

Subjective
Affected by existing opinions, feelings, and beliefs.

Subordinates
People you supervise at work.

Subtext
In a narrative, the unspoken meaning of action or dialog.

Subtractive color
A color model or system used for painting, in which all colors begin with white and colors are removed to achieve black.

Superimposition
Two shots or clips laid one on top of the other so both images can be seen at the same time.

Surrealism
A style of storytelling that visualizes the workings of the subconscious mind.

Sweetening
Adding a small number of sound effects to enhance a project.

Symbols
Something used to represent something else.

Synchronized sound system
A system that allows sound and picture to be recorded at the same time, ensuring that the sound would be synched with the video.

Synchronizing
Aligning. In audio and video production, it refers to sound that matches the image because it was either recorded simultaneously at the same rate of speed or recorded afterward carefully to match the image. Also called syncing.

Syncing
Aligning. In audio and video production, it refers to sound that matches the image because it was either recorded simultaneously at the same rate of speed or recorded afterward carefully to match the image. Also called synchronizing.

Tail
In editing, the last frame of an outgoing clip. Also called the end, out-point, or A-side.

Talent
Performers who appear onscreen or whose voices are recorded in association with a media project. Also called actors.

Talking head
An interview.

Talking head shot
A medium shot or MCU in which the subject looks slightly off-axis to the camera. Usually used for interviews. Also called an interview shot.

Tally light
A light on a television camera that indicates which camera (angle) the program is switched to so that the operator and the talent are informed.

Target audience
The group of people most likely to buy your product or service.

Team
A group of two or more people who work together to achieve a common goal.

Telephoto lens
A lens with a longer focal length than a normal lens and a narrower angle of view, which compresses space and makes objects appear closer. Also called a long lens.

Temp track
A track of temporary music created by the director to give the music supervisor or composer a sense of what they are aiming for stylistically.

Thank-you letter
A letter you write to thank a potential employer for considering you for the position.

Theme
The underlying idea explored by a media piece, or a musical composition associated with a character or storyline.

Three-act structure
A set of rules for organizing a narrative into three parts.

Three-point lighting
A classic style of Hollywood studio lighting that uses a key light, fill light, and back light.

Tilt
The vertical movement of a camera from a stationary point.

Time management
Organizing a schedule so there is time to complete all tasks and meet all responsibilities.

Timecode
A coded signal on videotape or film giving information about such things as frame number, time of recording, or exposure.

Title cards
Text that stays static on a media presentation screen, popularized during the early silent era of movies, and originally printed on actual cards.

Title roll
The end credits of a media presentation listing the names of the cast and crew and other contributors.

Titles
Text displayed onscreen.

Title-safe zone
The area in the frame where all text and graphics should be contained. Usually 10% in from each edge of the frame.

Total running time (TRT)
The length of a media project, which may need to meet a specific requirement for broadcast television, festival inclusion, or distribution.

Trace
The visual pattern that an incoming chrominance signal draws on a vectorscope.

Track
A layer in a video editing program where video or audio clips are placed.

Tracking shot
A shot in which the camera stays with the characters as they move.

Trademark
A symbol that indicates that a brand or brand name is legally protected and cannot be used by other businesses.

Traitor
In a narrative, a character who begins as an ally to the protagonist (or antagonist) but changes sides, typically flipping the balance of power.

Transcoding
The conversion of media from one codec to another.

Transcript
An official record of the courses you took in high school and the grades you earned.

Transferable skills
Skills that can be used and transferred from one situation or career to another.

Transition
In video and audio editing, a bridge from the end of one clip to the beginning of the next clip.

Transitions
In a screenplay or media project, how the writer or director expects to move from scene to scene, for example, using a cut or a dissolve.

Transmitter
Part of a wireless audio kit that stays with the talent in a pocket or clipped to a belt or waistband and sends the audio signal to the receiver.

Transparent continuity
A smooth cut between scenes. Also called a seamless cut.

Treatment
An outline or first draft of a screenplay or script.

Trimming
Cutting frames off a clip either to transition to another clip or to improve the rhythm of a sequence of clips.

Tripod
A three-legged stand that stabilizes a camera.

TRRS connector
An audio connector for mobile phones that have a built-in microphone.

Tuition
The cost of education.

Two-shot
A shot in which the faces of two characters are both included.

Unbalanced audio connection
A connection that cannot support phantom powering and requires the microphone either be dynamic or powered by another source, such as an AA battery.

Uncompressed format
Files, such as audio, video, or graphics, that are not compressed.

Undercranking
Shooting fewer frames per second and playing back at standard speed (24 fps) to achieve a fast-motion effect. Also called fast-motion.

Unidirectional
A type of microphone with a pickup pattern or polar pattern that allows the mic to pick up sounds from a narrow angle or a single direction.

Variation
A theme or visual element in a media production that changes throughout the narrative to reflect developments in the story. The leitmotif.

Verbal communication
The exchange of messages by speaking or writing. Also called oral communication.

Version
To keep separate copies of each version of a project after editing or revising.

Versioning
The duplication of edited work at specific points in the workflow in order to maintain backup copies of each version.

Victim
In a narrative, a character who represents the dire consequences if the protagonist does not achieve the goal.

Video assist
A small charge-coupled device (CCD) built into the camera to tap into the view of the lens, allowing directors to see what the camera operator sees. Also called a video tap.

Video tap
A small charge-coupled device (CCD) built into the camera to tap into the view of the lens, allowing directors to see what the camera operator sees. Also called a video assist.

Viewfinder
A display that allows the camera operator to determine the limits or edges of what is in the shot.

Vignette
An effect that darkens the corners of an image to bring the audience's attention toward the center of the frame.

Voiceover
Narration that does not correspond to someone speaking in the scene.

Walla
Crowd noise in the background of a scene.

Waveform monitor
An oscilloscope that measures the strength of a video signal.

White balance
A camera setting that lets you adjust the balance of RGB so that white objects appear white.

Wide lens
A lens with a shorter focal length than a normal lens and a wider angle of view. Also called a wide-angle lens.

Wide shot
A short-lens shot used to establish space, as in a master shot, or a whole location.

Wide-angle lens
A lens with a shorter focal length than a normal lens and a wider angle of view. Also called a wide lens.

Work ethic
The ability to show respect to everyone around you while you perform your responsibilities as best you can. Also called professionalism.

Writer
The original creator of a story or project. The writer visualizes the plot and theme, and creates the characters, visual descriptions, and dialogue.

XLR connectors
A three-pin connector used in professional audio recording to connect an XLR cable.

Z-axis movement
Moving toward or away from the camera.

Zoom lens
A lens that allows the operator to change focal length from wide to telephoto without switching out the lens.

Zooming
Changing focal length during a shot from wide to telephoto, or vice versa.

Index

A

Index

Q–R